This story, like all stories,
involves a subject and an object.

A subject is a person taken
into consideration for specific reasons.

Maria D. Rapicavoli
Surface Tension

A subject imposes itself
only by opposing itself.

An object is everything that the subject
perceives as different from itself.

Some stories never end.
How did this story begin?

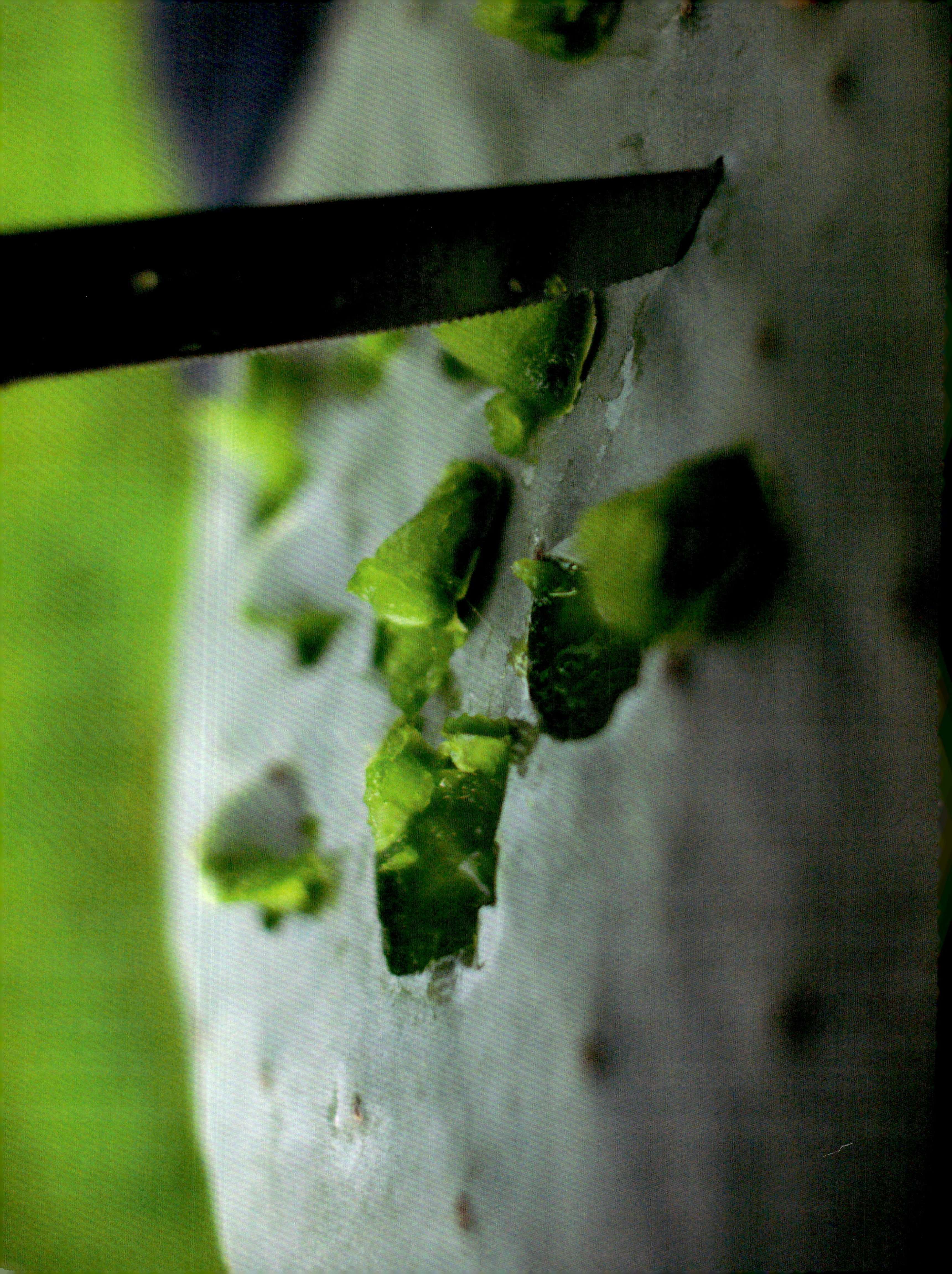

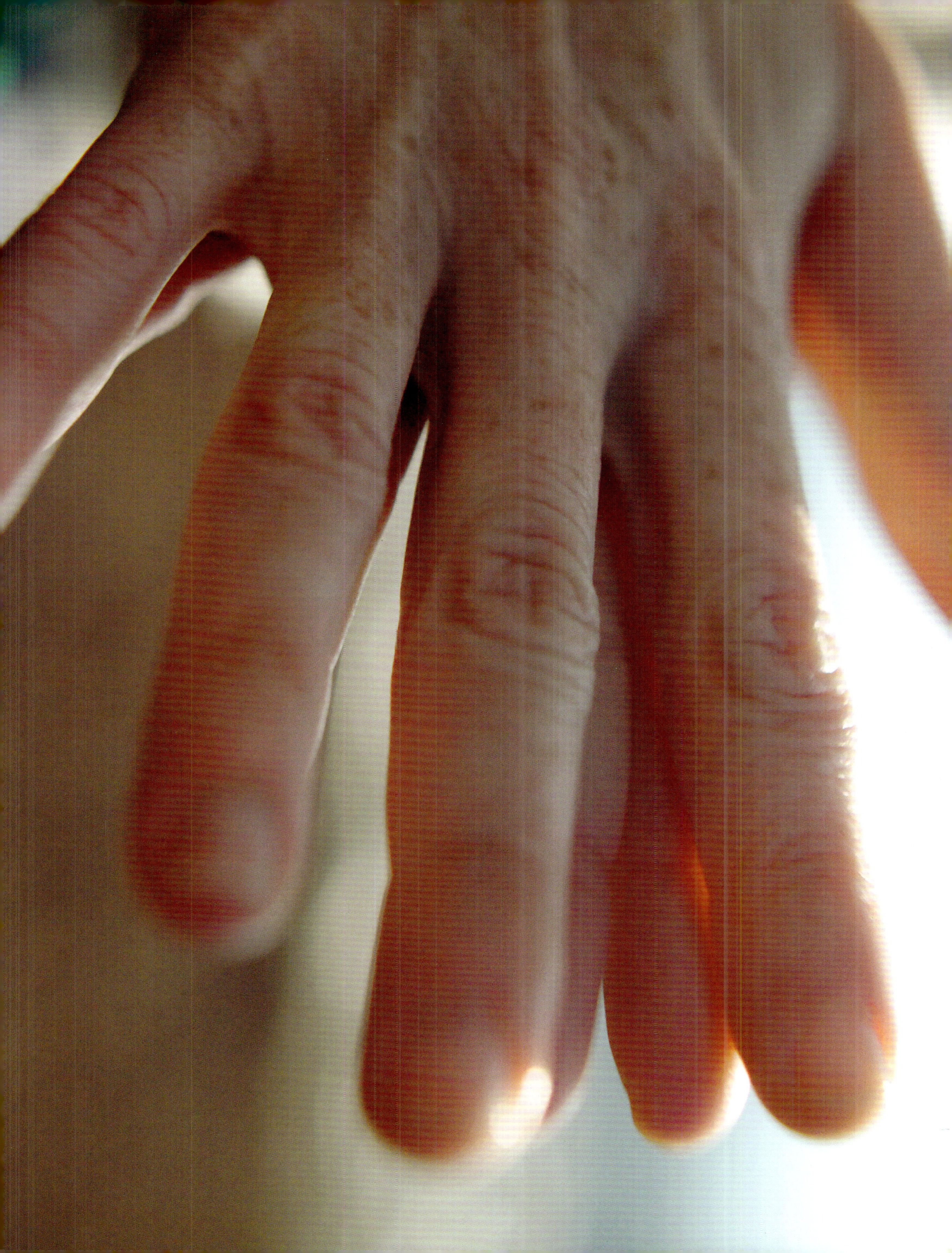

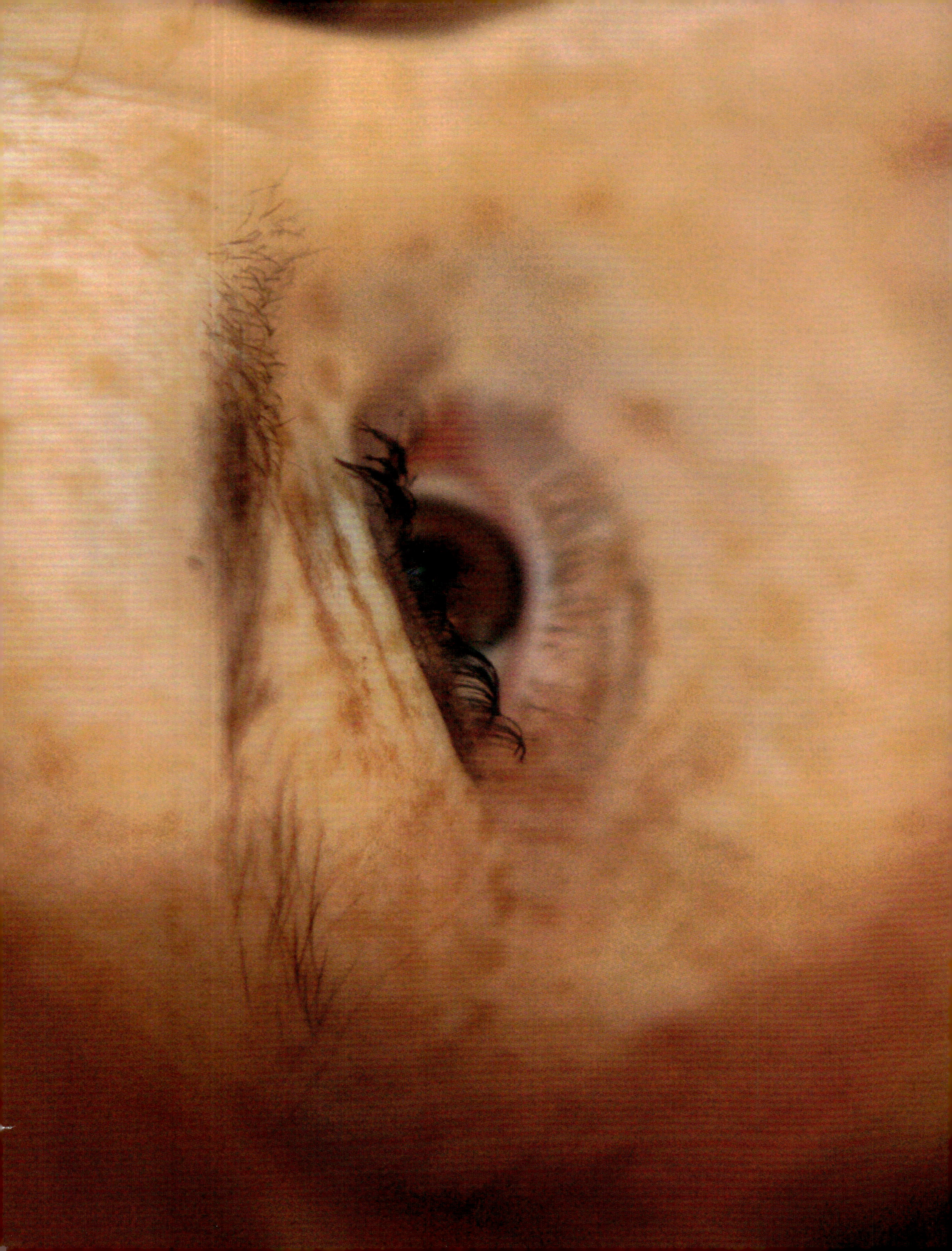

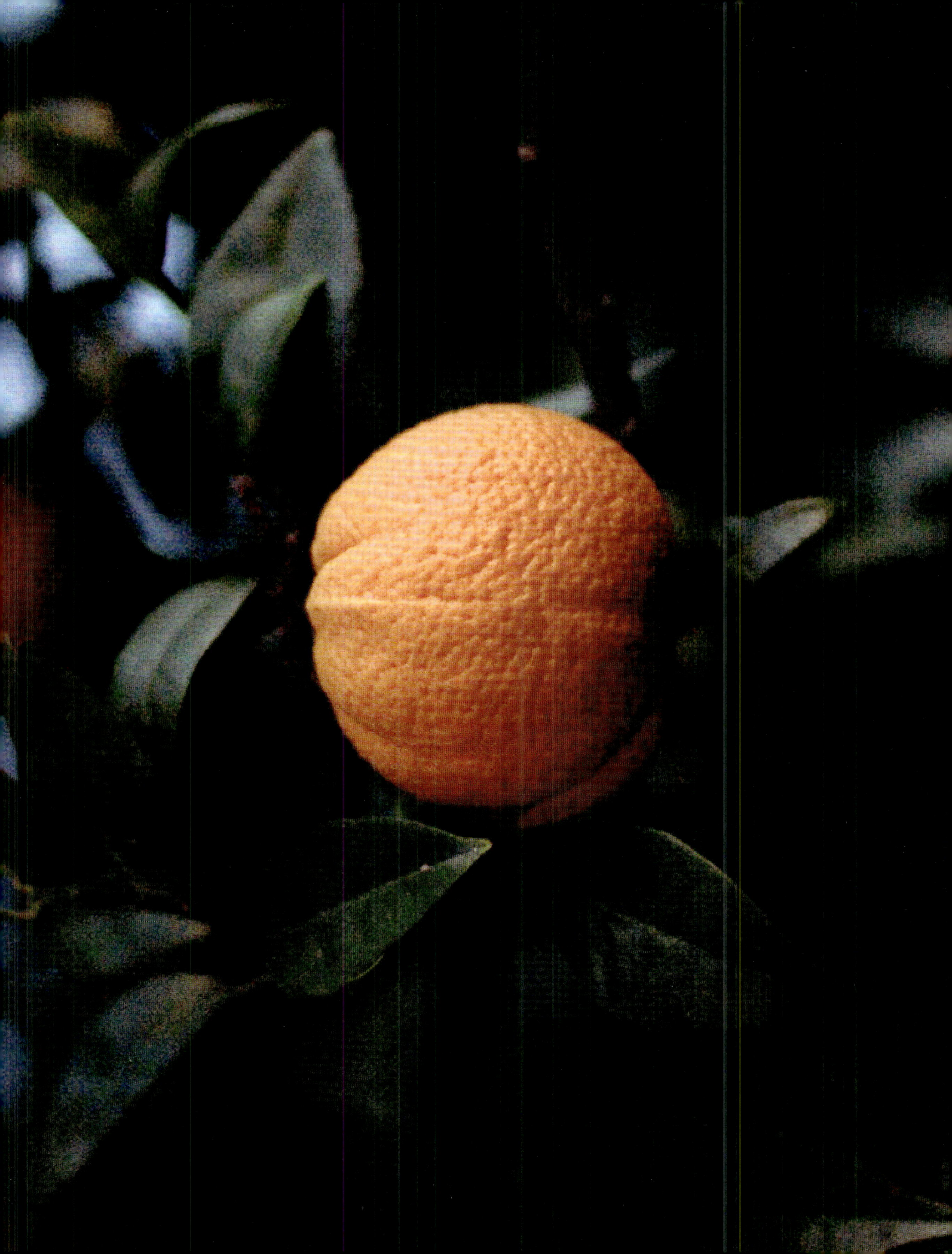

I was never allowed to speak.
The voice you hear is not mine.
Neither is the story I tell.

It might as well be mine.
It is made up of the memories of those who knew me
and those who have heard of me.

The sole purpose of violence is the assertion
of power of the attacker.

"Remember to breath"
I repeated to myself.

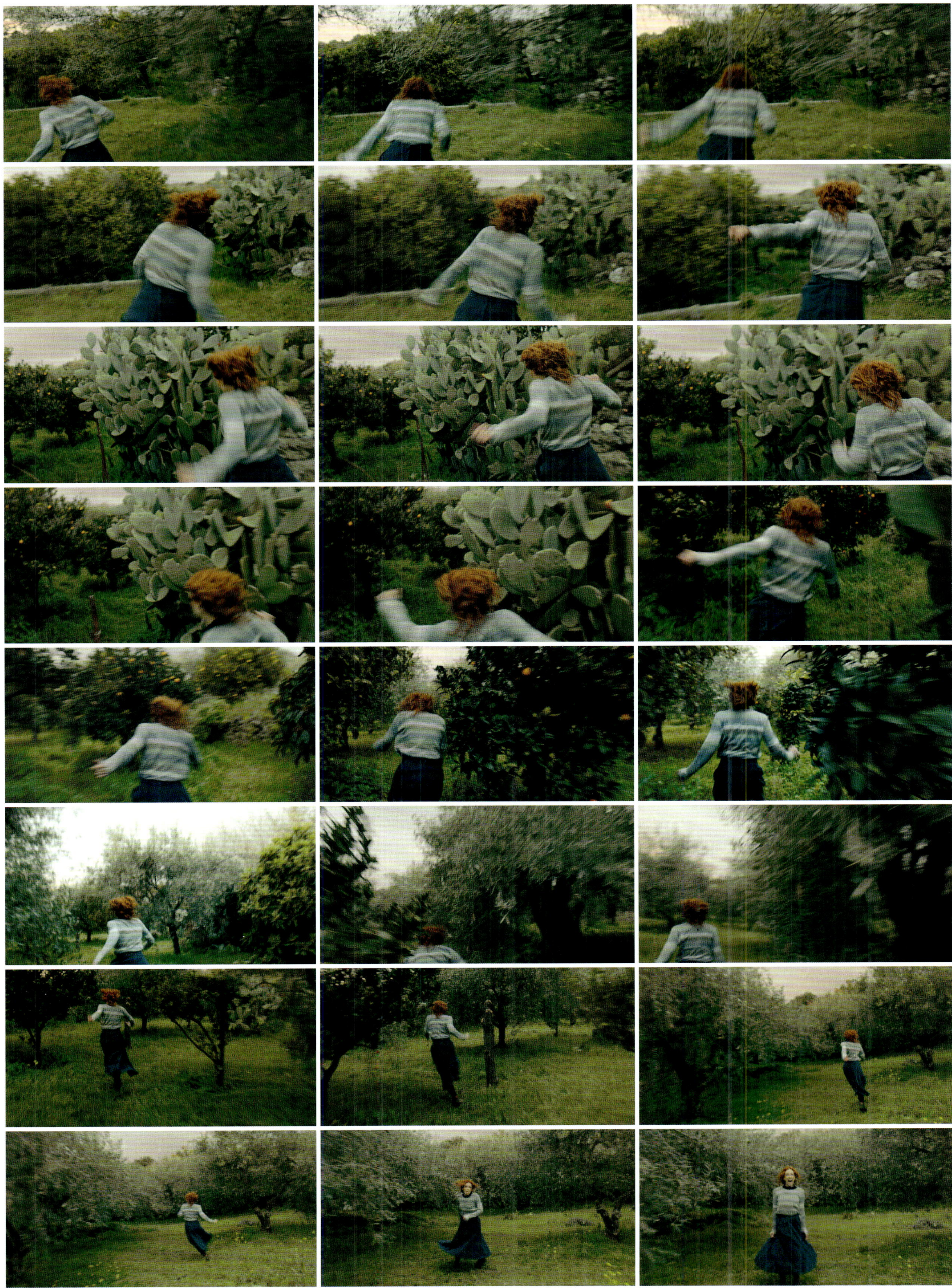

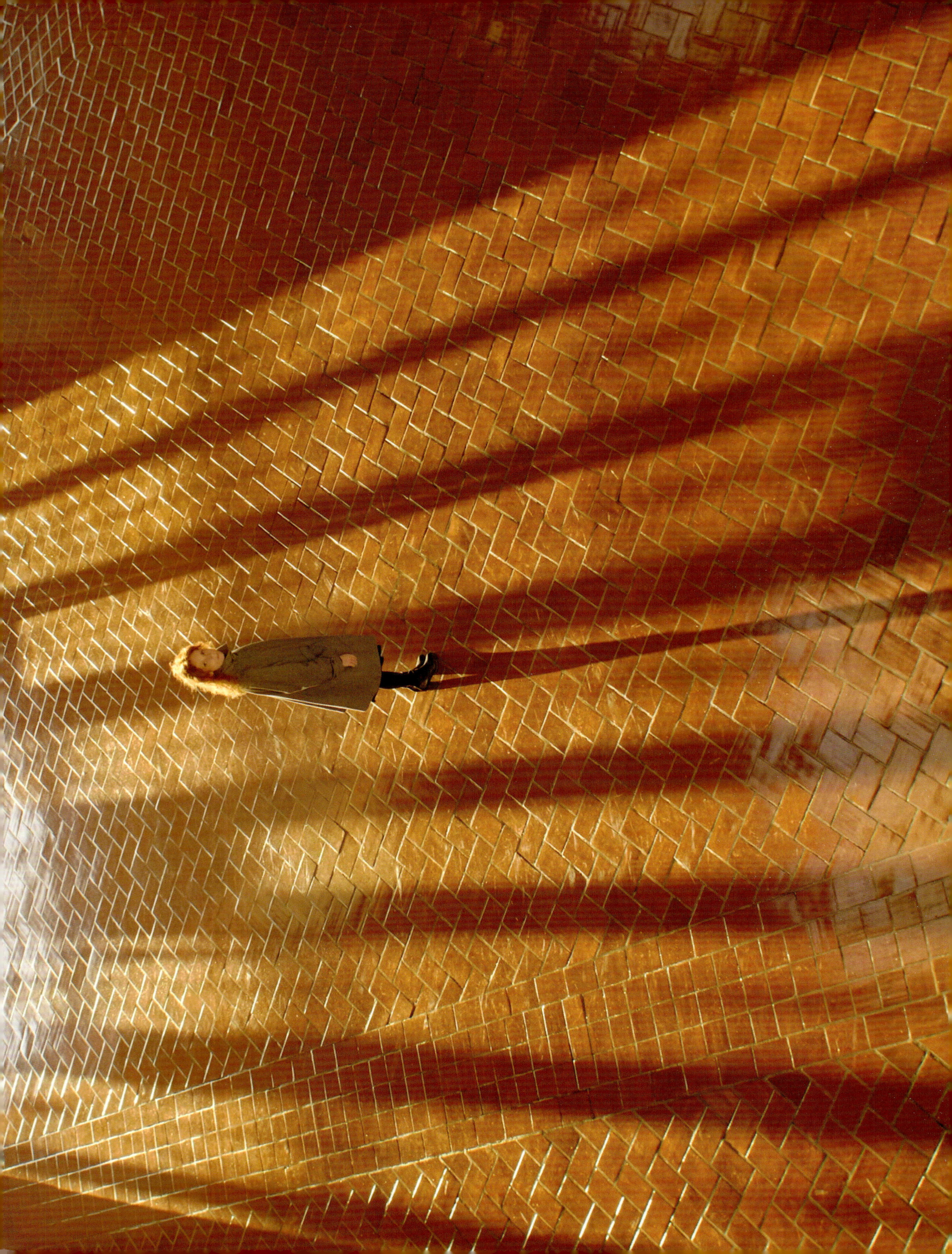

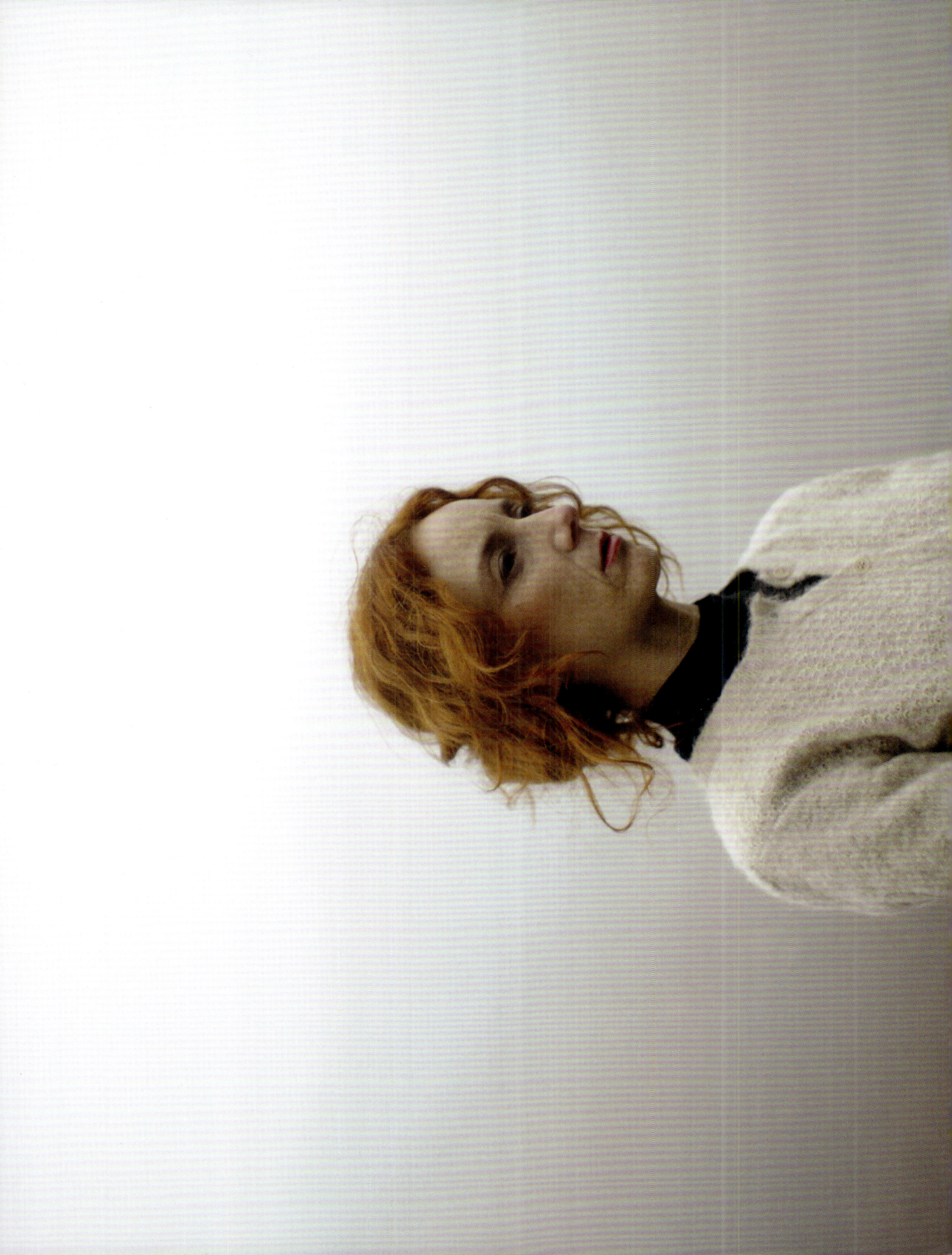

Duality of gender is apparent in conflict
in claiming superiority, you impose yourself as absolute
The Other is left out

What is authority?

Authority is the power vested in whoever
exercises command functions.

It is the action that determines
the will of those in power

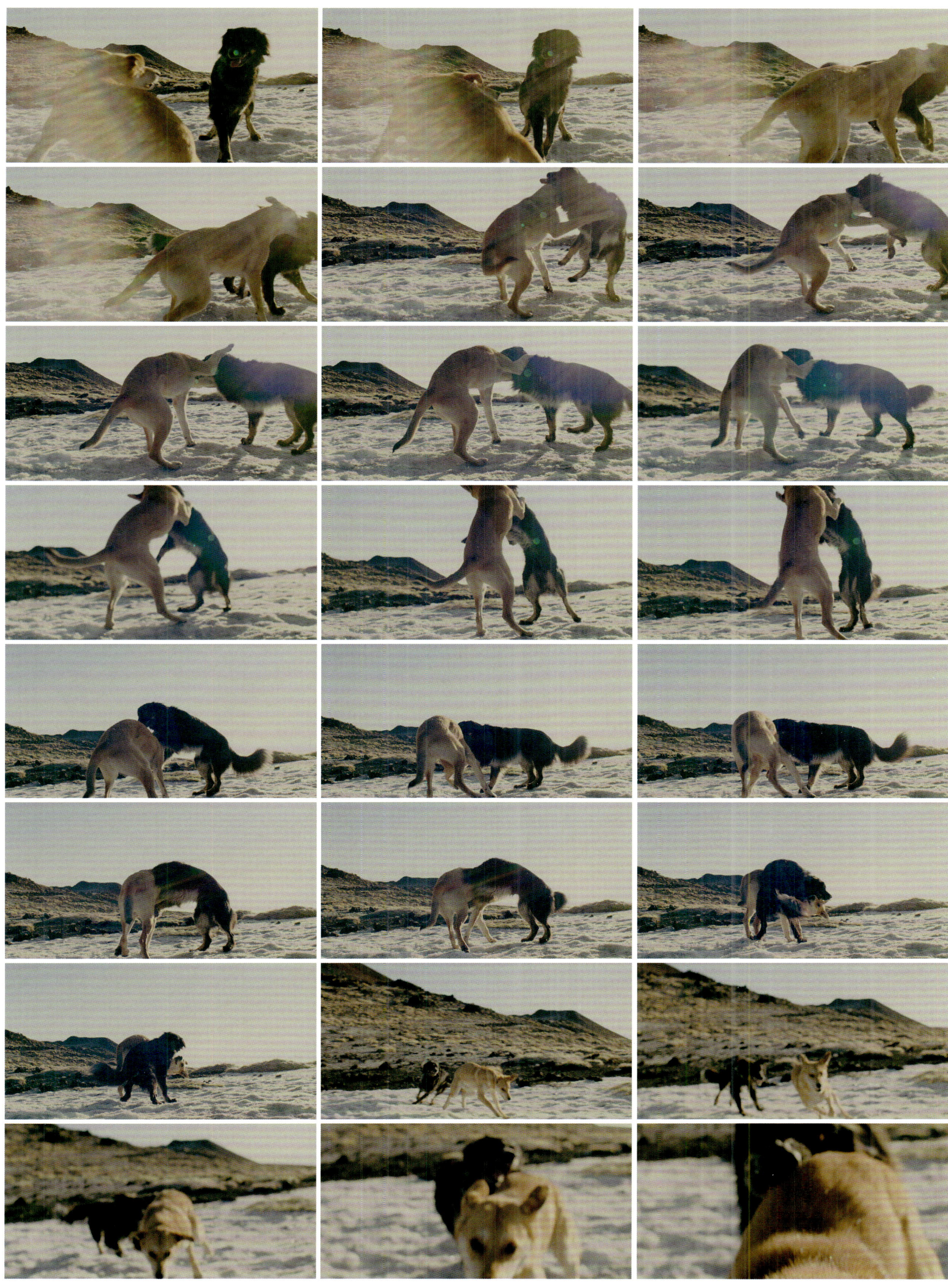

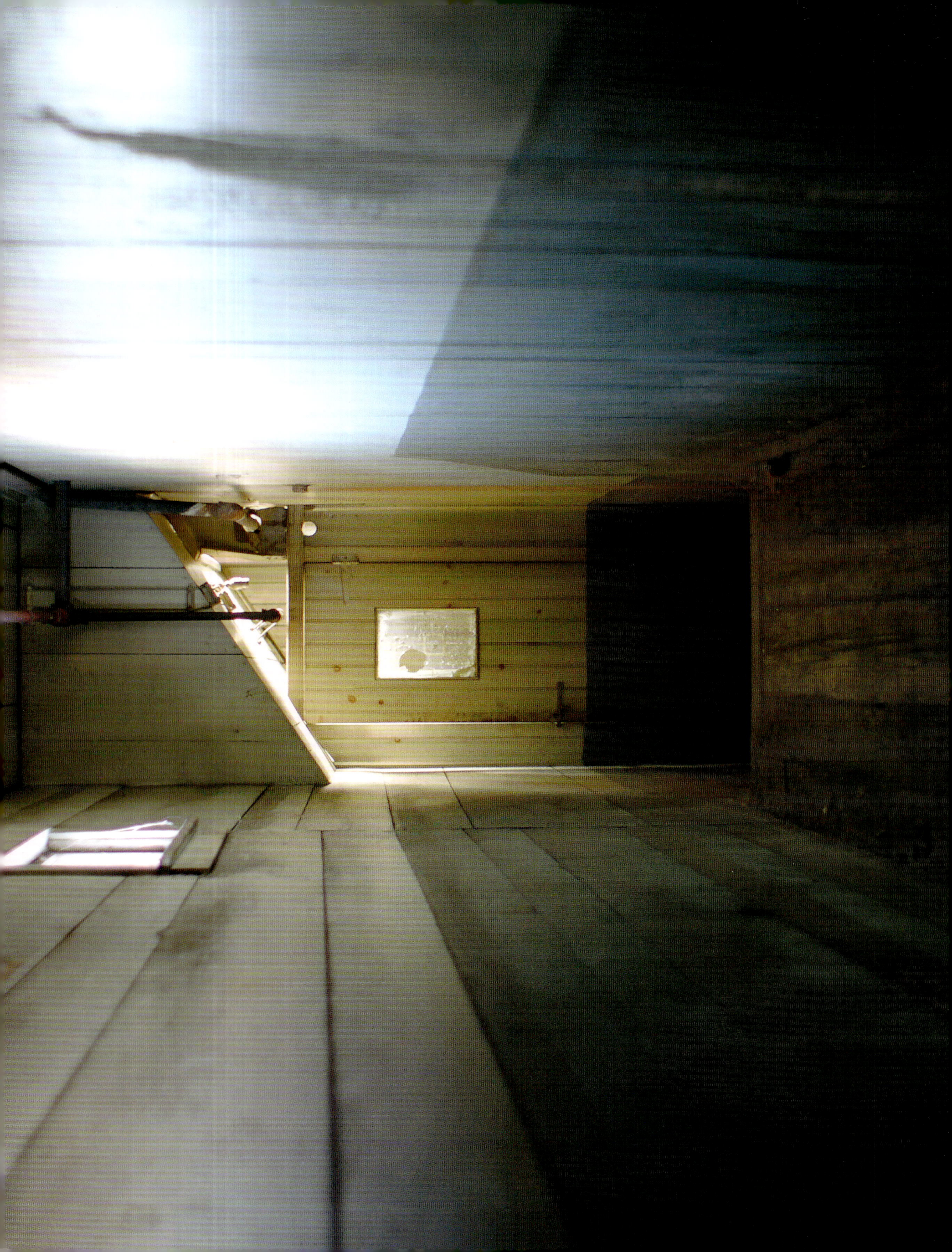

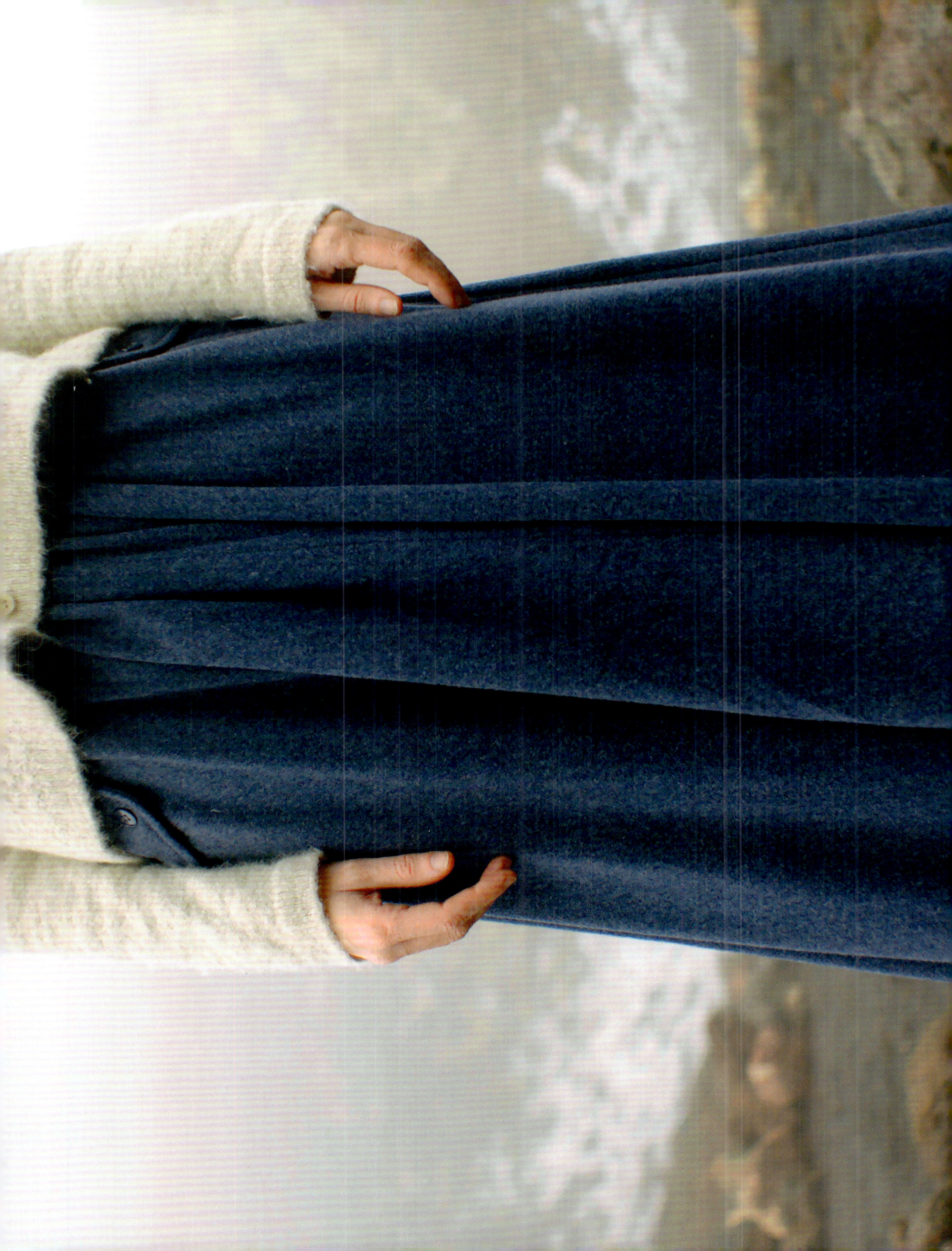

How is authority exerted?

Through the constant imposition of fear
in the object that succumbs.

The damage caused by violence is permanent.
I wondered how one human being
could contain all that evil

Fear.

Fear is an emotional state of insecurity,
repulsion, strong anxiety
in proximity of a perceived danger.

Memory of the danger generates fear.

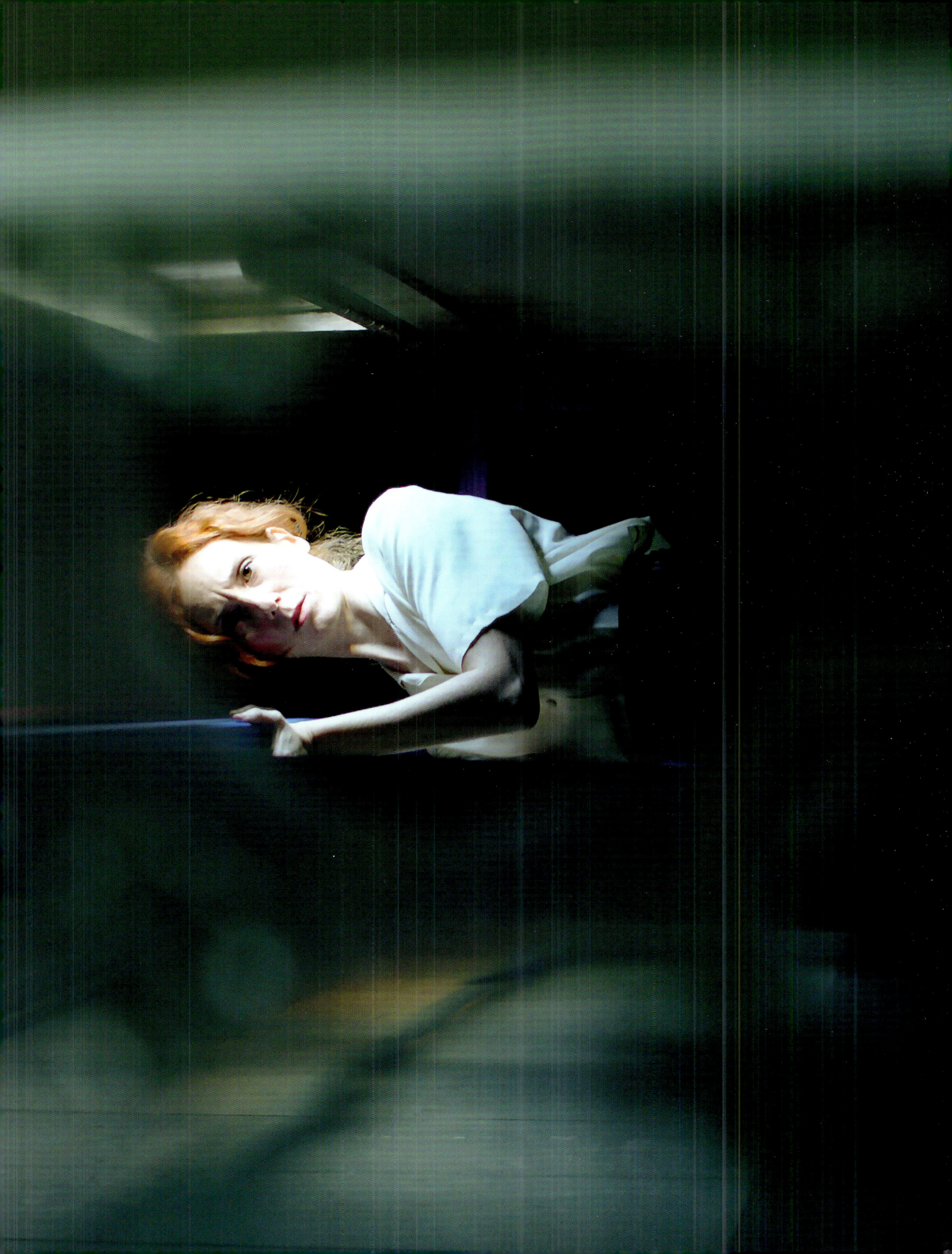

Liz Park, former Curator
University at Buffalo Art Galleries

Kristina Scepanski, Director
Westfälischer Kunstverein

New York–based artist Maria D. Rapicavoli has been drawing on her native Sicily as a place of departure and arrival for the past two decades. Since graduating from the Academy of Fine Arts in Catania in 2001, the artist has sought new contexts for exploring the invisible structures of power that shape her understanding of rootedness and migration as well as notions of domesticity and feminist politics. This search took her to London, where she received her MFA from Goldsmiths, University of London, in 2005, and to New York, where she participated in the Independent Study Program of the Whitney Museum of American Art in 2011–12. As cohorts in the Whitney program, we shared our research, artistic and theoretical concerns, and politics in seminars and informal conversations that took place day and night. This project, *Surface Tension*, is but one point in a continuing trajectory of our collaborative and intersecting practices and intellectual engagement. The artist's first monograph was produced on the occasion of the exhibition *The Other: A Familiar Story* at Westfälischer Kunstverein in Münster, Germany, and the artist's first career survey at the University at Buffalo Art Galleries, New York, titled *Surface Tension*.

Rapicavoli's video work *The Other: A Familiar Story* (2020), together with an accompanying sculptural installation, was the linchpin of her eponymous exhibition at Westfälischer Kunstverein. Based on a true story from the early twentieth century of a woman from Sicily who was forced to follow her husband to the United States, this tale of migration, oppression, misogyny, and economic inequality still feels far too familiar to us today, a century later. Even the work's reference to the catastrophic 1918 influenza outbreak after World War I allows us to draw parallels to our current pandemic, in the wake of which we all too clearly see how history rhymes.

Rapicavoli's images of barren volcanic landscapes in Italy and historic sites in the United States are already impressive, but her real achievement lies in her deployment of their suggestive power to palpably convey the protagonist's despair, fear, and anxiety. At Westfälischer Kunstverein, the artist showed the two-channel, synchronized video installation on a pair of projection surfaces that hung at an obtuse angle in the middle of the gallery, allowing visitors to walk around and view the work from different angles. Objects that appear in the video—some as props, others as found objects—were scattered around. Via large mirrors, exhibition space and cinematic space became blurred, and invited us all to become part of this "familiar story."

At UB Art Galleries, *The Other* was presented among other works produced over the past decade in order to contextualize Rapicavoli's larger practice as a photographer, media and installation artist, and sculptor. In addition to showcasing the range of her artistic output, *Surface Tension* presented the artist's engagement with a constellation of topics such as the effects of advanced military technology in Sicily, layers of colonial relations that undergird Mediterranean crossings to and from Europe and Africa, and gender and sexual politics embedded in personal and family histories. The exhibition thus presented a multifaceted view of an artist who is interested in both larger global politics, militarization, and migratory patterns, and intimate, domestic spaces and the inner psyches of individuals under duress. Rapicavoli's fierce, unflinching look at structures of power, which might seem too large to tackle in one individual's oeuvre, manifest as works of

art that are contemplative and embracing. As an arm
of a research university where seemingly irresolvable
questions are part of healthy daily discourse, UB Art
Galleries is committed to supporting projects that grapple
with some of the most challenging issues of our times.

In this volume, we are fortunate to have thoughtful
and illuminating texts by Sara Reisman, Wendy Vogel, and
Sarah Lookofsky—three interlocutors whose understanding of the artist's practice stems from their own interest
in and research on feminist histories and global politics.
Reisman situates *The Other* within Rapicavoli's earliest
video works from the early 2000s and discovers recur-
ring interests and artistic approaches to dealing with the
domestic realm and how women's roles are inscribed in
them. To fully consider Rapicavoli's *The Other* as a contri-
bution to current and urgent discussions of gendered and
sexual violence, Vogel dives into past legal victories as
well as standing statutes in Italy and the United States to
underscore the systemic ways in which men are granted
impunity in cases of spousal abuse. Just as Rapicavoli was
finishing the filming for *The Other*, a global pandemic was
declared, severely influencing all our lives. Reflections on
these developments mark the beginning of a conversation
between the artist and Lookofsky, which touches upon
the intersections of artistic practice, power, and purpose
across the different bodies of Rapicavoli's work.

We have many people and organizations to thank
in realizing this project. In addition to contributing an
essay, Reisman was instrumental in beginning this
journey and supporting the production of Rapicavoli's
The Other as the former Executive and Artistic Director
of the Shelley & Donald Rubin Foundation. An Italian
Council grant (2019, 6th edition) was critical in the
production and presentation of the work at the Rubin
Foundation's gallery, The 8th Floor, New York, as well
as in this publication. We acknowledge the continued
support of past and present Rubin Foundation staff:
George Bolster, former Director of Programming and
External Affairs; Anjuli Nanda Diamond, Curator;
William Furio, Manager, Events and Communications;
Matt Johnson, Director of Collections; James P.
McCarthy, former Treasurer and Secretary; Thomas
P. Mitchell, Vice President, Secretary, and Treasurer;
and Susan Szalai, Manager, Grants and Operations;
as well as Jessica Bailey and Amie Tzanidakis for
their invaluable administrative guidance and expertise.
Additionally, we extend our gratitude to Zach Milner
and Raul Zbengheci for their aid in the installation and
configuration of the work in *To Cast Too Bold A Shadow*.
A special thanks goes to Shelley and Donald Rubin
for their unwavering support and commitment to art
and social justice.

At Westfälischer Kunstverein, we would like
to thank the Kunststiftung NRW, namely Dr. Andrea
Firmenich and Dorothee Mosters, for their generous
support of the exhibition and publication as well as for
their gracious understanding of the challenges posed
by the pandemic. The entire team at the Westfälischer
Kunstverein deserves our heartfelt thanks for their fantas-
tic work: Tono Dreßen, Assistant to the Director and
Board; Jenni Henke, Production and Communications
Manager; Jana Peplau, Project Assistant; and Bernhard
Sicking, Gallery Assistant. The exhibition was installed
by our dedicated technician, Robin Völkert, and Anne
Krönker, Artistic Assistant, with support from the staff
of our neighboring LWL-Museum für Kunst und Kultur
(Westphalian State Museum): Johann Crne, Thomas

Erdmann, Frank Naber, Thomas Püth, Stephan Schlüter, and Beate Sikora. For the documentation of the exhibition, we would like to thank our photographer, Thorsten Arendt, and our videographer, Philipp Wachowitz. We also owe thanks to Judith Waldmann, who meticulously translated *The Other*'s Italian voice-over into German for additional subtitles.

At UB Art Galleries, we acknowledge the generous support of the Andy Warhol Foundation for the Visual Arts and the Q-International Grant of Fondazione La Quadriennale di Roma. Ongoing support for the galleries is provided by the UB College of Arts and Sciences, the Visual Arts Building Fund, the UB Anderson Gallery Fund, and the Seymour H. Knox Foundation Fine Art Fund. We could not have mounted the beautiful and ambitious exhibition without the tireless work of the staff: Robert Scalise, Director; Lynn Lasota, Finance and Operations Manager; Emily Reynolds, Marketing and Communications Manager; Nicholas Ostness, Registrar; Thomas Anderson and Jason Seeley, Preparators; Jim Snider, Tech Assistant; Amanda Speicher, Office Assistant; and Paul Wilcox, Maintenance Assistant.

Finally, we extend our sincerest gratitude to our comrade and companion, Maria D. Rapicavoli, for the opportunity to share her work with audiences on both sides of the Atlantic.

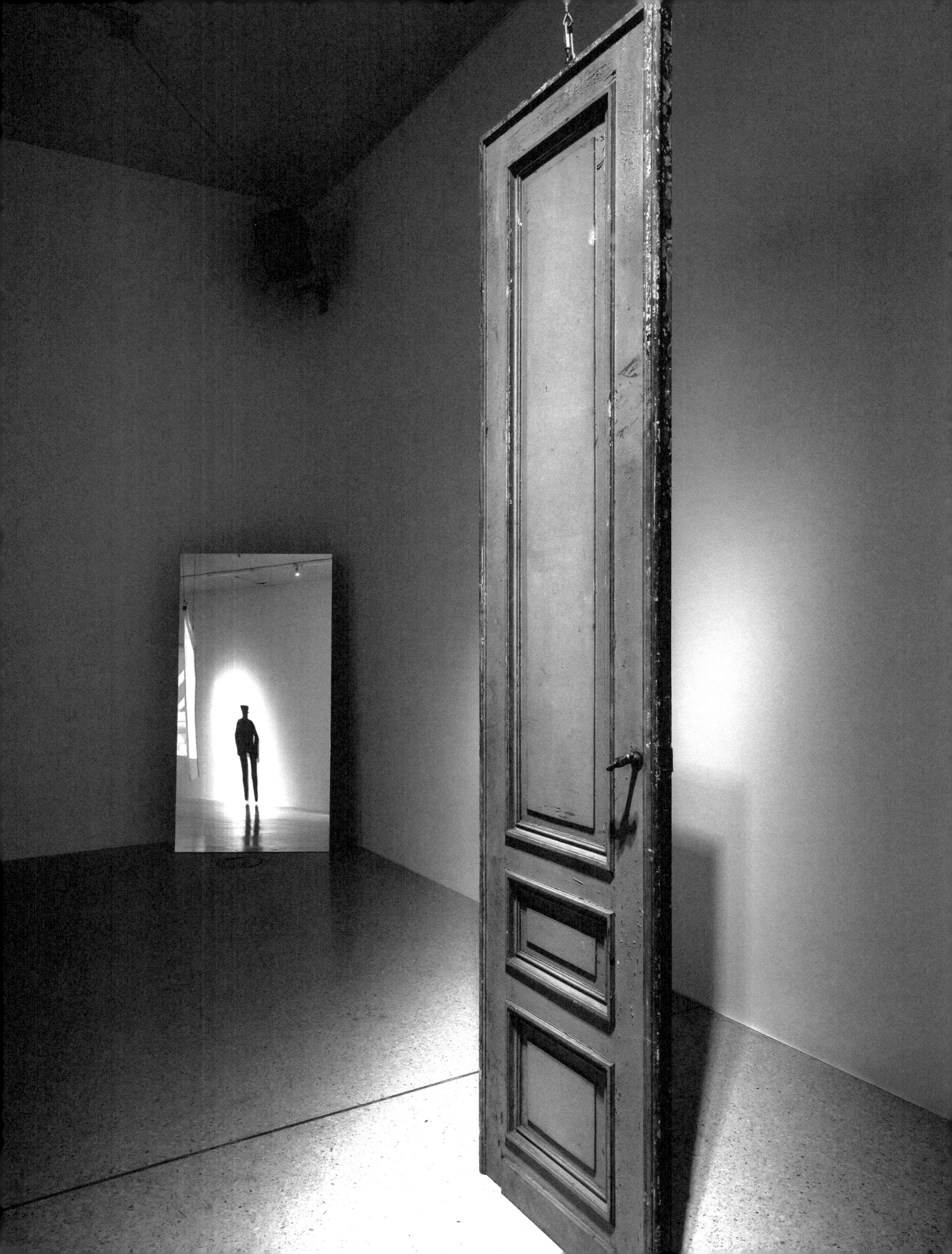

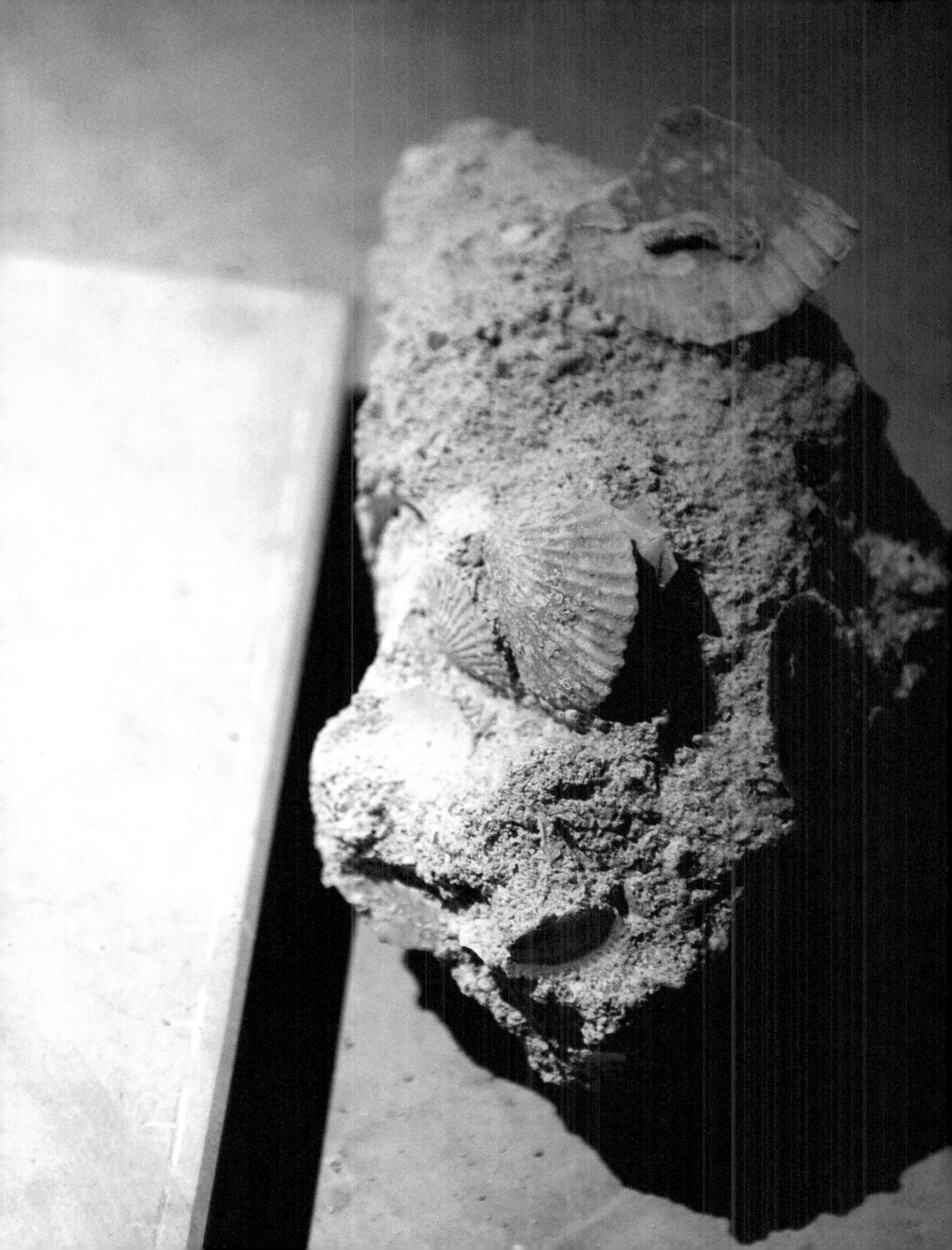

Some stories never end

Sara Reisman

To encounter Maria D. Rapicavoli's *The Other: A Familiar Story* (2020) is to follow a series of reversals, the urgency of which was not immediately apparent when Rapicavoli and I first discussed the project in March 2019. Commissioned for an exhibition I was preparing at the time—a show that expressly considered the impacts of misogyny in a range of cultural contexts—the video installation turned out to be much more historical and personal than I initially understood. In no way a documentary, *The Other* takes as its starting point the personal narrative of an unnamed member of Rapicavoli's extended family who was forced to leave her children in Nicolosi (Catania), Italy, and follow her husband to Lawrence, Massachusetts. This relative was coerced into marriage by a man who raped her. This confounding story at the center of *The Other* embodies

The Other: A Familiar Story (stills), 2020

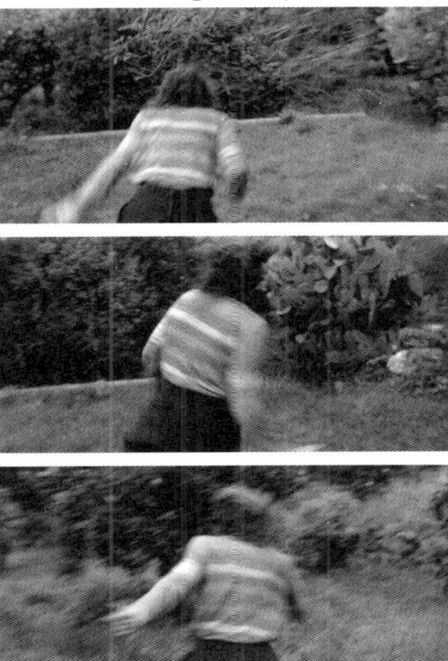

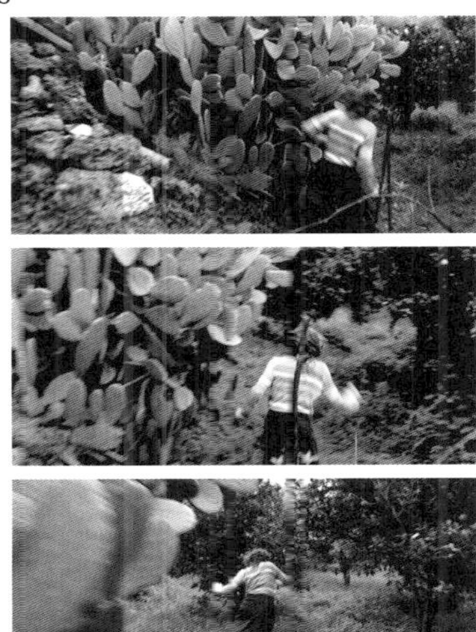

multiple, intertwined forms of oppression that are integral and widespread in the history of humanity. These kinds of transgressions are often unacknowledged, even as they play out around us.

Beginning with the first line of the voice-over—"Some stories never end"—the course of the protagonist's emotional landscape is mapped out in myriad spaces that allude to the uncertainties of her experiences of migration. The locations where the video was shot range from a domicile to natural environments. The protagonist is seen running through an orchard and

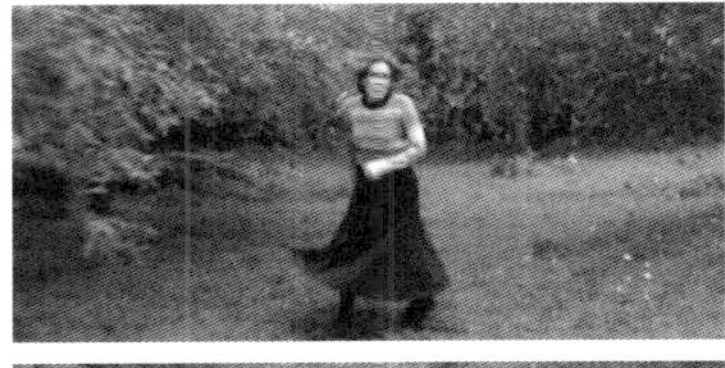

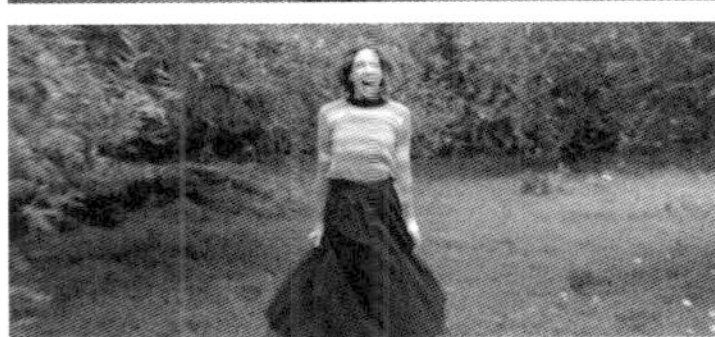

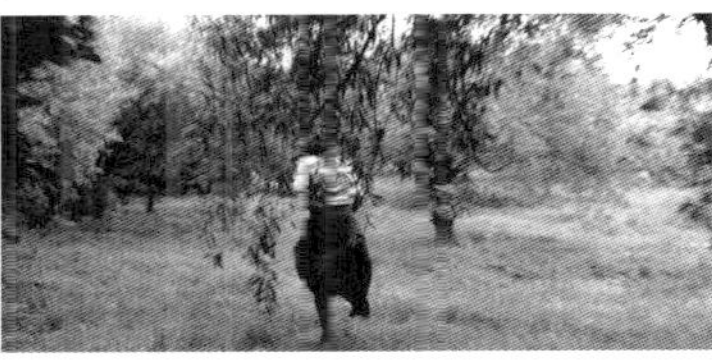

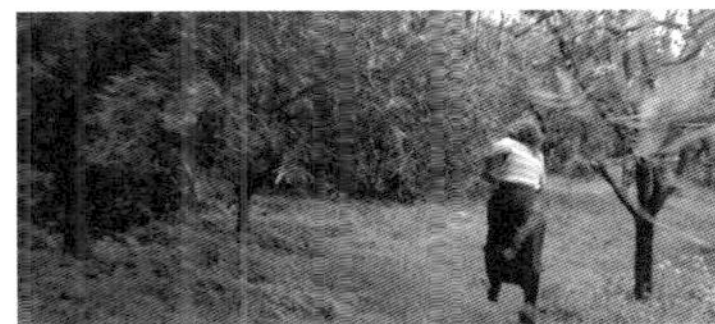

walking inside the interior of a cave. A wide-angle view captures the open sea, an empty factory, a too-narrow hallway where she struggles to move an Yves-Klein-blue bed frame, as if to make a space of her own, and a room in the hallway beyond the bedroom. The views of the landscape open to vast expanses, as if to release the subject into a realm of freedom and autonomy. This character is a prism for Rapicavoli's exegesis of philosopher Simone de Beauvoir's notion of "the Other": "It is not the Other who, defining itself as Other, defines the One; the Other is posited as Other by the One positing itself as One. But in order for the Other not to turn into the One, the Other has to submit to this foreign point of view."[1]

Simone de Beauvoir, *The Second Sex*, trans. Constance Borde and Sheila Malovany-Chevallier (New York: Vintage Books, 2011), 27.

Rapicavoli's late relative, whom the artist refers to in informal discussions by her first name, Mena, is like many women across geography and time whose lives map trajectories not of their own design. Her transatlantic voyage was common for her era. Between 1880 and 1920, more than four million Italians migrated to the United States.[2] At that time, especially those from

"The Great Arrival: Italian: Immigration and Relocation in U.S. History," Library of Congress, accessed July 22, 2021, https://www.loc.gov/classroom-materials/immigration/italian/the-great-arrival/

the south were fleeing a combination of poverty, violence, and social disarray that followed the formation of the modern Italian Republic in the late nineteenth century. The rationale for this type of forced migration and the breaking of familial bonds may have been compounded by Mena's second-class status as a woman, or other. Rapicavoli's interest in de Beauvoir's *The Second Sex* (1949) lies in the theoretical unlocking of the woman's conventional status, which frees her from the "minor" status that forced her to be the other without the right or the opportunity to build another condition for herself. This duality becomes even more significant when the other is an immigrant like Mena. Her existence is split into two realities: one in which she has no right to a voice, and a second that is largely foreign to her. In Lawrence, Mena worked in one of the many textile factories, which at the time employed countless immigrants. Her otherness is therefore double: she was other to her husband and other in the social context of the United States, where she had to lead a new life. According to de Beauvoir, the

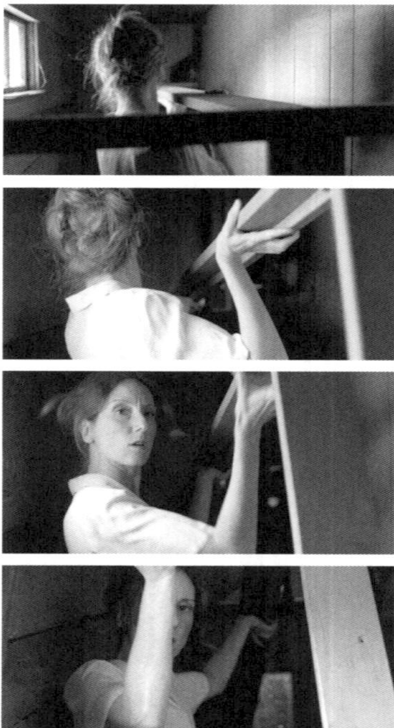

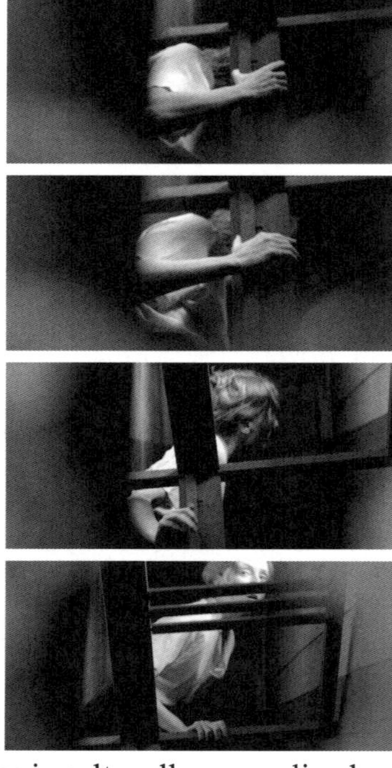

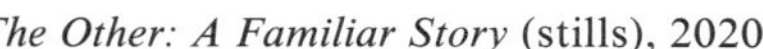
The Other: A Familiar Story (stills), 2020

woman's burden of otherness is culturally normalized, an inferior status of subservience to the dominant male figure.

During the development of the project, Rapicavoli made a conscious decision to remove Mena's name from the script. The lack of formal identification operates in parallel and contradictory ways. By making this fragmented narrative somewhat anonymous, the story can be more easily understood as universally familiar. This redaction within the video also ensures that this specific woman's history is not exploited. Yet it raises questions about the ethics of visibility and, conversely, invisibility, particularly in relation to immigration and

how being named can contribute to, or undermine,
an individual's sense of safety and legal protection.
Naming can potentially make the identified immigrant
vulnerable to authorities. In choosing to redact the name
of her protagonist, the artist grapples with an ethi-
cal dilemma in which larger political and social forces
prevent the names of individuals and groups from being
known, enabling further oppression and dehumanization
through omission. Rapicavoli notes that in the media,

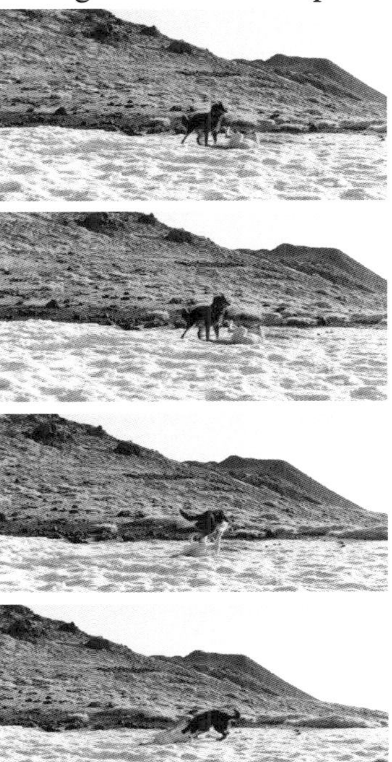

The Other: A Familiar Story (stills), 2020

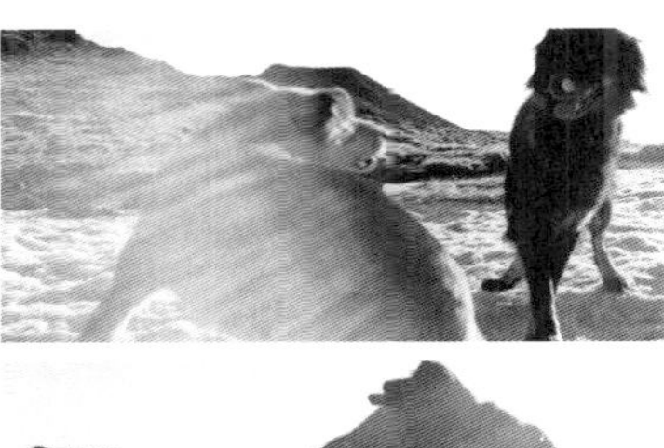

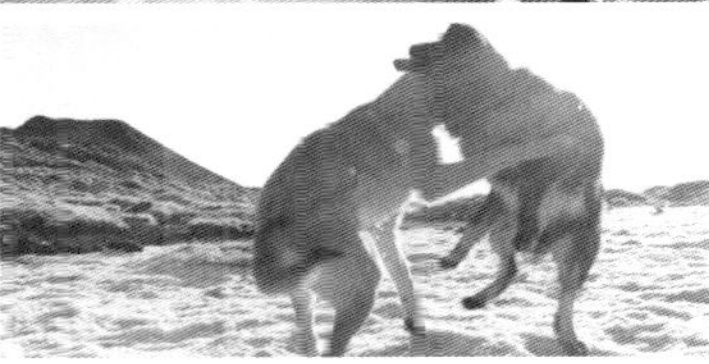

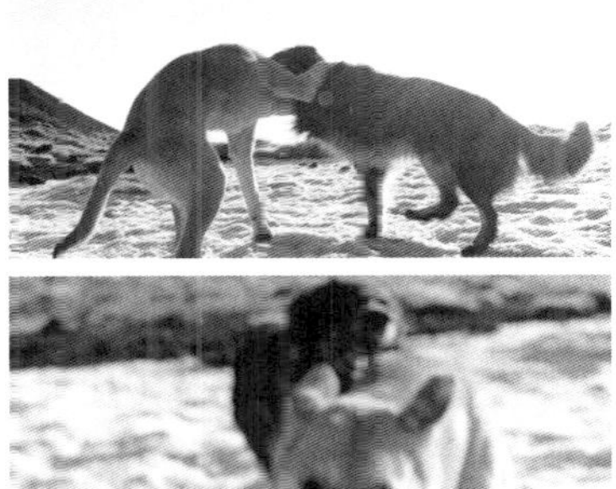

women who are victims of crimes often go unnamed,
as if to further diminish the importance of what they
have endured.

Within the script, "Some stories never end" is
followed by "not even when you die," pointing to the
epigenetic nature of generational trauma. Rapicavoli
shows us how the unresolved effects of the protagonist's
separation from her children, the labor conditions she
endured as a factory worker, and the suffocating and
inescapable relationship with her husband still rever-
berate more than a hundred years later. Looking back
on Rapicavoli's early video works, it becomes clear that
the intensity of *The Other*—in its writing and staging—
is a logical step in her progression as an artist. Three
of her earliest videos, *One, No One* (2005), *Four Virgins
and a Bed* (2007), and *My Ideal House* (2007), are experi-
mental works that tease out some of the key circumstances that shape women's lived experiences in both the
public and the private realms, while also revealing specific
tensions between traditional Italian cultural ideals and
contemporary life. These early artworks also coincide
with a time when her own experience of mobility within
Europe was novel. Having come to London in the early
2000s from a small village in Sicily where everyone knew
one another, the artist was not accustomed to being
asked "Where are you from?" She was fascinated by
Londoners' openness to other cultures and nationalities, and with their formality—a tendency to not have
deep conversations. *One, No One* was about breaking
that barrier. Rapicavoli gave strangers her camera and
asked them to film her, then asked them to guess who she
was. A project about the formation of her own identity,
it captures a moment when Great Britain was open to
every nationality as the European Union was expanding.

Within the video, Rapicavoli looks dispassionately
into the camera as each person attempts to describe her

from off-screen, a guessing game of sorts. The result
is a mixture of projected and imagined identities that
are generalized enough to describe the same person,
and, perhaps to a certain degree, a description of themselves. A deep, British-accented male voice speculates,
"The reason why probably an English person would think
[you're] perhaps not Spanish or Italian . . . your hair is
quite, well, like mine, quite pale skin. You don't look
like many southern European girls." A woman's voice
continues: "I would say you're maybe around twenty-six
years old. . . . I think you're some sort of student here
in London, maybe from Germany or something. I think

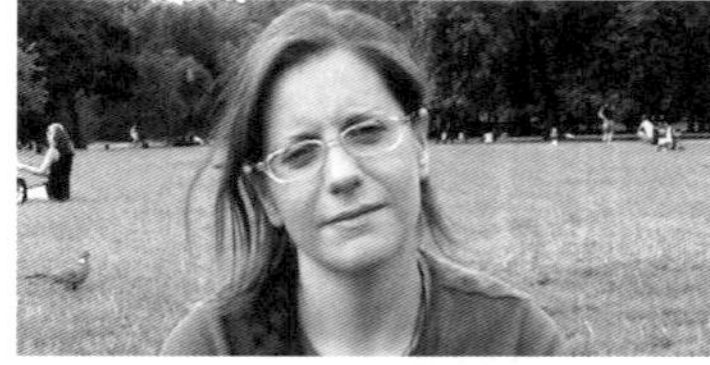
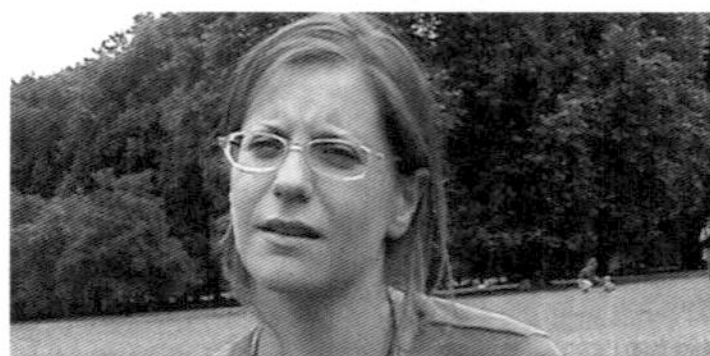
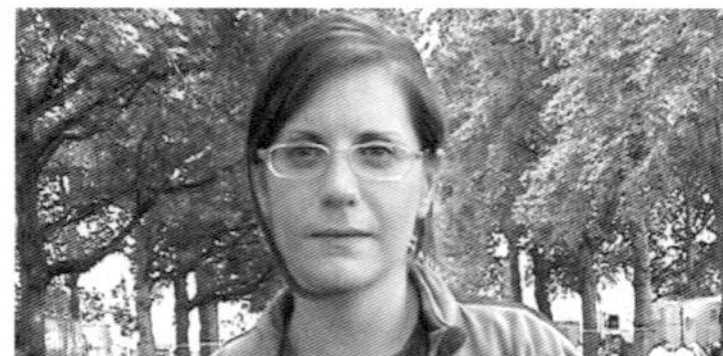
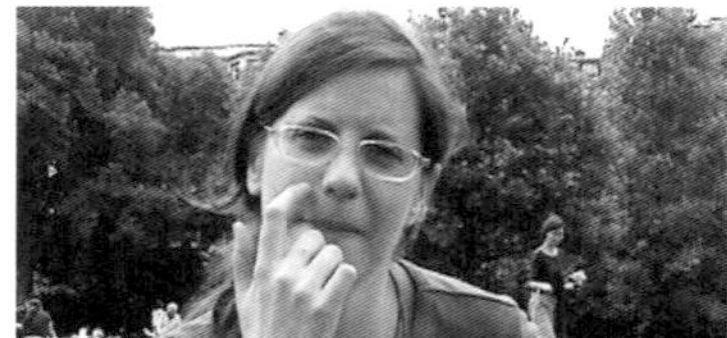

One, No One (stills), 2005

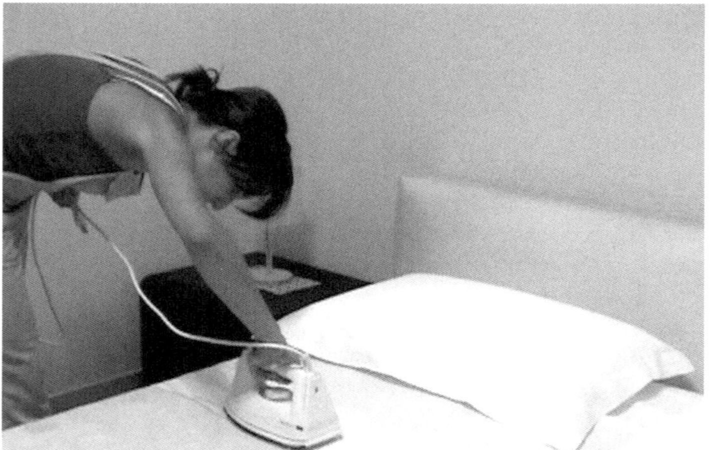

Four Virgins and a Bed (still), 2007

your accent is a little bit, maybe German or Holland,
or something like that." This woman's voice has an
ambiguously European accent, inflected with Dutch.
The first voice, with its British cadence, continues: "I think
you're different. I've never come across anyone like you
before. Um, you wear glasses. You have green eyes, or are
they blue eyes? You have a nice figure." This composite
of impressions expresses how identity can be constructed
in the most superficial of ways, from observations made
by near-strangers, through the lens of perceived nationality, race, and gender. Part of what is captured through
this one-sided exchange is Rapicavoli's own experience
in graduate school at Goldsmiths while she was still
learning English. It also points to the projections that
are made when reciprocity is not possible. Her enig-
matic expression alludes to the misrecognition that

often occurs in public between strangers—for instance a silent, quizzical look in response to being told she has a nice figure. Watching this, I wondered if this observation was welcome. Rapicavoli recalls an Ethiopian man who made an assumption about her marital status —"You are married, with one guy"—and later sang the Italian song "Susanna" to her off-camera. The lyrics of Adriano Celentano's song are about a tourist's affair with an Italian woman, making a flirtatious reference to the historic colonial relationship of their respective cultures (Italy occupied Ethiopia in the 1930s). In this relatively contemporary moment, gender dynamics, presumably heteronormative, hold fast.

Four Virgins and a Bed documents a Sicilian tradition that customarily takes place several days before

Four Virgins and a Bed (stills), 2007

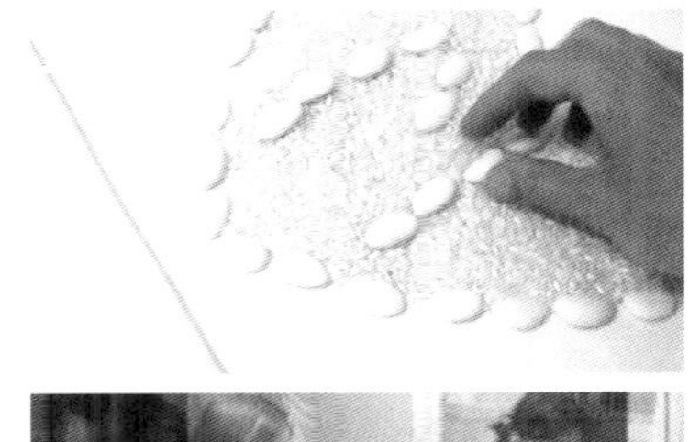

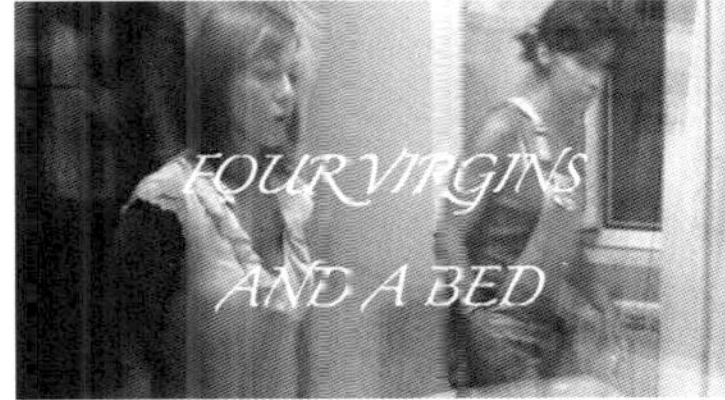

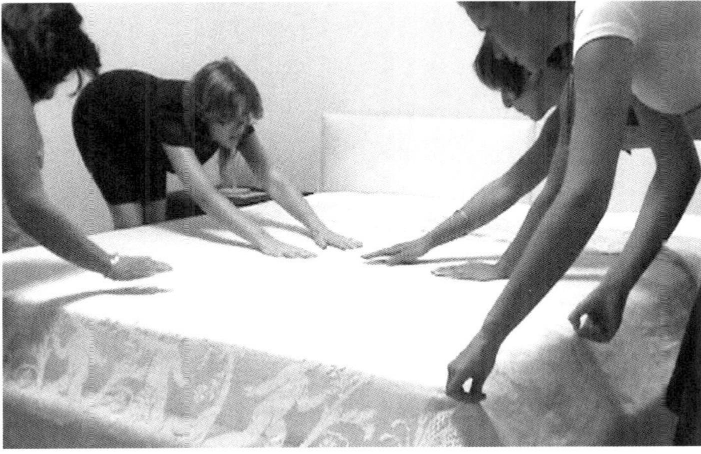

a wedding. Four maidens—virgins, in other words— make up the bed for the couple's wedding night, and a married "advisor," along with the bride's and groom's mothers, are supposed to inspect the bed to make sure it is suitable for the newly married couple. This archaic ritual puts women in a position of guilt if they are not virgins. In Rapicavoli's video, the four "virgins," including the artist, make the bed, dusting every surface, smoothing every crease. Together, they circle the bed in a choreography of patting and tucking and untucking the corners, going so far as to iron the top sheet, and eventually floating a lacy, off-white bedspread over the top. Under the pillows, the women arrange rice and candied almonds in the shape of hearts, one for the bride and one for the groom, complete with their initials, for good luck. The fantasy of the virgin Italian bride dates back to the Middle Ages, and continues to haunt the popular imagination, from Harlequin romance novels to Francis Ford Coppola's *The Godfather* movies. While Rapicavoli's performance video reads as a cheeky critique of this retrograde double standard (the bride must be a virgin, yet the groom's virginity is never discussed), it alludes to a tradition of wedding-night virginity tests in which the bride must prove her chastity by showing a bloodstained sheet. Failing this test, a bride could be divorced or disowned, and yet the notion that bleeding proves virginity is not scientifically sound. In many parts of the world—the Middle East, South Africa, and South Asia—these practices persist. Tests are implemented in preparation for weddings and in high schools, with repercussions that range from public humiliation to putting young women's lives at risk.[3]

Sophie Jones, "Virginity Testing: A Global Crisis," *Marie Claire*, October 30, 2019, https://www.marieclaire.com/politics/a29491715/virginity-testing-laws-regulations/

3

Somewhere between refusal, refuge, and fantasy, Rapicavoli's *My Ideal House* proposes an escape from the complications of marital bondage and reproductive obligation implied by *Four Virgins and a Bed*. It is comprised of scenes of the artist getting comfortable in different rooms (which turn out to be in a furniture showroom) containing classic Modernist design pieces, including a Mies van der Rohe Daybed and Philippe Starck's translucent Ghost Chairs. Rapicavoli stretches out in bed, touches her toes, plays solitaire, curls up with a

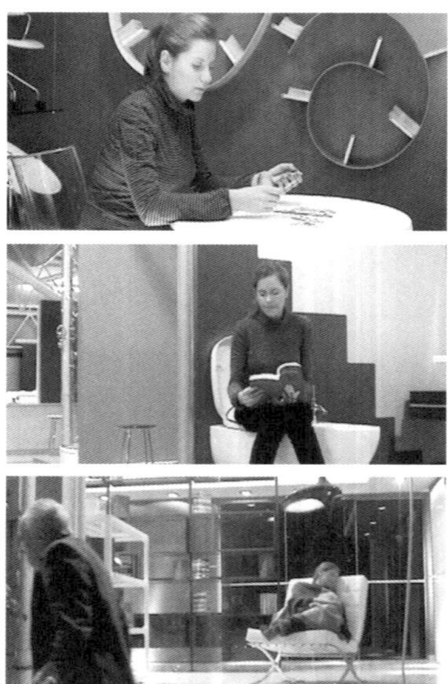

My Ideal House (stills), 2007

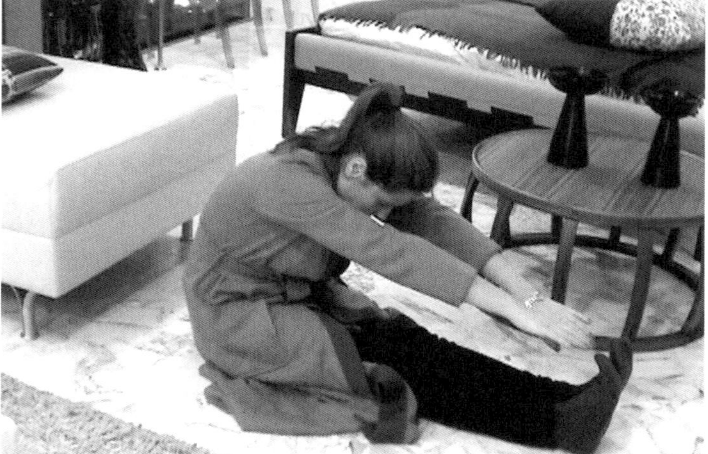

book in a Knoll Barcelona Chair, and eventually moves to the bathroom, where she continues reading on the toilet. These slightly comical gestures of daily life enact philosopher Walter Benjamin's characterization of the arcades as having originally served commercial functions that ultimately "become places of habitation."[4] In another

Walter Benjamin, *The Arcades Project*, ed. Rolf Tiedemann, trans. Howard Eiland and Kevin McLaughlin (Cambridge, MA: Harvard University Press, 1999), 5.

area of the "ideal house" adjacent to a sales desk, Rapicavoli intently files her nails while two customers browse nearby. Throughout the video, segments of which are shot at night, light is reflected from the windows and mirrors that are part of the store displays, doubling the artist's figure and actions and extending her audience to include passersby on the sidewalk outside. Finally she settles into a chair in front of one of the store's windows, wraps herself in a blanket, and turns inward to sleep, still visible to the outside world. As if an antidote to *The Other*, *My Ideal House* feels like a homecoming, an arrival to a place of comfort, in spite of the exposures and reflections that amplify her presence. *My Ideal House* is set to a soundtrack of the Velvet Underground's "I'll Be Your Mirror" (1967), in which Nico's melancholic voice affects a mixture of relief and resignation:

I'll be your mirror
Reflect what you are, in case you don't know
I'll be the wind, the rain and the sunset
The light on your door to show that you're home.

Rapicavoli's movements through a house of reflective surfaces—mirrors, windows, and hard, shiny industrial design—are at times humorous, but they lend gravitas to the complicated way in which women are typically seen as subjects of their circumstances, culturally bound up in appearances and so often involve mirroring their male counterparts. A poignant aspect of *My Ideal House* is the sense of comfort expressed in the artist's solitude—how being alone, rather than bound by familiar domestic trappings, can enable a greater sense of freedom. Taken together, this trilogy of Rapicavoli's earliest video works, alongside *The Other*, reveal the artist's depth of sensitivities to the gendered nature of contemporary life, making clear that even if some stories never end, circumstances can change.

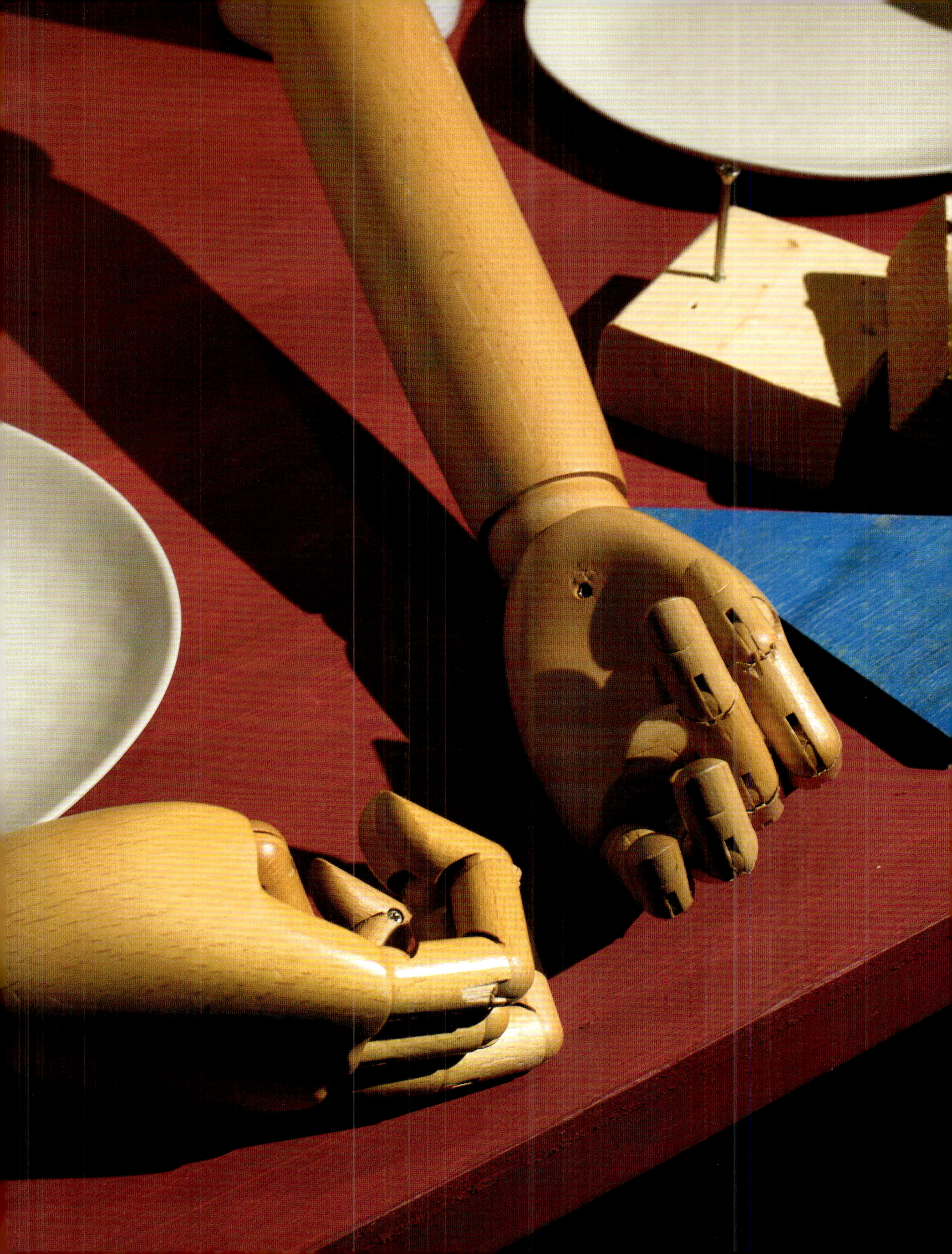

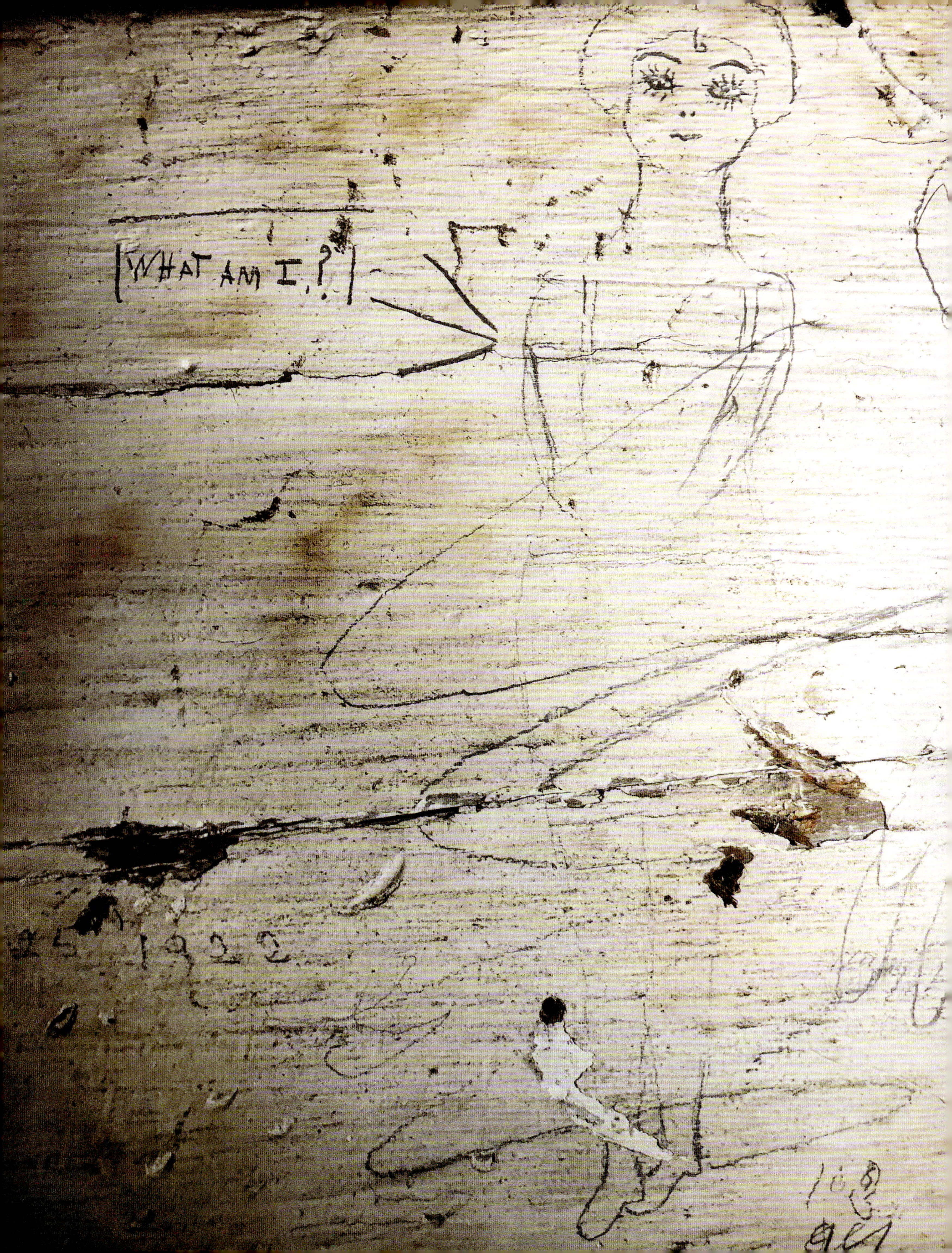

WHAT AM I ?
1922

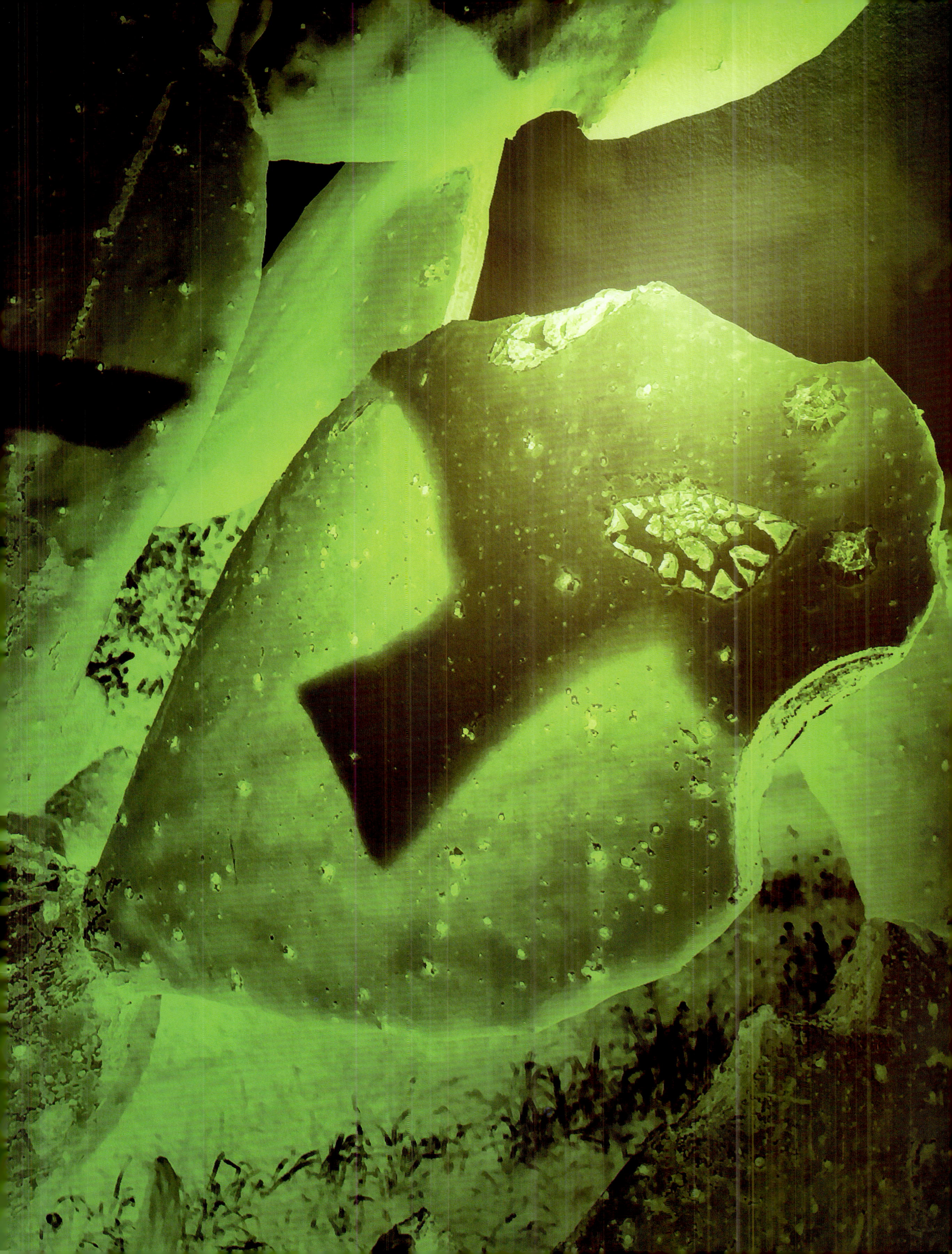

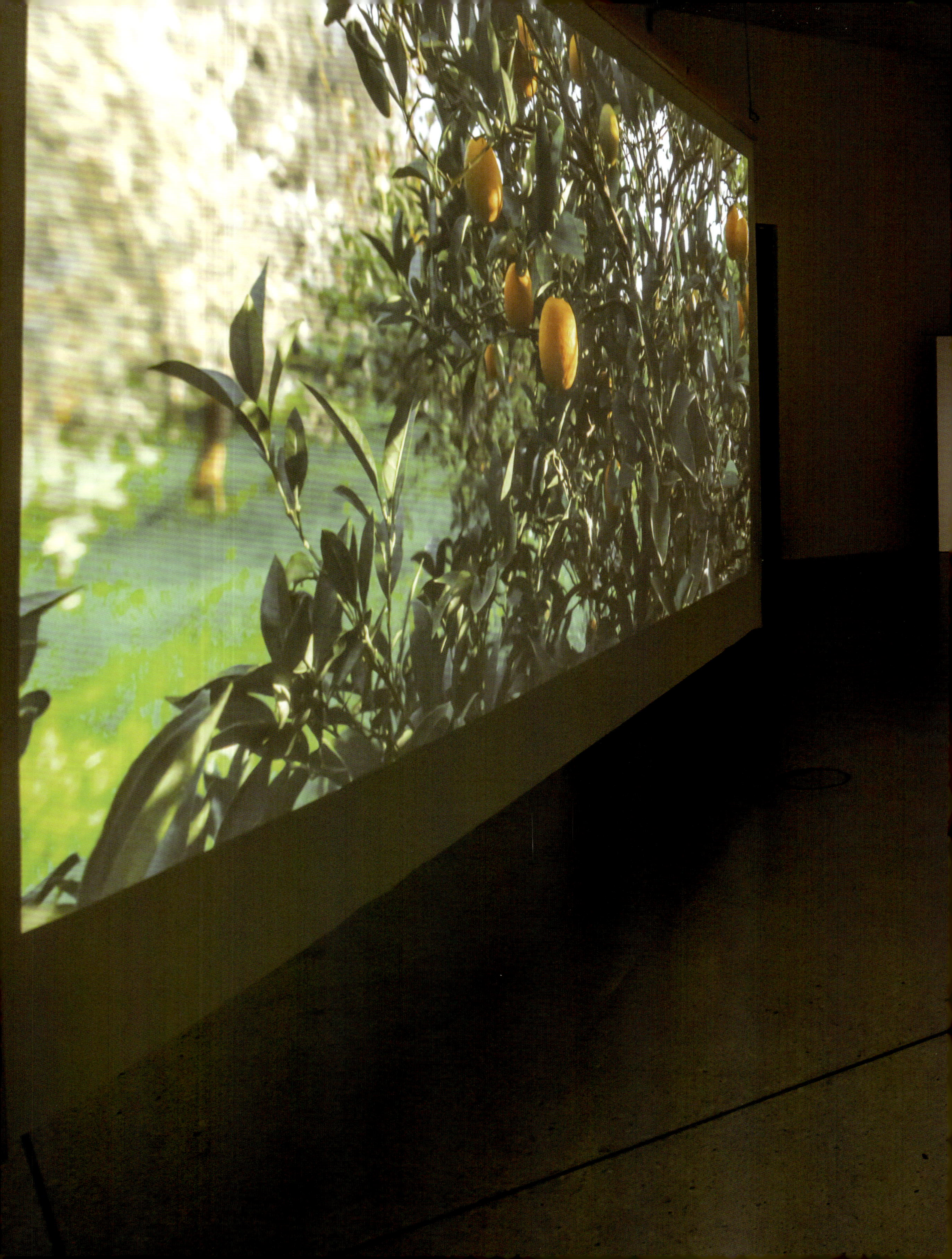

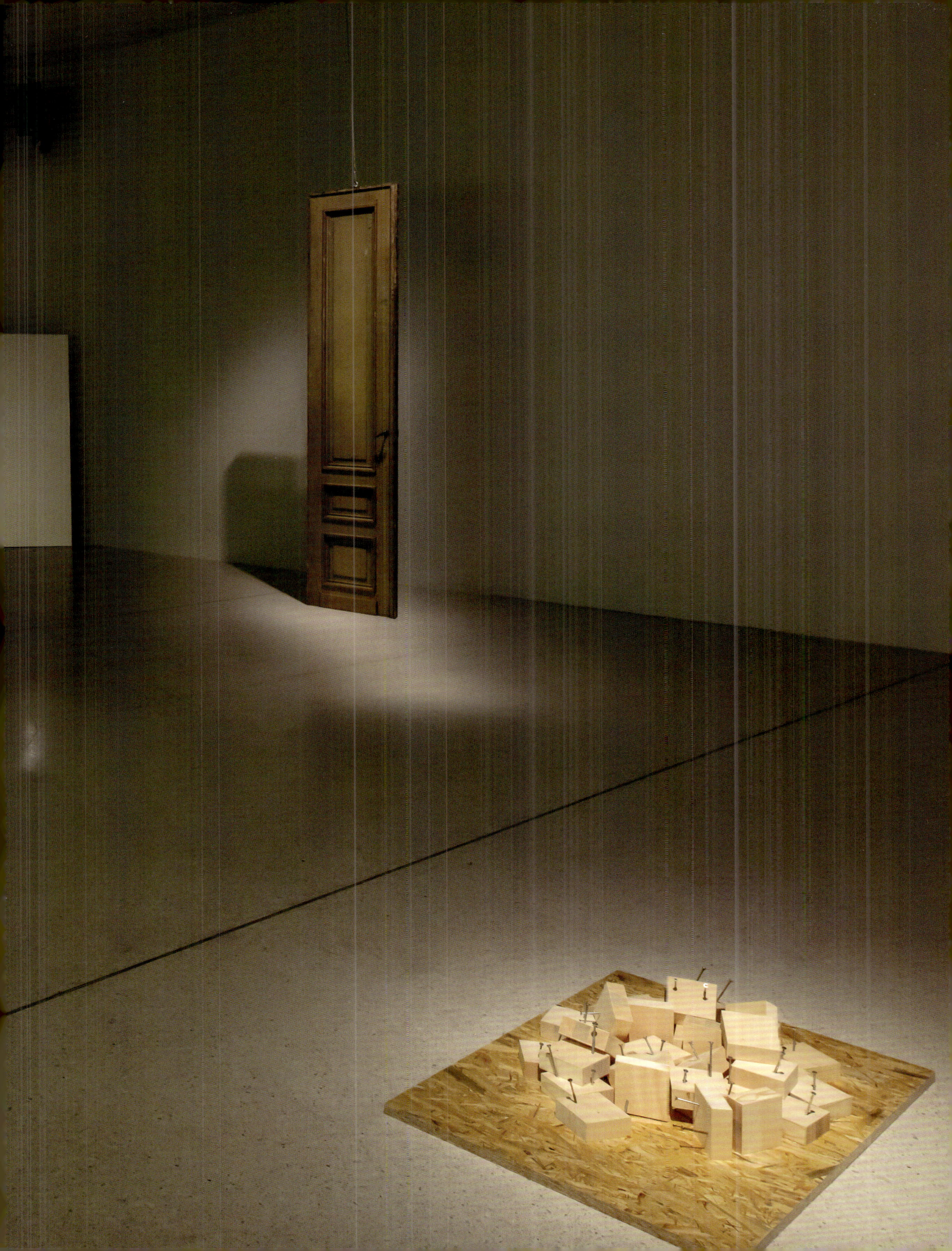

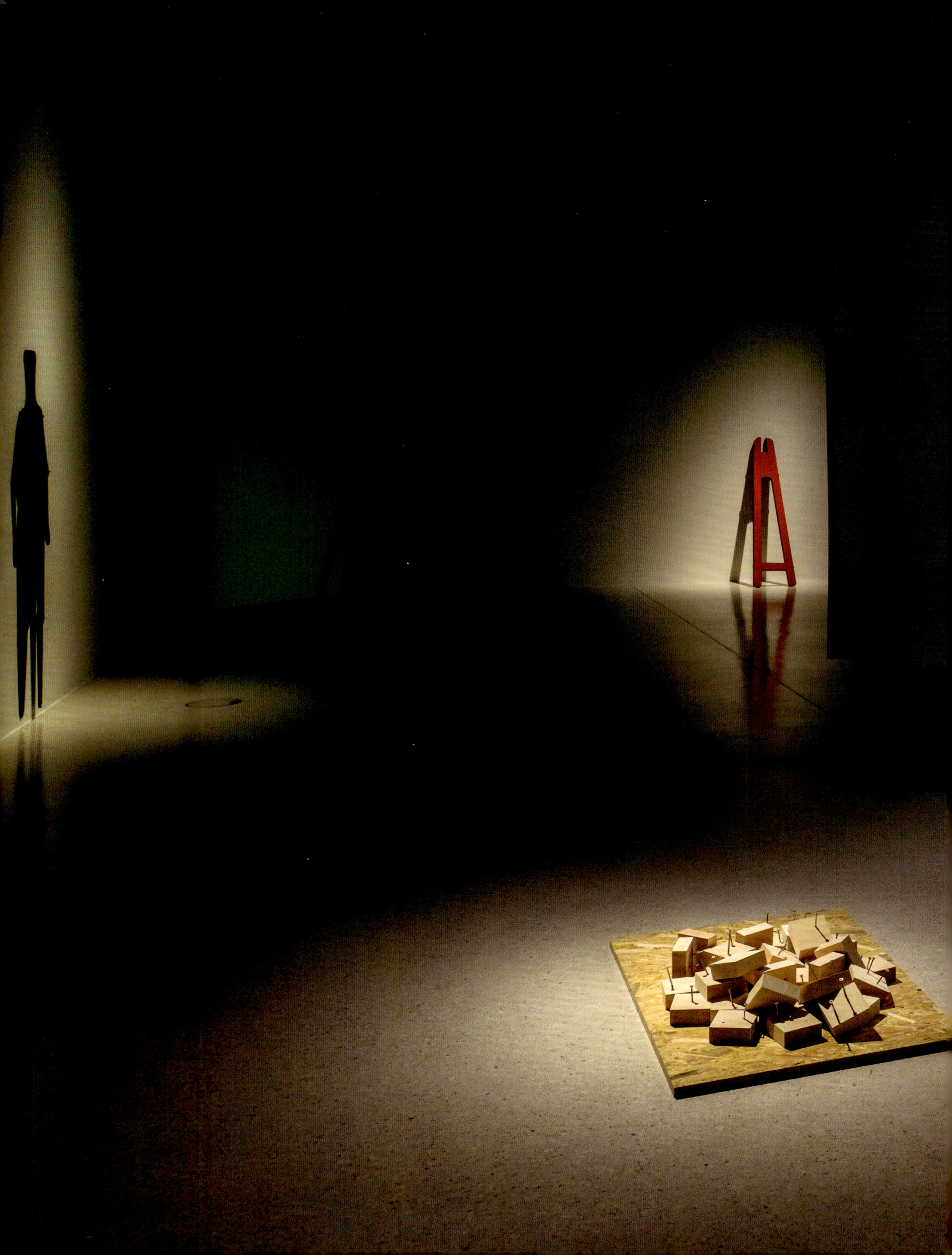

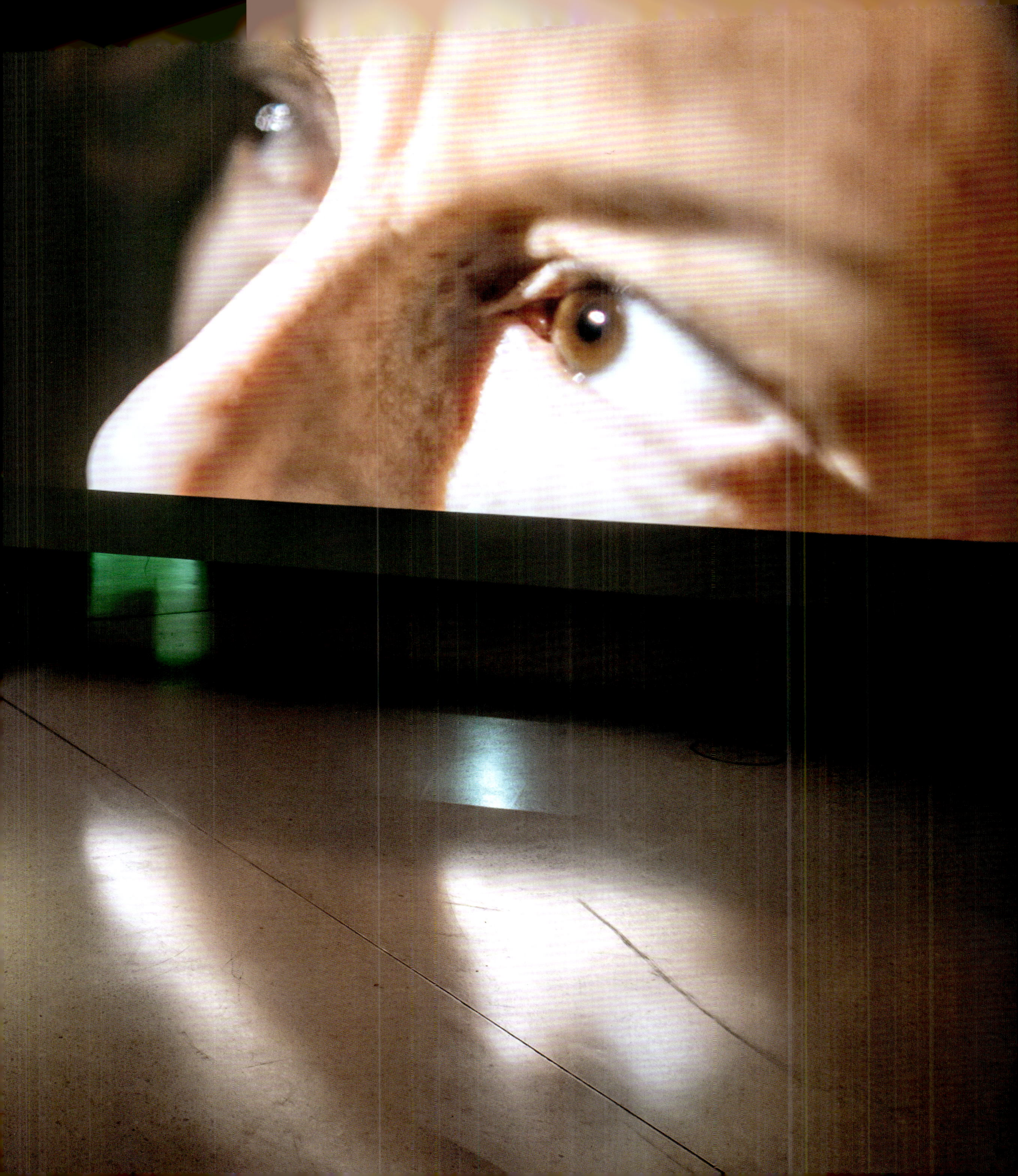

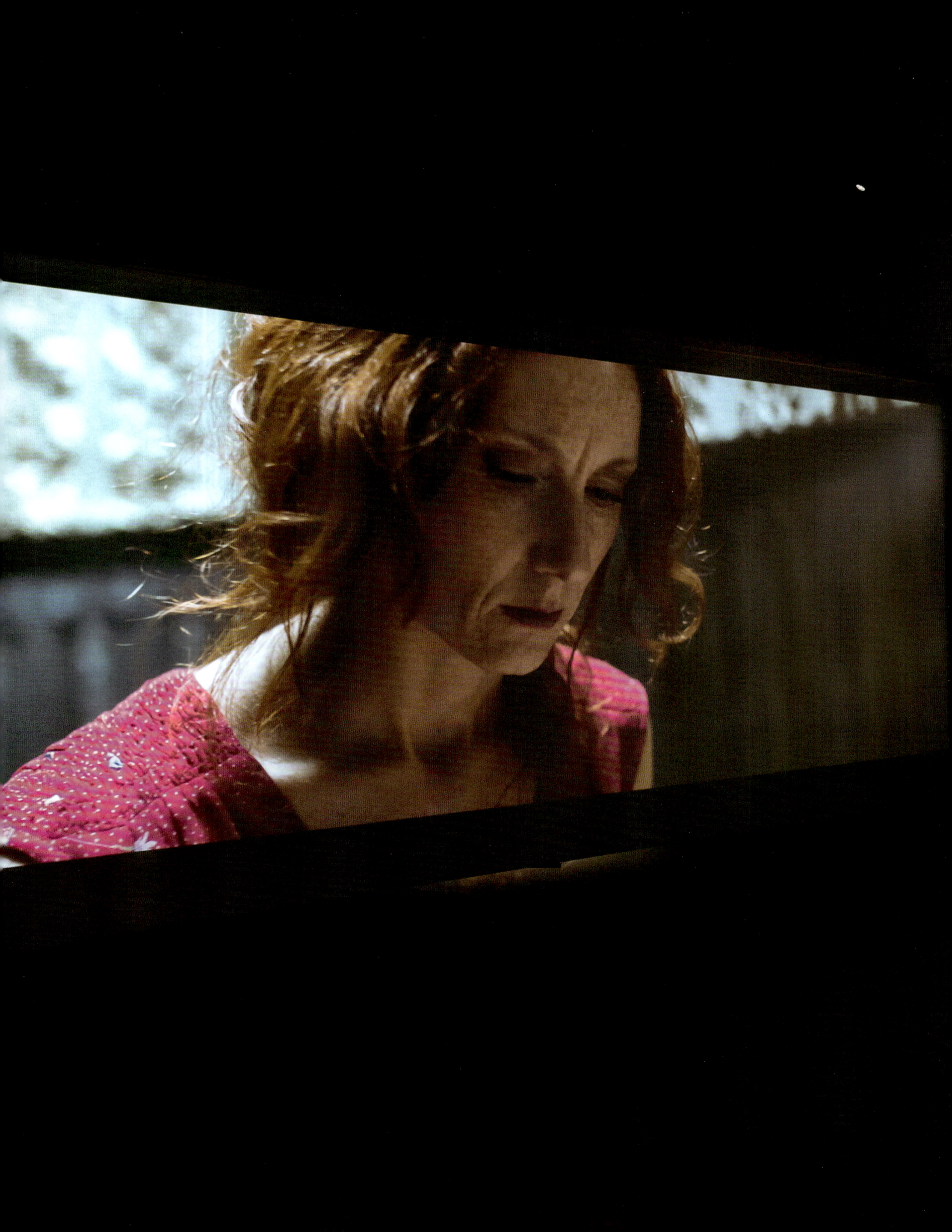

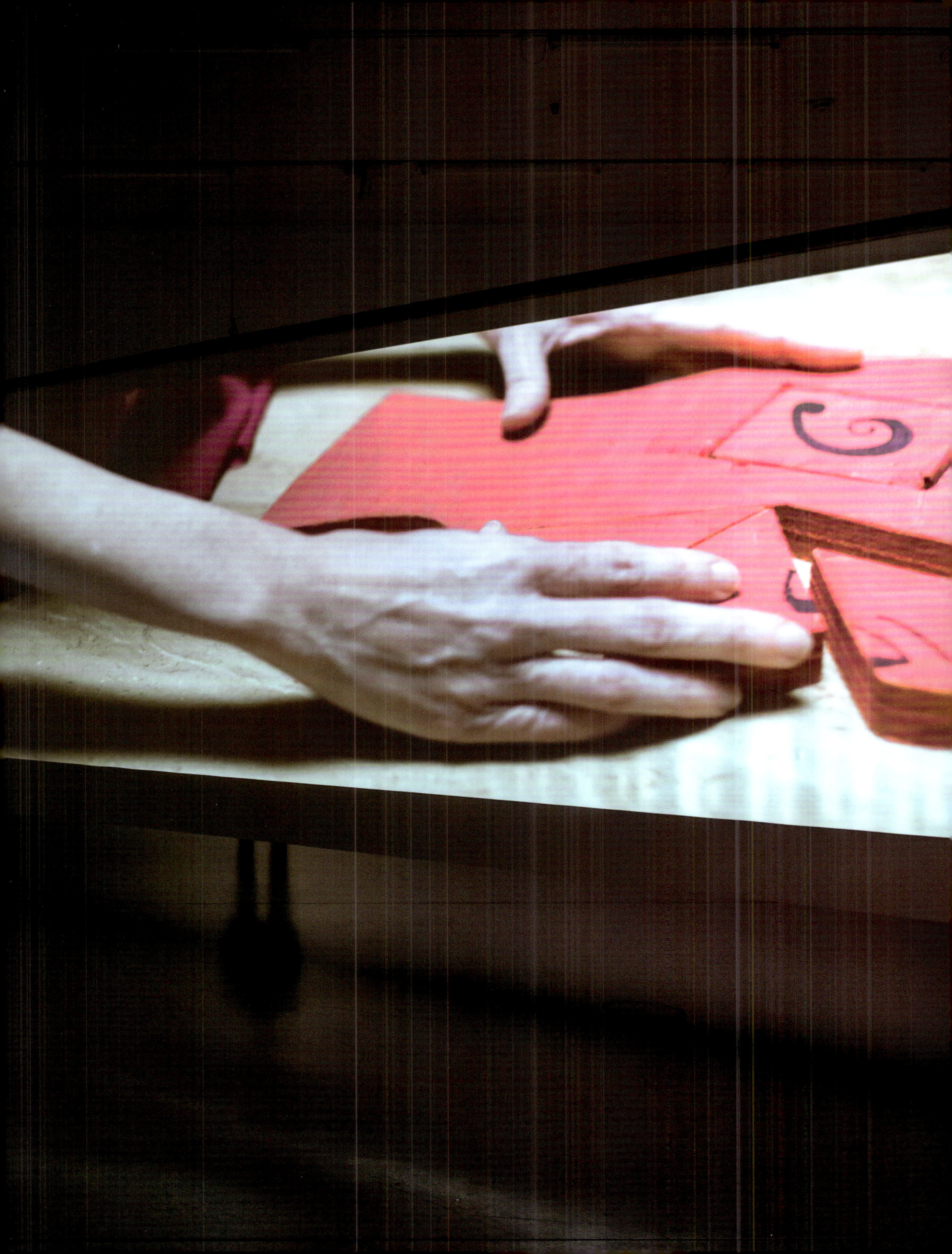

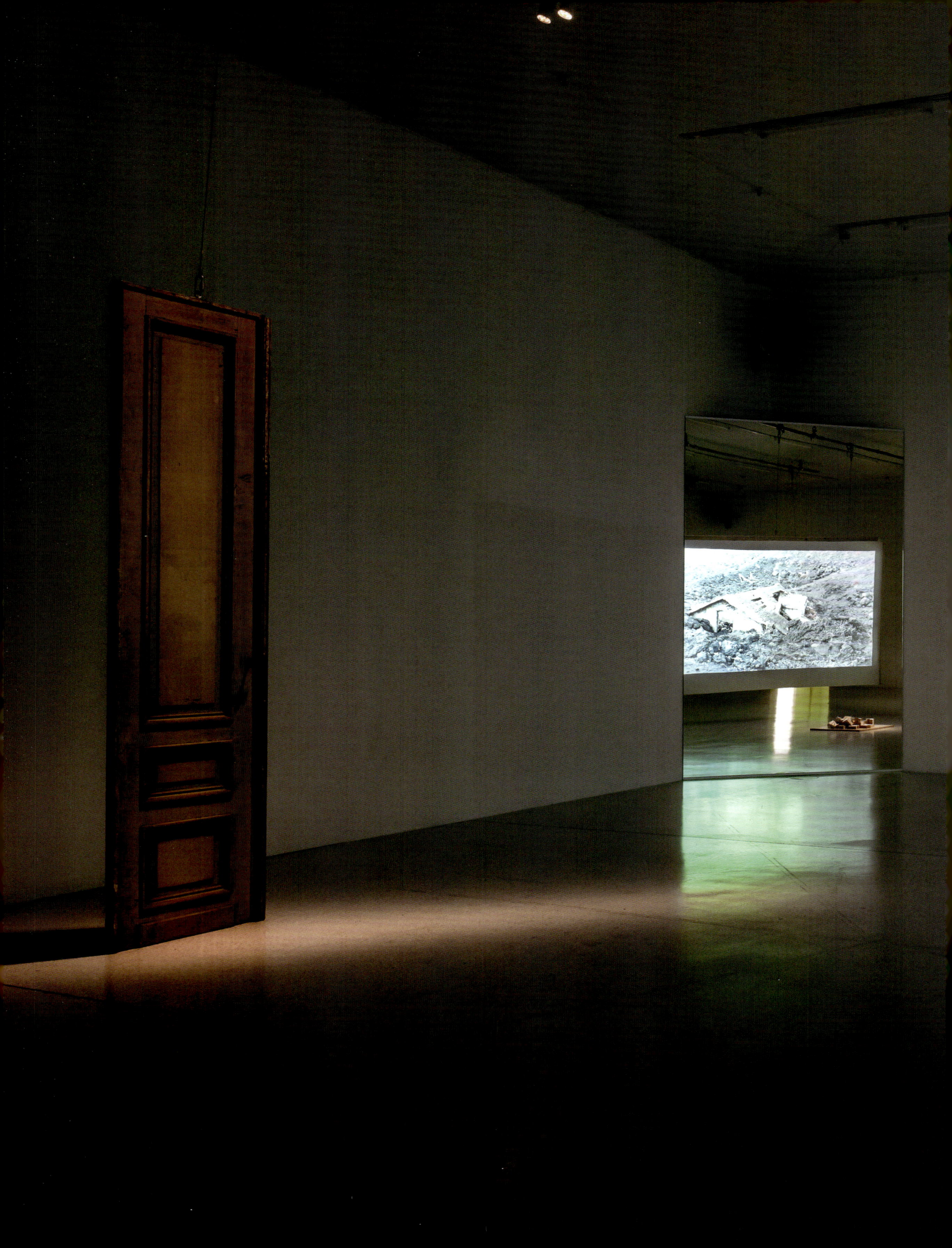

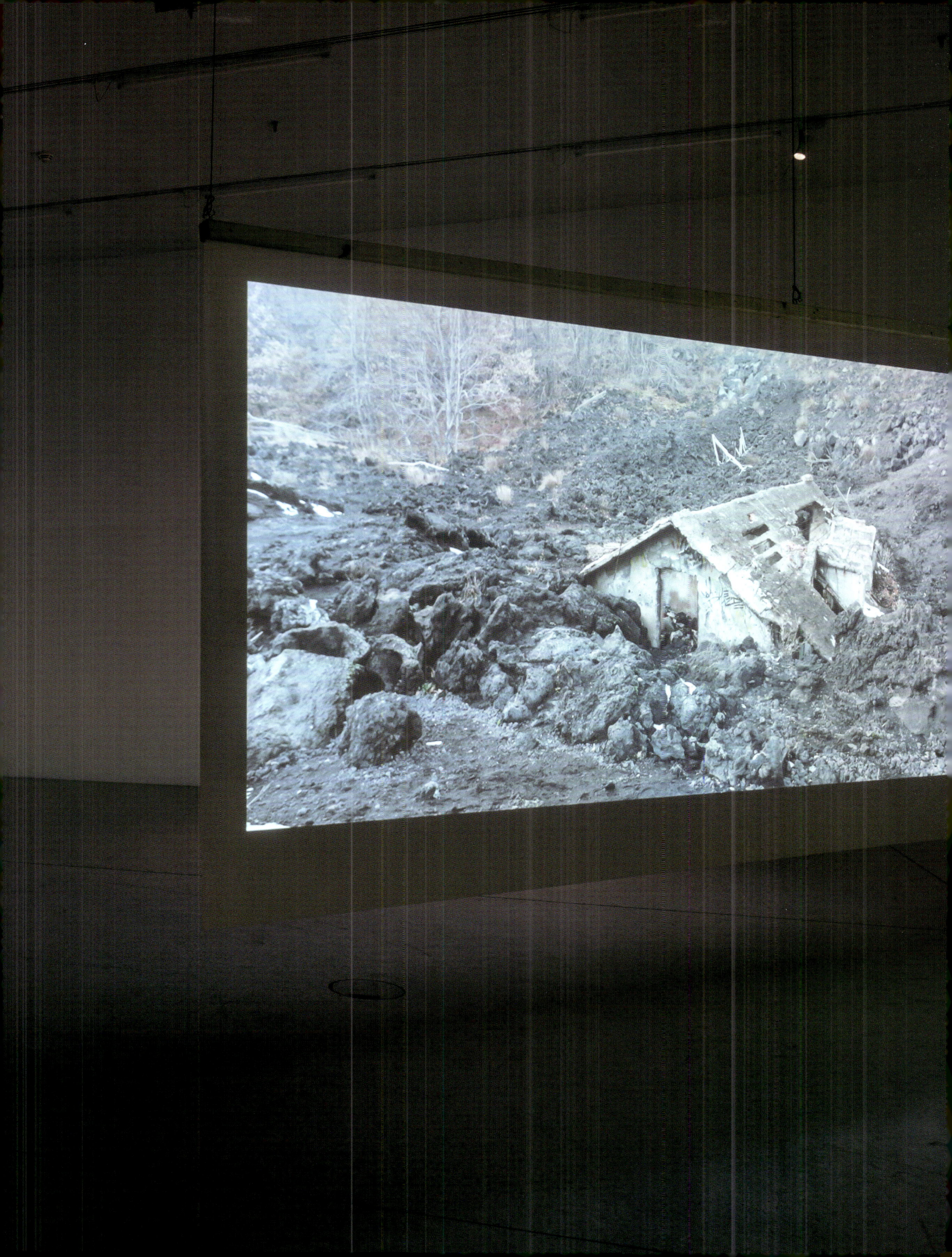

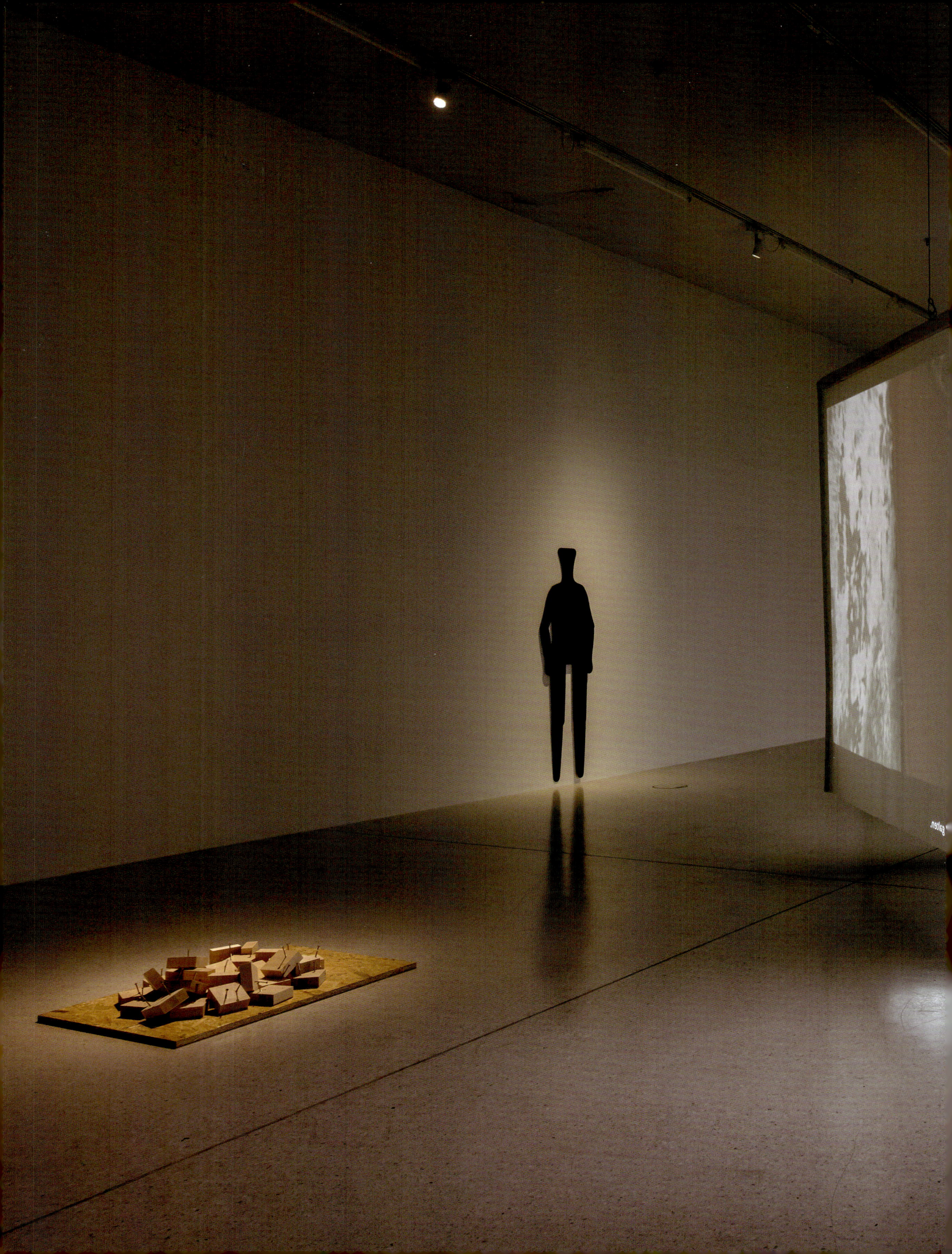

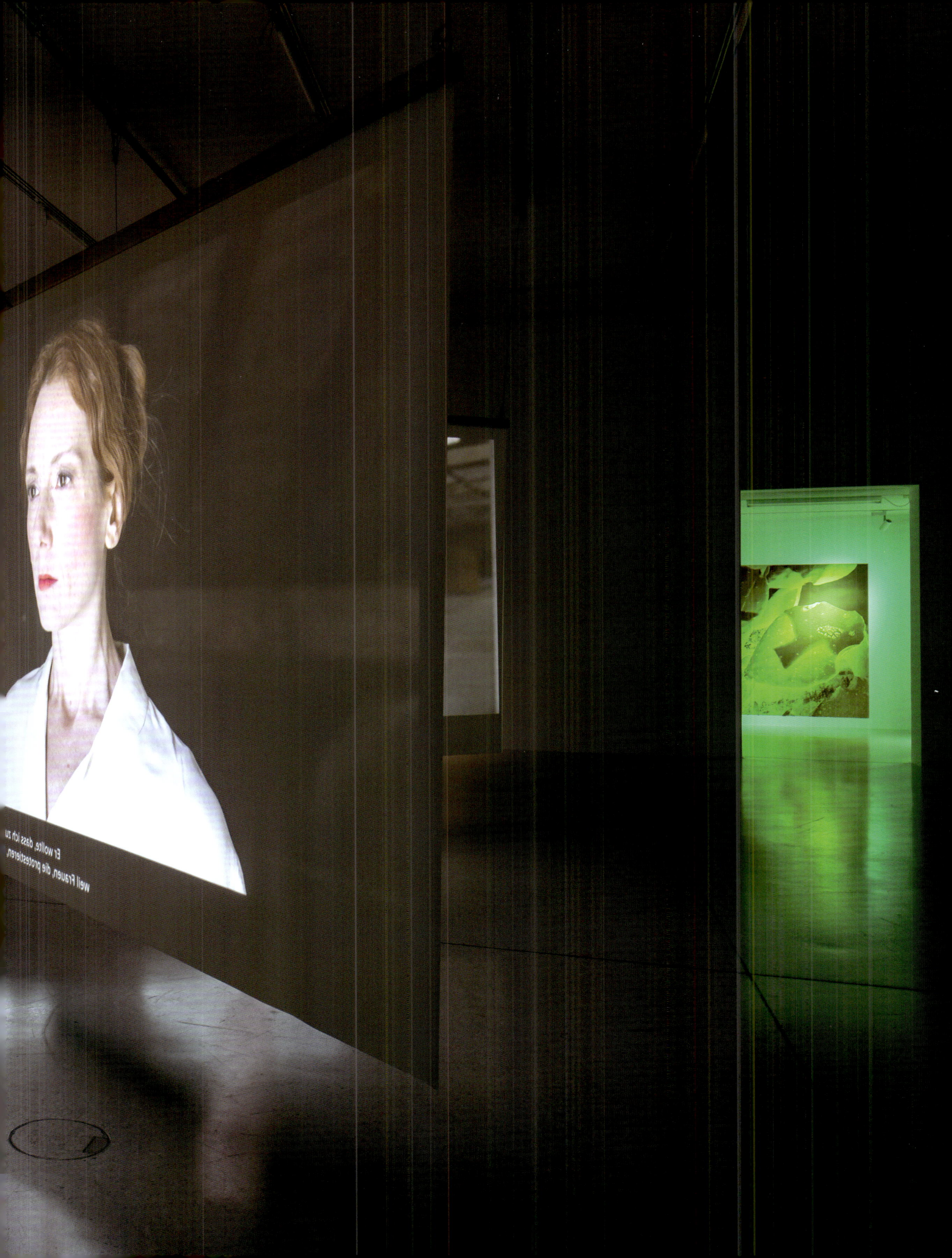

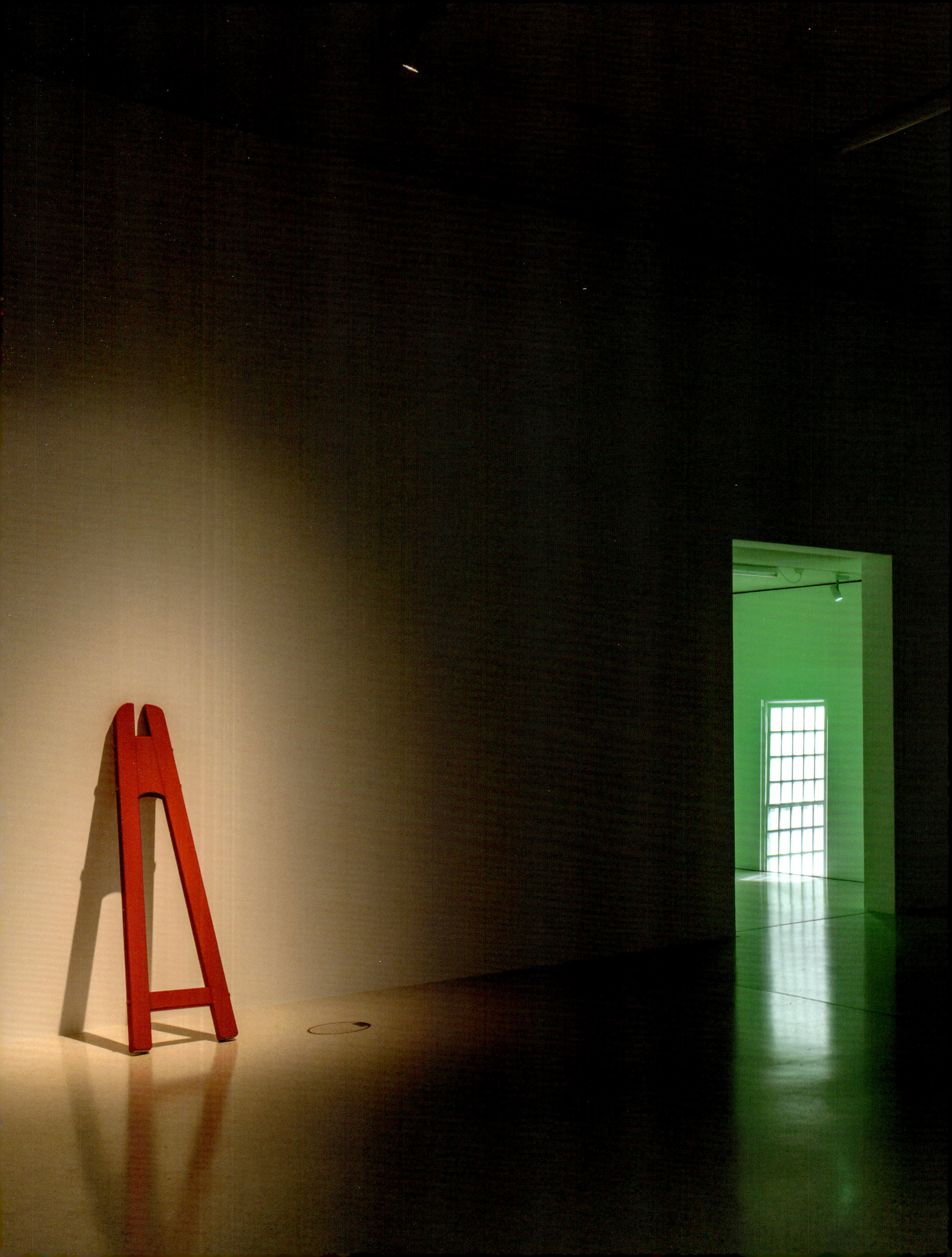

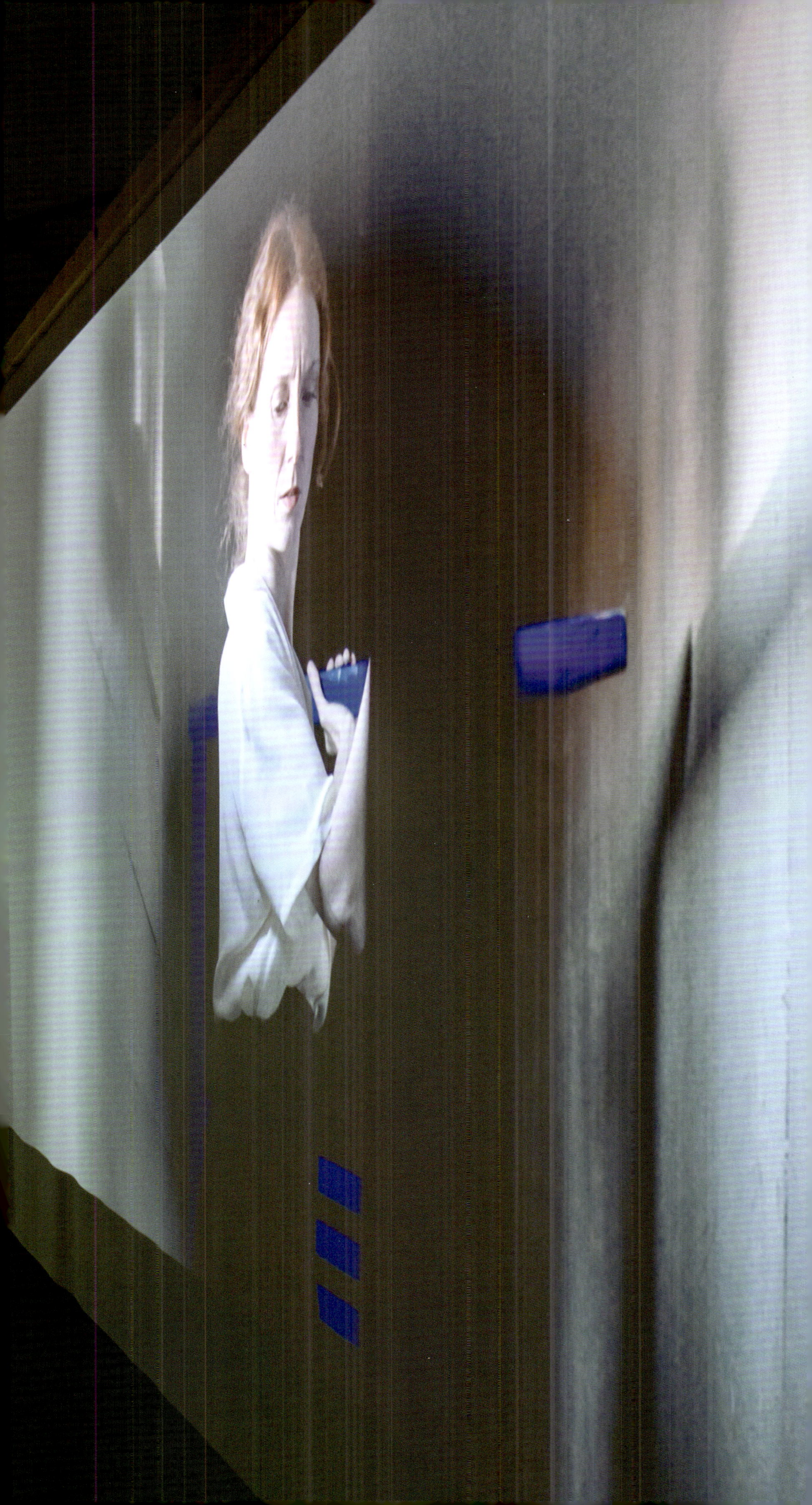

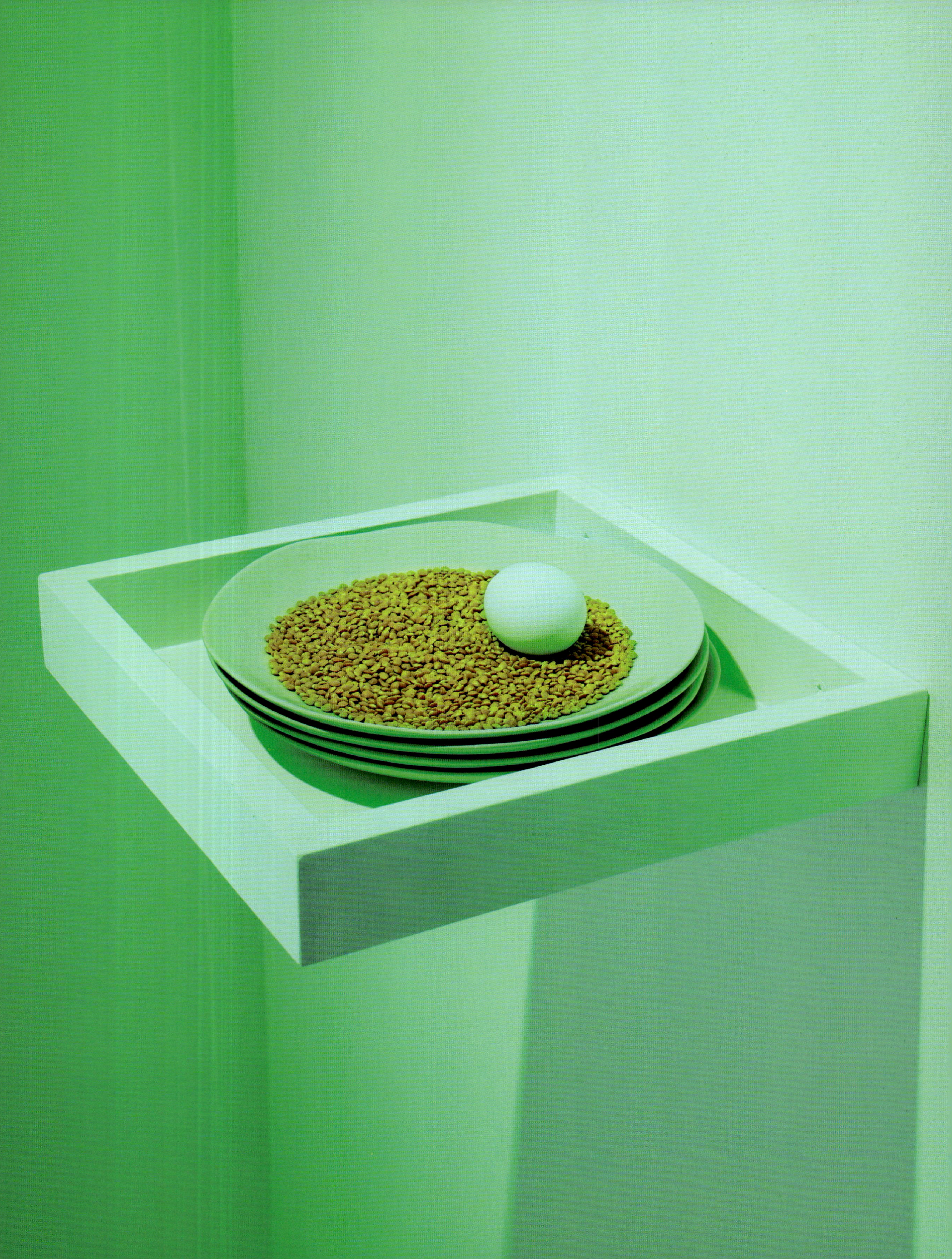

Overly Familiar

Wendy Vogel

Official stories are always biased, artificially constructed. Almost always affected by the alternatives against which they are stated. They exist in opposition with the Other, that despite its invisibility, is still tangible in those fragments we tend to call history.
—*The Other: A Familiar Story*

Maria D. Rapicavoli's two-channel video *The Other: A Familiar Story* (2020) imagines the harrowing psychological landscape of a Sicilian woman who enters into a forced marriage and, in 1907, travels with her husband to Lawrence, Massachusetts, in the United States. After the long journey by sea, she survives further abuses as an immigrant, wife, mother, and underpaid laborer at a textile factory. In 1912 she witnesses the factory's history-making strike, later dubbed the Bread and Roses Strike. This politicized event sparks her consciousness about the conditions of gender-based and racial discrimination. The video concludes with a series of open-ended questions about womanhood and cycles of dehumanization.

Based on a true story, *The Other* is a "familiar" tale on multiple levels. The protagonist, Mena (who goes unnamed in the work), is distantly related to Rapicavoli; both were born and raised in Nicolosi, a small village on Mount Etna close to Catania. Both immigrated to the United States as adults. Drawn to Mena's life, Rapicavoli conceived the work partly from family lore, including information gathered from Mena's now-elderly granddaughter. But the video makes explicit that there is an unbridgeable distance between the work of art and Mena's experience. "I was never allowed to speak. The voice you hear is not mine. Neither is the story I tell," the voice-over announces in the first few minutes. Rather, the story is "made up of the memories of those who knew me and those who heard of me." From that point onward, the script shifts between diaristic confessions of Mena's hardships and an overarching analysis of hegemonic power structures. Rapicavoli describes this clash in the video between the personal and the impersonal as related to "the Freudian uncanny . . . where estrangement and familiarity coexist."[1]

[1] Maria D. Rapicavoli, "A Discussion on Maria Rapicavoli's New Film *The Other: A Familiar Story*," The 8th Floor, New York, December 1, 2020, https://static1.squarespace.com/static/5bb3c259e666696713768624/t/5fc9517e508d-50110260d24c/1607029119542/12.01.2020+Event+Transcript.pdf

As the artist explains, such contradictions occurred often in Mena's life. The video's two-channel structure serves to formally highlight this disjunction.[2]

[2] Sometimes the two screens show different imagery, and sometimes a single scene or image stretches across both channels simultaneously.

Moreover, the video illustrates the all-too-familiar social phenomenon of othering—systemic marginalization based on gender, racial, sexual, and/or class identity. As her story unfolds, Mena gradually accumulates identities of otherness. First and foremost, her status as a woman is marked by sexual assault. *The Other*'s plot begins with her rape and marriage to her assailant. This act of forceful possession alienates her as an object, laying the foundation for subsequent abuse. As the voice-over explains, "It was called kidnapping for the purpose of marriage. It always ended in rape. In this instance, society imposed a demure, reparative wedding, without a white dress, as I had ruined my reputation." The Italian tradition of *matrimonio riparatore*, alternately translated as a rehabilitating or reparatory marriage (in colloquial US English, a "shotgun wedding"), absolves the rapist's crime if he marries his victim. This custom, abolished only forty years ago in Italy, still exists in countries around the world. The legal scholar Rachel A. Van Cleave summarizes traditional attitudes supported by Italian law around sexual assault and reparatory marriage: "The main harm was that suffered by the family. The privacy and autonomy of the victim were not of central concern, if they were even considered at all."[3] By privileging family status

Rachel A. Van Cleave, "Rape and the Querela in Italy: False Protection of Victim Agency," *Michigan Journal of Gender and Law* 13, no. 2 (2007): 283. [3]

above individual bodily autonomy, the assault survivor becomes a second-class citizen. In Mena's story, we see this and other processes of dehumanization repeated again and again.

In 1966, the Sicilian teenager Franca Viola became known as the first woman to publicly contest a reparatory marriage in Italy. Viola's former fiancé, a Mafia associate named Filippo Melodia, violently broke into her house with over a dozen friends on December 26, 1965. The men abducted Viola, then seventeen years old, and Melodia raped her repeatedly over the course of eight days. Viola's father verbally agreed with Melodia's associates to a reparatory marriage, but then at his daughter's request he contacted the police, who arrested Melodia and the kidnappers. The case received intense media attention, and the family suffered both personal and legal intimidation. In the lead-up to the trial, the Viola family's vineyard and barn were torched. Melodia's defense team attempted to discredit the victim, contesting that she had agreed to an elopement—*fuga d'amore*, literally "love escape"— and questioned her sexual history. But in a historic turn, Melodia was convicted of rape in 1966 and sentenced to eleven years in prison (later bargained down to ten), and seven of his accomplices received four-year sentences. The story inspired Damiano Damiani's 1970 feature film *La moglie più bella* (The Most Beautiful Wife).[4]

"La storia di Franca Viola," *Il Post*, January 10, 2018, https://www.ilpost.it/2018/01/10/franca-viola/ [4]

Viola's case was instrumental to changing public opinion about reparatory marriage. Article 544, the statute that legalized the practice, was repealed under Italian law in 1981. Only in 1996 did an additional law prohibit kidnapping for the purposes of marriage. This legislation carried symbolic importance as well, as it recategorized sexual assault from a crime against public morality to a crime against an individual.[5] These recent

Van Cleave, "Rape and the Querela in Italy," 289. She adds: "In addition, this categorical change represents the state's primary goal of protecting individual sexual liberty, in those terms, and not simply protecting public morals by prosecuting sexual offenses" (289). [5]

laws underscore the extent to which female bodies have been seen as property—first of their birth family, then in the bond of matrimony.

Italy is far from the only country to offer recent condemnation of marital rape. As of 2017, at least ten countries still had laws that permitted marital rape, and nine countries excused rapists from criminal action if they married their victims.[6] In the United States, attitudes

According to a report published by the nonprofit Equality Now, "At least 9 [countries] appear to have laws under which a perpetrator of rape or sexual assault can escape punishment if he marries the victim. . . . At least 12 appear to have laws under which a perpetrator can be exempt from punishment by reaching a 'settlement,' financial or otherwise, with the victim or the victim's family. At least 8 appear to have laws under which a perpetrator of rape or sexual assault can escape punishment if he received forgiveness from the victim" (17). "Marital rape is specifically characterised as not a crime (i.e. explicitly permitted) in at least 10 [countries.] Marital rape is only explicitly criminalised if the parties are separated in at least 6 [countries]" (25). Equality Now, "The World's Shame: The Global Rape Epidemic," 2017, accessible at https://d3n8a8pro7vhmx.cloudfront.net/equalitynow/pages/208/attachments/original/1527096293/EqualityNowRapeLawReport2017_Single_Pages.pdf?1527096293 [6]

have also been slow to change about a spouse's right to sexual consent. Although nineteenth-century anarchists and first-wave suffragettes spoke out against marital rape, feminists did not take up the issue again until the 1970s. By 1993, all fifty states had outlawed marital rape, although legal loopholes provide spousal exemptions to several acts that would otherwise be criminal. Up to twenty states exempt spouses who sexually assault partners who lack the ability to consent (if intoxicated or unconscious, for example), and up to eleven states have marital exemptions for sexual assault of partners capable of consent.[7] Child marriage laws

7 Teresa M. Garvey, Holly M. Fuhrman, and Jennifer Long, "Charging Considerations in the Prosecution of Marital Rape," *Aequitas* 34 (September 2019): 2, accessible at https://aequitasresource.org/wp-content/uploads/2019/09/Charging-Considerations-in-the-Prosecution-of-Marital-Rape-2.pdf

are the most egregious vestige of these laws. As of 2021, only five states and two US territories have banned marriage for individuals under eighteen years old. Many of these marriages—sixty thousand since the year 2000—make legal sexual activity with minors that would otherwise be criminalized, either because of one partner's age or because of the age difference between partners.[8]

8 Unchained at Last "United States' Child Marriage Problem," April 2021, https://www.unchainedatlast.org/united-states-child-marriage-problem-study-findings-april-2021/

Mena's story, then, posits sexual violence as the ground upon which additional intersectional oppressions are built. In addition to demanding that Mena immigrate with him to Massachusetts, Mena's husband forced her to leave their four children behind in Sicily. Once across the ocean she bore more children, whom her husband also mistreated. The video recalls his attempts to restrict their portions of food and alludes to further familial violence, including psychological gaslighting. The remainder of the work tackles such topics as the treatments of migrants (as the voice-over says of Mena's arrival in the United States, "We were seen as an inferior race—assassins and anarchists"), a global pandemic (the family survived the worldwide influenza outbreak of 1918), and labor struggles to organize for better working conditions (the Bread and Roses Strike).

Rapicavoli filmed in Sicily, in the abandoned factory where Mena and her husband worked and in a former mental hospital. The story's vivid locations, along with the piercing portrayal of Mena by actress Lucia Cammalleri, lend gravitas to the production. But *The Other* is not a traditional realist narrative. Mena is filmed as an isolated figure. Her internal monologue is recited in voice-over against dramatic scenery empty of other human characters. The specter of her husband appears as a shadow early in the video, and later as a cutout silhouette tacked to the wall. In a single scene shot in a dining room, mannequins stand in for her children born in the United States.

The opening scenes show Mena in the fairy-tale-like Sicilian environs of luscious gardens, mysterious caves, and the sea. After revealing the circumstances of her rape and marriage, Mena appears in the rubble of volcanic Mount Etna. "The damage caused by the violence is permanent," the voice-over says, as Mena paces outside a house destroyed by an eruption. She observes a fine line drawing that resembles her own face on the outside of the house. This scene presages the climax of the video, in which she discovers graffiti of nude women on the beams of the Lawrence textile factory.

Later scenes gradually strip away realism in favor of highlighting Mena's psychological torment. As her voice-over describes the boat transport to the United States, she appears in an isolated room completing a puzzle—a common intelligence test at Ellis Island that immigrants would need to pass in order to stay in the country. When the video segues to Mena's life in Massachusetts, the settings become more surreal. Footage of Mena hiding money in her modest home are juxtaposed with sequences of her cutting holes into cacti or retreating deep into a cave. In the starkest scenes revealing her despair, she physically struggles to maneuver a blue-painted wooden bed frame. The unwieldy object operates as a metaphor for the symbolic struggle in a patriarchal society. The voice-over makes clear that sexual violation was a consistent form of abuse in Mena's marriage: "Every time he ordered me to go to the bedroom with him, I imagined moving the bed to another room, making it vanish so we did not have to lie down next to one another."

She performs the lonely gesture of rolling the bed frame through the empty factory space as sunlight perversely streams in through large windows. In a subsequent scene she navigates the frame through a narrow hallway. The voice-over describes the claustrophobic experience of being cooped up in the house during the 1918 pandemic: "The more you stayed at home, the more breathless you became." Once again, Mena's story resonates with contemporary conditions: the National Commission on COVID-19 and Criminal Justice reports that domestic violence rose 8.1 percent during pandemic-related lockdowns in the United States.[9]

National Commission on COVID-19 and Criminal Justice Impact Report: COVID-19 and Domestic Violence Trends, February 23, 2021, https://covid19.counciloncj.org/2021/02/23/impact-report-covid-19-and-domestic-violence-trends/

The video imagines Mena's reaction to the 1912 textile strike as an exposure of the inequalities she suffered in private. As the voice-over states, the event "disrupted the ordinary, bringing all invisible struggles to the surface." The three-month protest, instigated by women workers and led by International Workers of the World organizers, brought together workers representing more than fifty nationalities to bargain for shorter work hours and better wages. The video, however, does not show the protagonist's participation in the strike. Instead, Mena's on-screen revelation about her objectification comes through an encounter with the aforementioned graffiti in the abandoned factory, much of which depicts scantily clad or nude figures. The camera lingers on an illustration of a woman with wide eyes surrounded by halos of eyelashes. Her body's contours, by contrast, are hastily drawn in, and subtly erased by time. "What am I?" a speech bubble asks. Mena appears to ask the same of herself.

Throughout *The Other*, Mena's story unfolds through the actor's proximity to objects and landscapes. In these objects—from a cactus to mannequins to graffiti—she recognizes herself, her family, and her patriarchal adversaries. In the two presentations of the video to date, Rapicavoli has situated it in installations that dramatize the work's sensations of doubling, mirroring, and collapsing of physical and psychological distance. *The Other* debuted in 2020 at The 8th Floor in New York, in the group exhibition *To Cast Too Bold a Shadow*, curated by Sara Reisman. This exhibition brought together artworks exploring histories of misogyny. Rapicavoli projected the two-channel video against adjoining walls that formed a corner, creating a triangulation between the projection and the viewer. In a small adjacent space, she presented various scenographic elements from the video. Three mirrors propped against the wall created a disorienting multiplication effect for the props: three mannequins, a puzzle perched on a table, several stools, the blue-painted bed frame, and unvarnished construction materials such as wood pieces and nails. The installation suggested the mental claustrophobia experienced by Mena in her inescapable situation of otherness.

For her exhibition at Westfälischer Kunstverein, Münster, in May 2021, curated by Kristina Scepanski, Rapicavoli reimagined *The Other*'s multipart installation across several rooms, immersing the viewer in the atmosphere of the video. She installed two screens in a V formation, with large mirrors in diagonal corners opposite the screens. As in the installation at The 8th Floor, the screens triangulated the viewers within them. The mirrors further implicated them in the sight lines of the video, as though they were characters in it. Sculptural elements from the sets were strategically curated and spread throughout the room: a cutout silhouette of a man, bits of rubble on the floor, a plate with lentils. Rapicavoli also included a found door of exaggerated height, similar in appearance to the door on top of which Mena hides money in the video. Because she was taller than her husband, she was the only family member who could reach the hiding spot; this prop celebrates her powerful stature and her cleverness.

The galleries also featured photographic components evoking Mena's psychological state. An alcove displayed an enlarged photograph of a Sicilian cactus with holes bored through its fleshy leaves. Rapicavoli tinted the image orange and lit it with a green gel. Its contrasting colors simulated the bewildering effect of an afterimage. In an adjacent space the artist projected an image of the windows of the Lawrence textile factory. This theatrical gesture foregrounded the importance of the industrial space that absorbed so many of Mena's waking hours—even after the strike, workers still labored fifty-four hours a week—and catalyzed her ability to question her situation. Printed photographs of the sexualized graffiti found in the factory's attic were shown in a smaller gallery space, spotlit and installed on darkly painted walls. While removing the imagery from the context of vandalism to that of autonomous art object, Rapicavoli's installation also called to mind the environment of the cave featured prominently in the video. Such a space offers both protection and, ironically, an environment of silencing.

Rapicavoli's *The Other* excavates the historical fragments of memory, piecing together a story situated at once in the present and in the past. The last line of the video makes this clear: "The story keeps on getting written." The struggles of othering and abuse persist to the present day. To make the struggles of the past "familiar," the artist puzzles out the story of a woman at once known to and estranged from her. She creates a context in which we might more closely examine the systems that perpetuate continued oppression based on gender, race, citizenship status, and class.

Something fragile is something that can be broken but is not yet broken

Sarah Lookofsky in conversation with Maria D. Rapicavoli

The following conversation took place over email and in a shared online document in July and August 2021. The virtual dialogue absorbed and reflected upon the formats of pandemic life, which were also the conditions for the works and exhibitions it addressed. The exchange considers different intersections of practice, power, and purpose across several decades and bodies of Rapicavoli's work. It has been lightly edited.

SL

I want to begin with the site- and temporal specificity of this book and the fact that someone (hopefully!) will be reading these words many months after our correspondence. Typically, I would smooth over this temporal gap, but given this very peculiar moment, I think we'd best dwell upon the fissure. In this moment, we are emerging out of the pandemic (you were fully vaccinated in the United States; I had my first shot in Europe last week). A year ago, we were both enclosed in our respective homes in New York City as tens of thousands of people were dying; there was a general state of fear and paranoia, as the science about how the virus spreads and the mortality rate were subject to speculation. I believe the last time we saw one another was at a Black Lives Matter demonstration in June 2020, an incredible moment of physical togetherness after months of isolation. It was probably around this time that you took photographs in Manhattan in the aftermath of the demonstrations and looting that caused much of the city to shutter in a very dramatic way. It made the place strange. Let's begin by thinking back to that moment. Tell me about coming across these places and how the photographs came about.

MDR

I am currently on Mount Etna, in Sicily. I am very familiar with this place, because I was born here and grew up at the bottom of the volcano. An eruption just started. I hear the roaring; I see the smoke, and I feel tension mixed with excitement and fear. My external reality is out of my control. I have an urge to go outside and experience the moment.

I bring this up because last year, at the end of May, I was feeling the same sense of pressure. I was in my small apartment in Manhattan after two months of self-isolation, watching the news, when the murder of George Floyd took place. Tension in the city was palpable. I could not sleep because helicopters were all over and the police sirens sounded everywhere. There were demonstrations on every street corner. The media was focusing on the violence of these actions, but I was instead enjoying that revolutionary tension. I was fascinated by the sudden change that the city was experiencing. On one hand, streets filled with hundreds of people raising their voices. On the other hand, boarded-up facades were protecting the businesses inside from vandalism and looting. Banks and luxury stores locked their doors first, followed by shopping centers, restaurants, and art galleries. Corporate logos and fancy vitrines were disappearing behind anonymous panels of wood. There was no competition to attract customers. Capitalism was, for the first time, rejecting people, and people were finally rebelling. For days I was in between these two universes, photographing hundreds of barricaded buildings in the morning, then taking part in the demonstrations at night.

SL

One image that is particularly striking captures the Apple Store entrance on Fifth Avenue. Usually a glass cube facing Central Park, it is covered in wood panels painted white. I once wrote an essay about that store and the shift of the signifier of transparency from modernist architecture to the corporate facade. But corporate illusions of transparency could not withstand the threat of broken glass.

MDR

Most of the sealed-off stores used unpainted, natural wood. Only a few of them painted their panels as a mark of distinction (for instance Tiffany & Co. was wrapped in turquoise). The Apple Store wrapped itself in white. The building became a tall, white, wooden fortress.

Only the top of the glass was left unprotected—a show
of some sort of vulnerability? Or maybe as a watchtower
to control the area? The white walls were surrounded
by metal chain-link and plastic barriers. Dozens of police
cars were surveilling the area. Wow, what a statement,
I thought. At first glance, it looked like a big white
bumper protecting itself from possible intruders. To me,
that opacity was a reactionary act repelling any form
of revolution. A symbol of white supremacy revealing its real nature, which has nothing to do with transparency. What a stark contrast with many boarded-up
small businesses in Lower Manhattan that had sprayed
"BLM" on their raw wood panels.

SL

You were at the protests, witnessed some of the moments of vandalism, and have described these experiences as very vivid. But, as in most of your work, your photographs
are devoid of people. Why did you decide to not picture people, here and in the majori-
ty of your other projects?

MDR

A key concern of my artistic production has always
been how to make the abstractions of global capitalism
tangible. Most systems of power are not easy to grasp,
as they manifest through representations rather than
directly. But they do leave traces by establishing their
principles on accumulations of goods, spectacles, and
dispossession, and enforce their power by expanding
everywhere in society. I don't depict people because I
want to focus on making visible the consequences that
these abstract entities leave in physical space, not on
people's reactions. I can better isolate, analyze, and
highlight the system this way.

In 2013, I worked on a series of photographs of
the M.U.O.S. (Mobile User Objective System), a system
of satellite communications at ultra-high frequency
that enables enhanced long-distance communication
with drones. It was under construction in Niscemi,
Sicily. The photographs were taken during a demonstration followed by a peaceful occupation of the military
base in protest of the construction of the ground sta-
tion. The photographs don't depict people protesting;
instead, they reveal the big surveillance device and a police
helicopter flying over. The reason *why* people were
demonstrating seemed more important than the act
of demonstration per se. Moreover, by photographing
the M.U.O.S. from that point of view (only accessible
through the base), I was implicitly showing that I was
demonstrating inside the military area.

SL

I'm glad you brought up your M.U.O.S. satellite dish photographs. Considered alongside
the boarded-up storefronts, they exemplify how the sites and objects you isolate in your
photographic practice bear a metonymic relationship to larger systems of power: a satellite
for global surveillance, a boarded-up Apple Store for capitalism in crisis, a boat for the migrant crisis (I am speaking here of the series *Load Displacement* [2012], which features ves-
sels in Sicily used to carry migrants). Do you think of these works as connected? How has
your work migrated between these different sites and systems?

MDR

My practice employs multiple media, including video,
sculpture, and photography, to investigate how, through
spatial and temporal forms of montage, such elements
can be configured to generate a space for both aesthetic
experience and critical discourse. The process that
moves me is always the same: I seek to explore how
abstract—and often invisible—social, economic, and
political structures and forms can be represented or
figured through art. I seek to make these systems of
power visible, because they generate in me a state of
discomfort that must be expressed. If the representation of reality surprises us by being contradictory and

paradoxical, it means that we are not passive observers and perhaps can have a critical perspective on things. I believe that art, as a practice, can provoke a social response. It can have consequences and be a transformative experience.

This conception has influenced all of my artistic research, from my early work about the Sicilian Mafia (someone once described the Mafia as the best example of capitalism), to my work about the brutal conditions under which millions of migrants are forced to cross the Mediterranean Sea, to my images of the military system of surveillance that regulates and controls our sky, to the patriarchal systems reiterated in my most recent work.

<table>
<tr><td>SL</td><td>Let's talk about the sculptural piece If I Am In Pieces Is It Easier To See? (2020), which was also made during the pandemic but has a much more affective resonance. It points to two distinct tendencies in your work: the documentary approach to infrastructural power, and works that take on the psychological effects of such power systems. How do you reflect upon this particular piece and the very different (sculptural, manually labor-intensive) working mode it involved?</td></tr>
</table>

SL

Let's talk about the sculptural piece *If I Am In Pieces Is It Easier To See?* (2020), which was also made during the pandemic but has a much more affective resonance. It points to two distinct tendencies in your work: the documentary approach to infrastructural power, and works that take on the psychological effects of such power systems. How do you reflect upon this particular piece and the very different (sculptural, manually labor-intensive) working mode it involved?

MDR

When the pandemic started, I found myself isolated in my apartment, unable to go to my studio because of the lockdown. I was forced to stay in a restricted place and both live and work there. In the meantime, I was asked by the Magazzino Italian Art Foundation to take part in a project called *Homemade*. I was not sure if I could focus on any new project. A sense of uncertainty and anxiety was all over. Because of this big shift in my reality, I thought that by sharing my feelings I was somehow sharing the reality around me.

The first boarded-up storefront I came across was at the beginning of the lockdown in New York, in March 2020, three months before the BLM demonstrations. It was an abandoned building in SoHo, not far from my apartment. A nearby postal worker told me it had been vandalized the night before. An accumulation of broken glass was still on the street. The last trace of an urban drama in a city that was just starting to hold its breath for a long time. Those shiny little pieces of glass caught my eyes. I brought them home but then got rid of them right after; a deep fear of the virus prevented me from keeping them. Like the storefront, I needed to protect my place from the external reality. But the longer I stayed home, the more I felt the rupture and loss that the broken glass so accurately represented. I then ordered fifty pounds of clay and modeled thousands of small, sharp, geometrical pieces of ceramic to reconstruct the glass shards. I processed the feeling of rupture with resilience, spending hours meticulously modeling broken pieces of glass with clay so as to reconstruct reality.

My apartment became a workspace: my kitchen table a desk, and my bed a shooting set. My space shrank; my time expanded. The manual labor helped me to understand that new rhythm of time and give shape to fears that were otherwise difficult to grasp. I realized how fragile I am, and how the world is all connected to individual fragilities. I saw fragility as the perception of a possibility that a rupture can happen. Something fragile is something that can be broken but is not yet broken. And once it *is* broken, it loses its fragile nature and becomes something else. So, while modeling hundreds of pieces of "broken" clay, I somehow erased the potentiality of its fragile nature, and I overcame the loss of the storefront glass found on the street, with its representation of a broken reality.

These reflections are also interesting in relation to the works we first addressed: the glass storefront that is protected from being smashed, revealing a fragility in the capitalist system, and your careful rendering of the physicality of broken glass in clay (taking away its transparency!). This act evokes a kind of care and repair but without restoration. Meticulously allowing something to remain broken.

The global aspect of the pandemic has been fascinating to me. It brought an extended, common focus to the whole world; everyone was facing a shared threat. Just as you describe it, I also experienced this as an affective dimension of globalization that felt unprecedented. (Of course, that common threat did not just produce unity internationally. It also led to explosions of nationalist fervor in many places and the push to hoard resources.) What I've also found interesting is that despite the global nature of the pandemic, the experience of it was so different depending on context, not only because of economy and infrastructure—the availability of oxygen, vaccines, et cetera—but also due to cultural specificities. Different intersections of science with various cultural traditions led to wildly different mandates about masking, distance, closures, and so on.

> I agree. It generated an economic war that revealed conflicts and disparities across countries, turning a viral threat into a pandemic of inequality.

Yes, absolutely. Regarding how to imagine or picture the international or the global, an undercurrent in your work, I think, could be described as an examination of the local in a global age, and by extension, the specificities of place in relation to mobility and distributed power. Most of your work is devoted to two localities—your native Sicily and your diasporic home of New York—and to examinations of those places as well as to tracing connections between them. Can you talk about what the connection to these places and the local means to your practice?

> Specific locations (geographic and, recently, also mental) are often a starting point that helps me describe a more universal situation. My Sicilian background has moved me to investigate various structures of power that involve Italy (Sicily in particular) and its connections with the United States, especially since 1943. This was the year in which the two countries started an economic and military pact that still has a strong impact not only on their politics specifically, but also globally. My photos of M.U.O.S. mentioned earlier are a perfect example of the physical consequences of this agreement: an extremely powerful system of surveillance that controls the entire planet.
>
> Working mostly with site-specific installations, I think about places in terms of spaces. Analyzing the problems of space concerns different scales and registers in my work: from how one experiences architectural space phenomenologically to how space can be geopolitically defined through bordered or controlled areas (both aerial and terrestrial). This idea of space extends to questions of proximity and contact: how we perceive the here and there, the near and far away, and how such binaries are continually shifting and changing. Capitalism, by way of nation-states, generates both visible and invisible borders, yet at the same time dissolves them through the flows of trade and finance. How can the notion of a particular site and place be conceived in relation to this space of flows (both material and immaterial) and, politically, how does the control of space function on the levels of the personal, social, or national (both concretely and imaginarily)? In this sense, maps and charts have often been important sources in my research, which I decode and abstract to transform their geographical specificity into a more universal model.
>
> In 2012, I came across a formerly classified US aerial chart of the sky above Sicily: a sky I always imagined as free and open to all. But seeing those demarcations, even just on paper, made them real to my

eyes. I then started an ongoing project, *A Cielo Aperto*, a site-specific installation delineating, among other restricted and prohibited sites, the flight corridors used by military drones. The installation consists of wall projections of a single still image, a photograph of the sky, and a network of strings that cut through the space above the viewer's head and cast shadows on the walls. My aim is to invite the visitor to experience a sensorial reality that otherwise would have remained an abstraction.

The immersive installation *Intimacies (Mediterranean Civilization)* (2017) was conceived as an environment in which sea and sky are the main elements of the geography that separates the Libyan and Tunisian coasts from Sicily. The geographies marked in the sky map the off-limits areas and the routes of military drones, whereas the marks in the sea (drawn on the floor using pumice powder) trace the routes of migrant boats.

SL

There is an interesting tension here, and in your work in general, between the urge to reveal and make transparent and, on the other hand, the formal abstraction that you are clearly drawn to in your immersive and sculptural practices. Abstraction can serve to render something nonspecific and thereby general, or, as you say, universal. But abstraction also has to do with the nature of the infrastructures these works address. Although they have tangible effects (drone killings, war, and so on), there are, of course, no actual lines in the sky or the sea; borders are not there but constructed. When faced with such systems, you provide not knowledge per se, but an awareness of these overarching realities that exist beyond comprehension and immerse the viewer in the web of the system. Before we end, I have to ask: Could you imagine making work about a place with which you are not intimately familiar?

MDR

As I said, structures of power can have different names and geographies, even though I believe that they determine human nature in consistent ways. In my recent work *The Other: A Familiar Story* (2020), although the video is, again, representing a link between Sicily and the United States, I give no reference to places or names. The main character could be any migrant woman, past or contemporary, facing gender and sexual violence and alienation because patriarchy is still, unfortunately, universal. I believe the idea of a macrocosm represented by a microcosm will always be part of my research, but not necessarily in relation to Sicily or the United States. So, yes, I see myself as open to new geographies.

Maria D. Rapicavoli was born in Catania, Italy, and lives and works in New York. She was a fellow in the Whitney Independent Study Program in 2011–12, and holds an MFA from Goldsmiths, University of London (2005), and a BA from the Academy of Fine Arts in Catania (2001). She has exhibited in several group shows, including at Socrates Sculpture Park, New York; Magazzino Italian Art, Cold Spring, New York; Whitechapel Gallery, London; Yerba Buena Center for the Arts, San Francisco; Museo di Villa Croce, Genoa, Italy; Fondazione Sandretto Re Rebaudengo, Turin, Italy; Museo d'Arte Contemporanea di Villa Croce, Genoa; Palazzo Reale, Milan; Guest Projects, London; Museo d'Arte Contemporanea della Sicilia, Palermo, Italy; Strozzina, Fondazione Palazzo Strozzi, Florence; Sala Rekalde, Bilbao, Spain; and the Italian Cultural Institute, London and New York. She is the recipient of many awards and grants, including the Italian Council grant, 6th edition (2019); nctm e l'arte (2013); DE.MO/Movin'UP (2011); and the Renaissance Prize Award at the Italian Cultural Institute, London (2008). She has participated in the AIRspace residency program at Abrons Arts Center, New York (2015); the International Studio and Curatorial Program, Brooklyn (2014); and the Lower Manhattan Cultural Council Swing Space residency program, New York (2013). Currently she is an artist member at the Elizabeth Foundation for the Arts in New York.

Sarah Lookofsky is an art historian and curator, and dean of the Academy of Fine Art at Oslo National Academy of the Arts (KHiO). Previously she served as associate director of the International Program at the Museum of Modern Art, New York, where she focused on research and publications devoted to art and art histories beyond North America and Western Europe. Prior to that, she was a faculty member and the instructor for curatorial studies at the Whitney Museum of American Art Independent Study Program. She has curated and written for a variety of venues and formats and served as general advisor to the 9th Berlin Biennale, curated by DIS collective, and as arts editor for *DIS Magazine*. She holds a PhD and an MA in art history, theory, and criticism from the University of California, San Diego, and a BA in film and media studies from the University of Copenhagen.

Liz Park is Richard Armstrong Curator of Contemporary Art at Carnegie Museum of Art, Pittsburgh. She was previously curator of exhibitions at the University at Buffalo Art Galleries, State University of New York and associate curator of the 2018 Carnegie International at Carnegie Museum of Art. She has curated exhibitions at a wide range of institutions, including Western Front, Vancouver; The Kitchen, New York; Institute of Contemporary Art at the University of Pennsylvania, Philadelphia; Miller Institute for Contemporary Art at Carnegie Mellon University, Pittsburgh; and Seoul Art Space Geumcheon. Her writing has been published by *Afterall* online, *Afterimage*, *ArtAsiaPacific*, *Performa* magazine, *Fillip*, *Yishu: A Journal of Contemporary Chinese Art*, Pluto Press, and Ryerson University Press, among others. She was a Helena Rubinstein Fellow at the Whitney Independent Study Program in 2011–12 and Whitney-Lauder Curatorial Fellow at ICA Philadelphia in 2013–15. Her research interests include mobility and migration as well as representations of violence in the colonial present.

Sara Reisman is a curator, educator, and writer based in New York, where she is chief curator and director of national academician affairs at the National Academy of Design. Until recently she served as executive and artistic director of the Shelley & Donald Rubin Foundation (2014–21), and has held roles as director of the Percent for Art program at the NYC Department of Cultural Affairs (2008–14) and associate dean of the School of Art at the Cooper Union (2008–09). Reisman has curated exhibitions locally and internationally for venues including Dublin City Gallery The Hugh Lane; Futura Centre for Contemporary Art, Prague; the Queens Museum of Art, New York; Socrates Sculpture Park, New York; the Philadelphia Institute of Contemporary Art; Momenta Art, Brooklyn; and Smack Mellon, Brooklyn, among other venues. As a writer she has contributed to *ARTnews*, *BOMB*, and *artjournal* as well as writing for and editing book projects focused on such artists as Elia Alba, Pablo Helguera, and Suzanne Lacy. Reisman has been awarded residencies by Art Omi, the Foundation for Civil Society, Artis, CEC ArtsLink, Futura, and the Montello Foundation. She has taught art history and contemporary art at the University of Pennsylvania, SUNY Purchase School of Art + Design, and, since 2016, the School of Visual Arts MA Curatorial Practice program.

Kristina Scepanski is a curator and art historian from Cologne. Since receiving her MA in art history and German and English philology at the University of Cologne in 2009, she has worked for the European Kunsthalle Cologne, a discursive platform without a physical location, and for Kunstverein für die Rheinlande und Westfalen, Düsseldorf. In 2011–12 she was a Helena Rubinstein Fellow at the Whitney Independent Study Program, where she co-curated a show at The Kitchen, New York. In 2013 she was appointed artistic director of Westfälischer Kunstverein, Münster. She has been a visiting lecturer and tutor at Hoger Instituut voor Schone Kunsten (HISK), Ghent, Belgium; Jan van Eyck Academie, Maastricht, the Netherlands; De Ateliers, Amsterdam; Justina M. Barnicke Gallery, University of Toronto; Or Gallery, Vancouver; and RAT School of Art, Seoul. Parallel to her position in Münster, she has held teaching positions at the Kunstakademie Münster and the Hochschule der Künste Bern in recent years, as well as the Chillida Visiting Professorship at Goethe University Frankfurt in 2019.

Wendy Vogel is a writer, critic, and independent curator living in New York. A former editor at *Flash Art International*, *Modern Painters*, and *Art in America*, she regularly contributes to *Artforum* and *art-agenda*, among other publications. Vogel teaches in the photography department at Parsons School of Design, New York. Her work considers legacies of feminism, sexual agency and identity, and structural biases in contemporary art. She is a 2018 recipient of the Creative Capital | Andy Warhol Foundation Arts Writers Grant in short-form writing.

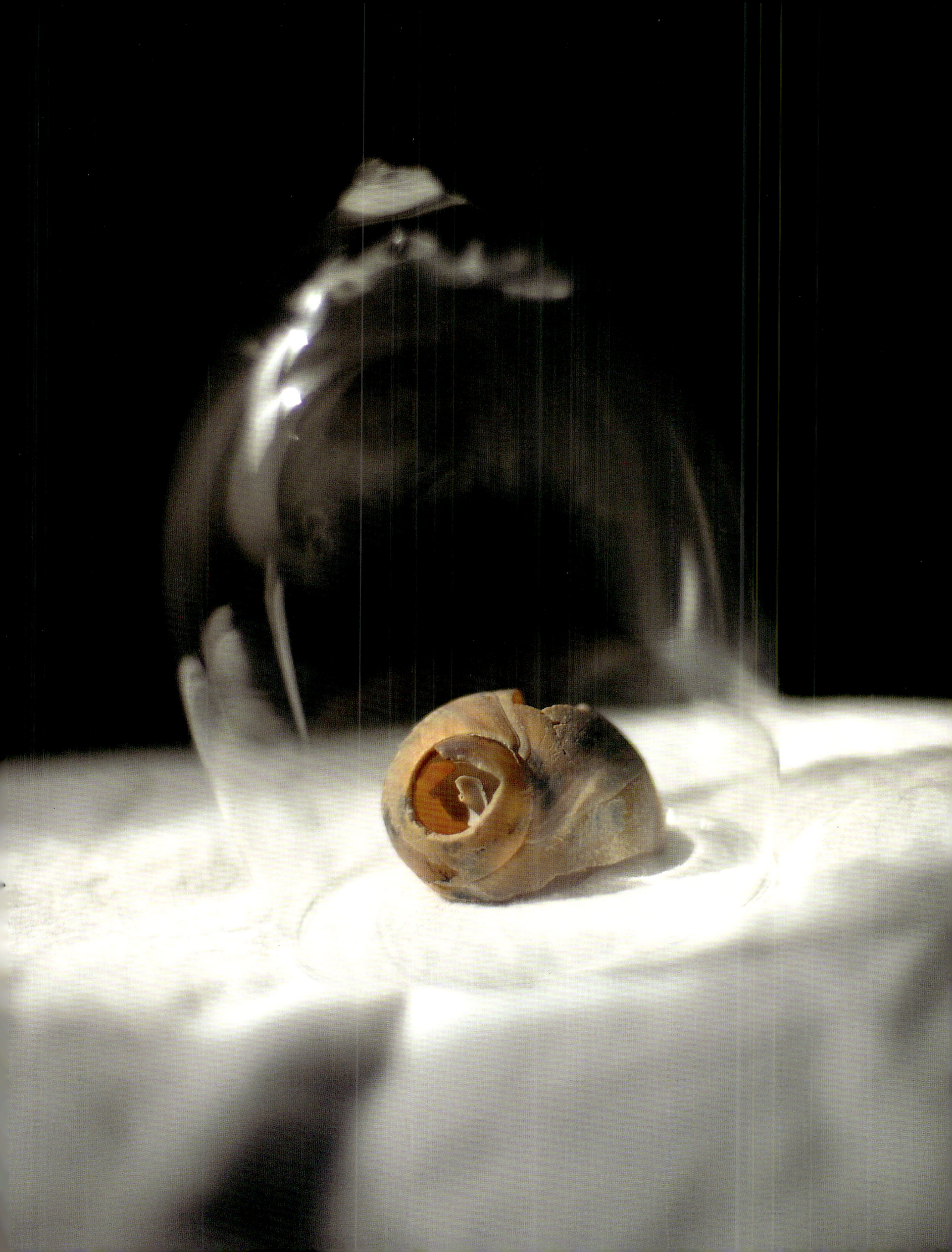

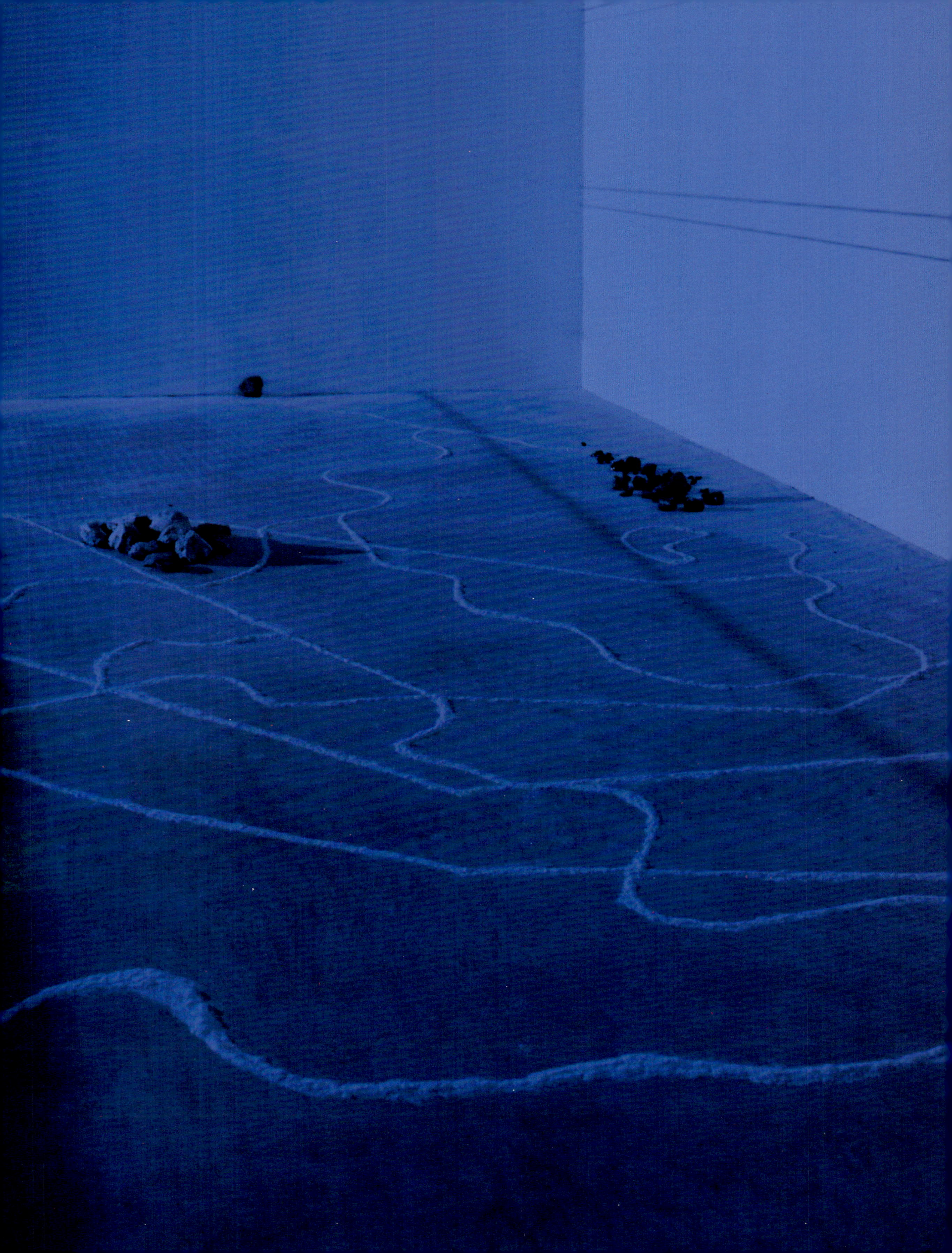

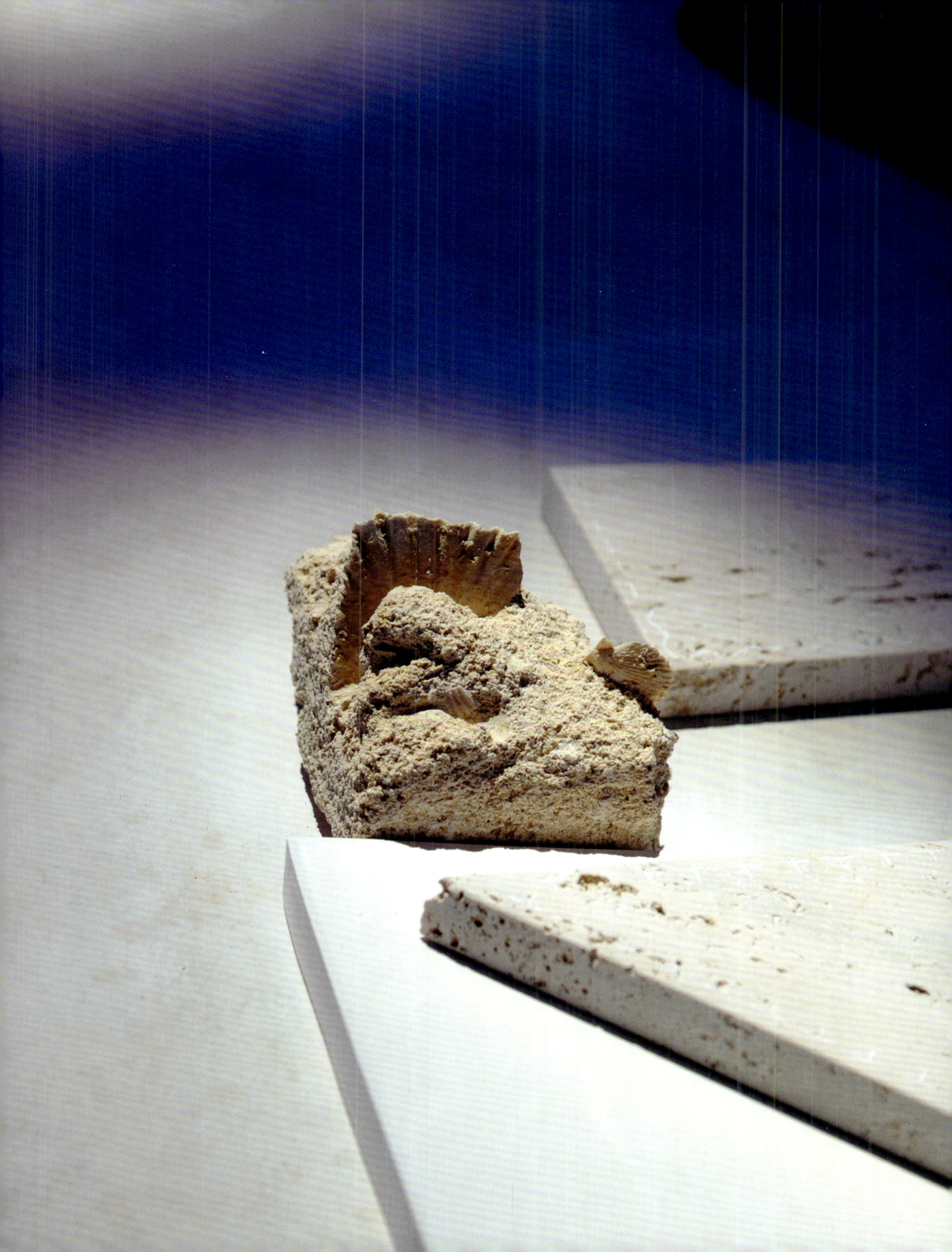

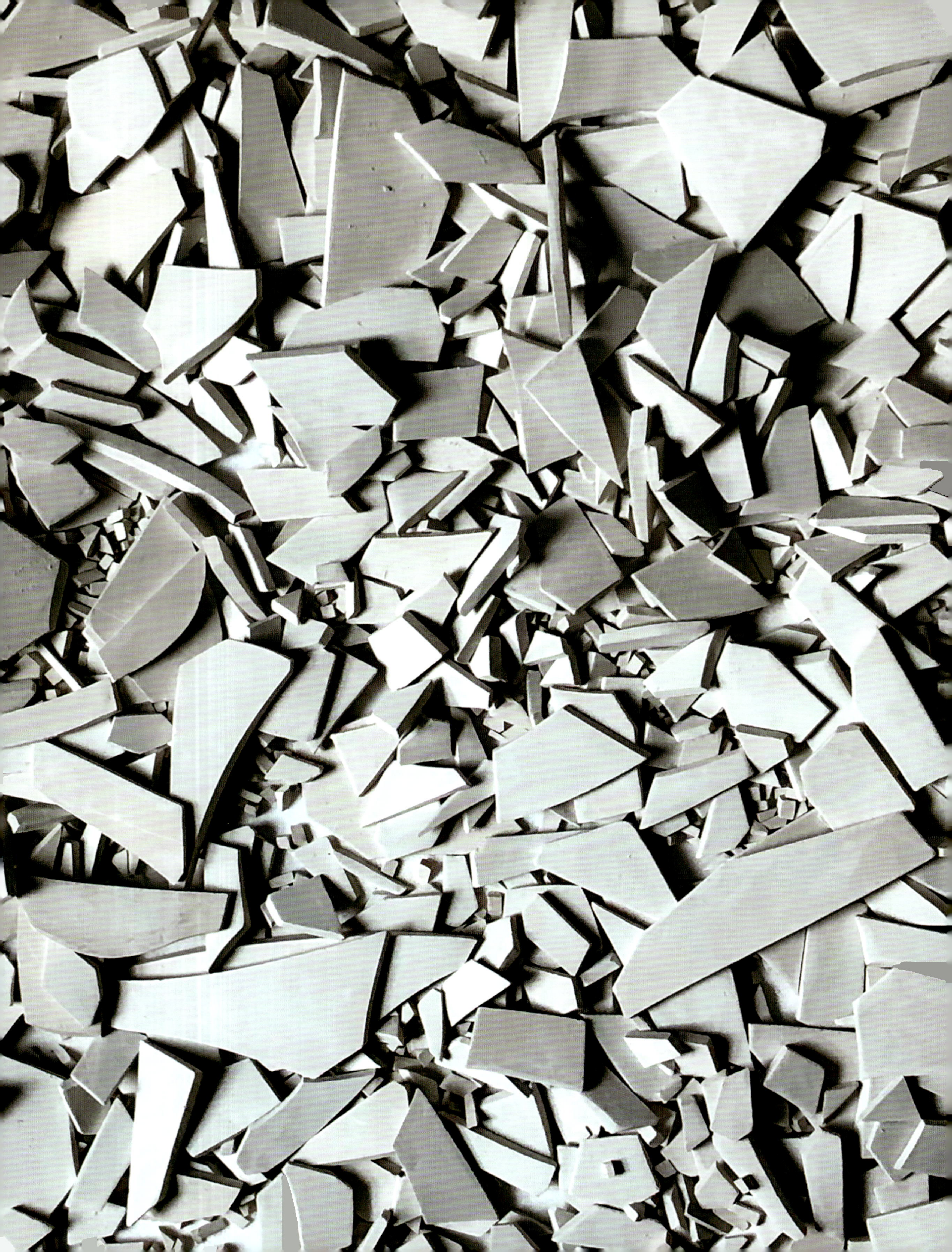

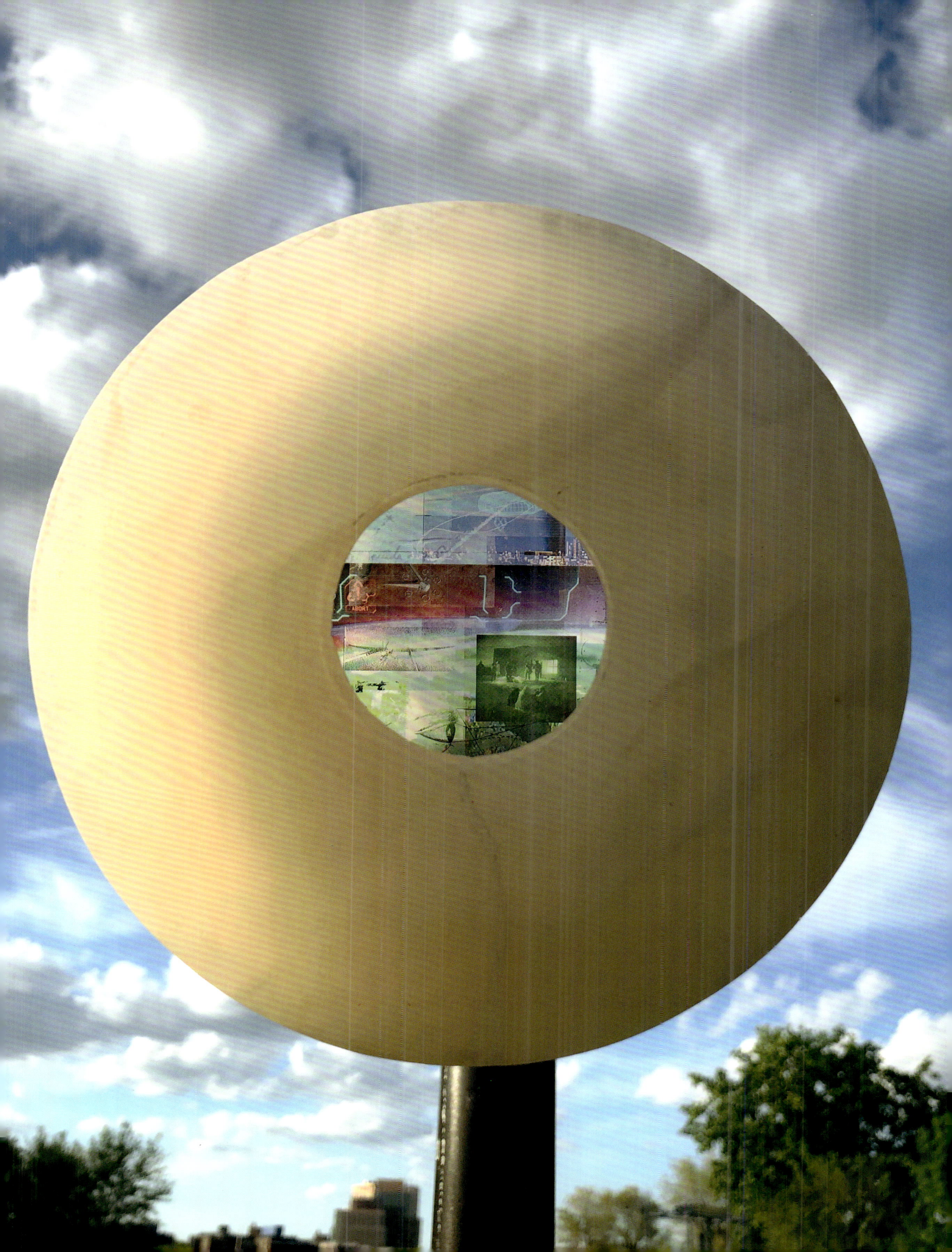

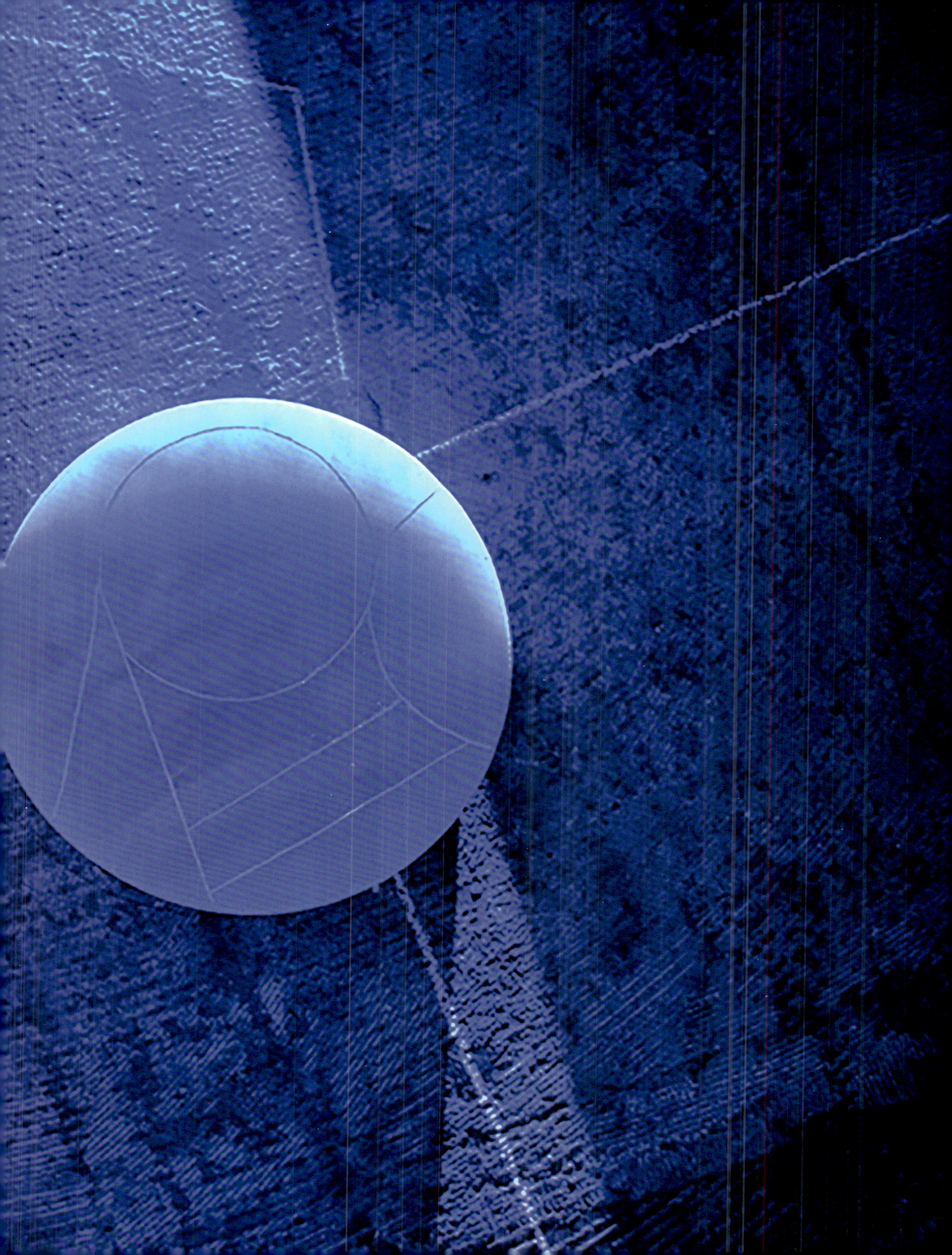

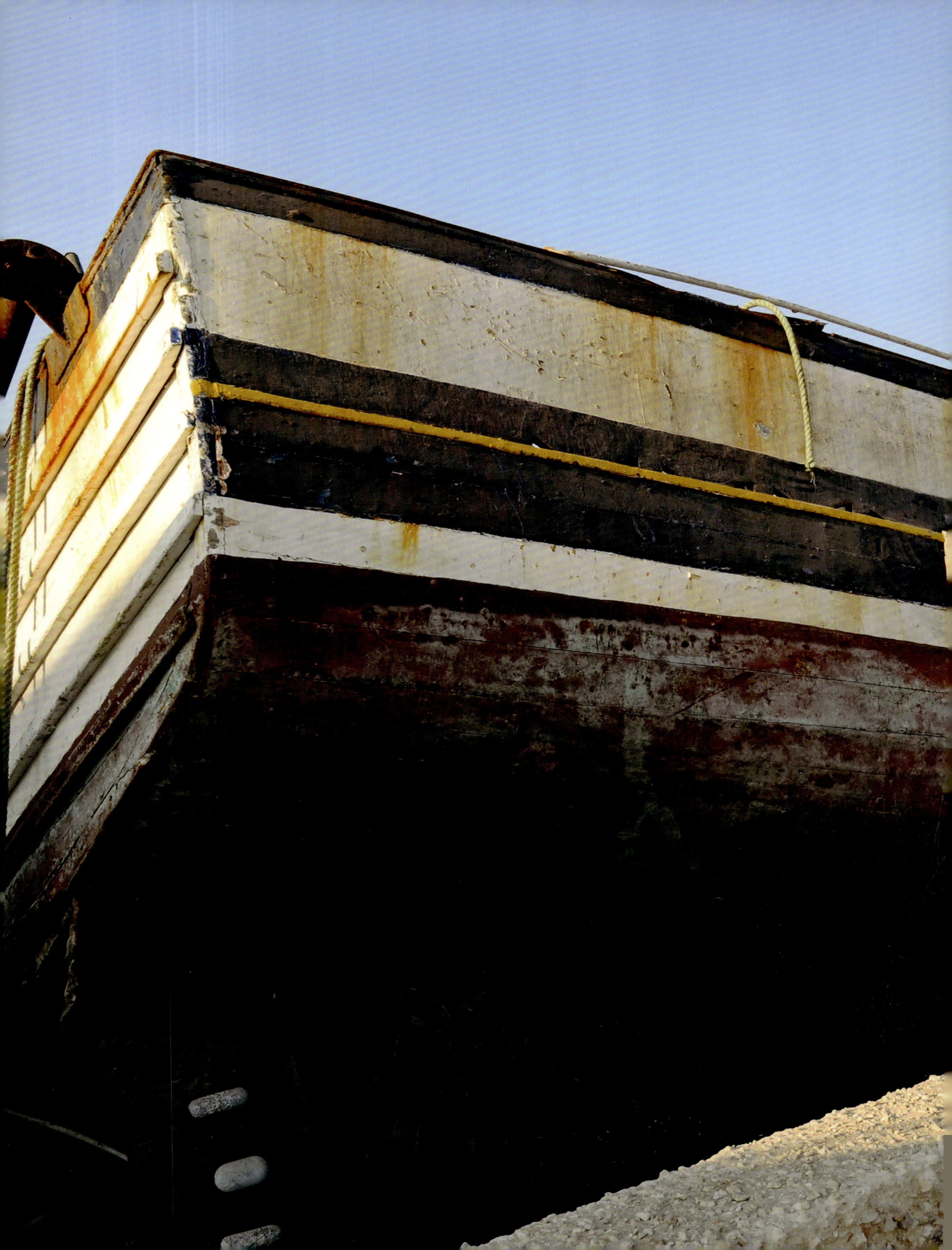

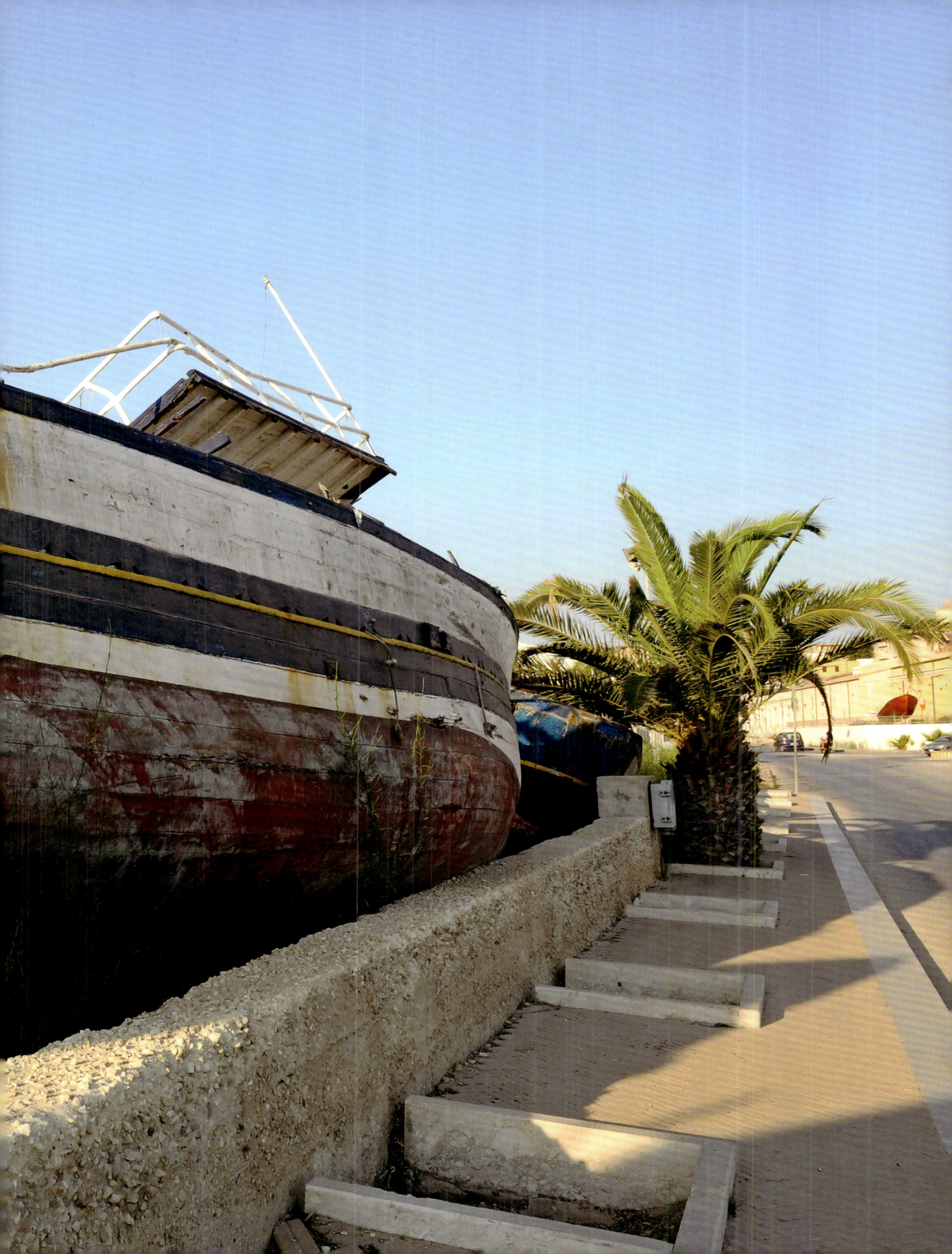

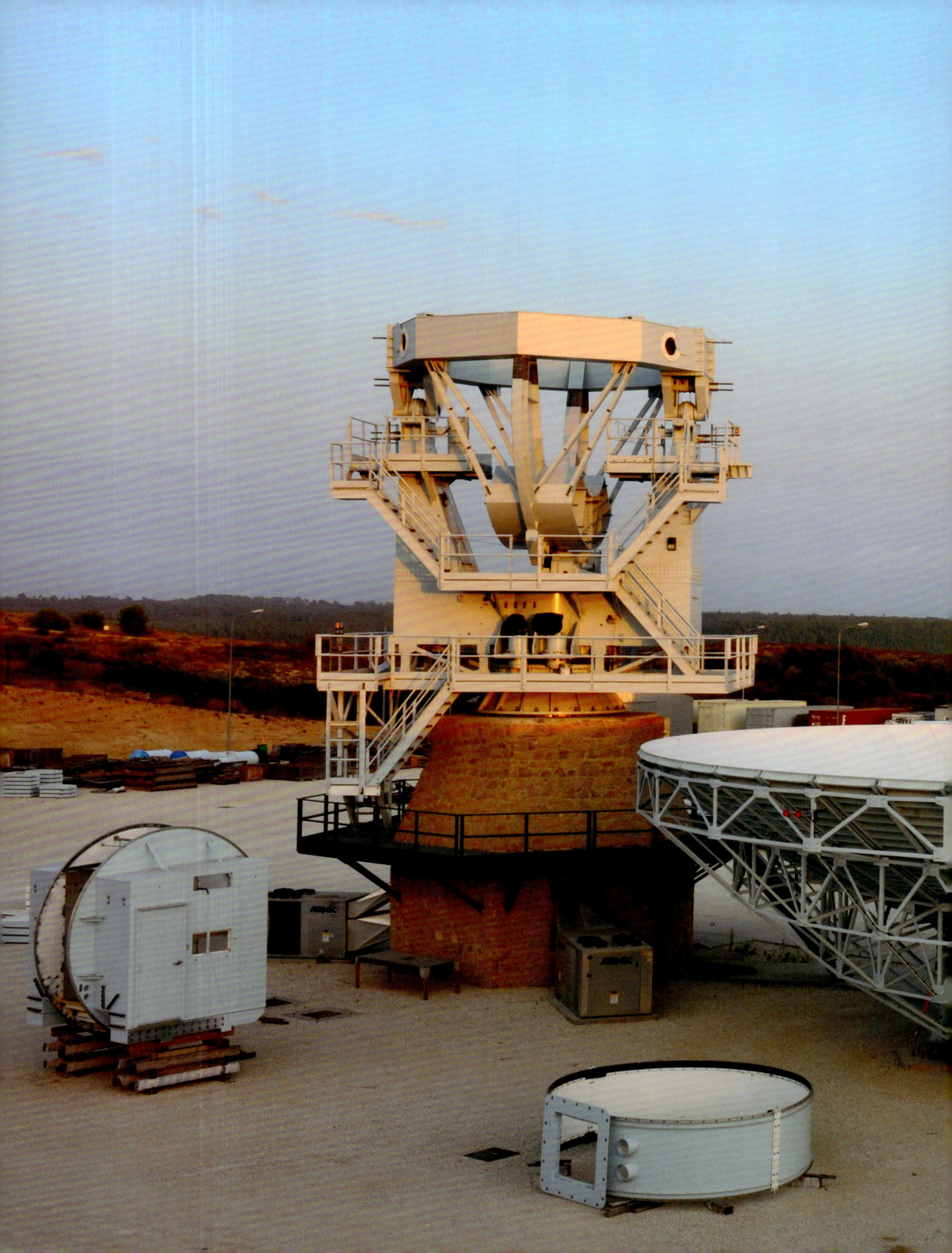

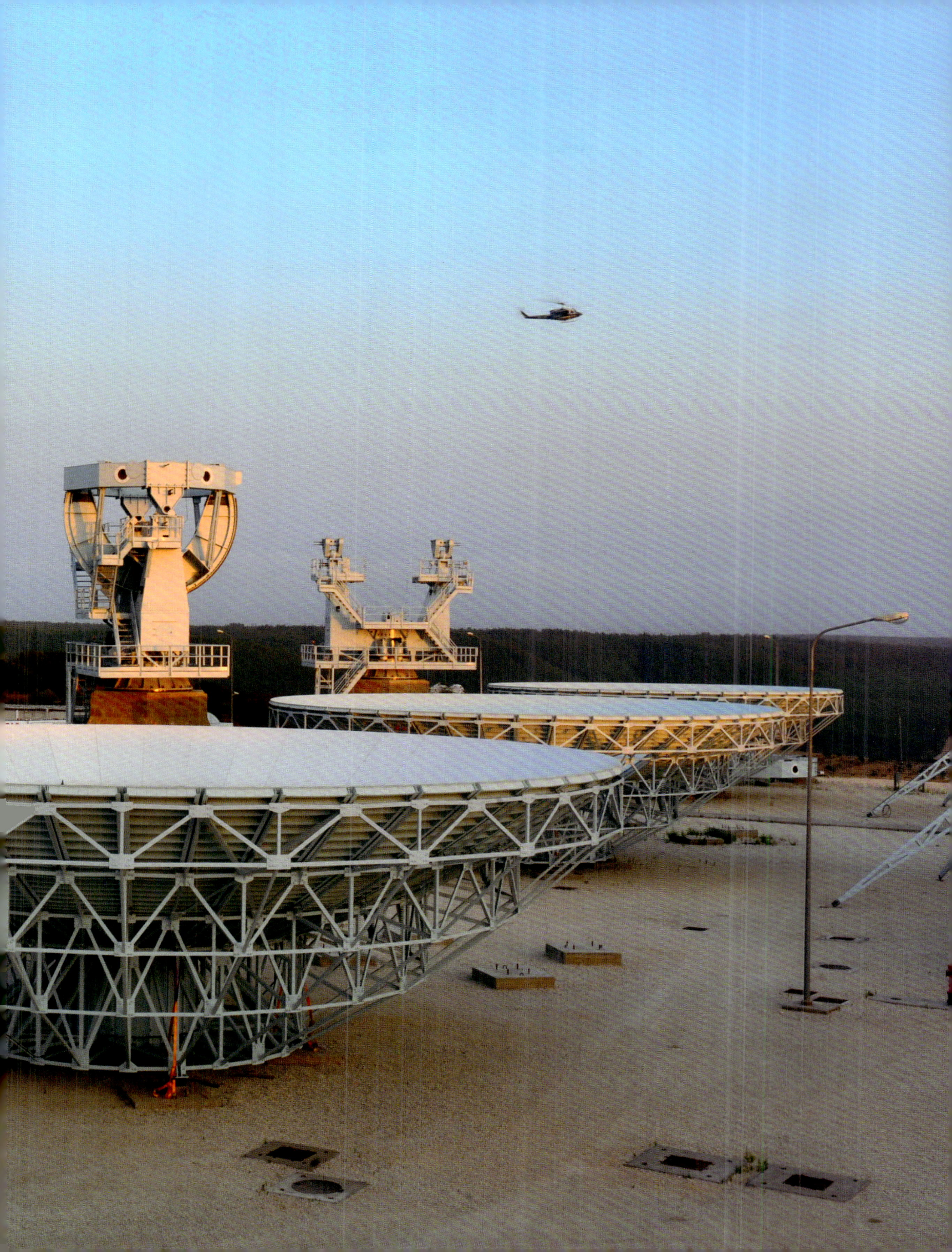

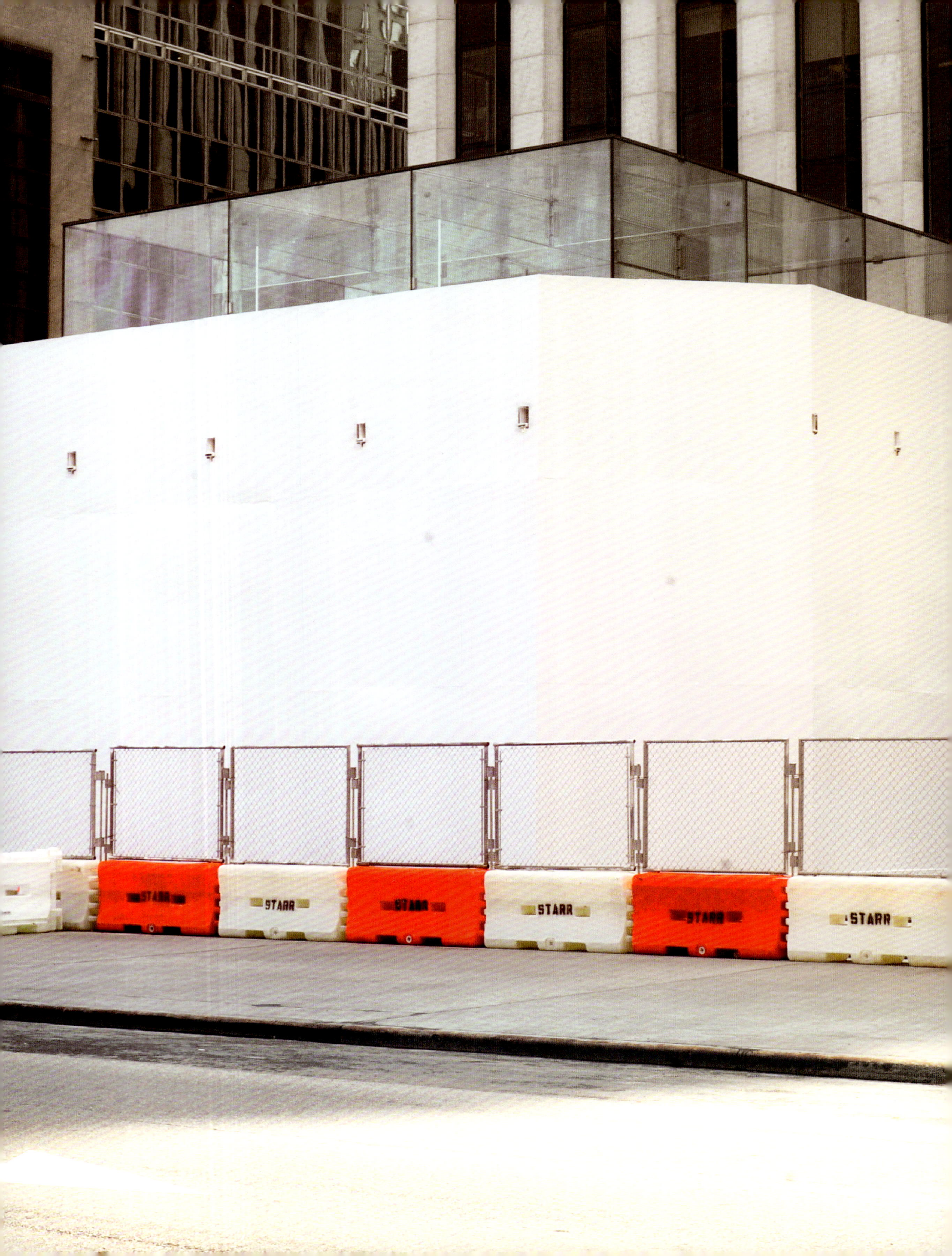
STARR
STARR
STARR
STARR
STARR
STARR

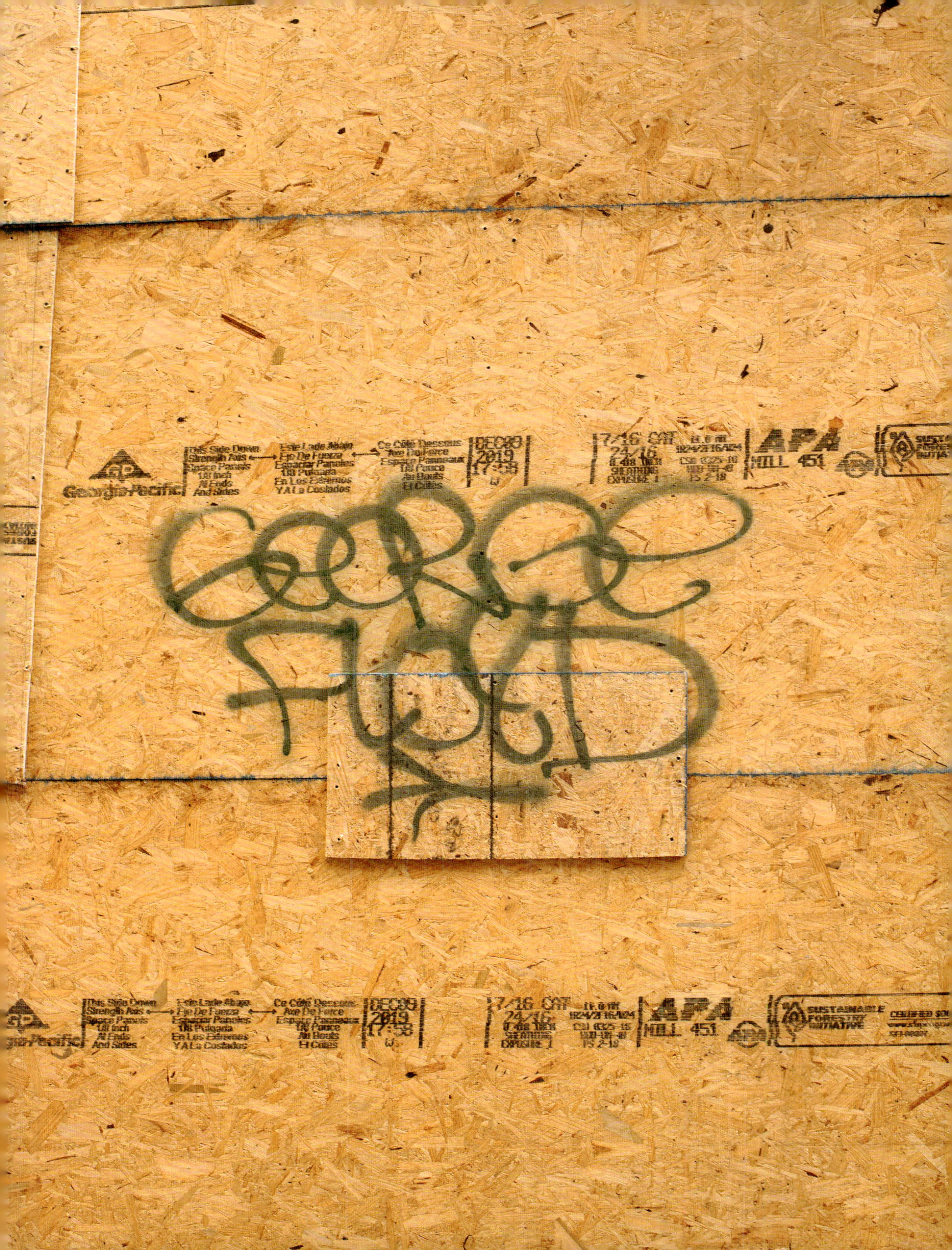

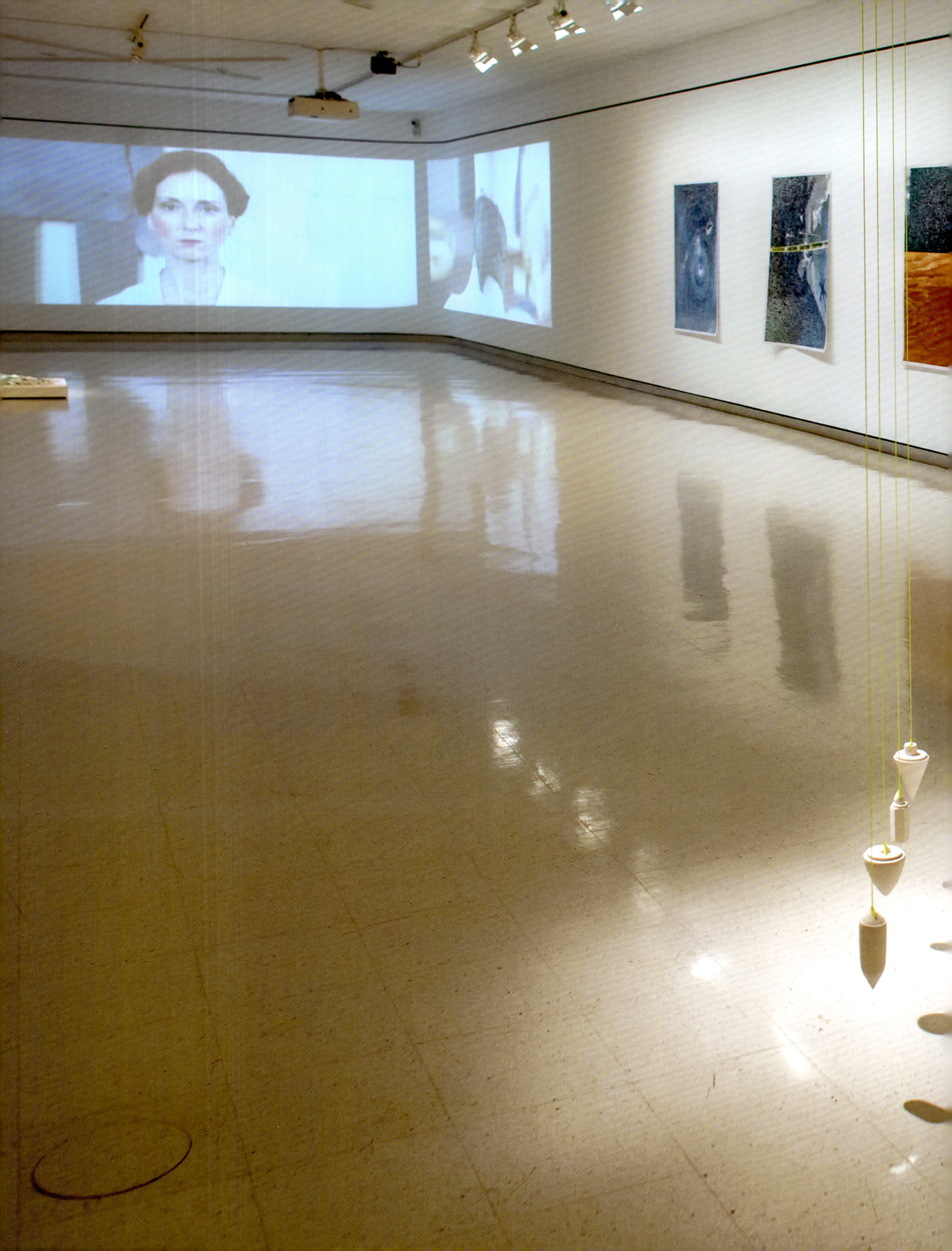

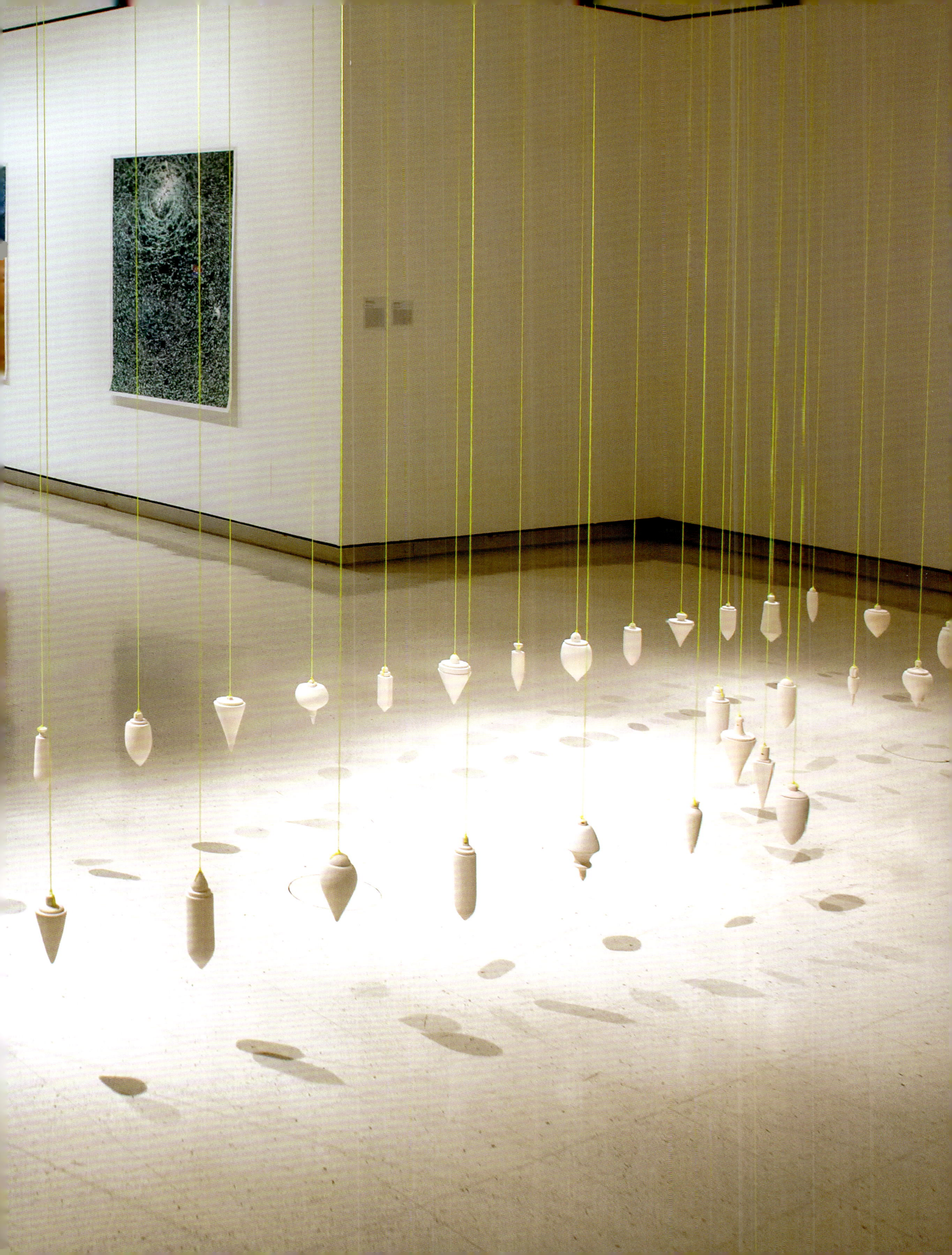

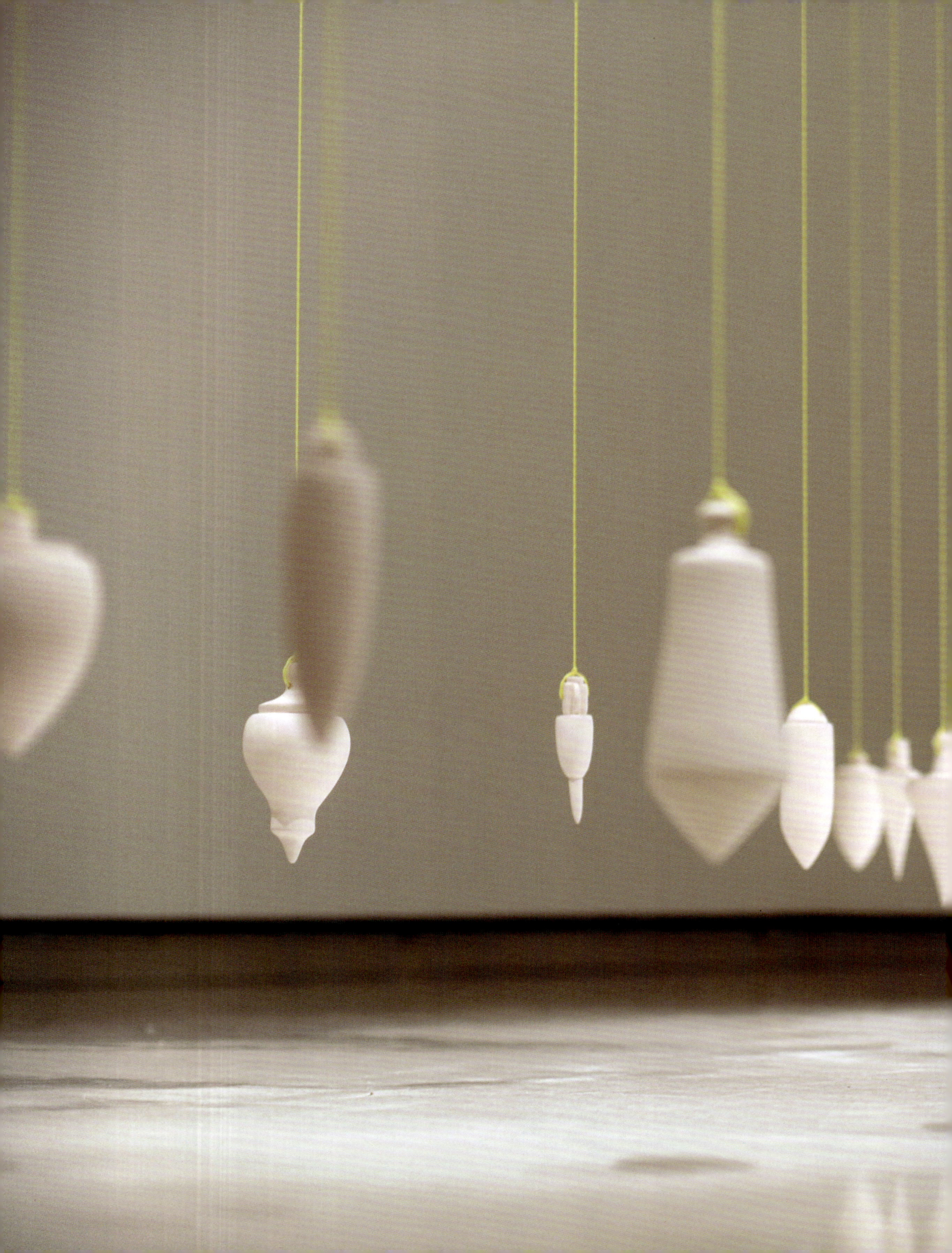

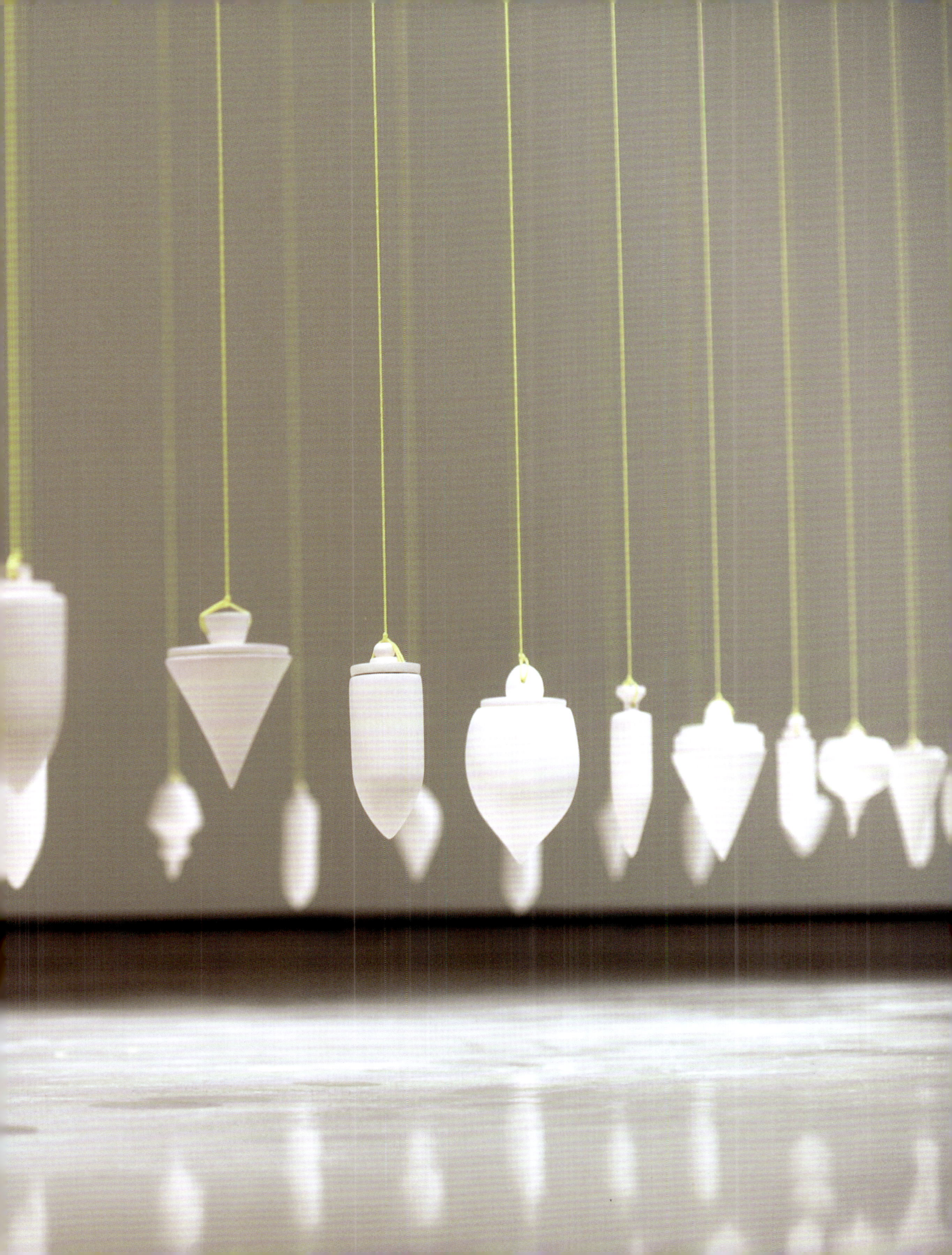

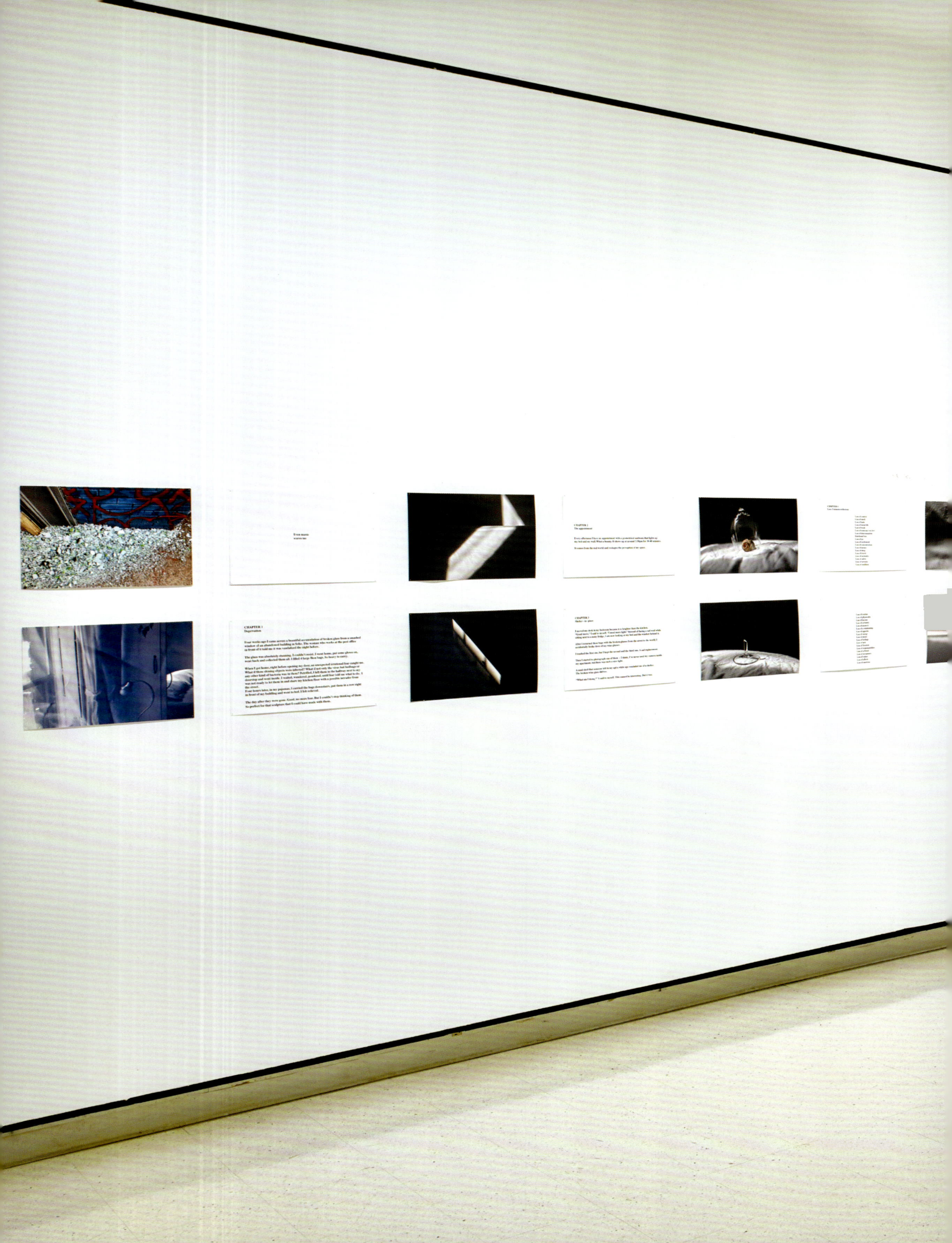

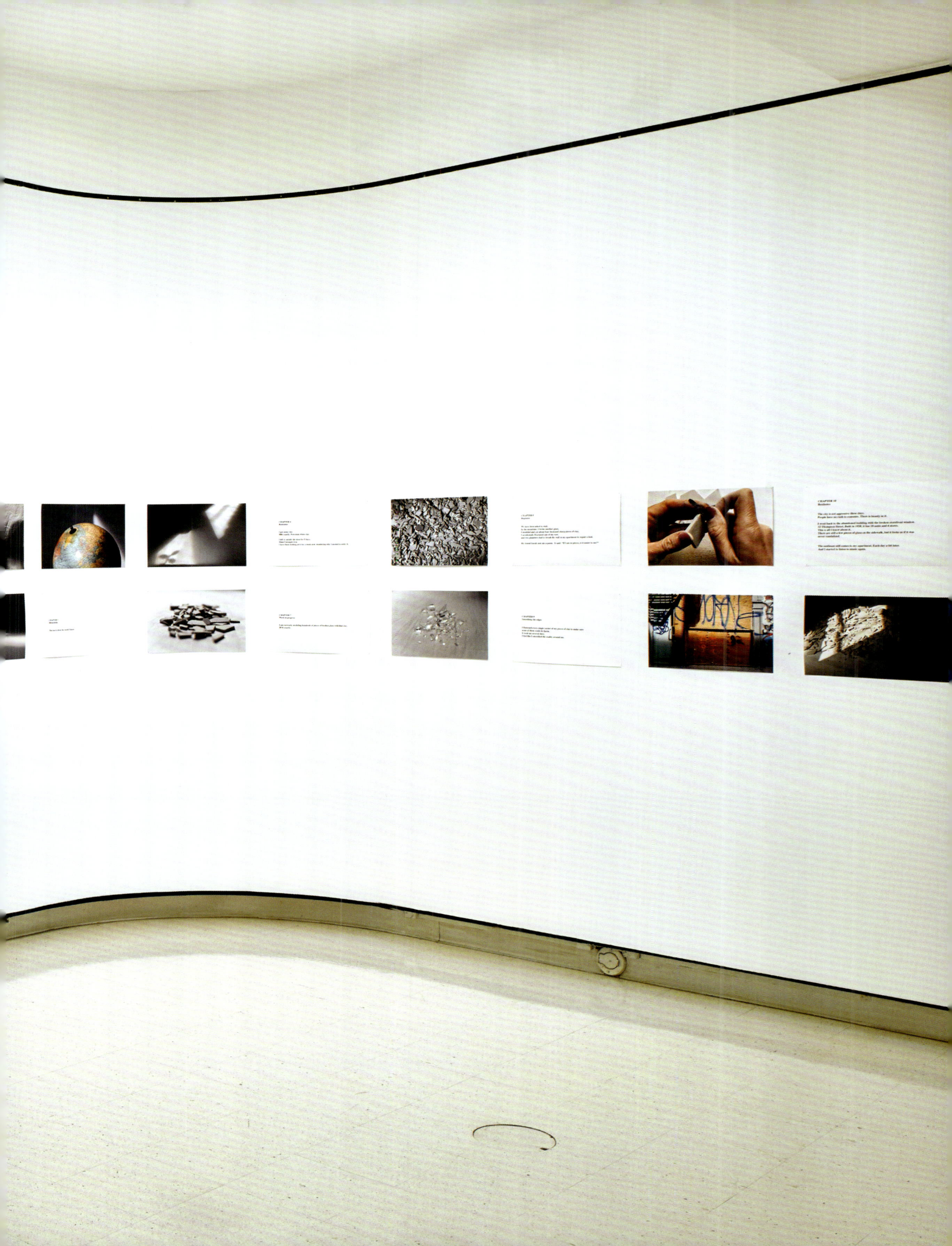

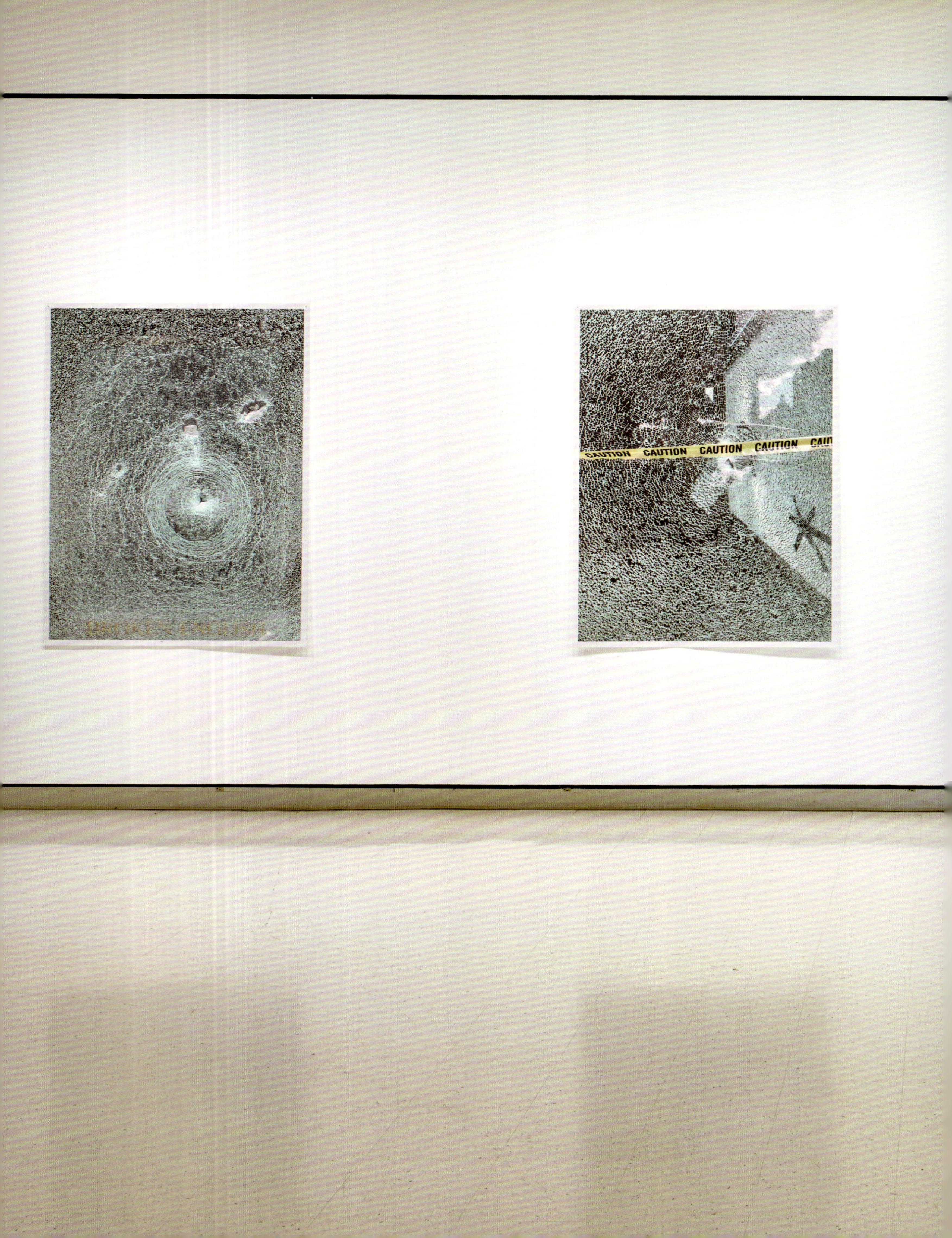
CAUTION   CAUTION   CAUTION   CAUTION   CAUT

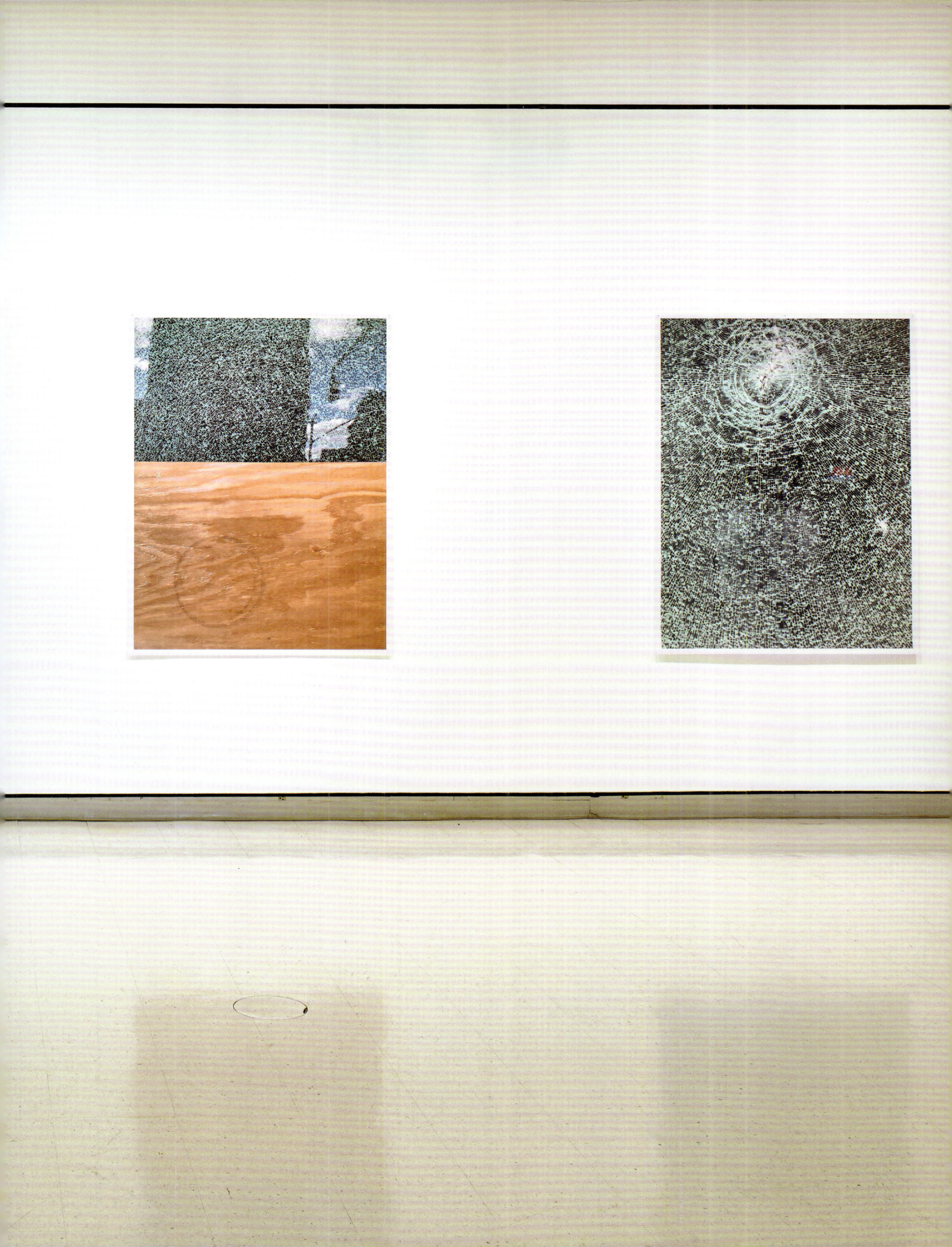

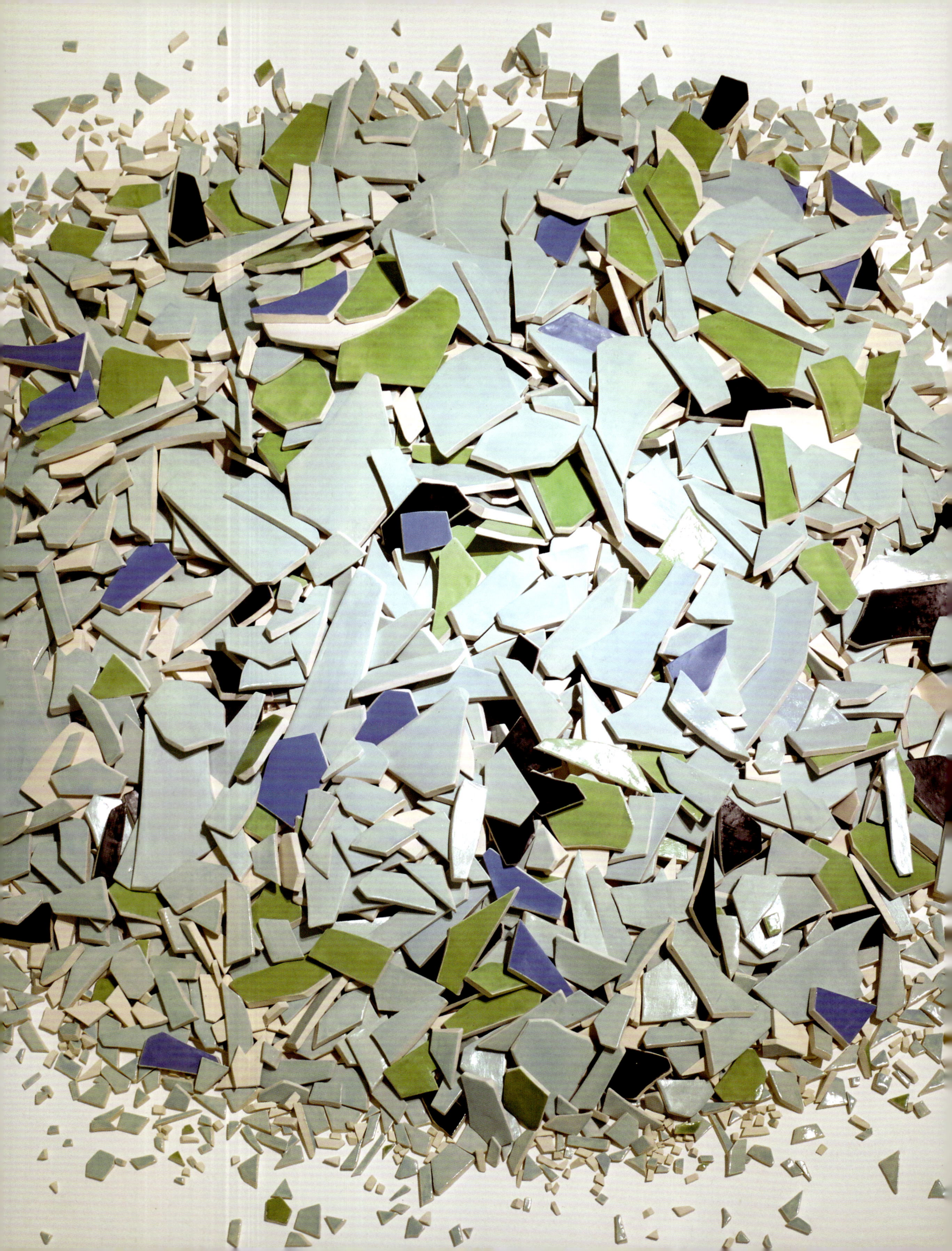

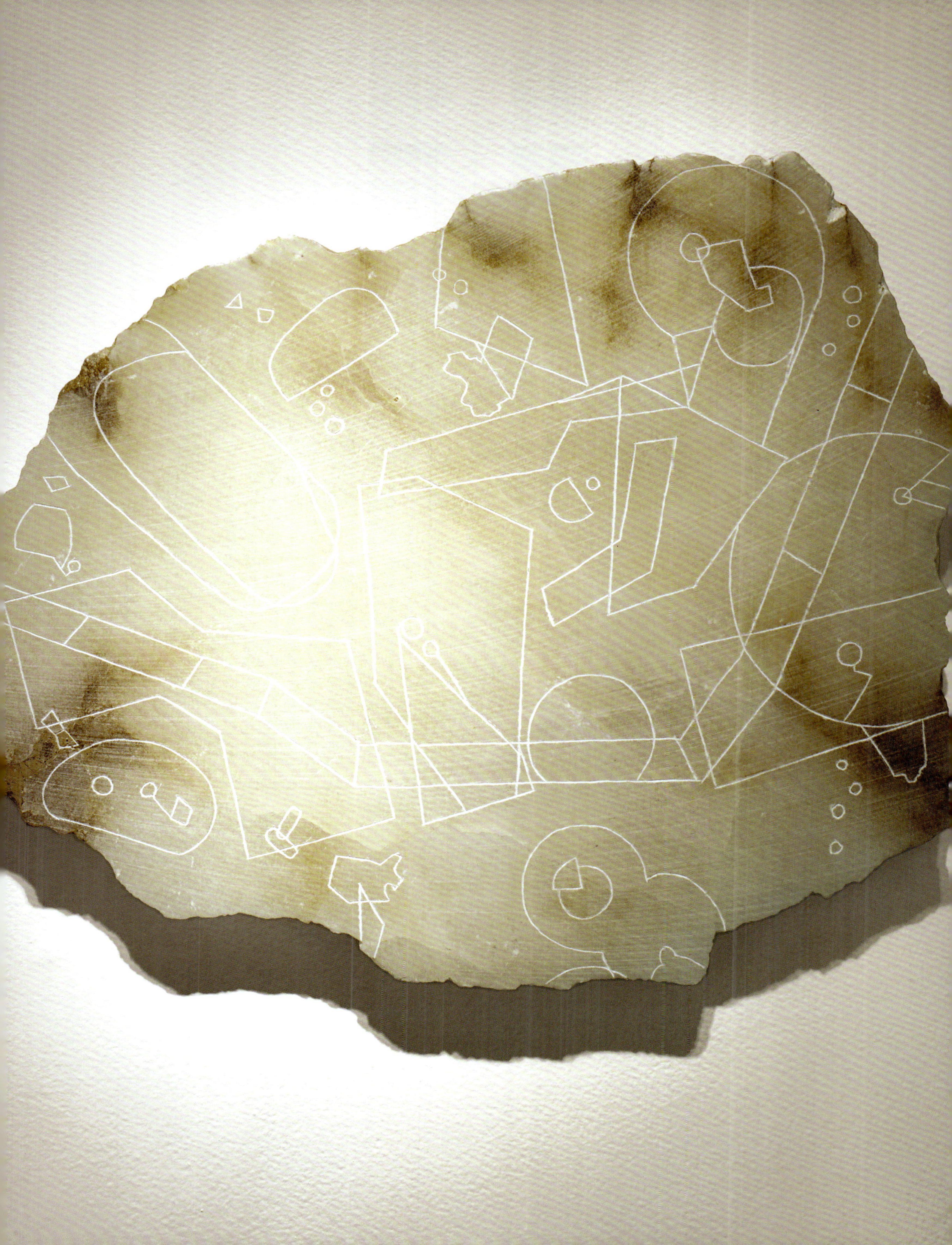

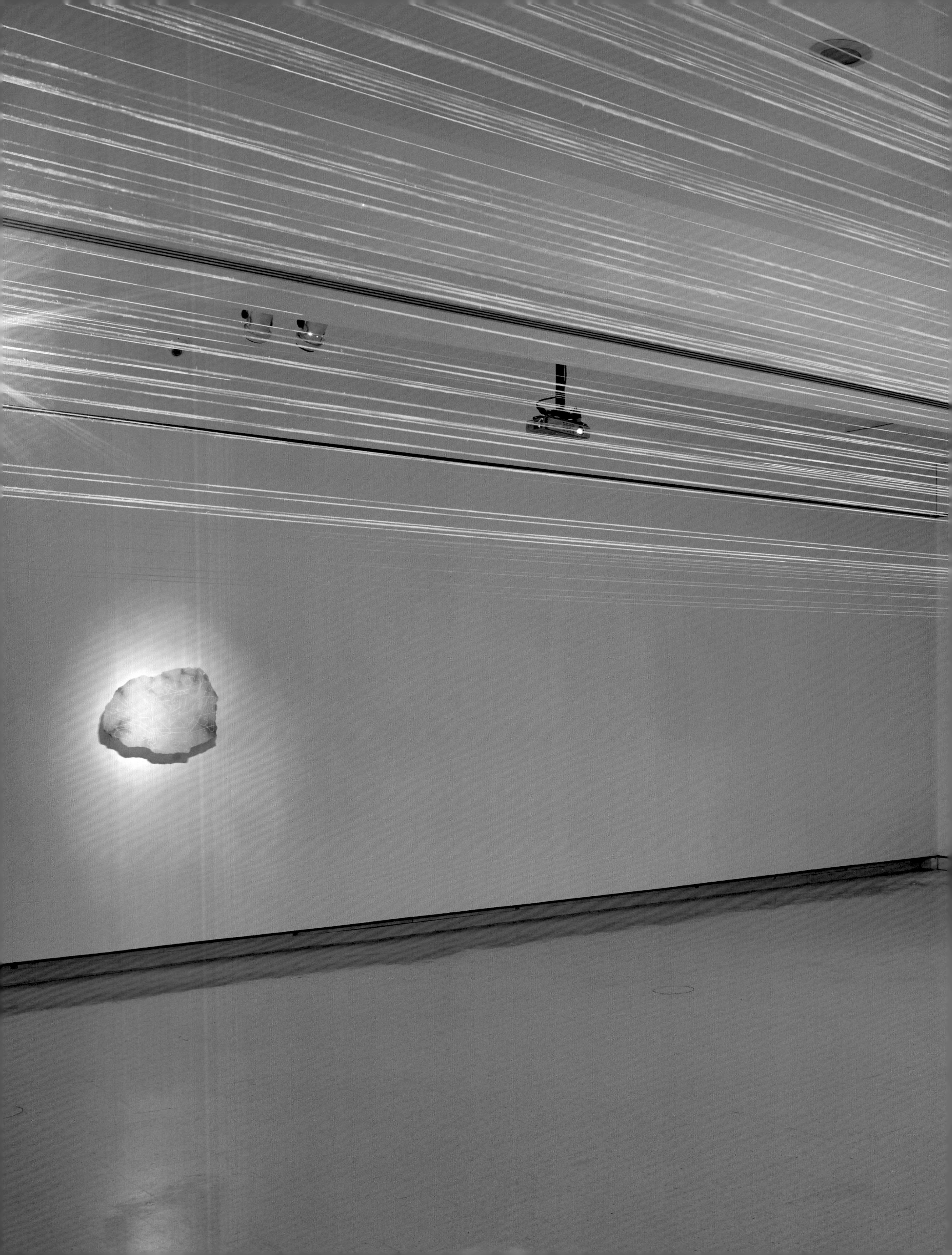

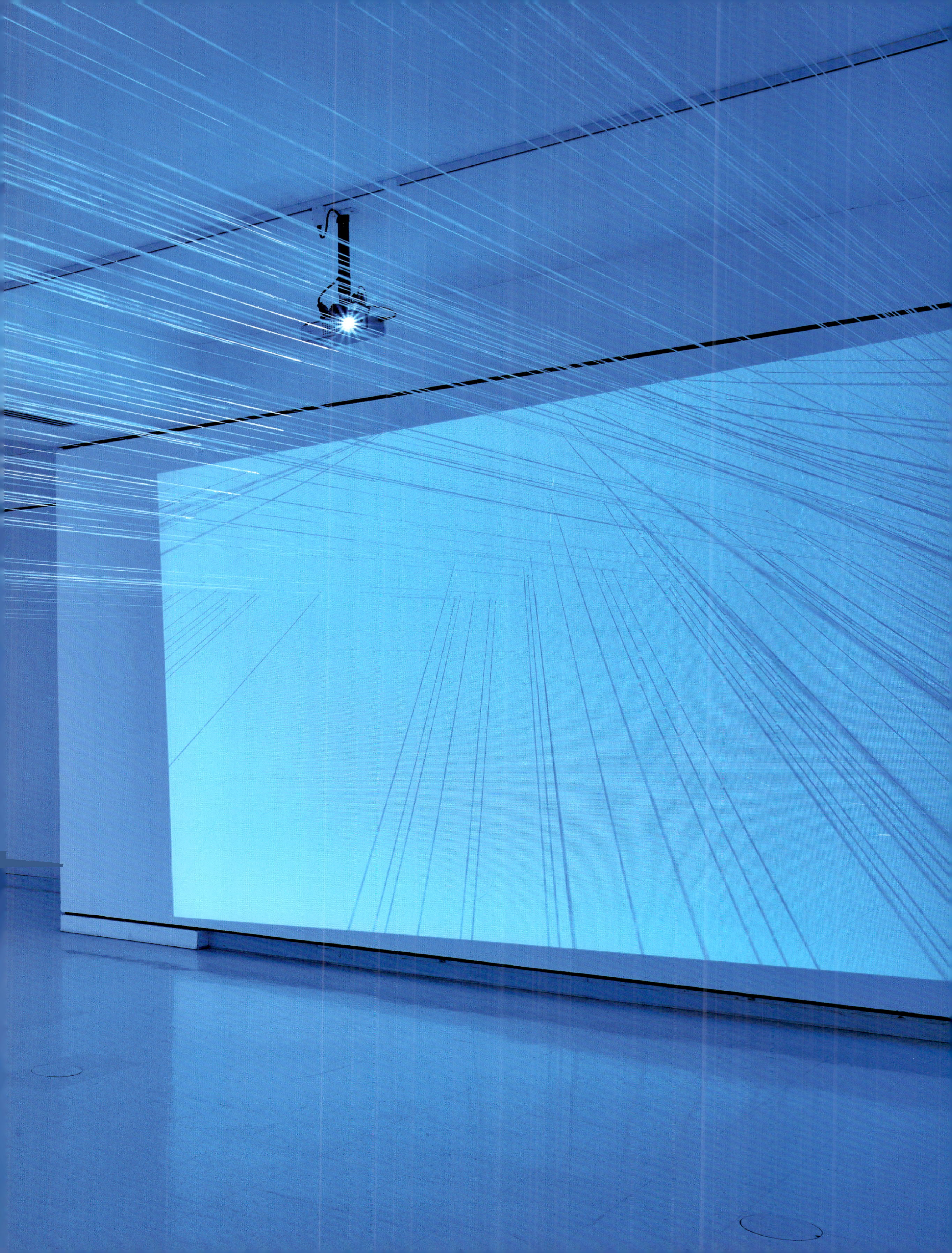

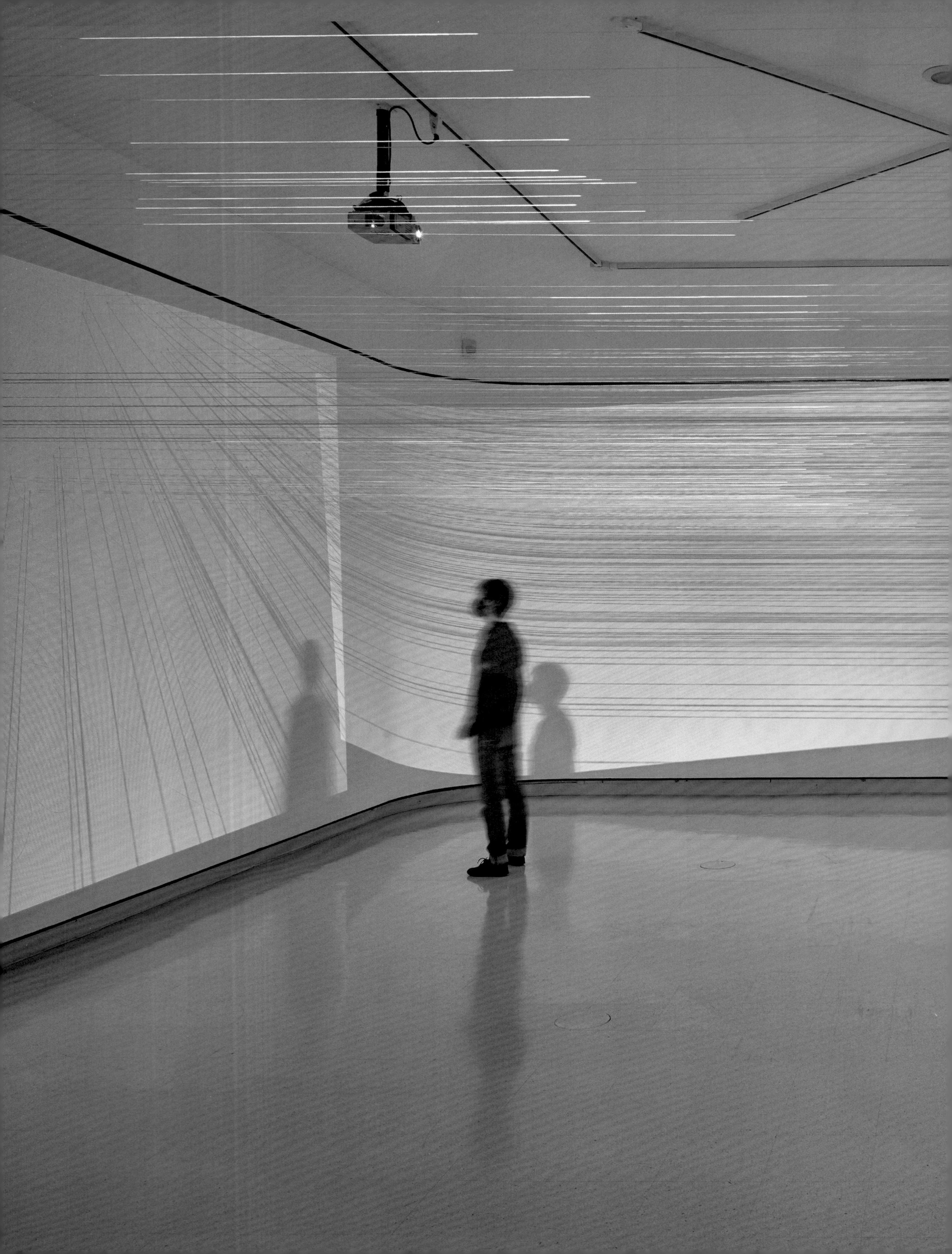

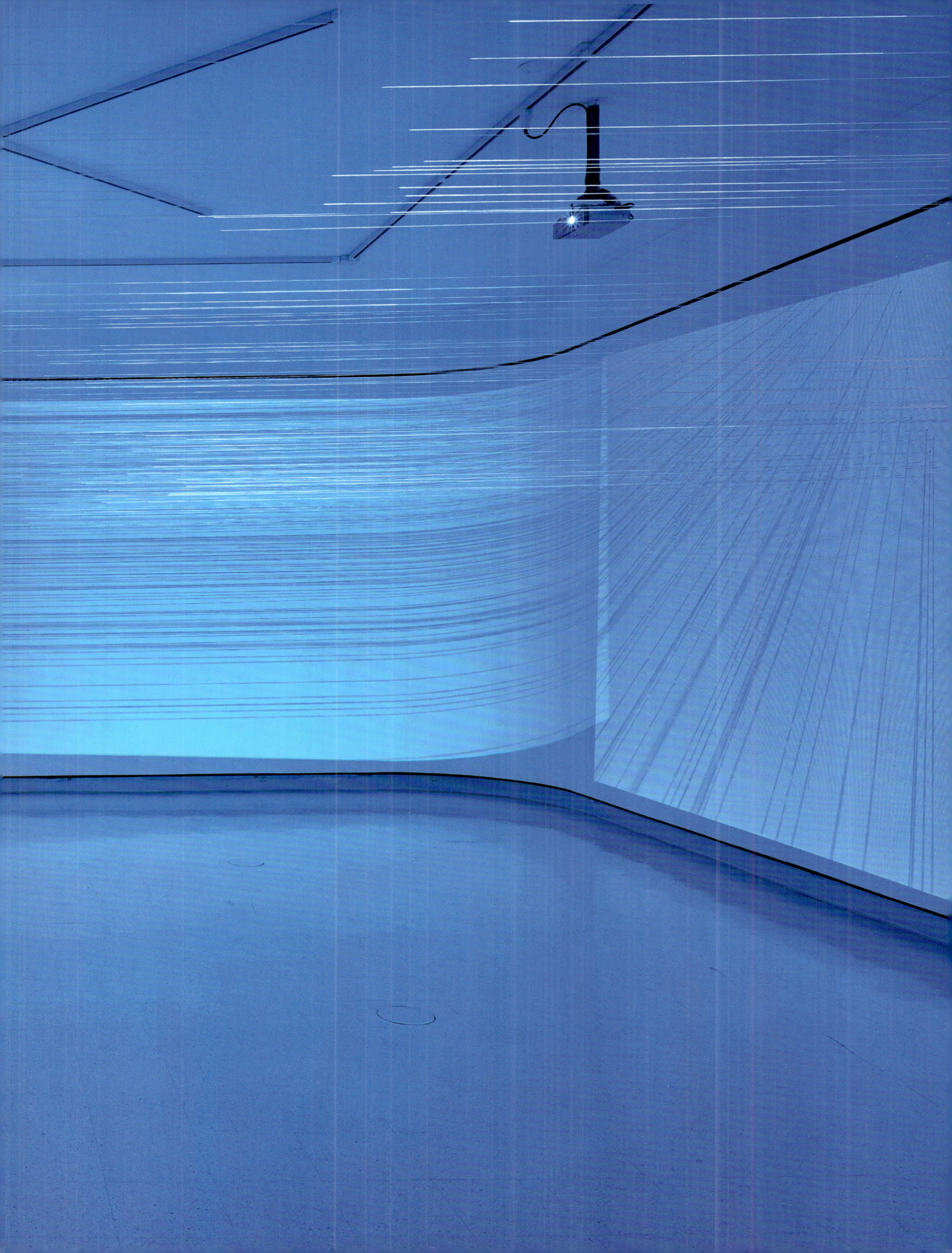

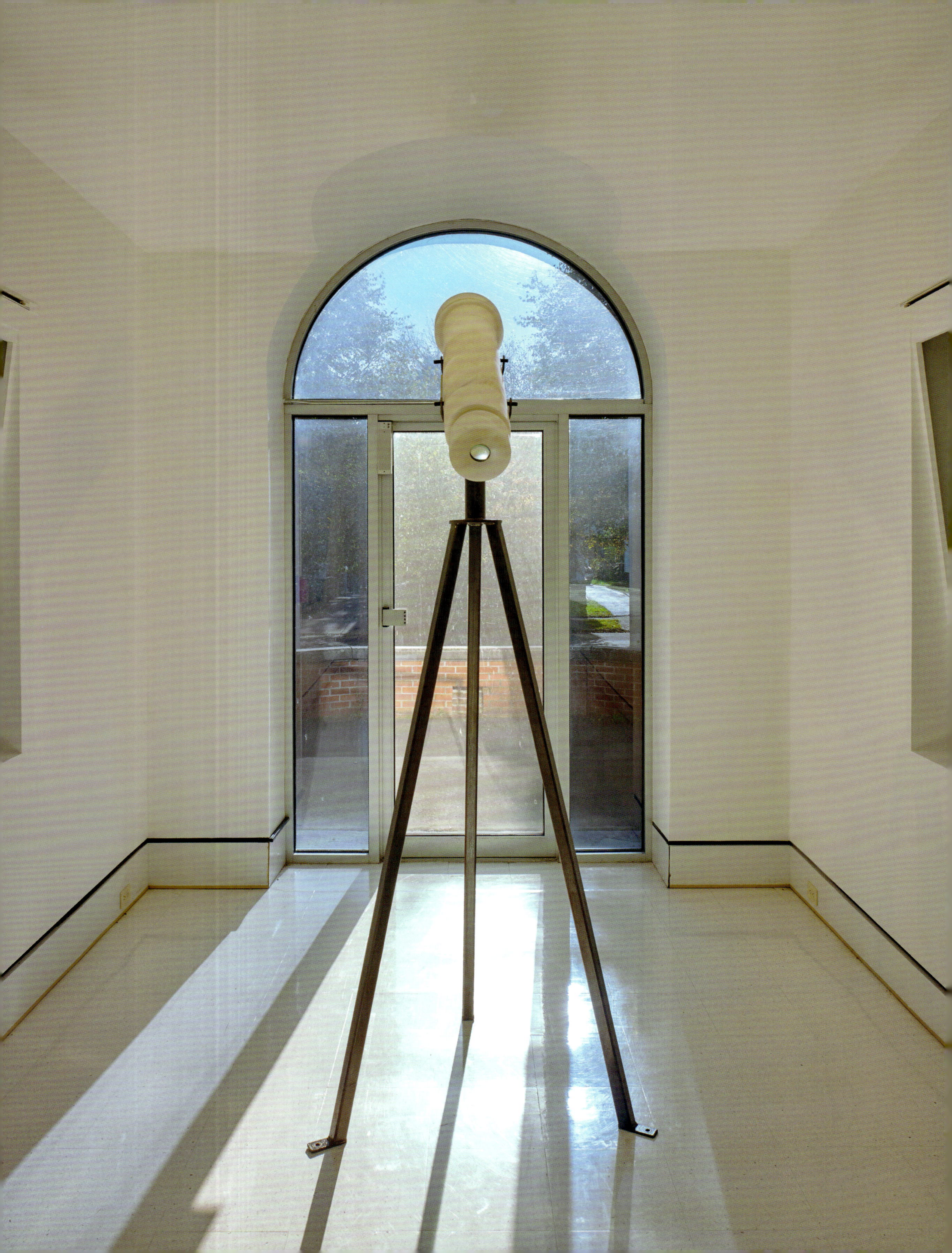

p. 1–15
The Other: A Familiar Story (stills and excerpts from
the script), 2020
2-channel video installation, stereo sound
19:40

p. 22
Installation view, *The Other: A Familiar Story*
Westfälischer Kunstverein, Münster, 2021
Photo: Thorsten Arendt

p. 23
Del Capo d'Africa a Misurata (detail), 2017
Installation view, *Intimacies
(Mediterranean Civilization)*
Brodbeck Foundation, Catania, 2017
Photo: the artist
Courtesy: Brodbeck Foundation, Catania

p. 25–27
The Other: A Familiar Story (stills), 2020
2-channel video installation, stereo sound
19:40

p. 28
One, No One (stills), 2005
Video, stereo sound
7:40

p. 28–29
Four Virgins and a Bed (stills), 2007
Video, stereo sound
6:30

p. 30
My Ideal House (stills), 2007
Video, stereo sound
2:20

p. 33
The Other: A Familiar Story, 2020
Installation view, *To Cast Too Bold A Shadow*
The 8th Floor, New York, 2020
Photo: Alexa Hoyer

p. 34
what am I, 2021
Pigment print, mounted on aluminum
6 × 8 inches / 15 × 20 cm

p. 35
Forgotten Thought, 2021
Photograph printed on foil
78 × 60 inches / 198 × 152 cm
Photo: Thorsten Arendt

p. 36–47
Installation views, *The Other: A Familiar Story*
Westfälischer Kunstverein, Münster, 2021
Photo: Thorsten Arendt

p. 48
Meal, 2021
Plates, lentils, egg
Variable dimensions
Installation view, *The Other: A Familiar Story*
Westfälischer Kunstverein, Münster, 2021
Photo: Thorsten Arendt

This book is published on the occasion of

The Other: A Familiar Story
curated by Kristina Scepanski
Westfälischer Kunstverein
May 8–August 8, 2021

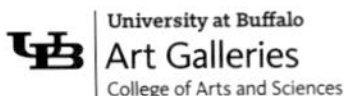

Rothenburg 30
48143 Münster
Germany
+49 251 46157
info@westfaelischer-kunstverein.de
westfaelischer-kunstverein.de

Maria D. Rapicavoli: Surface Tension
curated by Liz Park
University at Buffalo Art Galleries
November 6, 2021–March 13, 2022

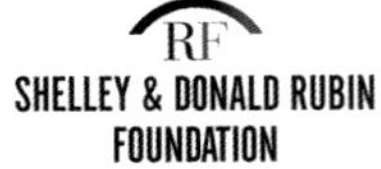

1 Martha Jackson Place
Buffalo, NY 14214
United States of America
+1 716 829 3754
ubartgalleries.buffalo.edu

With Partners

SHELLEY & DONALD RUBIN
FOUNDATION

THE 8TH FLOOR

Maria D. Rapicavoli
Surface Tension

Project supported by the Directorate-General
for Contemporary Creativity by the Italian
Ministry of Culture under the Italian Council
program (6th edition, 2019)

Head of Publications
Ilaria Bombelli—Mousse

Publishing Editor
Vittoria Mieli—Mousse

Texts
Sarah Lookofsky, Liz Park
and Kristina Scepanski,
Sara Reisman, Wendy Vogel

Copy editing and Proofreading
Lindsey Westbrook

Graphic Design
Gloria Favaro—Mousse

Published and distributed by
Mousse Publishing
Contrappunto s.r.l.
via Pier Candido Decembrio, 28
20137, Milan–Italy

Available through
Mousse Publishing, Milan
moussemagazine.it
DAP | Distributed Art Publishers,
New York
artbook.com
Vice Versa Distribution, Berlin
viceversaartbooks.com
Les presses du réel, Dijon
lespressesdureel.com
Antenne Books, London
antennebooks.com

© 2021, Maria D. Rapicavoli, Westfälischer
Kunstverein, University at Buffalo Art Galleries,
Mousse Publishing, and the authors of the texts

All works by Maria D. Rapicavoli
© Maria D. Rapicavoli

First edition
2021

Printed in Italy by
Intergrafica Verona S.r.l.

ISBN 978-88-6749-487-3

€ 27 / $ 30

All rights reserved. No part of this publication
may be reproduced in any form or by any electronic
means without prior written permission from
the copyright holders.

The Other: A Familiar Story

A film by Maria D. Rapicavoli
with Lucia Cammalleri

Narrator
Lucia Cammalleri

Cinematographer
Giacomo Belletti

Editing and Sound Design
Luca Fantini

Executive Producer
Veronica Diaferia

Production Company
tinygiant

Assistant Director
Annamaria Craparotta

Assistant Camera
Corey Stein

Sound Mixer
Pat O'Leary
Carmelo Sfogliano

Makeup Artist
Dario Cerfolli

Production Assistant
Christopher Newton
Corrado Vasquez

Post Production
tinygiant

Thanks to:
Chiara Messineo, Antonella Borzì, Rosetta Di
Gregorio, Rosa Longo, Giuseppa Longo, Silvana
Borzì, Claudia Gangemi, Carlotta Vagnoli, Michela
Lagalla, Emanuele Coco, Giuseppe Mazzaglia.

A very special thanks to:
Anna Longo, Millie Seman, Agatino Rapicavoli,
Michael Sullivan.

The work *The Other: A Familiar Story*
was commissioned by The Shelley & Donald Rubin
Foundation for The 8th Floor in collaboration
with Westfälischer Kunstverein. It has entered
the collections of the Museo Civico di Castelbuono
(Palermo) thanks to the Italian Council program
(6th edition, 2019).

Project supported by 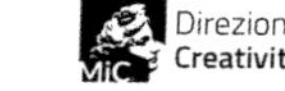 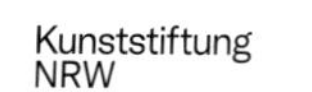

Kunststiftung
NRW
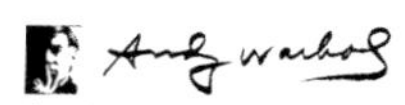

Q-INTERNATIONAL
LA QUADRIENNALE
DI ROMA

Sereina Steinemann
Works

Stadt Luzern
Kunstmuseum Luzern

1.

Die Welt tritt auf als «Welt» und wird betrachtet als Meute. Das ist eine sofortige Überwältigung. Mit Überwältigung beginnt ein Tag, so schreitet ein Tag voran und so endet er auch (ohne je wirklich vorbei zu sein).

Sie, die wir hier kurz begleiten, ist irgendeinem Märchen entsprungen, aber welchem nur? Das weiss sie jetzt auch nicht mehr. Ich habe Ahnungen, sagt sie, aber tatsächlich kann ich meinen Ursprung nicht präzise benennen. Der sei im Übrigen auch nicht so wichtig.

Sie wurde, sagt sie, irgendwie mit Märchen gefüttert, ja, wirklich kaum von der Mutterbrust, später sei auch die sogenannte feste Nahrung eher zweitrangig gewesen. Schon die Mutter habe sie mit Büchern ernährt, habe anstatt Zeit Bücher gegeben, folglich habe sie immer Bücher in ihrer Nähe gehabt. Es sei dann der Eindruck entstanden, sie gehöre den Märchen an, der riesigen Märchenfamilie, die ja eine internationale Gemeinschaft sei. Riesig, sagt sie, eine lange Linie, an der sie hänge. Im Übrigen sei es gar nicht so wichtig zu wissen, welchem Märchen genau sie entspringe, wichtig sei nur, der Welt etwas entgegensetzen zu können.

Sie sei ja eigentlich ein eher scheues Wesen und werde von der sogenannten Welt aufgerieben, über Gebühr. In ihrer Ziehfamilie aber: ablenkende, tröstliche, stärkende Erzählungen in Überfülle.

2.

Mal fühle sie sich ein wenig heimisch, dann aber wieder so dermassen fremd, dass sie sofort gehen, dass sie sofort das Weite suchen müsse. Und das, darauf weist sie deutlich hin, meine sie ganz ernst: also nicht einfach weggehen, sich nicht nur von einem Ort entfernen, sondern Weite suchen.

Denn wenn der Mensch mal gucken kann!

Guck mal hier, guck mal da.
Weite.
Sie sagt: Als wüsste ich noch, was das ist. Ich, sagt sie, bezeichne ja schon das als Weite, was nur die Abwesenheit der allzu aufdringlichen Enge ist, all der Dinge, Worte und Handlungen, die sich direkt auf mich zubewegen. In Gedanken, sagt sie, strecke sie ja die Hände immerzu nach vorn, abwehrend, sich eine Distanz erringend, die aber kaum zu verteidigen sei, denn wenn es ihr gelinge, nach vorn etwas Abstand zu erzeugen und diesen ein paar Minuten oder mitunter sogar Tage zu verteidigen, komme die Enge von der Seite, von hinten, oben, unten…

3.

Spricht man sie an, kommt sie ins Plaudern. Nach einer Weile sagt sie: Ich hoffe, ich habe Sie nicht aufgehalten. Dann überreicht sie ihre Visitenkarte: Melden Sie sich gern jederzeit.

SCHLÜSSEL UND MEHR.
Hauptsächlich Schlüssel.

Ja, sie sei eine Art Vertreterin für Schlüssel und sehe sich als eine Handlungsreisende. Das sage alles. Sie sei immer unterwegs. Selbst wenn sie sitze, wenn sie in ihrem Bett liege: immer unterwegs. Eine Rastlosigkeit, die ihr, hätte sie Muttermilch bekommen, als ein leibliches Erbe erschienen wäre. So aber: Immer wandere ihr Kopf entlang der Fäden, der Verbindungen zu ihrer angelesenen Familie, immer entdecke sie Verweise auf die Grösse ihrer Verwandtschaft: Wir sind überall. Einfach überall.

4.

Ihr Geschäft laufe so: Naja. Ihr Geschäft laufe so, dass sie noch ein zweites Standbein habe. Beide Beine gleichermassen muskulös und einander auf unterschiedliche Art stützend. Das Geschäft mit den Schlüsseln verstehe sie eigentlich nicht als Geschäft, aber es ist der Nachteil der Welt, hier alles zu einem Geschäft erklären zu müssen, um über die Runden zu kommen. Und bei den Ziehfamilientreffen, die sie regelmässig besuche, sehe sie sich jene genau an, die es geschafft haben, sich aus den Geschäften zu ziehen, die durch Klugheit, Schönheit, durch Witz oder durch eine Transformation in eine andere Wesenhaftigkeit hinein den Sprung durch alle Schichten, den Sprung in eine Unabhängigkeit erlangten, die sie auch haben möchte. Aber noch, sagt sie, weiss ich nicht, wie man springt.

5.

Sie fährt. Das ist doch immer noch am besten. Sie fährt beruflich oder sie kommt nicht umhin, beruflich unterwegs zu sein. Sie habe ihr Schlüssel-Geschäft nicht als ein so reiseintensives angelegt, aber es habe sich so ergeben. Und sowieso betrachte sie das Reisen als gute Basis, als Reminiszenz an einst mögliche Abenteuer, die in den Märchen stehen. Ja, die Märchen seien ihr Chronik und Lehrmaterial zugleich.

Sie pflege die ab und an als alt oder überholt anmutende Praxis der Reisebekanntschaften. Ja, sie komme beruflich gern mit allen möglichen Menschen ins Gespräch, so bringe sie die Schlüssel in die Welt. Denn dass der Mensch der Schlüssel bedürfe und die Schlüssel der Menschen – daran bestehe doch kein Zweifel.

1.

The world enters the stage as "World" and is regarded as a mob. That is immediately overwhelming. The day begins with overwhelm, and that is how it continues, and that is how it ends (without ever really being over).

She—the one we're going to join for a while—has sprung from some fairy tale or other, but which one? She doesn't know anymore. I have my suspicions, she says, but I really can't say precisely where I come from. And anyway, it's not that important.

She was, she says, somehow fed on fairy tales, yes, and scarcely on mother's milk, and later so-called solid food was of secondary importance to her. She says her mother fed her on books, gave her books instead of time, and thus she always had books close by. Then, it began to seem that she belonged to fairy tales, the enormous family of fairy tales, which is after all an international community. Enormous, she says, a long line from which she dangles. And besides, she says, it's quite unnecessary to know exactly which fairy tale she comes from, the important part is being able to set something against the world. She's really quite a shy creature and the so-called world wears her out; it wears her out unduly. But in her foster family: distracting, comforting, fortifying stories in abundance.

2.

Sometimes she feels at home, she says, a little bit, but then she feels so foreign again that she has to leave immediately, to get some distance. And that—she makes it very clear—is meant quite seriously: she doesn't just have to leave, she doesn't just have to go away from a place, she has to get some distance.

Because when you can really look! Look over here, look over there. The distance.

She says: as if I still knew what that was. I already call something distance when there's only an absence of the most insistent restrictions, of all the things, words and actions that are headed directly for me. In her thoughts, she says, she always stretches her hands out ahead of her, fending off, fighting for distance. But that distance is nearly impossible to defend. If she manages to carve out some space, holding it for a few minutes or even days, the narrowness inevitably closes in—from the sides, from behind, from above, from below…

3.

If you speak to her, she gets talking. After a while, she says: I hope I haven't held you up. Then she presents her business card: Please feel free to contact me at any time.

KEYS AND MORE.
Mostly keys.

Yes, she's a kind of sales rep for keys, and she sees herself as a travelling saleswoman. That tells you all you need to know. She's always on the road. Even when she's sitting down, even when she's in bed: she's on the road. A restlessness which she would—if she had been fed on mother's milk—regard as an inherited trait. But as it is: her mind always wanders along the threads, the connections to the family she read her way into, she's always discovering references to the numerousness of her relations: we are everywhere. Simply everywhere.

4.

Her business is going—well. Her business is going well enough that she can stand on her own two feet. Both feet equally sturdy, supporting her in different ways. She doesn't actually see the key business as a business, but the downside of this world is that you have to call everything a business just to get by. And at the foster family meetings she goes to regularly, she looks carefully at the ones who have managed to get out of doing business, through wisdom, beauty, wit, or through a transformation into another type of being, skipping through all levels of society, skipping into an independence which she'd like to have too. But, she says, I still don't know how to skip.

6.

Die Schlüssel: ihr Team. Ihre Mitarbeit-
enden. Eine plaudernde Menge. Die Schlüssel hochaktiv und konzentriert, du meine
Güte, sagt sie, das kann sich niemand aus-
denken, wie schön es ist, in Gesellschaft
der Schlüssel zu sein. Sie betreibe, wenn
man so will, eine andere Art von Schlüssel-
dienst, ja, vielleicht könne man das so
sagen.

Aber nein, sie sage das so eigentlich
doch nicht gern: kein Dienst, keine Dienst-
leistung. Man könne den Dienstleistungs-
sektor doch gar nicht mehr beruflich
betreten, ohne sofort als ausbeutbar und
herumkommandierbar betrachtet zu werden. Und sie sehe sich ungern als Dienerin,
schon eher als Begleiterin, so in etwa,
okay?

7.

Irgendwann habe sie nur noch an Schlüssel
denken können. Und nach Schlüsseln
Ausschau halten können. Das sei so etwas
wie ihre Ausbildungszeit gewesen. Sie
habe ihren Schlüssel verloren, habe allen
möglichen Stellen Bescheid gegeben, aber
nie wieder etwas gehört. Der Schlüssel
war und blieb weg, aber sie sage dennoch
weiterhin, dass nichts wirklich verschwinden könne.

Nichts kann verschwinden.

Sie sage das, wenn auch nicht voller
Überzeugung. Es so zu formulieren sei der
Versuch (glaube sie), sich auf grössere
Verluste vorzubereiten. Es sei der Versuch,
auf künftige Verluste, die es wohl geben
wird, es sei denn, sie gehe zuvor der Welt
verlustig (haha), mit einer Lüge zu reagie-
ren. Bevor die Verluste geschehen.

Und eine Lüge, das hätte sie gerade
vorhin noch bei Jean-Luc Nancy gelesen,
sei ja nicht per se schlecht: «Lügen heisst,
nicht die Wahrheit zu sagen. Aber die
Wahrheit, die von der Lüge verhehlt oder
verheimlicht, verändert oder entstellt
wird, die ist vielleicht gar nicht immer so
einfach zu entwirren. [...] Wenn die Ver-
urteilung der Lüge so tief in uns verankert
ist, dann vielleicht deshalb, weil wir einerseits wissen, dass die Lüge unvermeidlich
ist, und andererseits zugleich wissen, dass
es im Leben im Allgemeinen um die Wahrheit gehen muss.»[1]

8.

Nein, sie lüge nicht. Sie füge ihre Erzählungen der Welt hinzu.

Jetzt, sagt sie, sind die besten Zeiten,
um Erzählungen zu ergänzen. Sie schöp-
fe naturgemäss, weil sie ja zu dieser inter-
nationalen Märchenfamilie gehöre, aus
einem gewaltigen Vorrat. Und immer kommen neue Geschichten hinzu. Es genüge
aber im Übrigen nicht, aus Fakten Fiktionen
zu machen. Es gehe immer um eine Ver-
besserung der Welt. Das sei Teil all ihrer
Handlungen, das sei das Zentrum ihrer be-
ruflichen Tätigkeit.

Und nein, sie sage nicht einfach:
Hier, wollen Sie einen Schlüssel? Ich habe
welche dabei.

Meine Schlüssel, sagt sie, sind wie
Agenten, und ich schicke sie nicht in
unvorbereitetes Gelände. Ich überlasse sie
nicht gern denen, die mit ihrem neuen
Schlüssel nicht auf neue Schlösser aus
sind. Ein neuer Schlüssel ist eine Art Brille,
ein Werkzeug des Sehens. Sie habe keine
Schlüssel zu verschleudern. Sie verteile die
Schlüssel wirklich nicht beliebig. Wie ge-
sagt, das Schlüsselunterfangen ist ja kein
Business, sondern eher eine Kooperation.
In erster Linie eine Kooperation mit den
Schlüsseln.

9.

Sie werde hier nicht alles erzählen. Oder
sie habe schon alles erzählt. Ihr Schlüsselunterfangen sei ein symbolisches. Das sei
ja keine Neuigkeit. Sie arbeite mit den
Mitteln, derer sich ihre Ziehfamilie schon
seit Ewigkeiten bediene. Sie arbeite mit
den Mitteln, derer sich die ganze Welt bediene, die aber angeblich in Vergessenheit
geraten seien. Sie übergebe tatsächliche
Schlüssel, die sich vorrangig als Symbol
verstünden, als Erinnerung daran, dass
etwas aufgeschlossen werden könne, als
Erinnerung daran, dass dieser Schlüssel
irgendwo passe.

Derzeit sei sie allerdings etwas müde
und behalte die Schlüssel lieber bei sich.
Es schmerze sie die Vorstellung, die hoch-
geschätzten Schlüssel vielleicht in die
falschen Hände zu geben.

Die Schlüssel signalisieren, sie hielten
das aus. Aber sie, sie halte das nicht aus.
Sie wolle nicht die Vorstellung haben, der
Schlüssel liege an irgendeinem Taschen-
grund zwischen Krümeln, Powerbank, Papers
und Münzen und sehe nie das Tageslicht
und werde (und das sei das Schlimmste)
schlichtweg vergessen.

Ein Alptraum, sagt sie.

Wer nicht aufzuschliessen verlangt,
was noch gar nicht oder nicht mehr zu
sehen ist, hat die ganze Welt verloren.

Und irgendwann einmal hatte irgend-
jemand von aussen ein Herz in den Staub
des Zugfensters gemalt. Darüber einzelne Tupfer, Tapser, etwas wie eine versehent-
liche Spur, etwas wie ein Beat, ein Puls-
schlag, eine Schrift. Die fotografierte sie.

10.

Ja, der Eindruck täusche nicht: Sie arbeite,
als wolle sie den Kapitalismus müde machen, ja, das sei ihr Ziel. Ja, sie agiere als
eine, die den Kapitalismus derart heraus-
fordere, dass sie ihn (in Gestalt seiner frei-
willigen oder unfreiwilligen Apologet*innen)
wiederholen lasse, was er zu sagen ver-
lange. Sie lasse ihn seine Botschaften und
Glaubenssätze verbreiten, lasse ihn sich
entspannen und locke ihn in eine Situation,
in der er die eigenen Botschaften und
Glaubenssätze noch einmal und noch einmal sage, sie führe ihn in eine Art Zwang-
haftigkeit, die den Kapitalismus sich selbst
eine Enge erzeugen lasse.

Wie lässt sich etwas ermüden, das
ihr und allen, die sie liebe, so feindselig ge-
genüberstehe?

Was ermüden soll, müsse durch sich
selbst ermüdet werden.

Ja, sie sei definitiv auf einem guten
Weg.

Sie wisse jedoch nicht: Habe sie jetzt
alles schon einmal gehört? Oder lieben
die Menschen die Wiederholungen ihrer
selbst? Das sichere Gelände der Identität?
Diese Sicherheit behage ihr nicht. Ges-
tern habe sie neben einem gesessen, der
habe grosse Reden geschwungen und
nichts gesagt, was er nicht schon an ande-
rer Stelle gesagt habe. Dabei war er nicht
einmal ein Politiker, er war nichts als
ein Vertreter seiner selbst. Er habe Formu-
lierungen benutzt, wie: Das sage ich ja
eigentlich nicht öffentlich, aber ich sage es
hier. Sie sagte: Das hast du doch alles
schon einmal gesagt. Ich habe dich an drei
anderen Orten reden hören und nur einmal hörte ich, was du da sagtest, zum
ersten Mal. Er habe sie dann vor aller Augen
und Ohren darauf hingewiesen, dass er,
wohl im Gegensatz zu ihr, die bessere
Geschichte in petto habe. Sie hingegen sei
offensichtlich gezwungen, wieder und
wieder Neues zu erzählen.

Sie sei in einem Wechselbad aus Em-
pörung und Müdigkeit gewesen. Sie habe
ihn von seinem Stuhl schieben und ausser-
dem alle Schlüssel auffordern wollen,
ihn, diesen nach Identität Süchtigen, abzu-
schliessen. Dauerhaft. Ihre besten Verbün-
deten seien ja die Schlüssel.

11.

Wenn sie aus dem Zugfenster schaue, sehe
sie Höhlen, wo keine sind: Was sie für
den Eingang in den Berg hielt, war ein gros-
ser, voluminöser Baum, der dunkel vor
diesem Berg stand, der für Momente durch
die Abendsonne aus der ihm ähnlich se-
henden Landschaft hervorgehoben wurde.

Sie, die wir hier wirklich nur kurz begleiten, fuhr da schon eine Weile an einem
Fluss entlang, der ruhig floss, ganz ohne
Aufwühlung, ganz ohne den Wind der letz-
ten Tage. Der Fluss war ein Spiegel für
den mit dicker Haufenwolken bespielten
Himmel und zeigte dessen Färbung, orange-
rosa.

Wer, wie sie, der Märchenfamilie ange-
hört, ist an den Flüssen der Welt zuhause.

12.

Sie, die ja Schüssel eher verteile als ver-
kaufe, die Schlüssel also gegen eine sogenannte Schutzgebühr vergebe, aber lieber
verschenken würde, nur wisse sie ja leider,
dass die meisten Mitmenschen den Wert
einer Sache erst anerkennen können, wenn
sie dafür einen ihnen irgendwie angemes-
sen scheinenden Betrag bezahlt haben – sie
halte ja immerzu nach zu den Schlüsseln
passenden Schlössern Ausschau, die selten
so aussehen, wie man sie sich so vorstell-
te. Man müsse doch sowieso von allen
Erwartungen Abstand nehmen. Das habe
sie in ihrer Zeit als Handlungsreisende
gelernt.

13.

Es war einmal, so beginne sie mit der Erzählung über all die Dinge, die sie nicht mehr
anwesend wissen wolle. Und sie beende die
Erzählung so: Es war einmal und kommt
nicht wieder.

Sie sagt, sie versuche zu sein wie
jene guten Feen, jene guten Hexen, die mit-
tels der Sprache die Wirklichkeit veränder-
ten. Sie schaffe ab, erzeuge Weite, denke
neu. So gehe es los, das sei alles, worum es
ihr haupt- und nebenberuflich gehe. Und
privat übrigens auch. Da mache sie keinen
Unterschied

1 Jean-Luc Nancy, *Die Wahrheit der
Lüge. Für Kinder und Erwachsene*,
Passagen, Wien 2023, S. 15 und S. 18.

5.

She travels. After all, that's still the best way. She travels professionally or she cannot avoid being professionally on the road. She didn't set up her key business to be so travel-heavy, but it turned out that way. And anyway, she sees travel as a good basis, as a reminder of fairytale adventures that used to be possible. Yes, for her, fairy tales are both a chronicle and a textbook.

She cultivates the practice of travel acquaintances, which sometimes seems old-fashioned or obsolete. Yes, in her professional guise, she likes to talk to all sorts of people, that's how she brings the keys into the world. After all, she says, people need keys and keys need people—there can be no doubt about that.

6.

The keys: her team. Her coworkers. A chattering crowd. When the keys are highly active and concentrated, oh my goodness, she says, you just can't imagine how great it is to be in the company of keys. She offers a service, if you like, a key service, yes, perhaps you could say that.

But no, she doesn't actually like saying it that way: this is not a service, public or otherwise. The service sector—you can't even join that sector anymore without immediately making yourself exploitable, someone to be ordered around. And she'd rather not see herself as a servant, she'd rather be a kind of companion, something like that, okay?

7.

At some point, all she could do was think about keys. And look out for keys. That was, in a way, her period of apprenticeship. She had lost her key, she says, and she reported it to all possible authorities, but never heard anything back. The key was gone and it remained gone, but she still goes on saying that nothing can really disappear.

Nothing can disappear.

She says that, though not with full conviction. Putting it that way is an attempt (she believes) to prepare herself for greater losses. There will be future losses, they will certainly come, unless the world loses her first (haha)—and this is an attempt to react to those losses with a lie. Before they happen.

And a lie, she read just now in the work of Jean-Luc Nancy, is not a bad thing in itself: "Lying means not telling the truth. But the truth that is hidden or kept secret by the lie, changed or distorted, might not always be so easy to disentangle. [...] If condemning the lie is so deeply anchored in us, that might be because we know that lying is unavoidable, while at the same time we know that life in general must be about the truth."[1]

8.

No, she doesn't lie. She adds her stories to the world.

Now, she says, these are the best times to add to stories. Naturally—because she belongs to this international family of fairy tales—she can draw on a mighty store. And new stories are always being added. But it's not enough to turn facts into fiction. It's always about improving the world. That is part of everything she does on her travels, that is the core of her professional activities.

And no, she doesn't just say: Here, do you want a key? I have some with me.

My keys, she says, are like agents, I don't send them into territory that hasn't been prepared. I don't like to hand them over to people who aren't out to find new locks with their new keys. A new key is like a pair of glasses, it's a tool of vision. She doesn't have keys to waste. She really doesn't distribute the keys randomly. Again, the key project is not a business, but more of a cooperation. Above all, it's a cooperation with the keys.

9.

She's not going to tell the whole story here. Or she already has told it all. Her key aproject is symbolic. That's nothing new. She works with the tools that her foster family has been using forever. She works with the tools that the whole world uses, but which have supposedly fallen into oblivion. She hands over actual keys which regard themselves mainly as symbols, as reminders of the fact that something can be opened up, as reminders that these keys fit somewhere.

At the moment, however, she's quite tired and prefers to keep the keys with her. It's painful, she says, to imagine the possibility of placing the highly prized keys in the wrong hands.

The keys signal that they would be able to handle that. But as for her, she can't handle it. She does not want to imagine a key lying at the bottom of some bag between crumbs, a power bank, cigarette papers and coins, never seeing daylight, and being (that's the worst part) quite simply forgotten.

A nightmare, she says.

If you don't try to unlock what can not yet or no longer be seen, then you've lost the whole world.

And at some point, someone had drawn a heart in the dust of the train window from the outside. Above it were a few dots, prints, something like an accidental trail, something like a beat, a pulse, a bit of writing. She photographed that.

10.

Yes, the impression is correct: she's working as though she wanted to make capitalism tired, yes, that's her aim. Yes, she's acting as someone who challenges capitalism in such a way that she makes it (in the form of its voluntary or involuntary defenders) repeat what it wants to say. She lets it spread its messages and dogmas, lets it relax and lures it into a situation in which it will proclaim its messages and dogmas again and again, she leads it into a kind of compulsion which makes capitalism create constraints for itself.

How is it possible to tire something out that is so hostile to her and to everyone she loves?

If it is to become tired, it has to tire of itself.

Yes, she's definitely on the right track.

But she doesn't know: has she now heard everything before? Or do people love repetitions of themselves? The safe ground of identity? This safety unsettles her. Yesterday, she sat next to someone who was holding forth, talking big, and not saying anything he hadn't already said somewhere else. And he wasn't even a politician, he was nothing but a representative of himself. He used phrases like: I don't actually say this in public, but I'll say it here. She said: You've said all this before. I've heard you speak in three other places, and only once did I hear what you said for the first time. He then—in front of everyone—pointed out that he, unlike her, had the better story up his sleeve. She, meanwhile, clearly had to invent new things to talk about, again and again.

She was, she says, overcome with a mixture of outrage and weariness. She wanted to push him out of his seat, this identity addict, and also to order all the keys to shut him up. For good. Because the keys are her best allies.

11.

When she looks out of the train window, she says, she sees caves where there are none: what she thought was an entrance into the mountain was a big, voluminous tree, standing dark in front of the mountain, which blended into the similar-looking landscape and then stood out for a moment, because of the evening sun.

She, whom we're really only joining for a short time here, had been travelling for a while along a river which flowed calmly, quite unruffled, without the wind of the previous days. The river was a mirror of the sky, where thick cumulus clouds were gathered, and it showed the sky's colours, orange-pink.

Those who belong, like her, to the fairytale family, are at home beside the rivers of the world.

12.

She, who really distributes keys as opposed to selling them, who provides keys in return for a so-called cover charge, but would rather give them away, it's just that she knows that most other people unfortunately only recognize the value of an object when they've paid an amount for it that somehow seems appropriate to them—she's constantly looking out for locks that match the keys, which rarely look as you'd expect. Either way, you have to let go of all expectations. She has learned that, she says, in her time as a travelling saleswoman.

13.

Once upon a time, that is how she begins the story about all the things that she wants to consign to the past. And she ends the story as follows: once upon a time there was and will not be again.

She says she tries to be like those good fairies, those good witches, who changed reality through language. She gets rid of things, makes space, rethinks. That's how it starts, she says, that's all that matters to her, in her side job and in her main occupation. And in her private life too, by the way. She makes no distinction there.

[1] Jean-Luc Nancy, *Die Wahrheit der Lüge. Für Kinder und Erwachsene*, Passagen, Vienna 2023, p. 15 and p. 18. Quotation translated by LD.

Halt + Form

extra **stark**

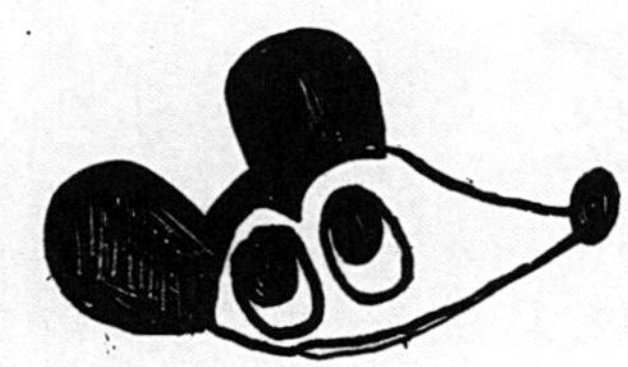

Der

Moment

gehört

mir.

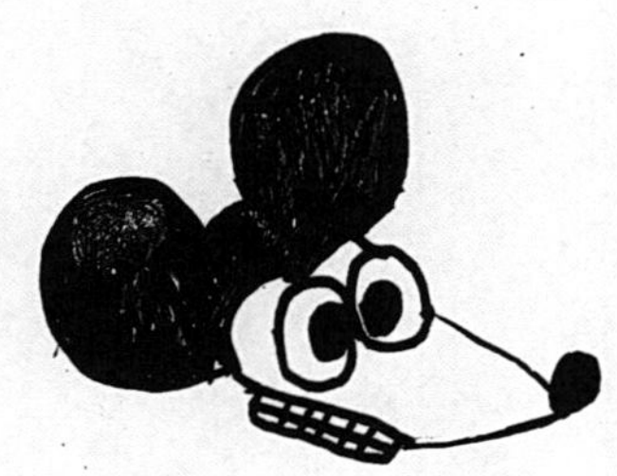

100 %.

refresh your
life style !

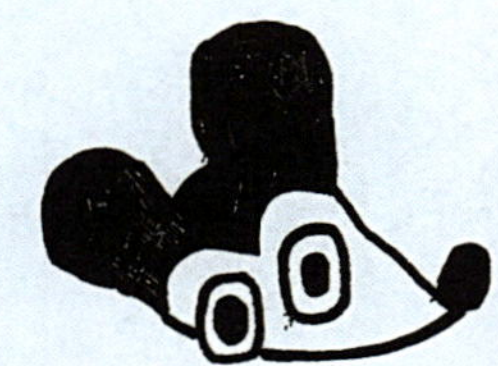

Taking
a break
from
boring

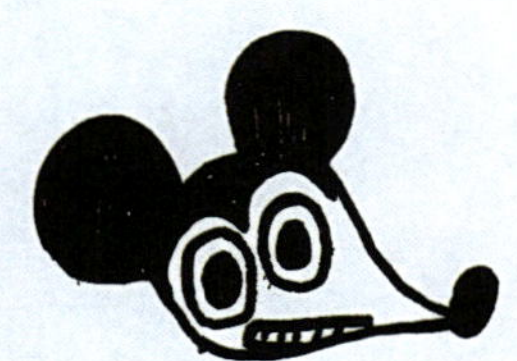

KAPITAL
erhalten
MEHRWERT
schaffen

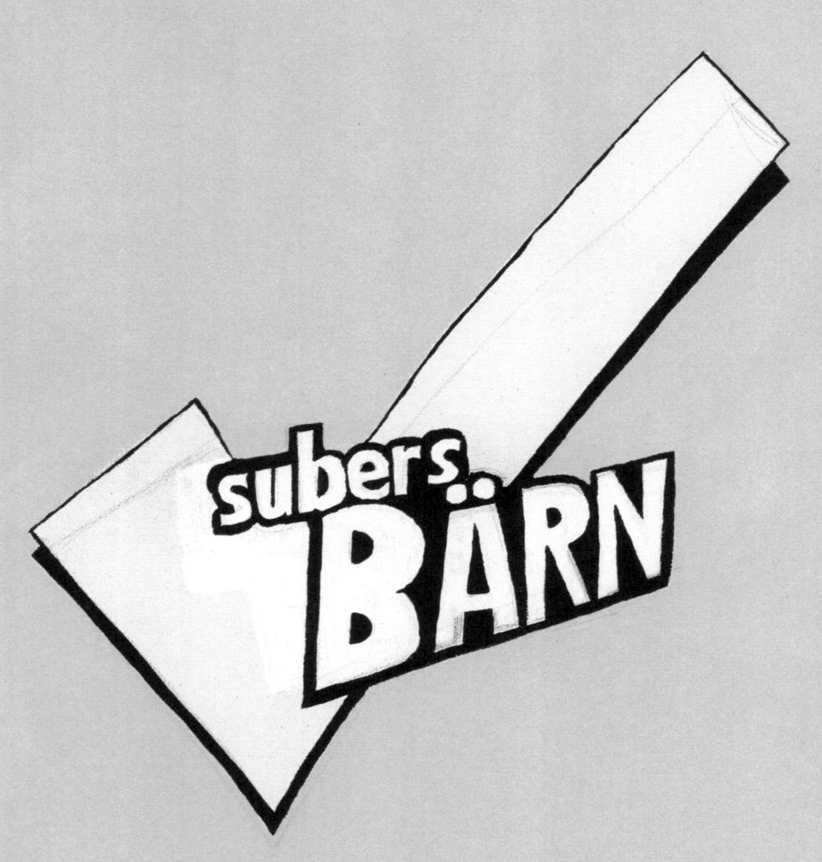
subers.
BÄRN

More
extra,
less
ordinary!

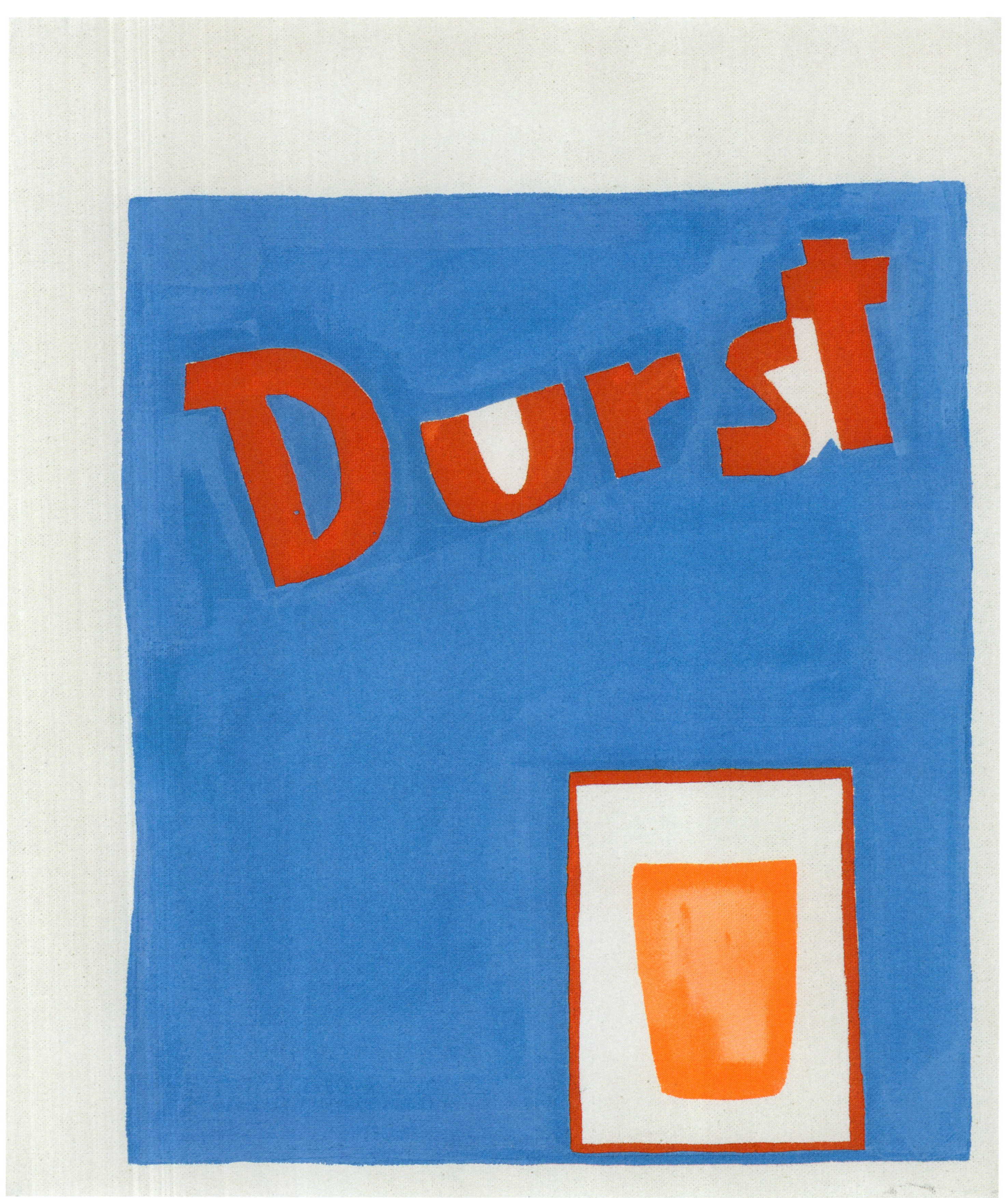

Durst

Das
beste
Plus
für
deinen
Sommer

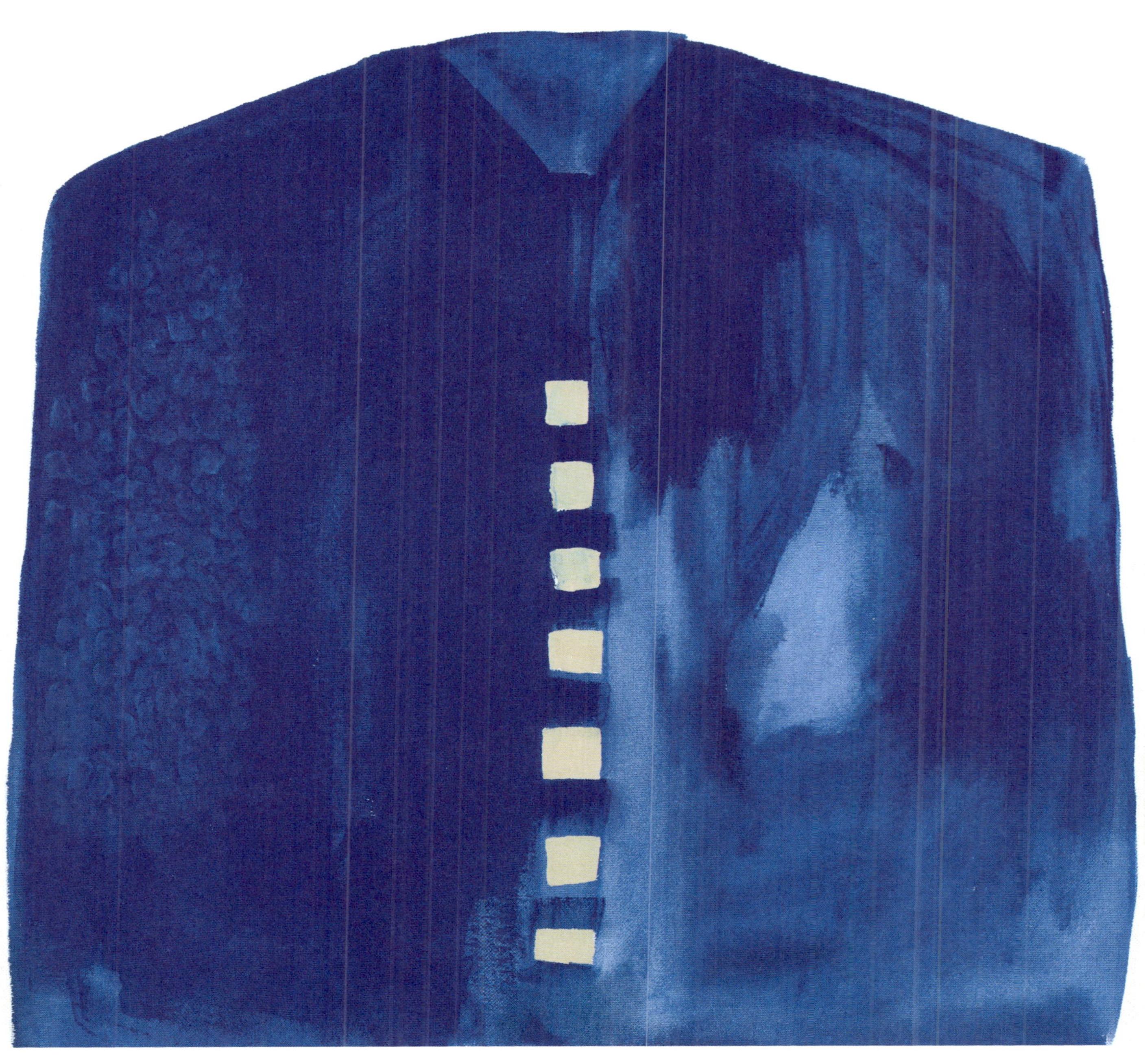

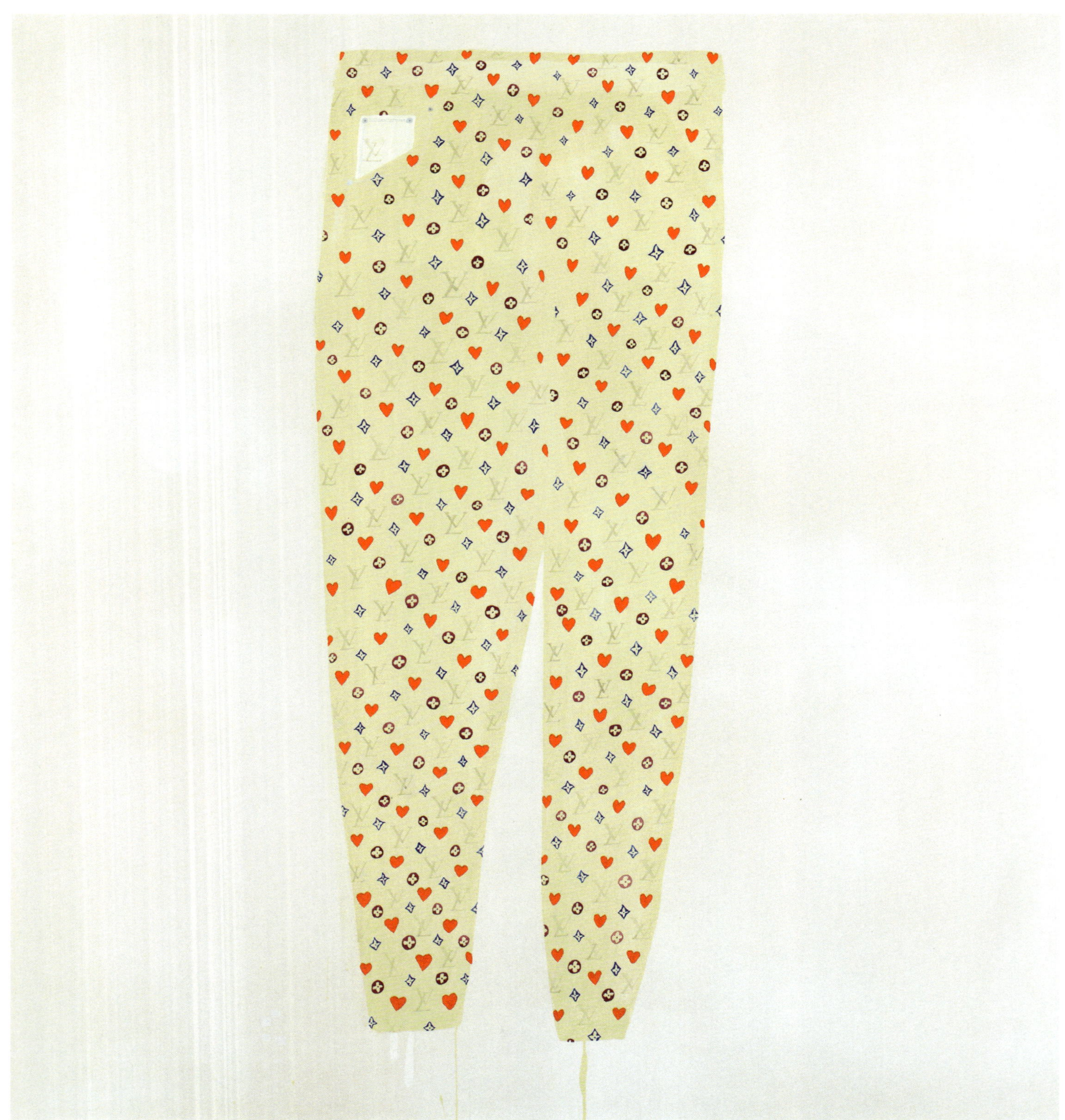

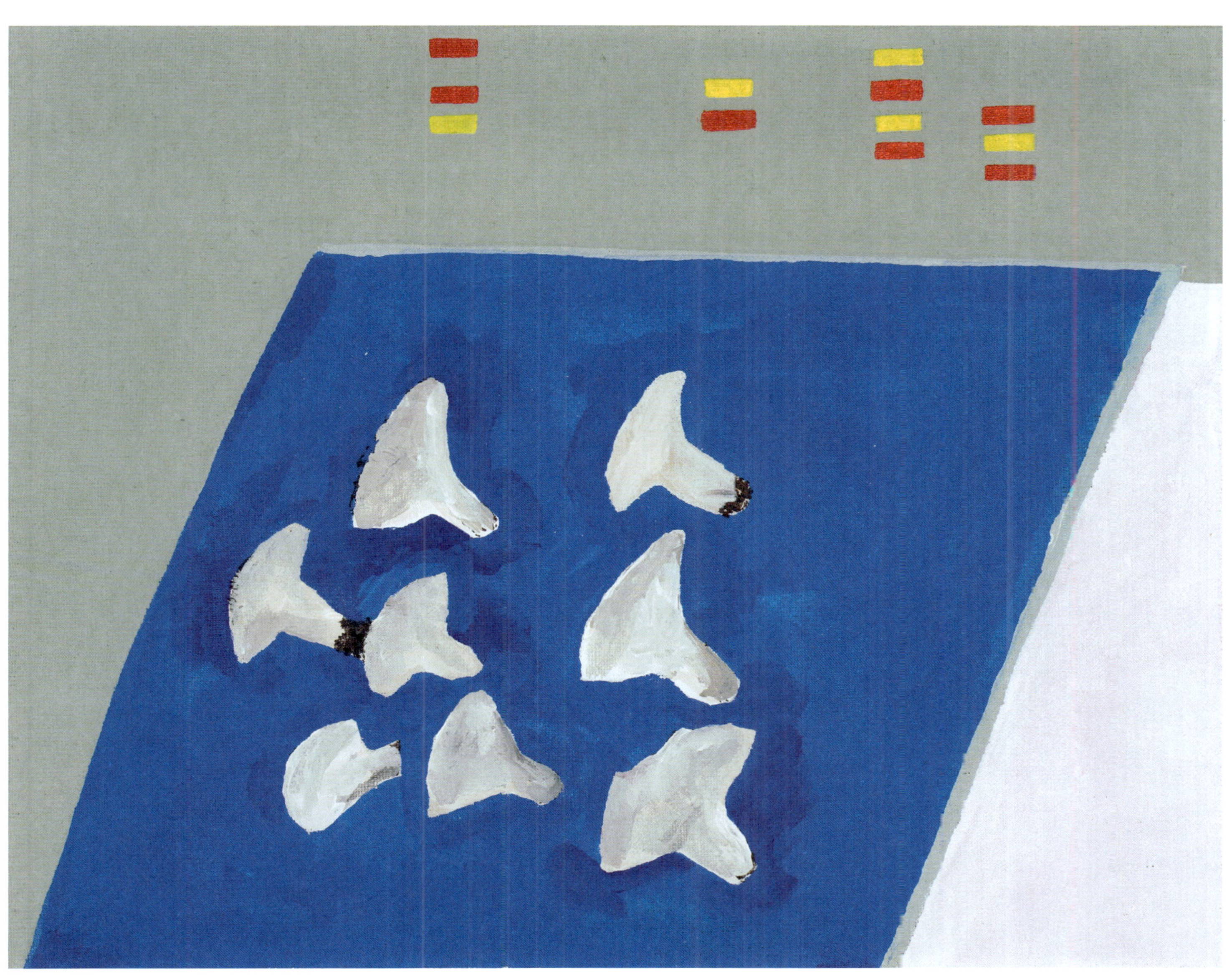

mir

Spruudle

vor

Idee ...

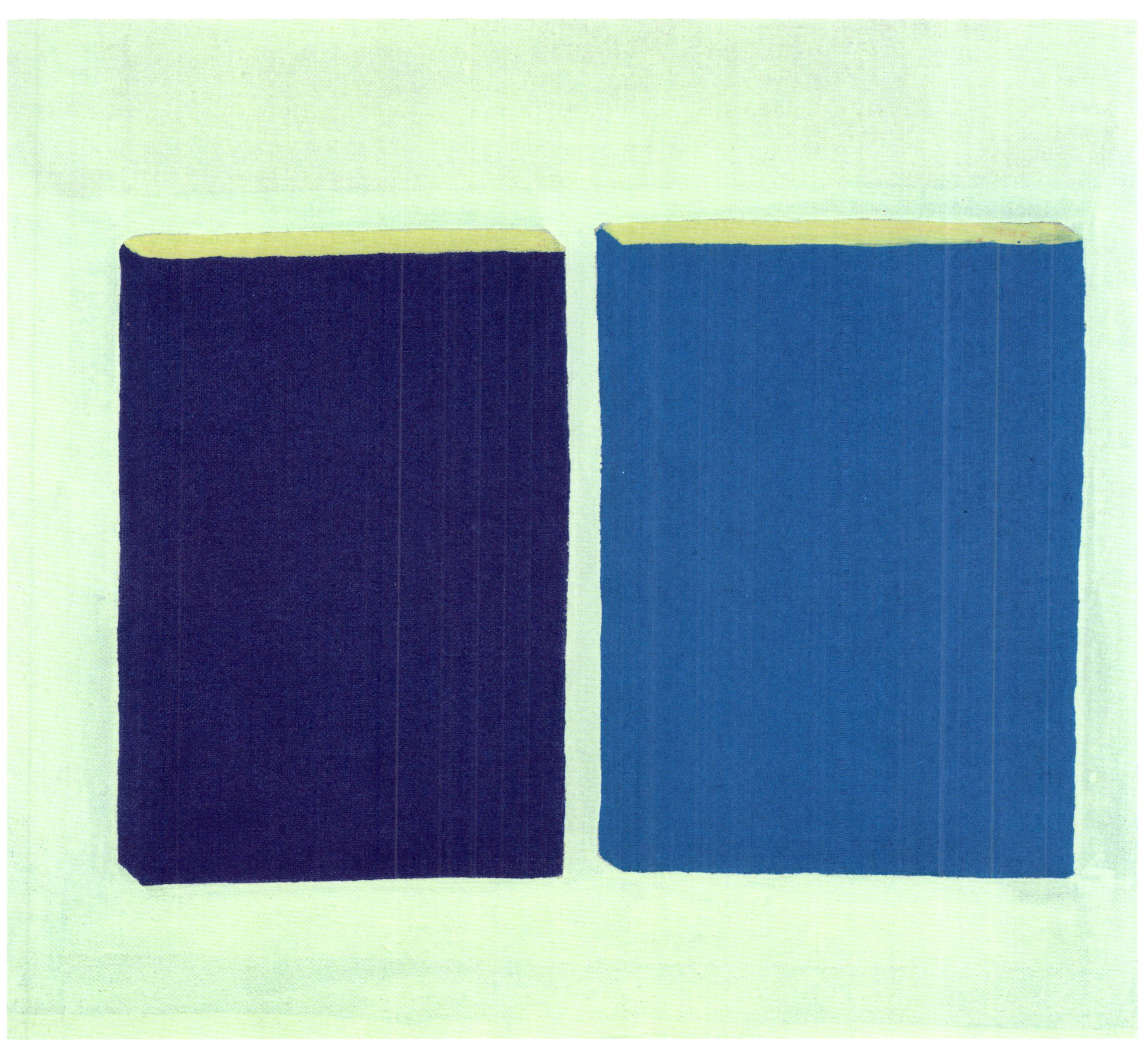

Be

the

beautiful

you

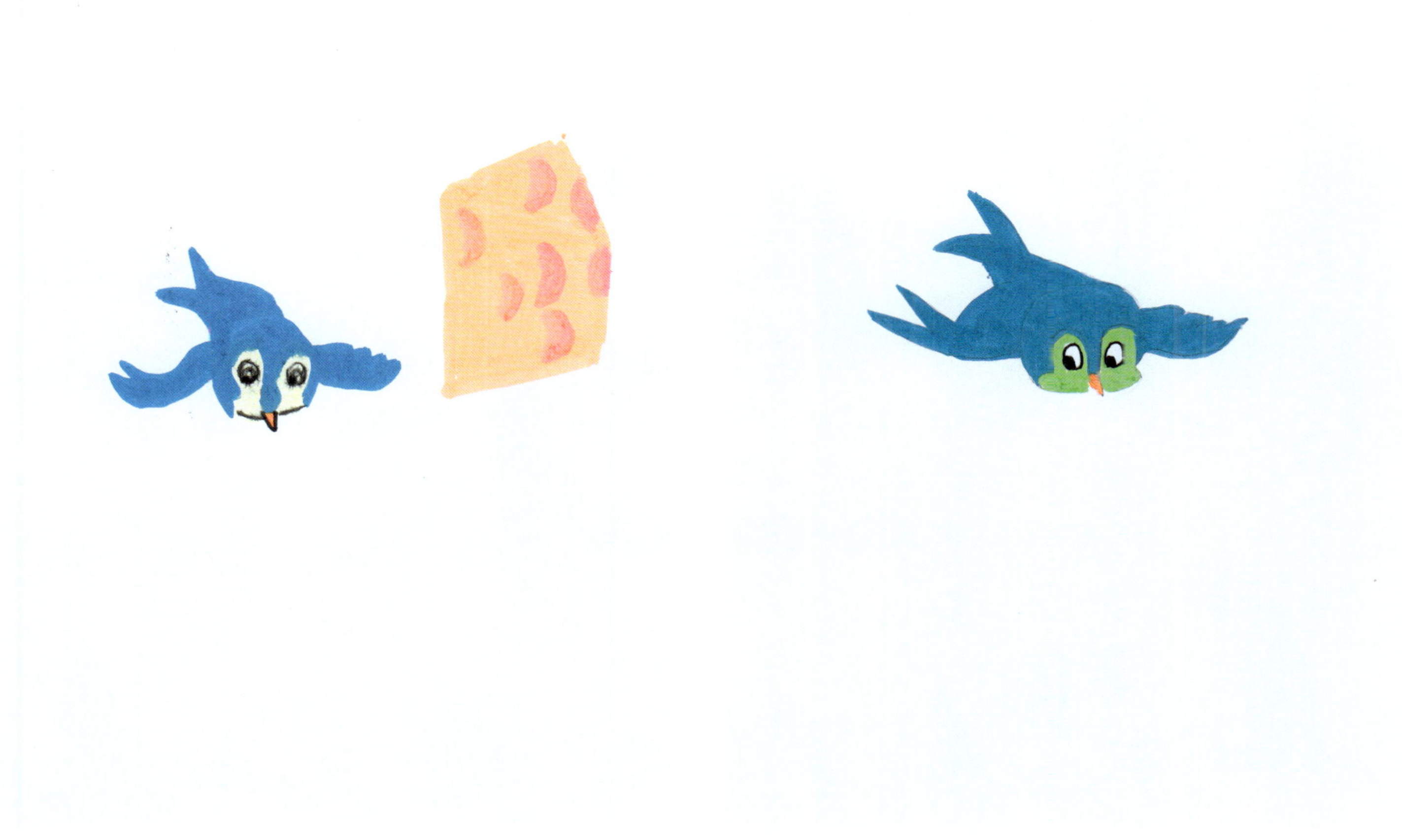

Endlich loslegen fühlt sich gut an.

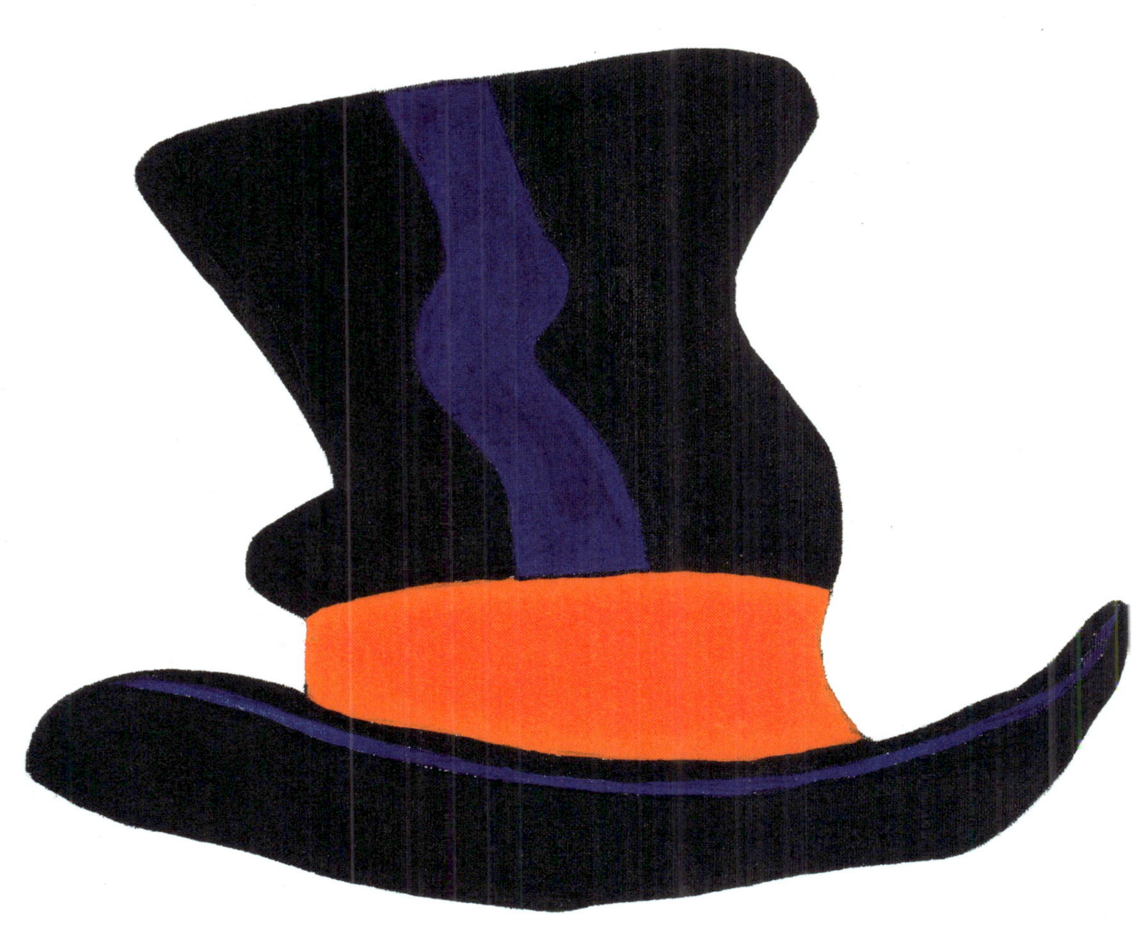

Smile with Strength

I know for certain this photo was staged. There is no way that Abby Walton is a lesbian. She is the straightest person I know. Staged just to get in Vice.

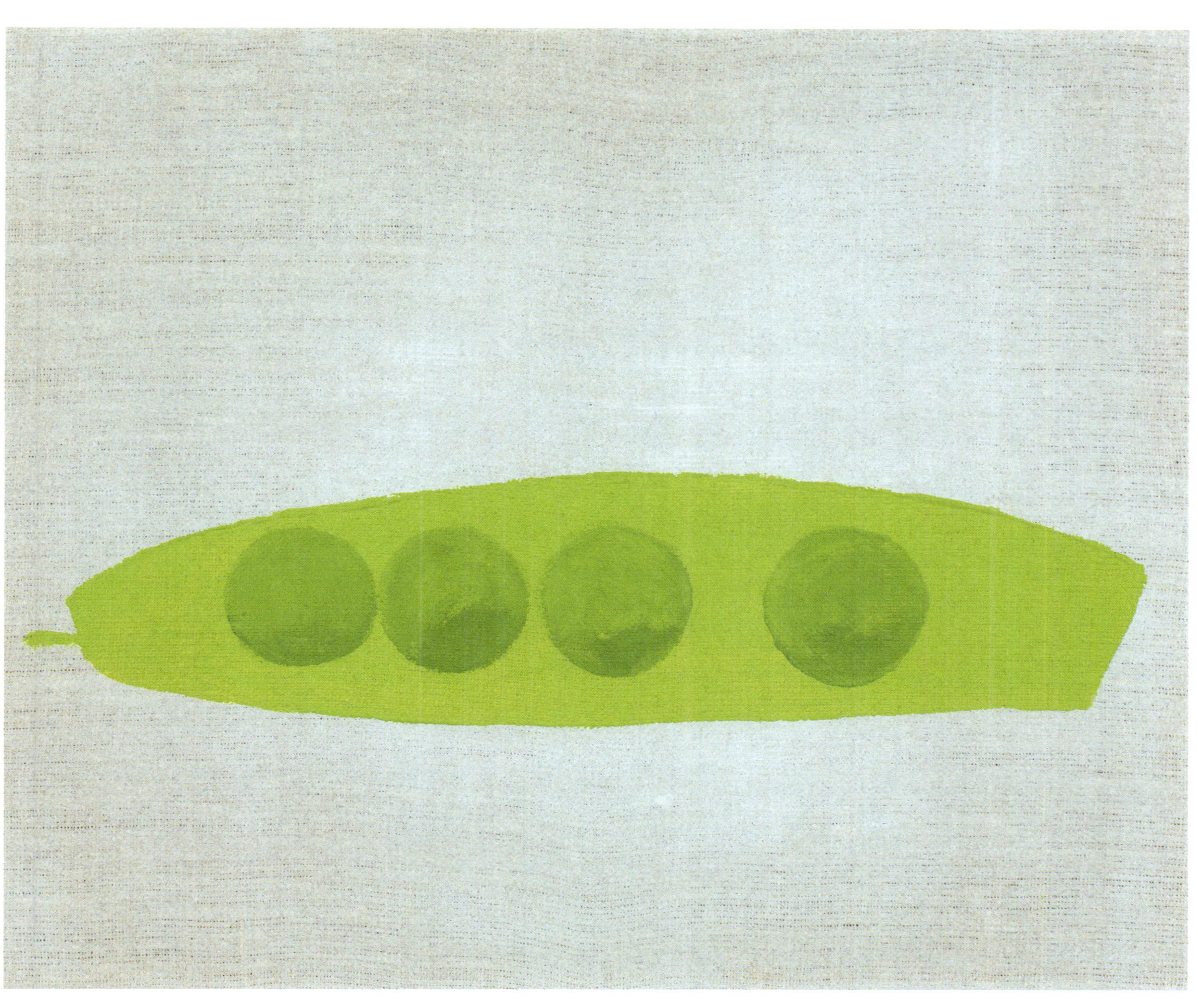

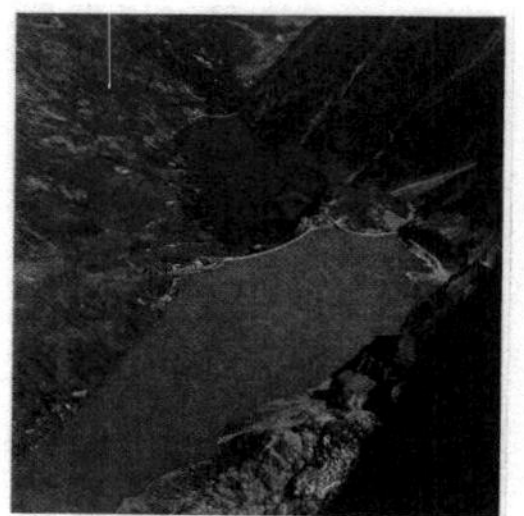

«blues» new album

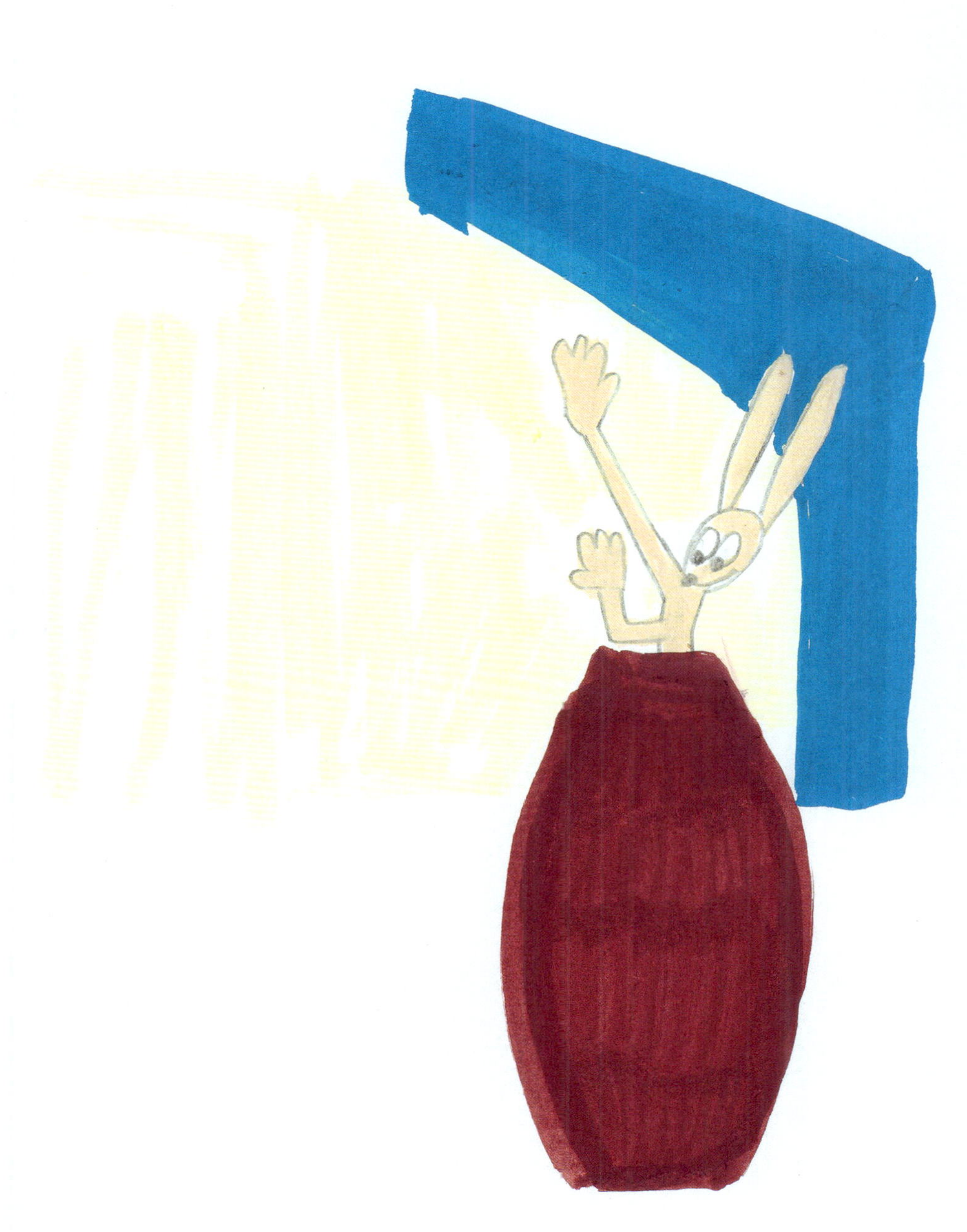

Sport

8/2022
© 5.St.
1. und
einzige
ausgabe
39/40
CHF 5

Wissenswertes & neue Fakten

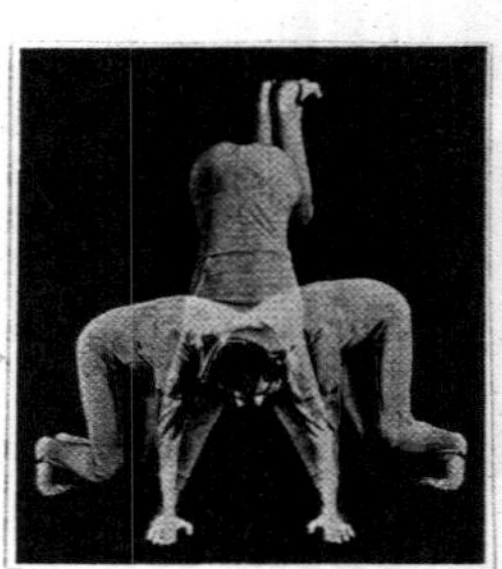

Falsches Ballaufnehmen

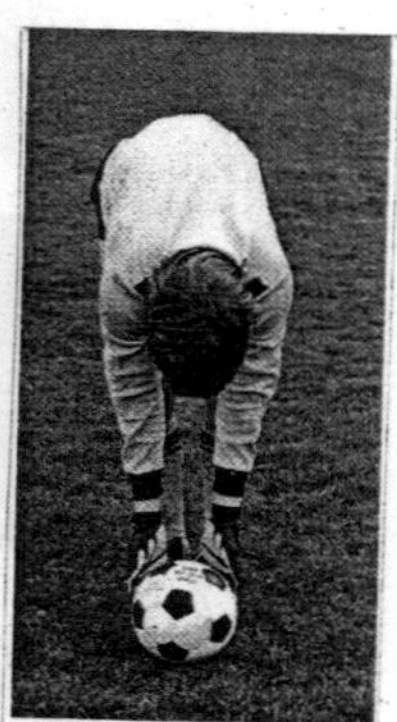

Richtiges Ballaufnehmen

- Hätten
  Sie's
  gewusst?

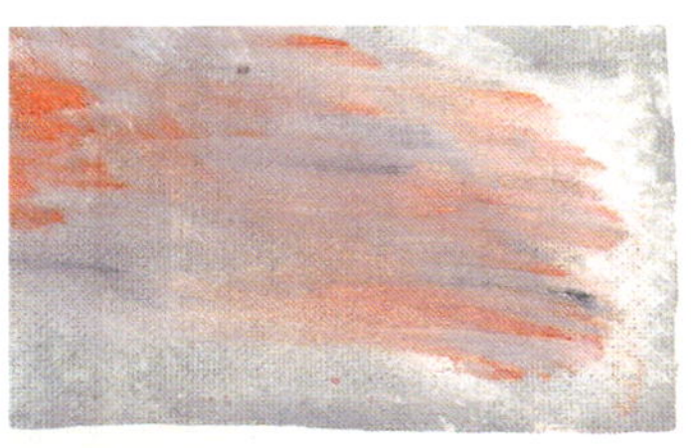

ELIZABETH MURRAY
MERET OPPENHEIM
STANLEY WHITNEY
LOUISE BOURGEOIS
PHILIP GUSTON
HENRI MATISSE
LYNETTE YIADOM-BOAKYE
LILY VAN DER STOKKER
RAOUL DE KEYSER
JUDITH HOPF
SEREINA STEINEMANN
SELINA LUTZ

8.9. — 17.12. THEÒSIS

WISSEN HEUTE

SCIENCE AUJOURD'HUI

Hier lacht der Betrachter

Hier runzelt der Betrachter die Stirn

Hier weint der Betrachter

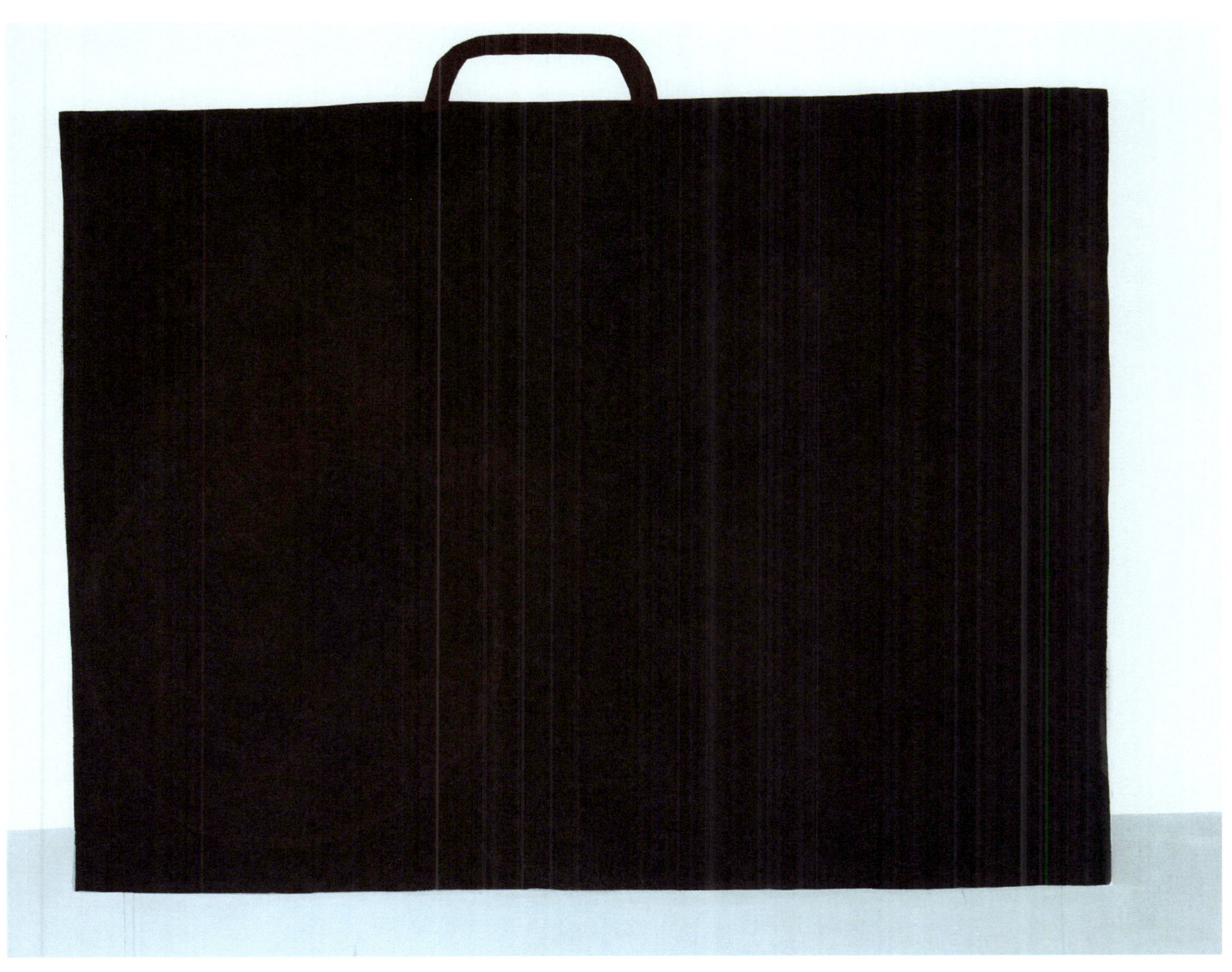

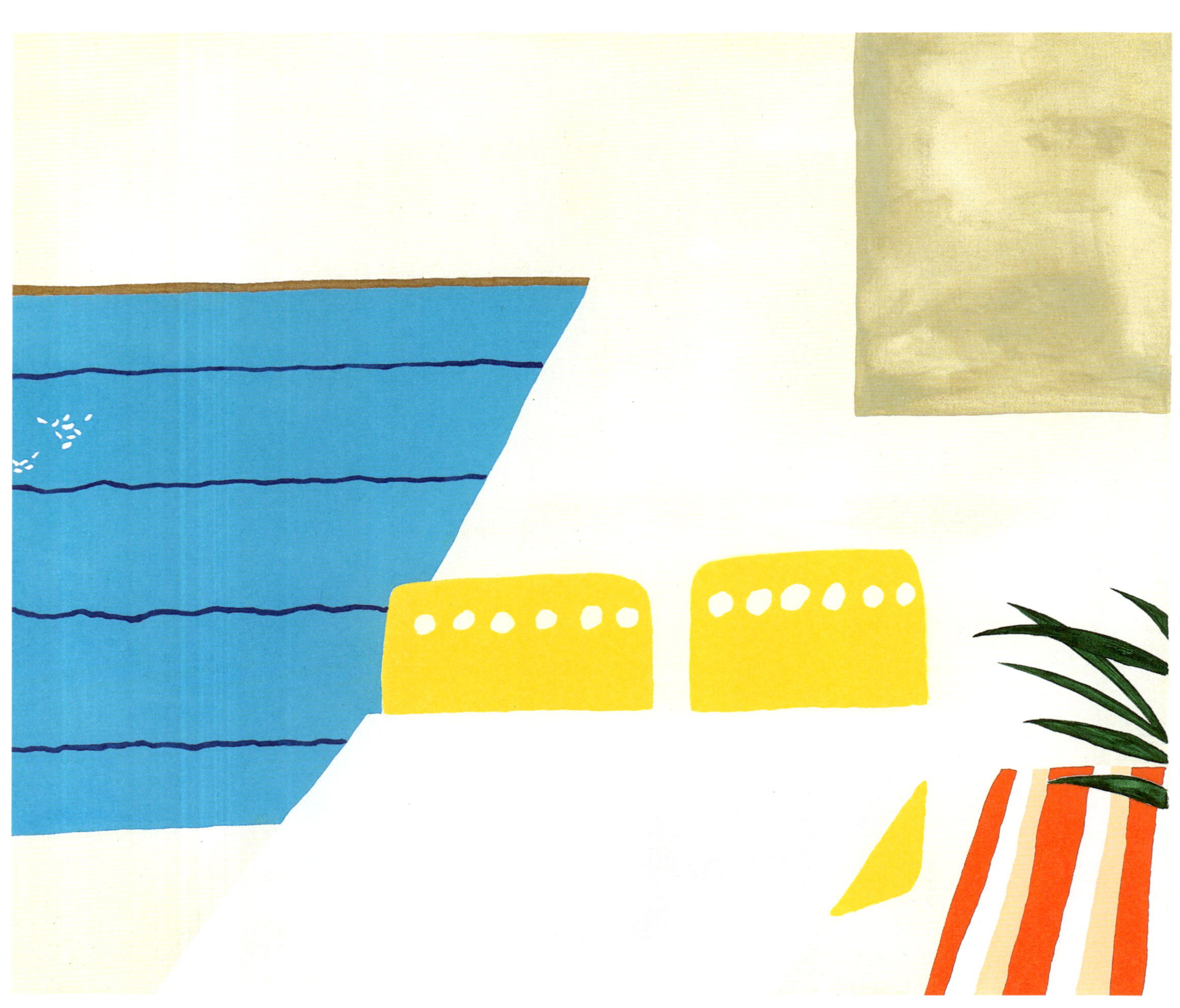

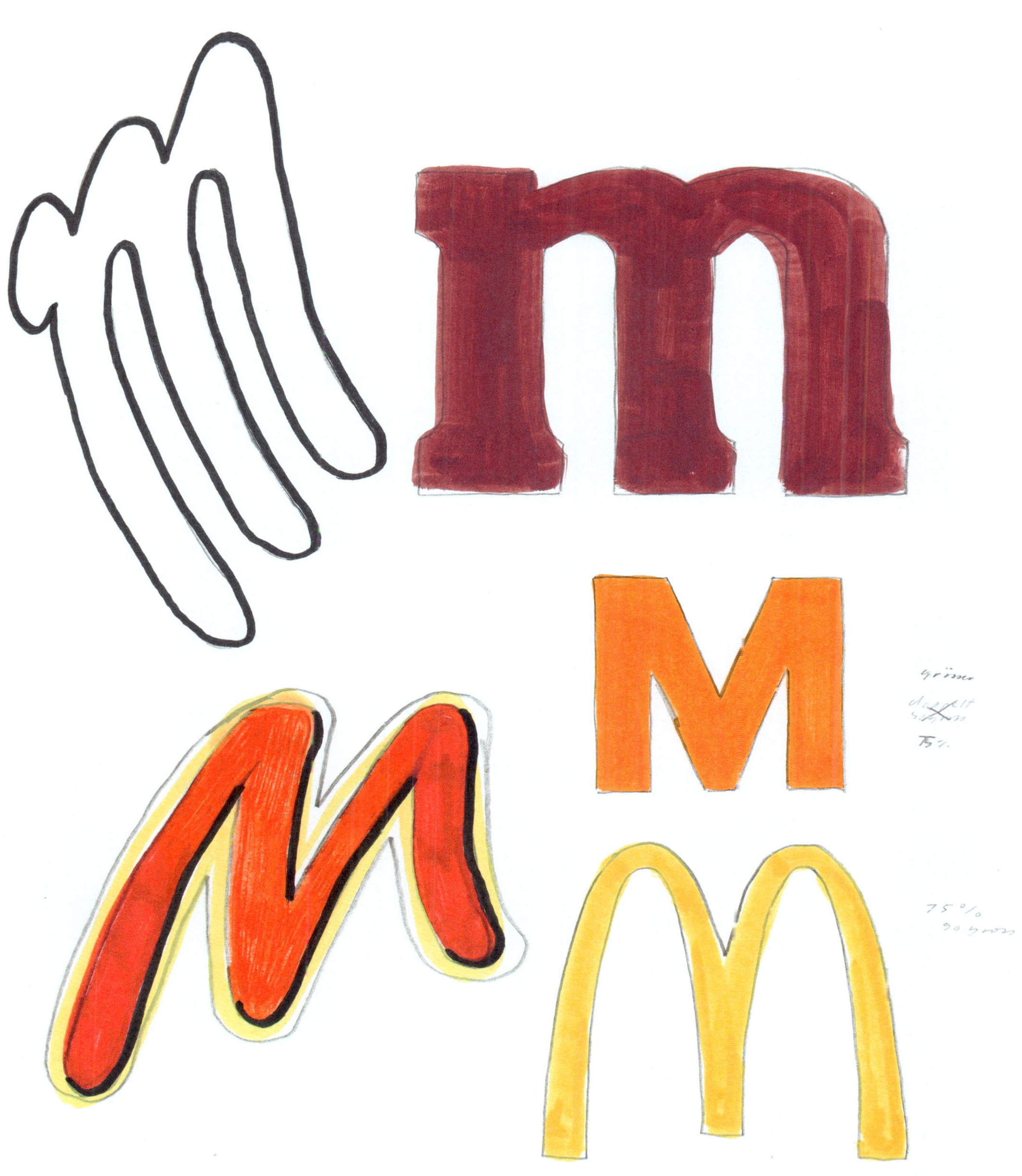

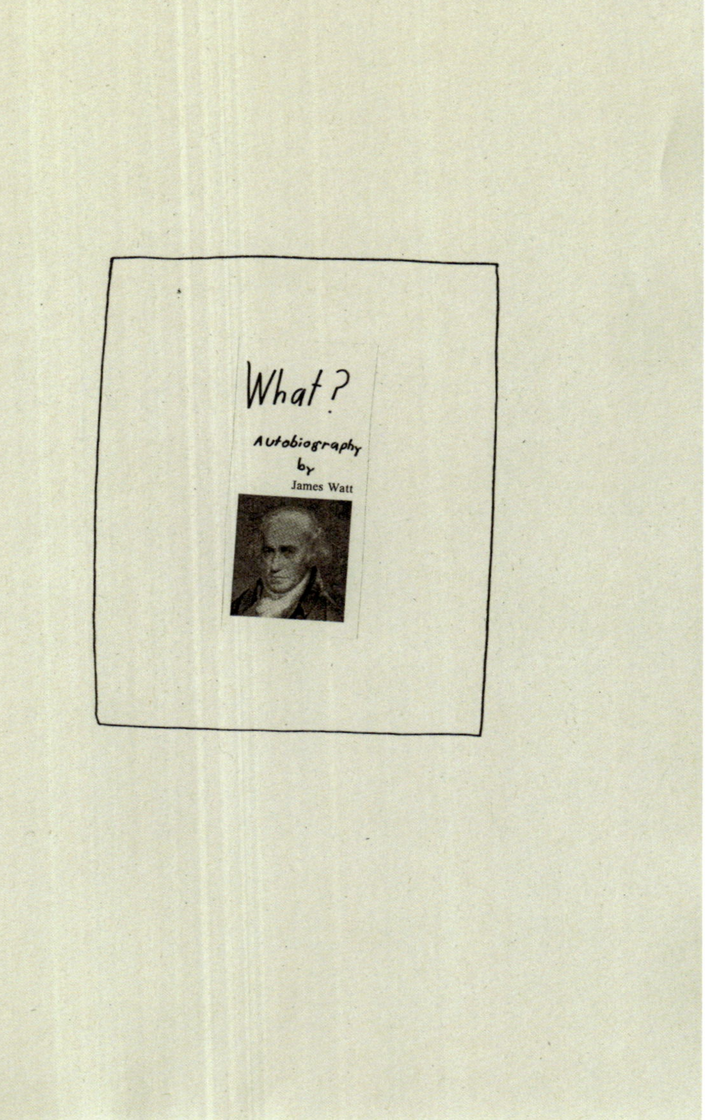

What?
Autobiography
by
James Watt

Abcdef g

HIJKL

MnN

OPQ

RSTUV

xyz

The Enthusiast

Look!
Look at that boy over there.
What a surprise!
Great!/Fantastic!/Fabulous!
How nice/wonderful!
That's lovely/great/etc.
Isn't that lovely/great/etc.

Poems

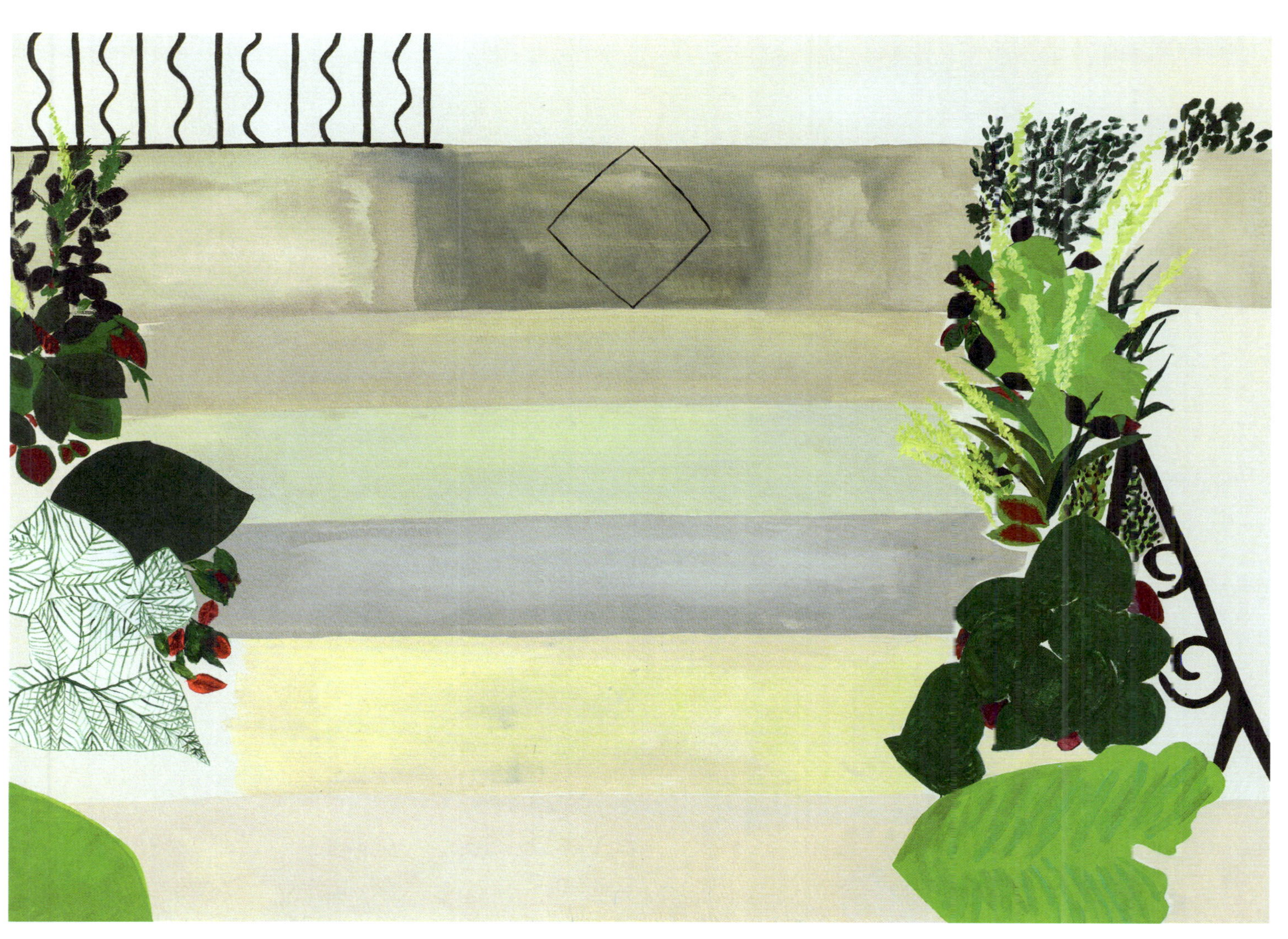

Das will
ich wissen

Ihre Suchanfrage

Meinten Sie: buchsbaum

Ergebnisse für: fuchsbaum

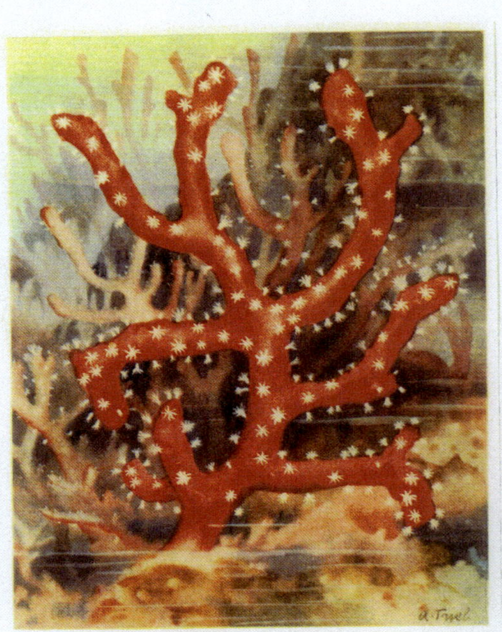

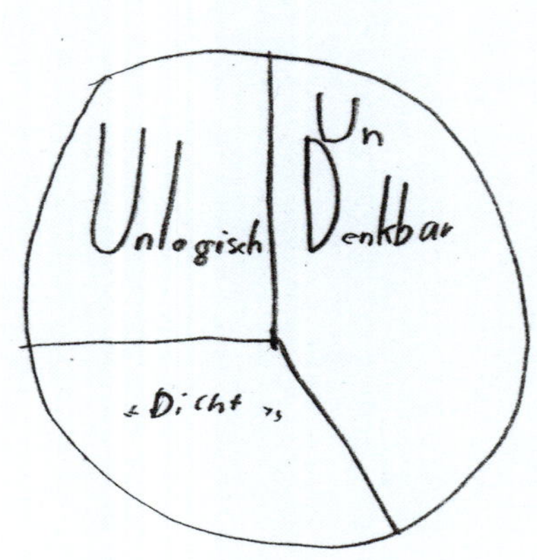

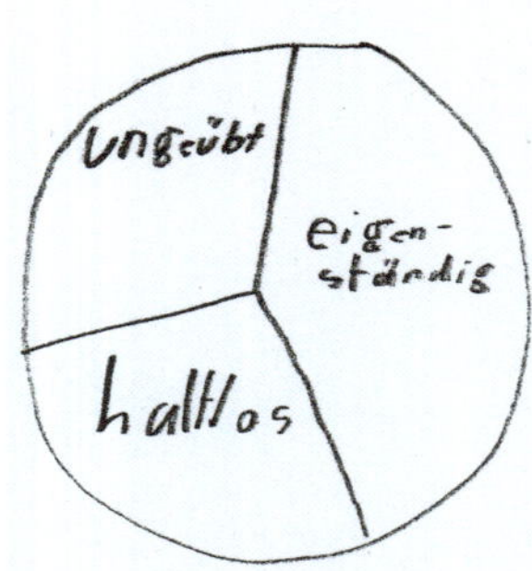

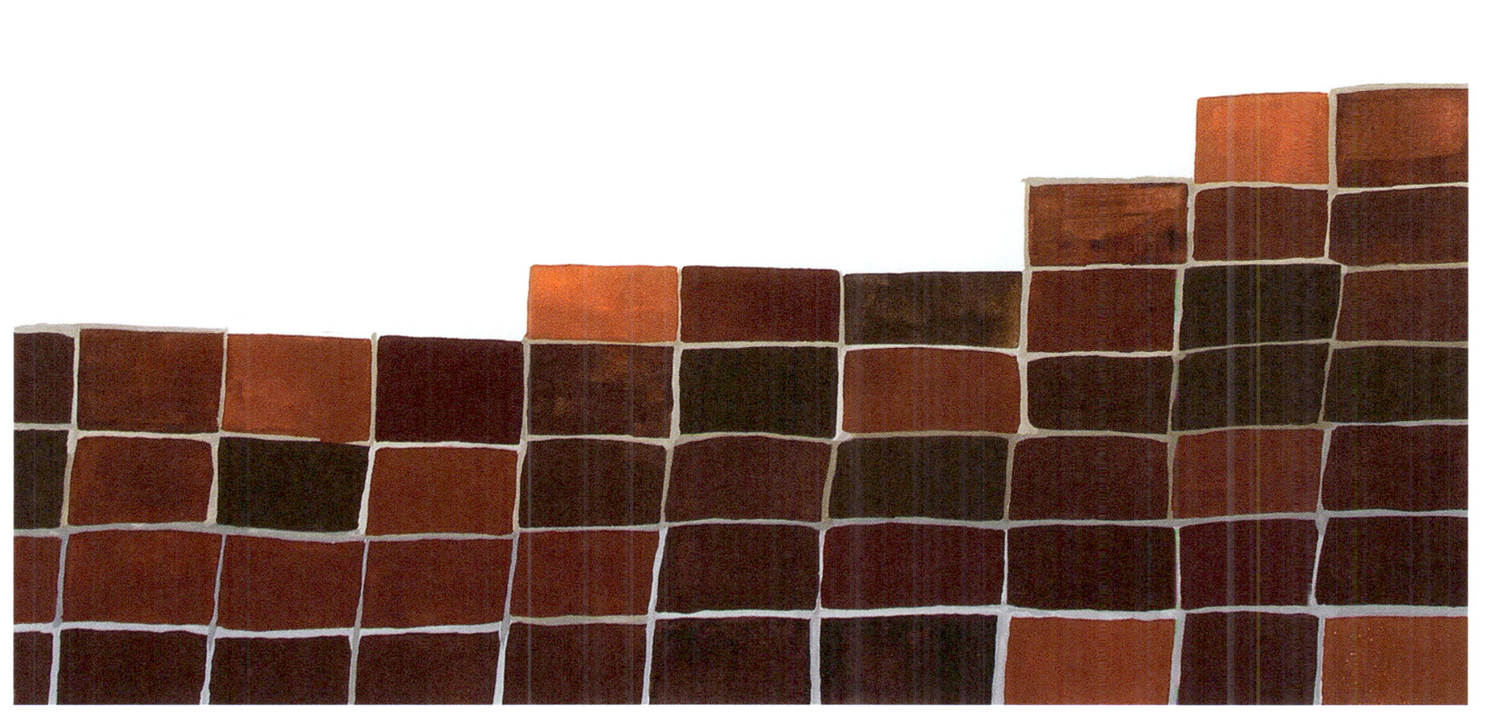

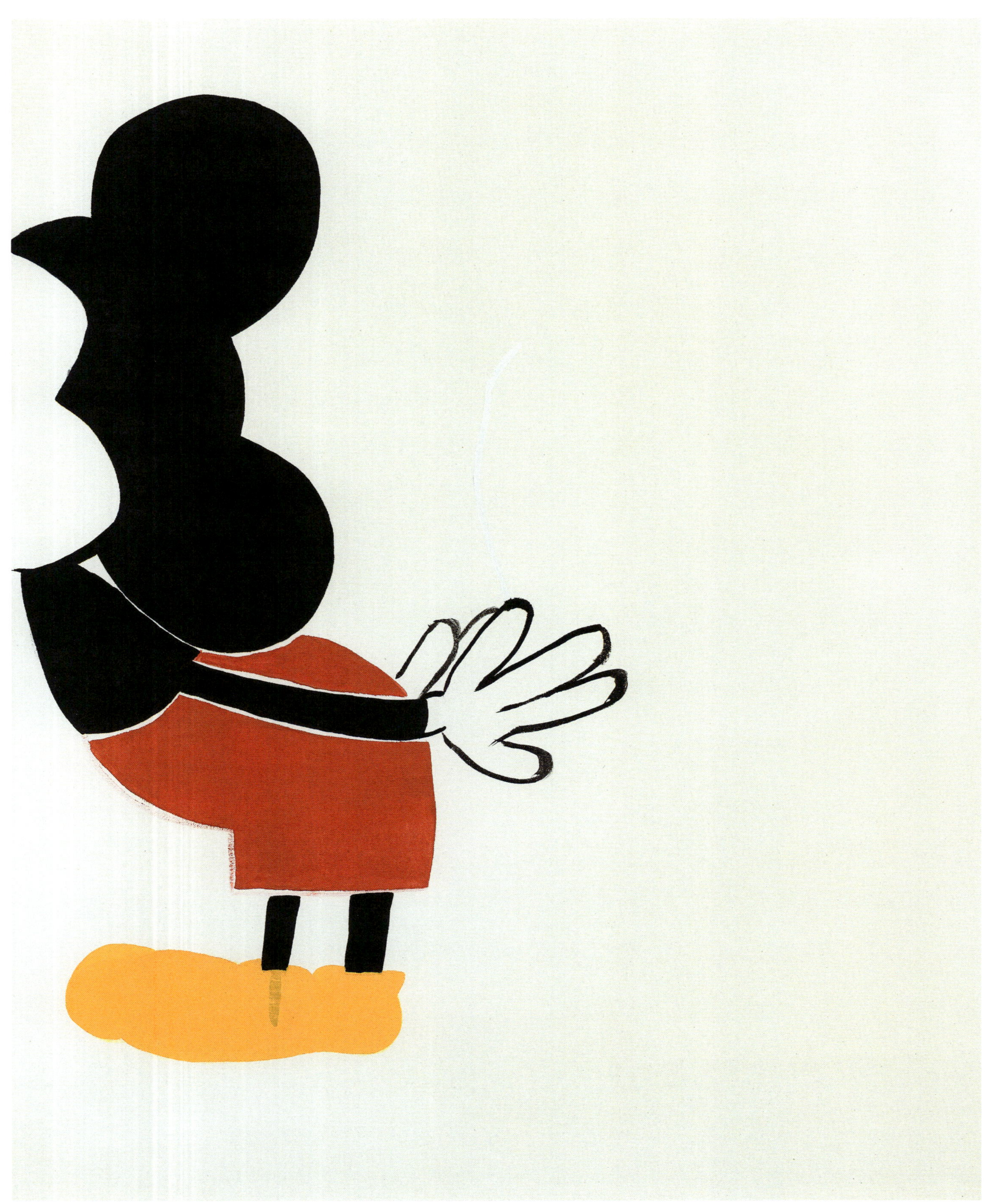

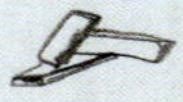

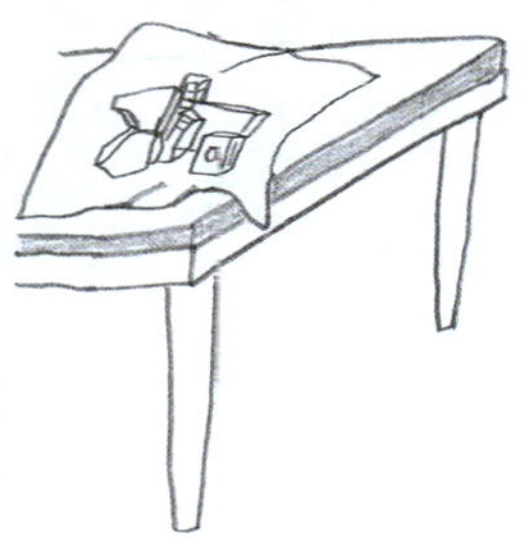

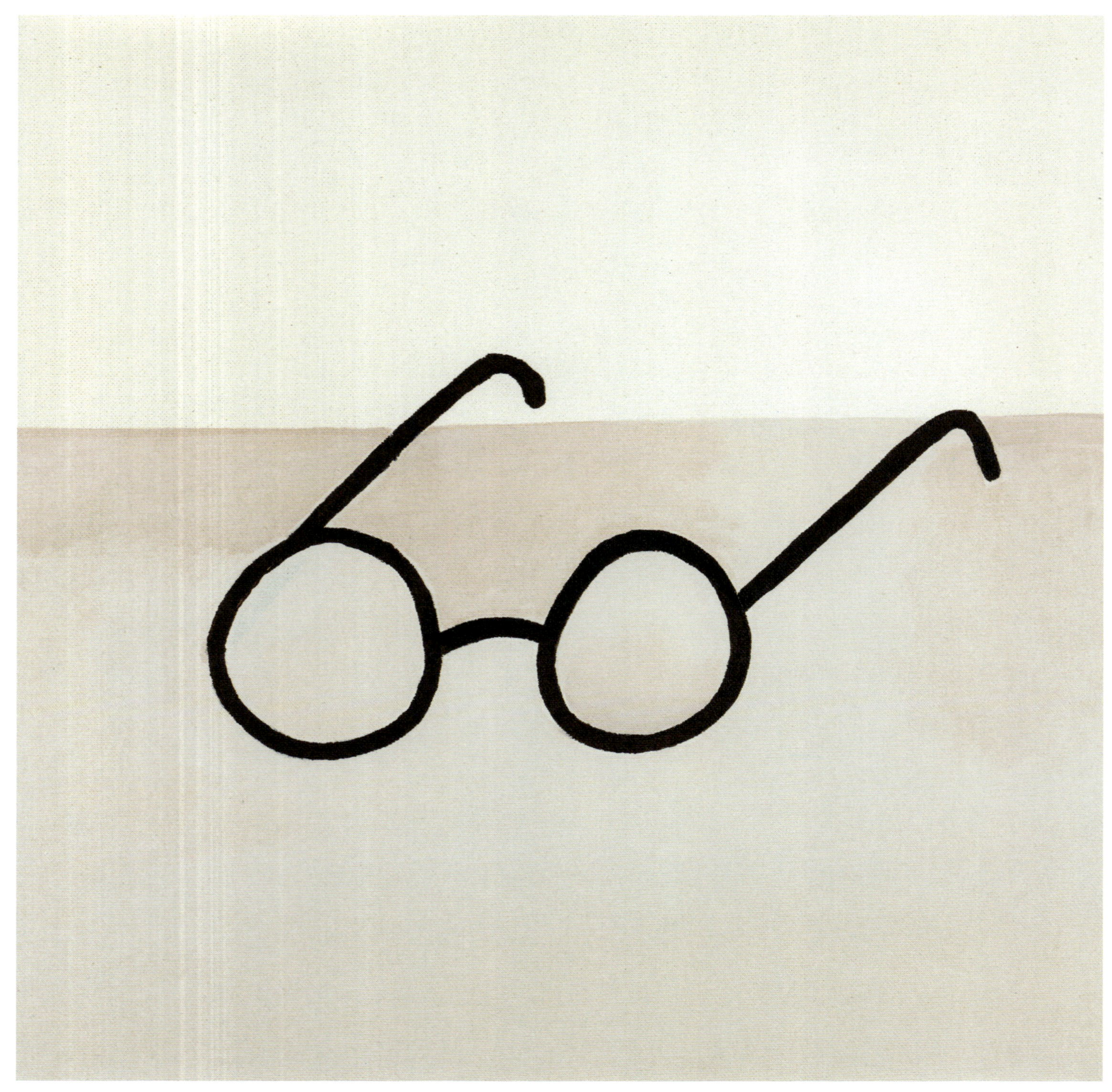

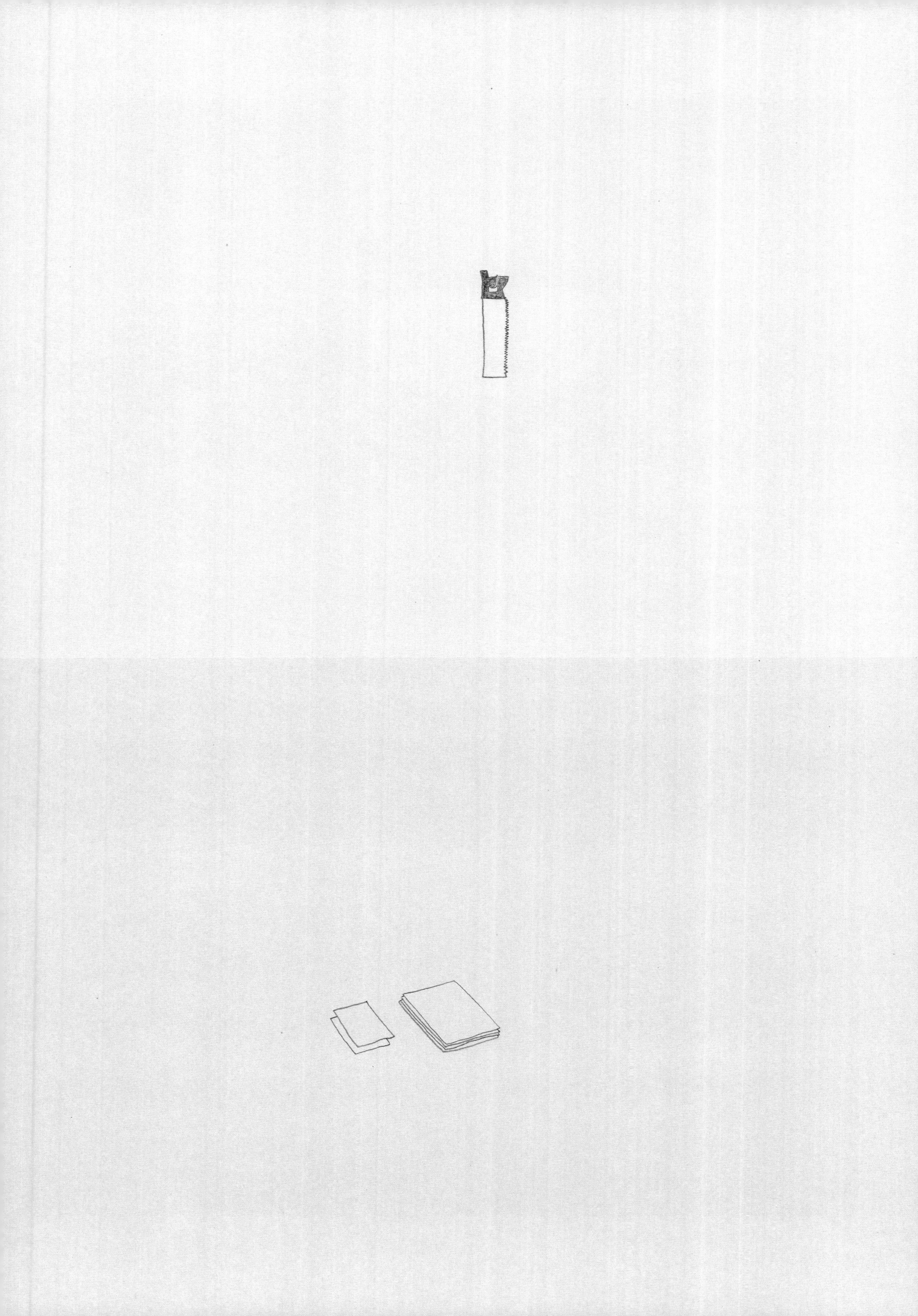

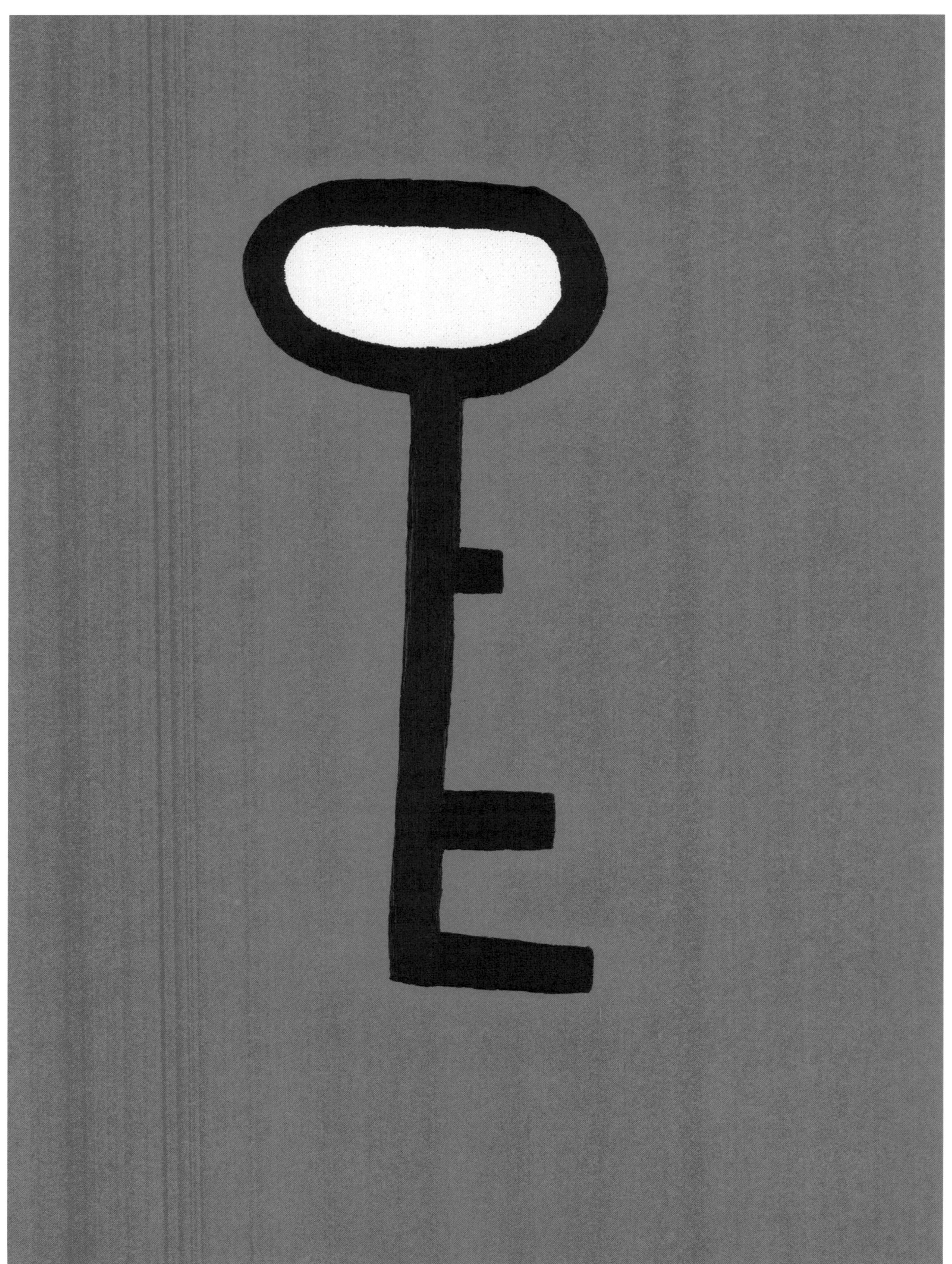

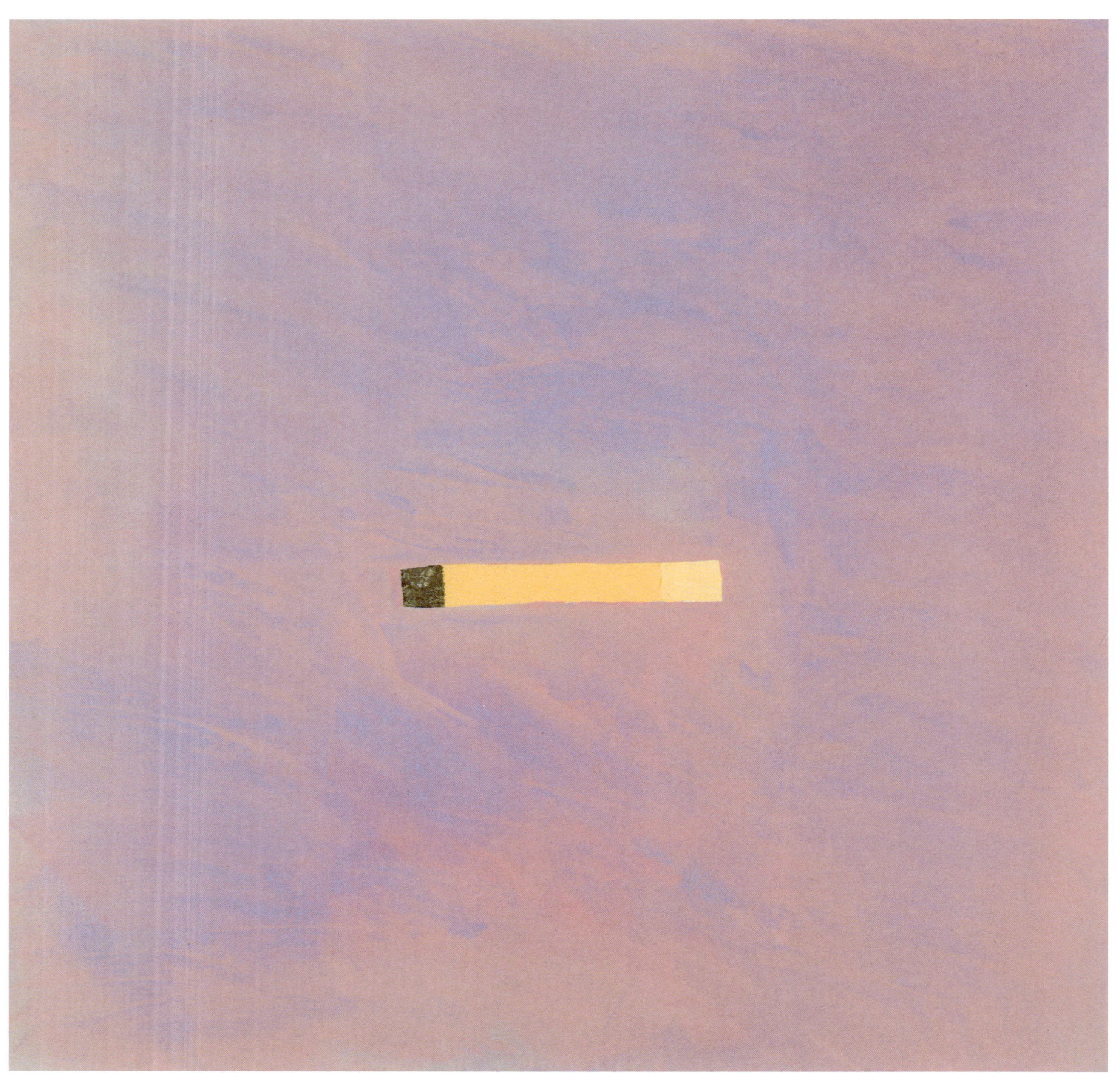

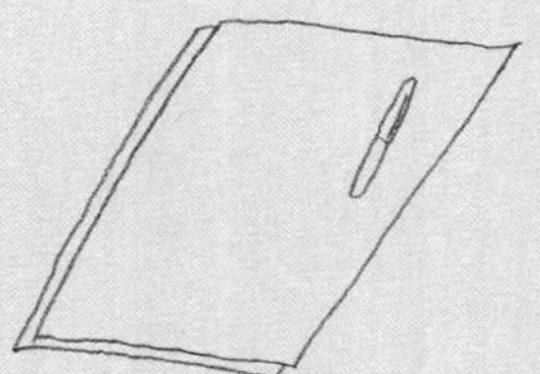

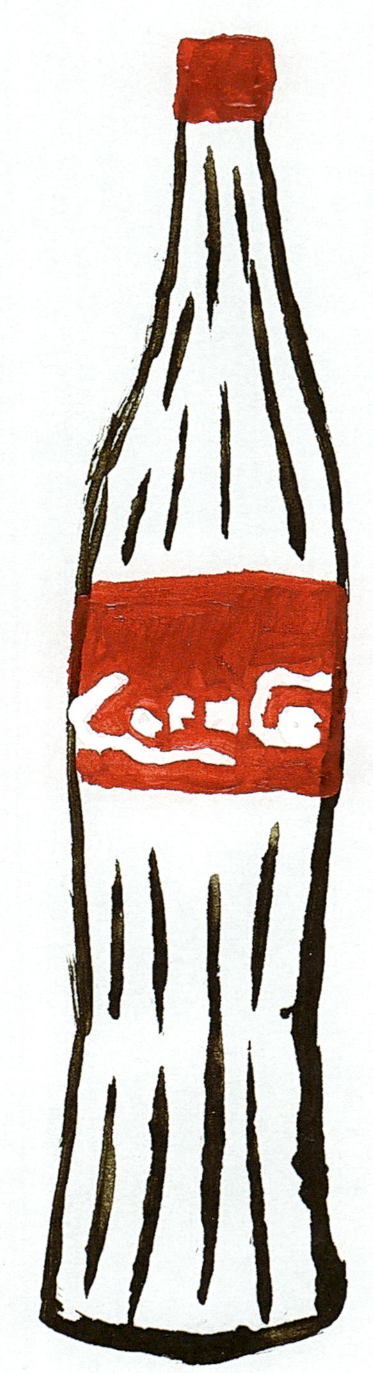

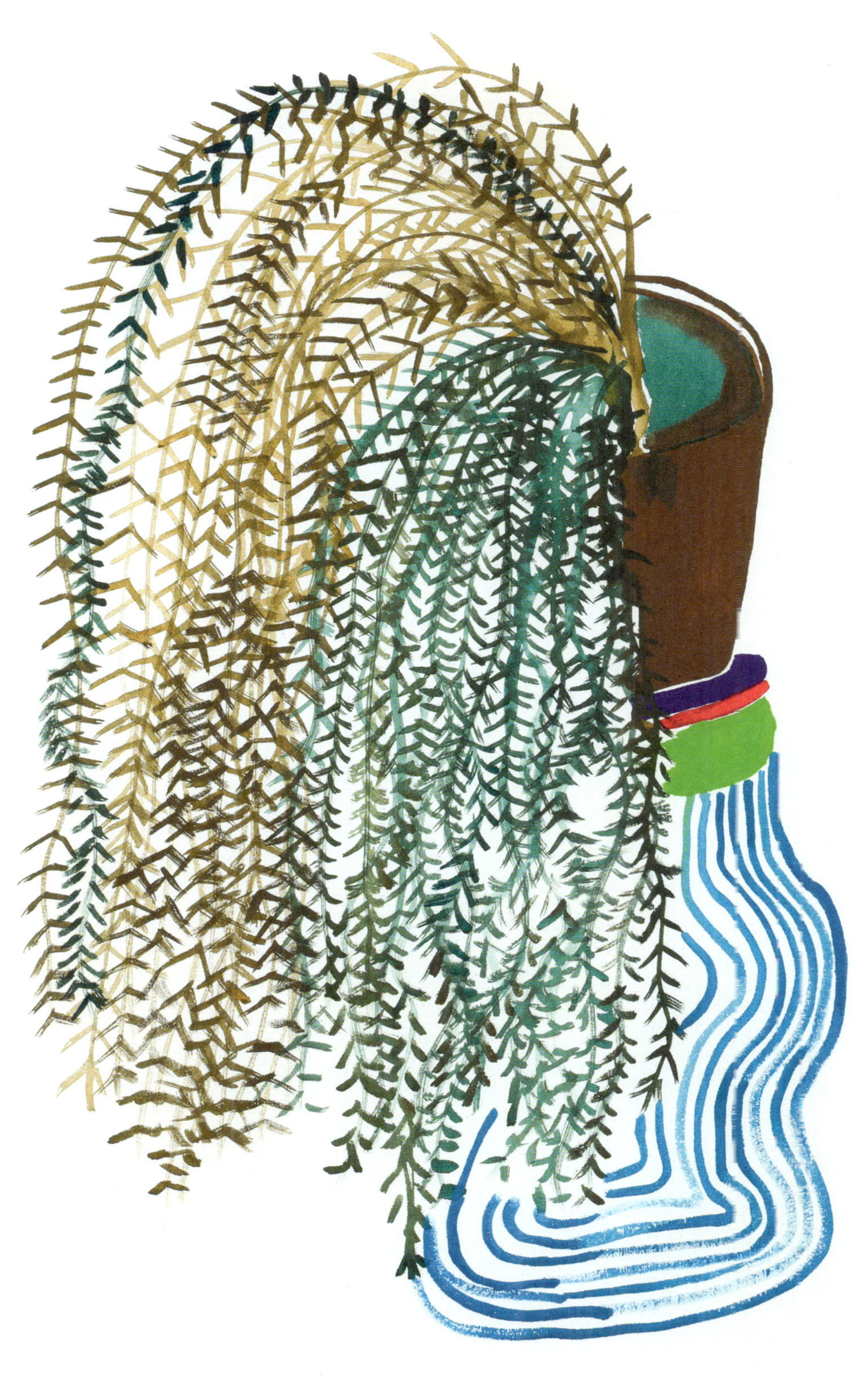

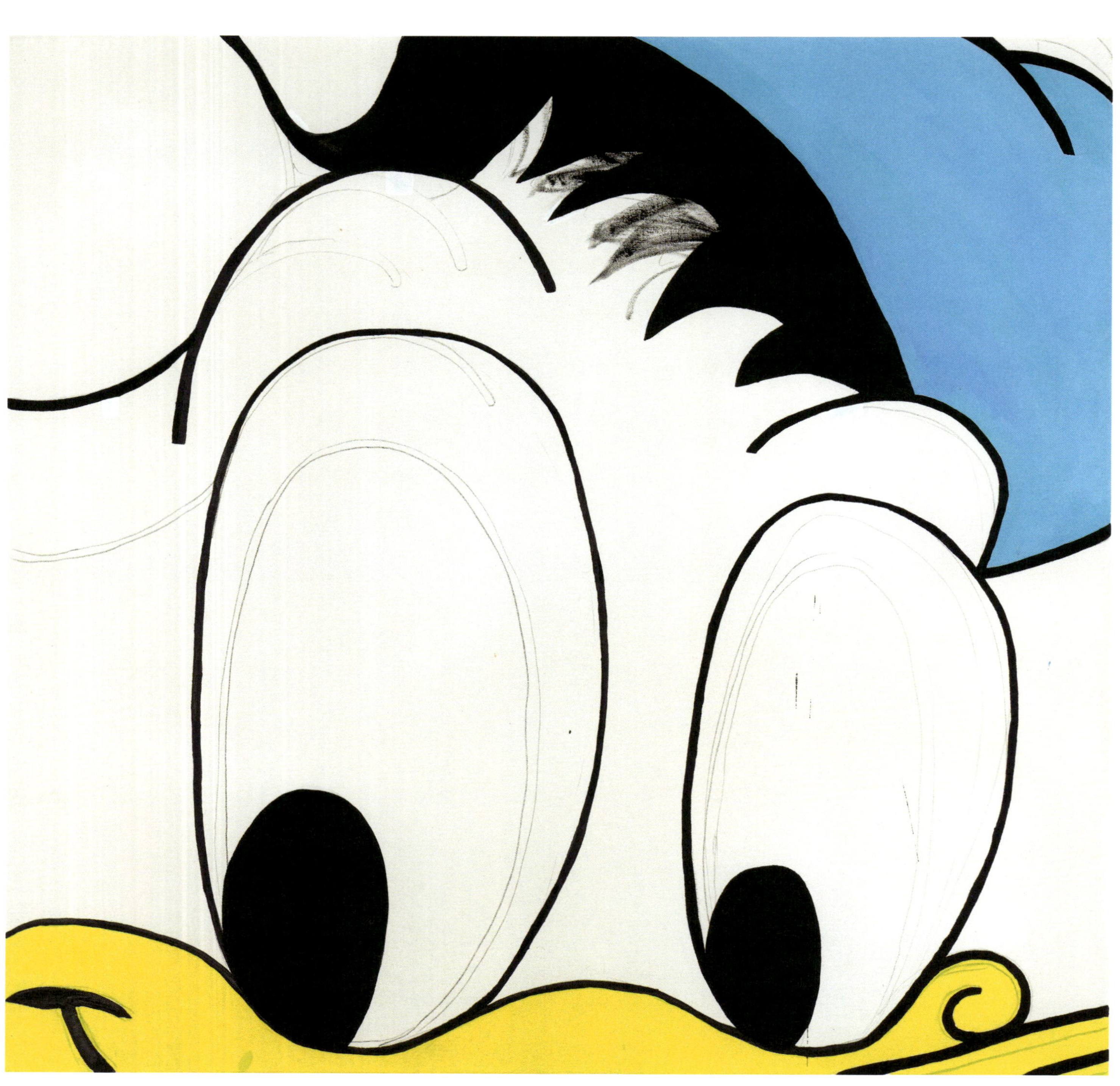

No one
builds a
legacy by
standing
still

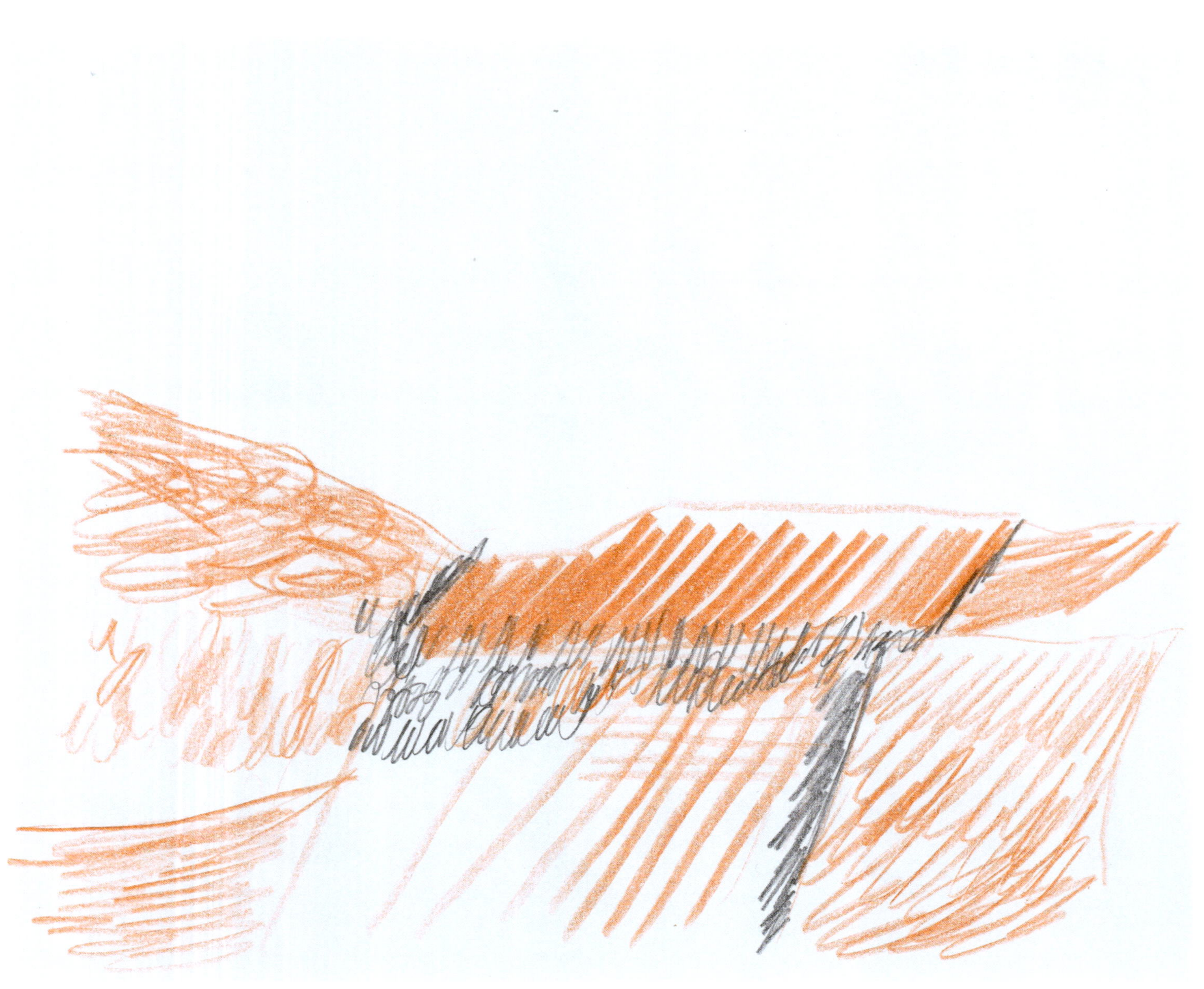

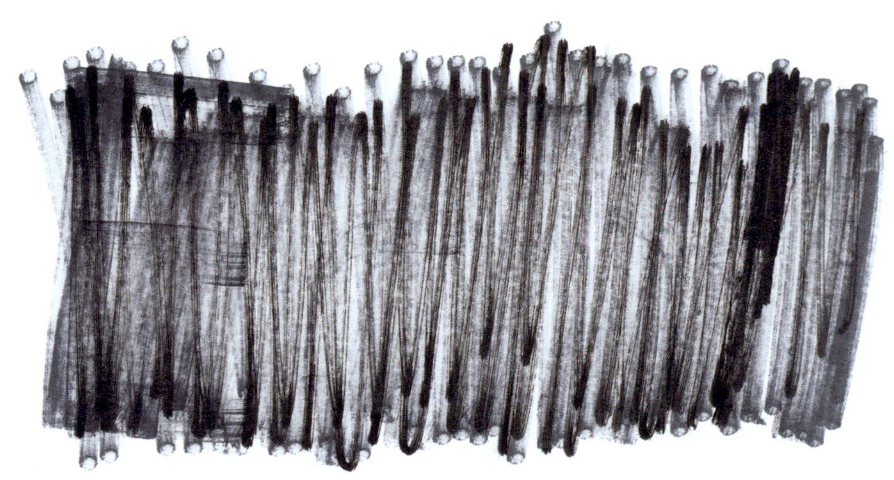

Qualität ist unsere Stärke

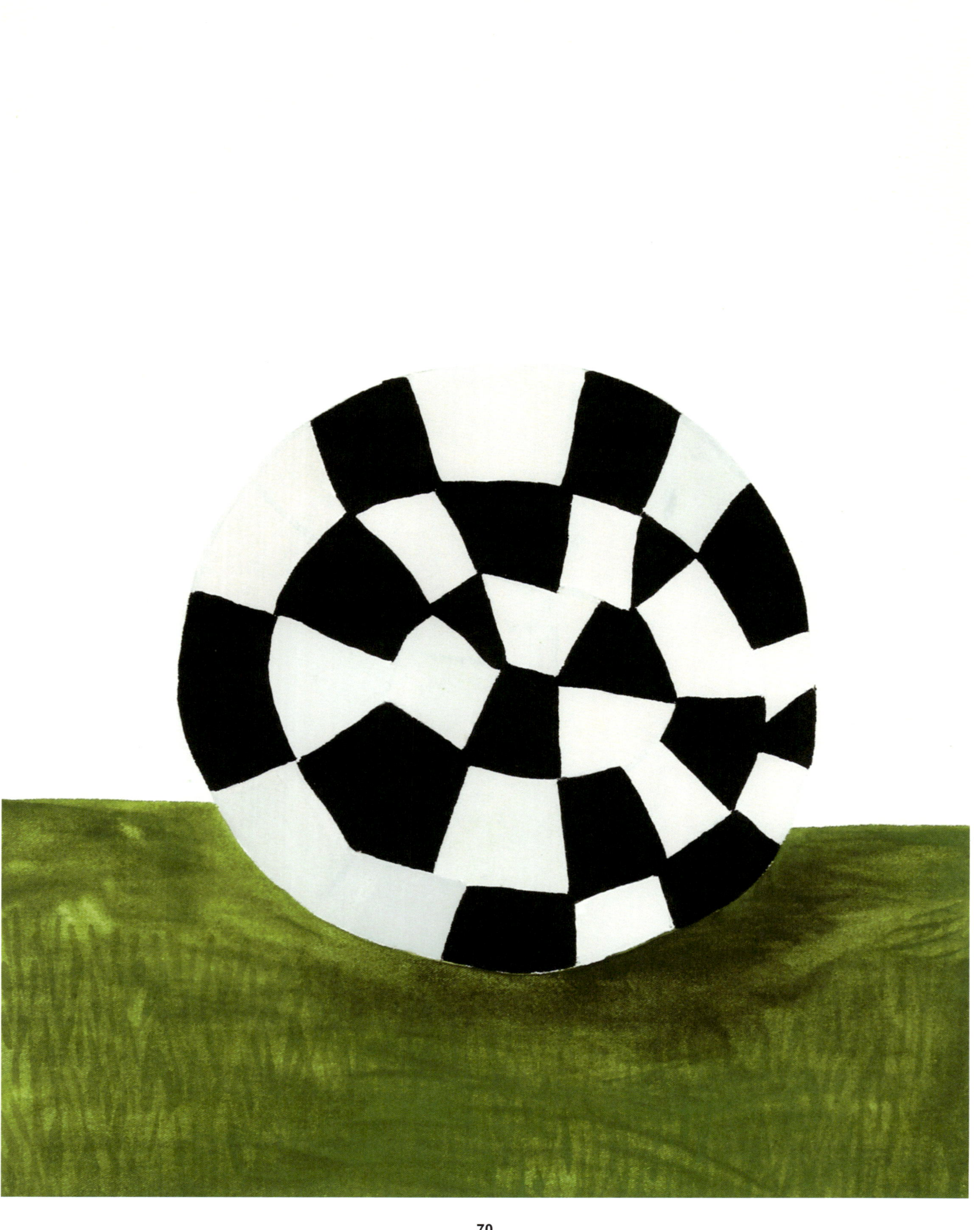

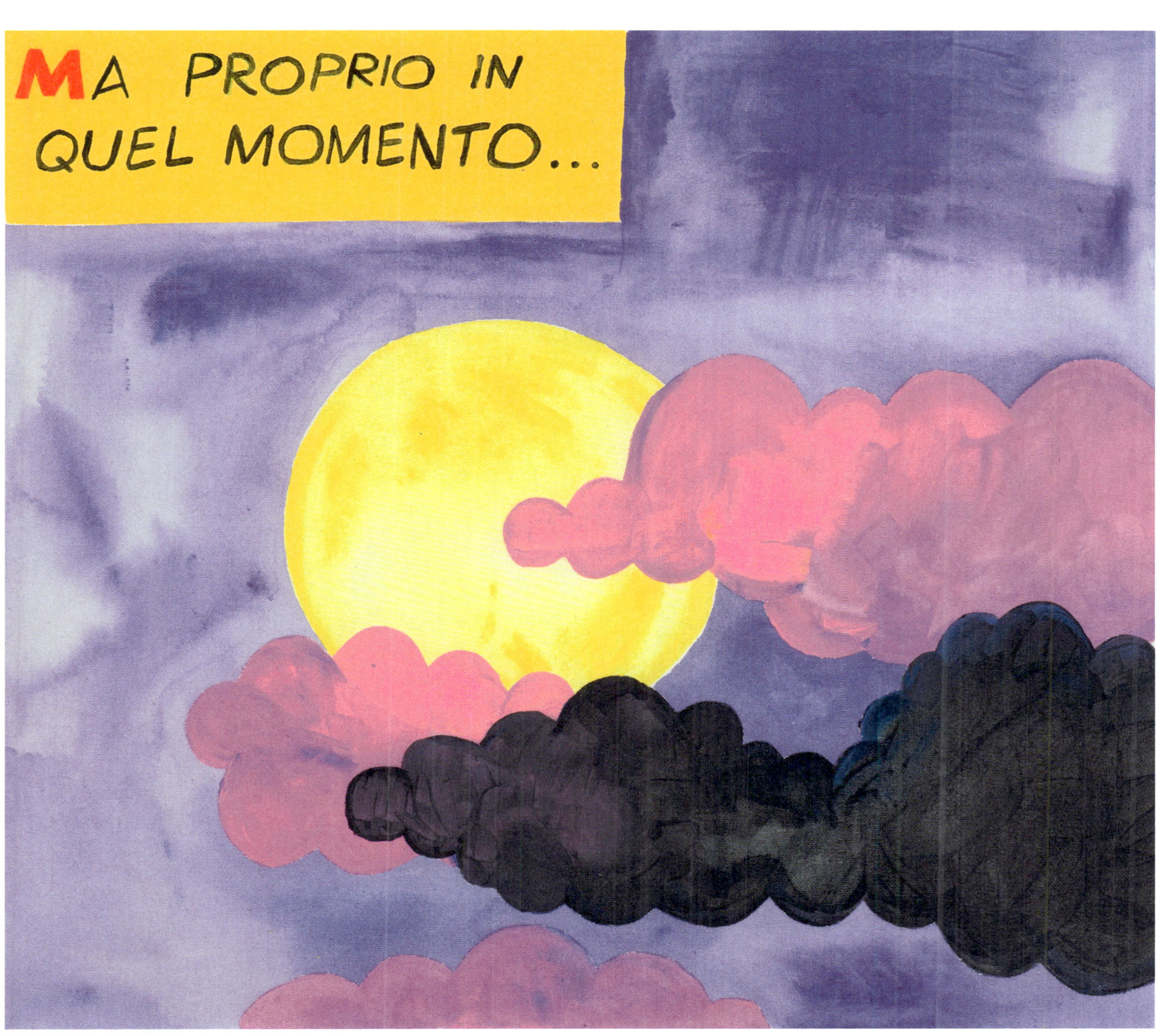

MA PROPRIO IN
QUEL MOMENTO...

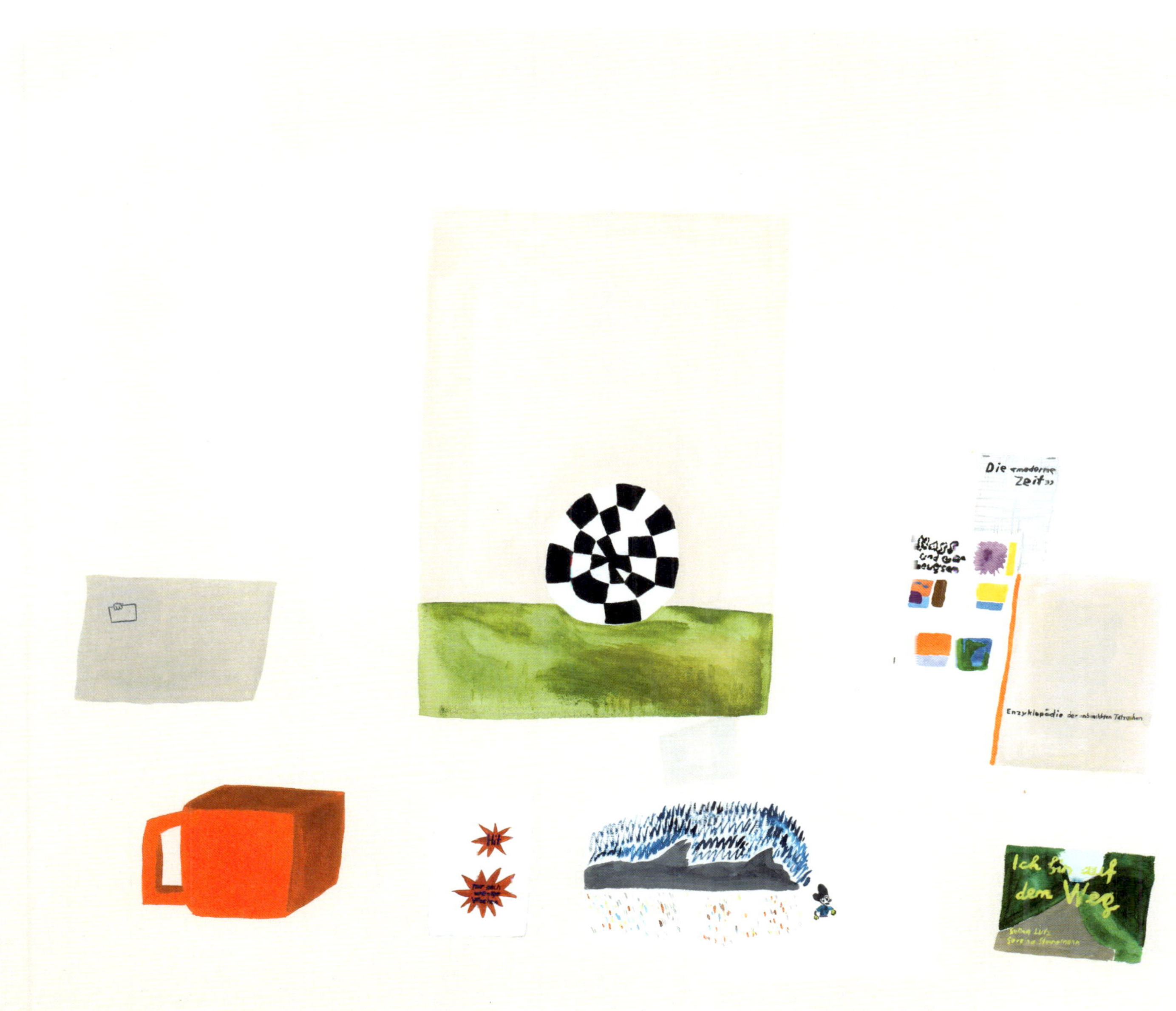

Die »moderne Zeit«
Enzyklopädie der unbeachteten Tatsachen
Ich bin auf dem Weg

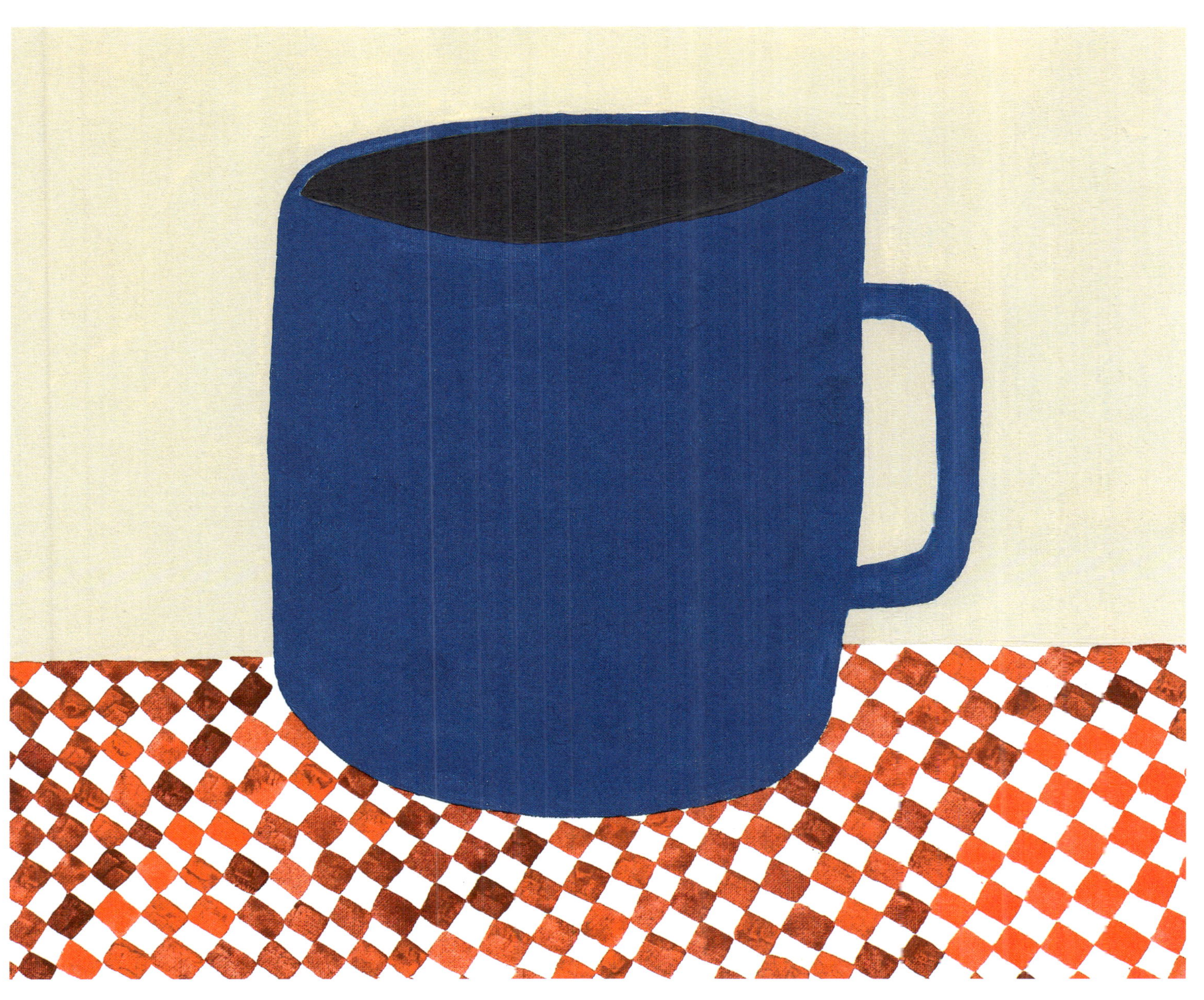

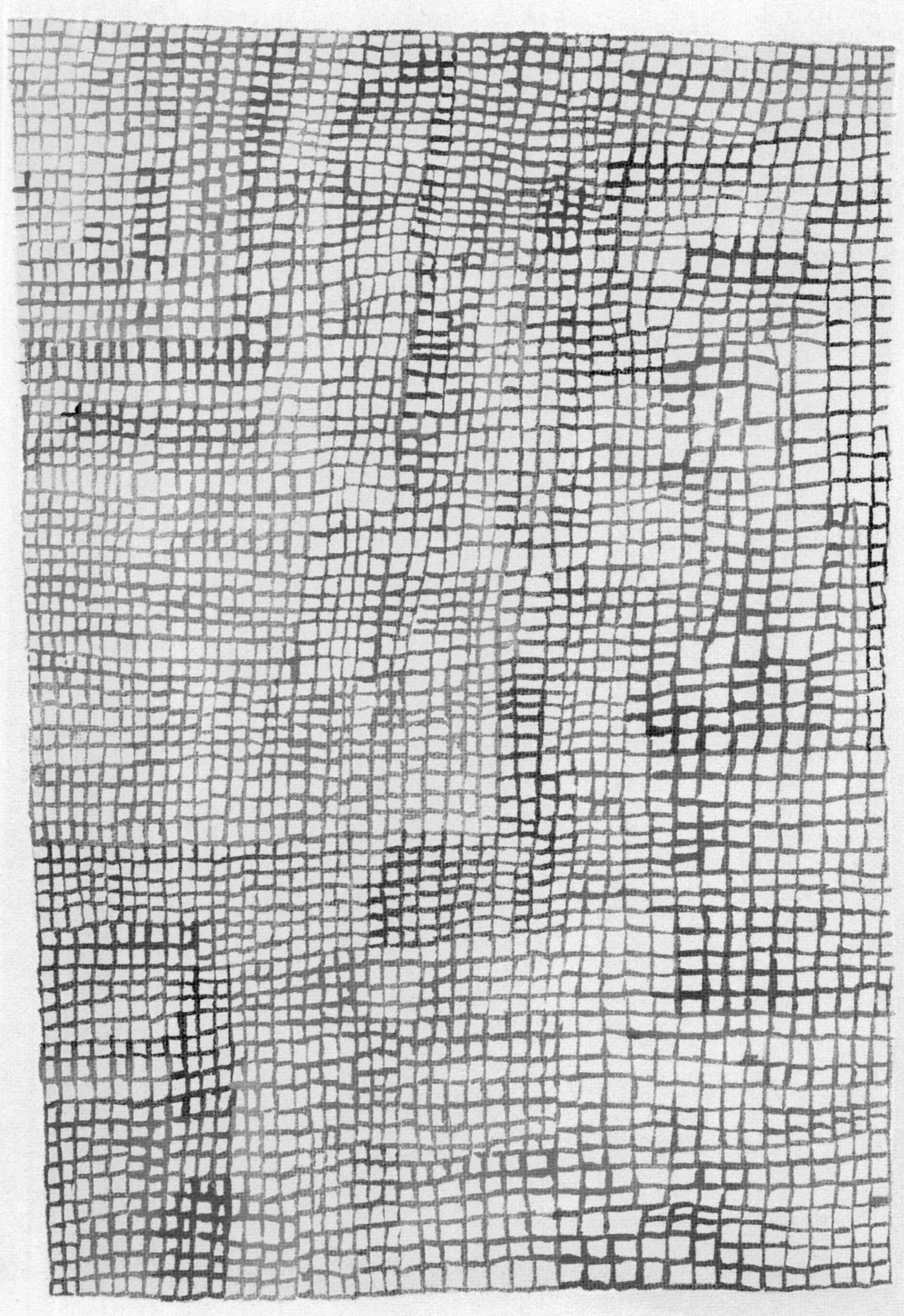

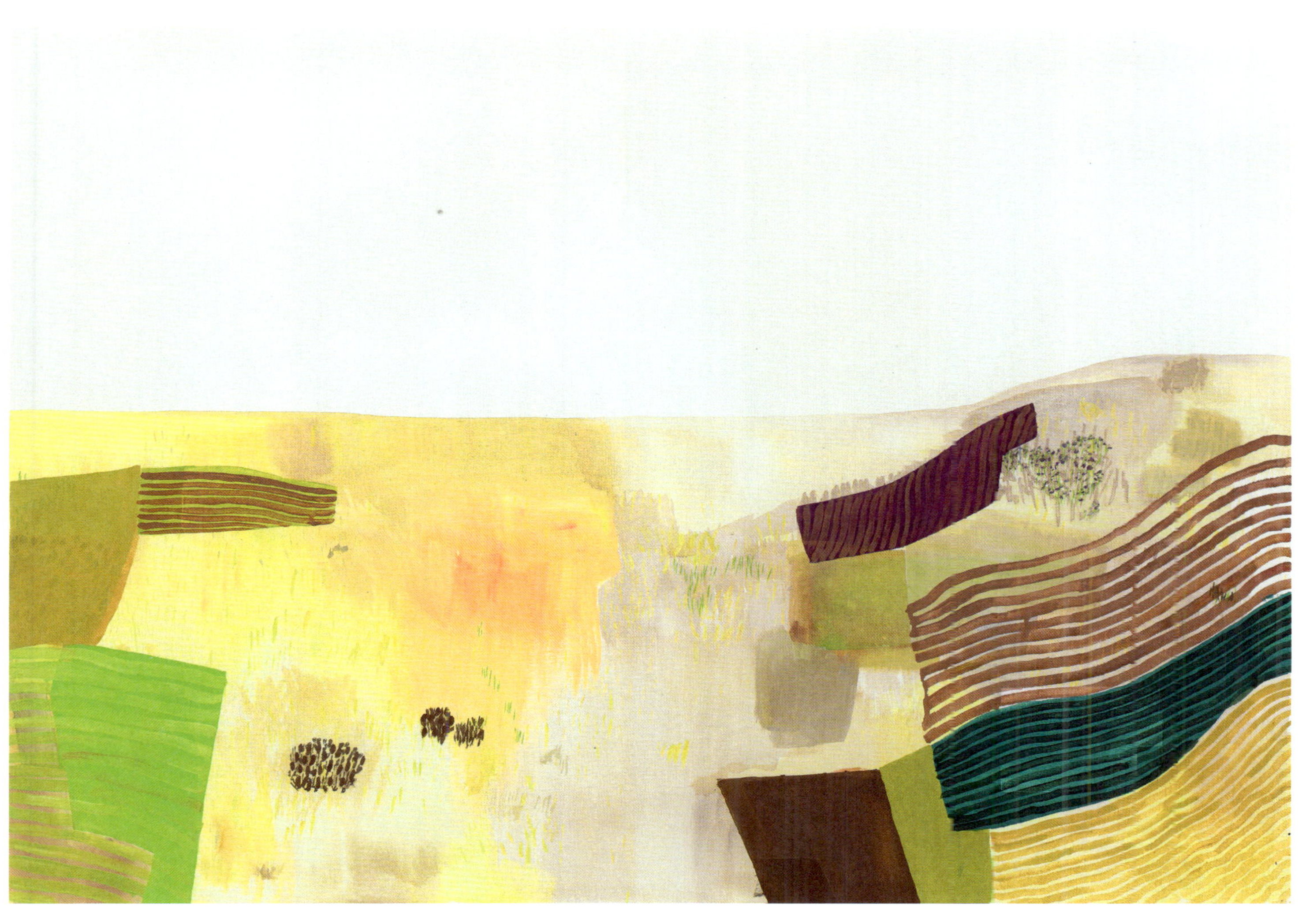

Aneinander hängen und ziehen

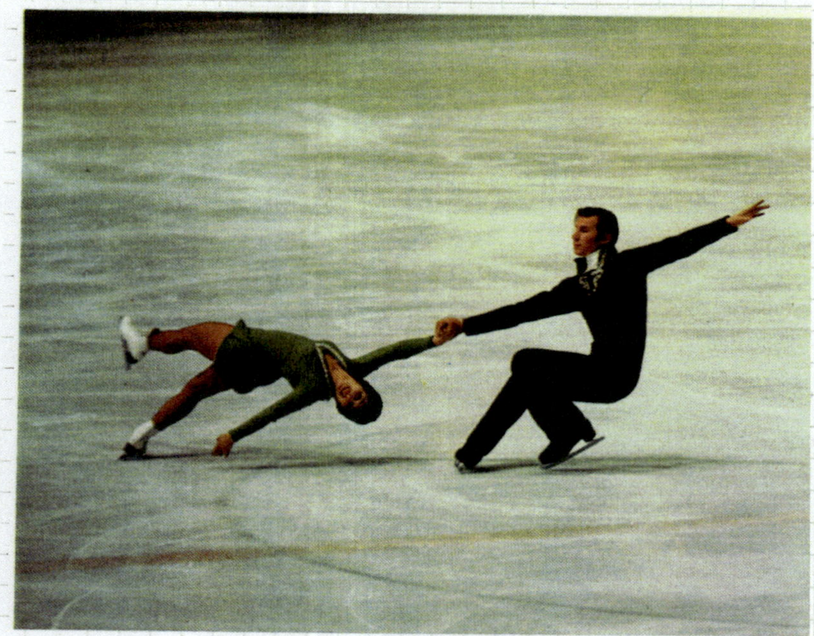

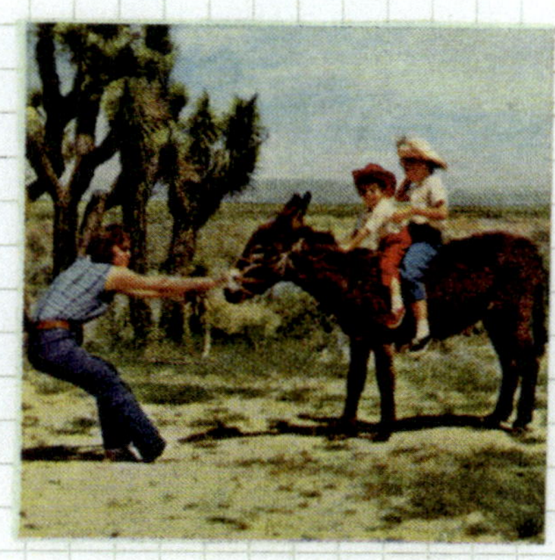

Aneinander hängen und ziehen

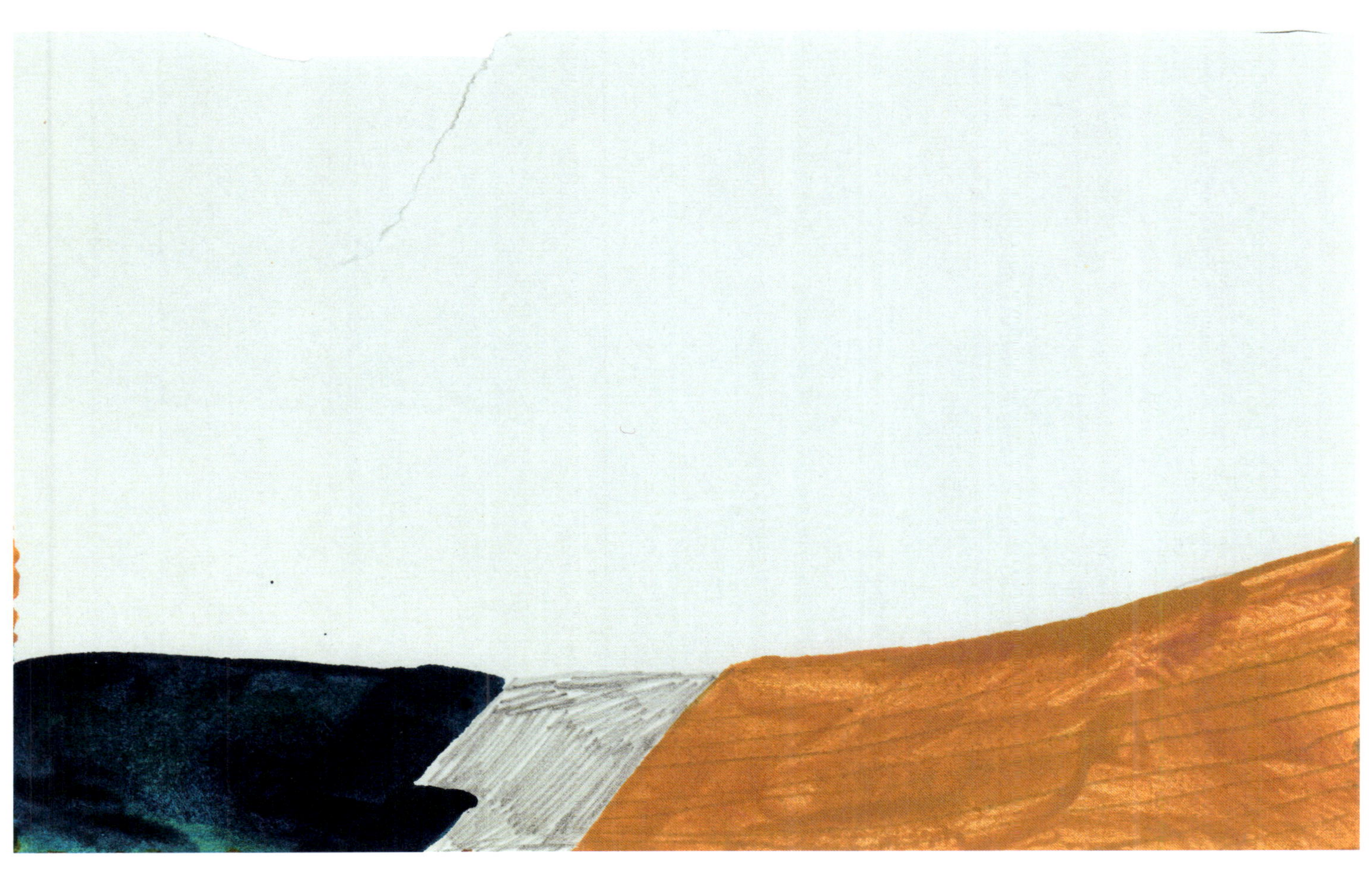

DIE WELT UND IHRE THEMEN

Das neue Heft
CHF 4   10/60
© S.-St.

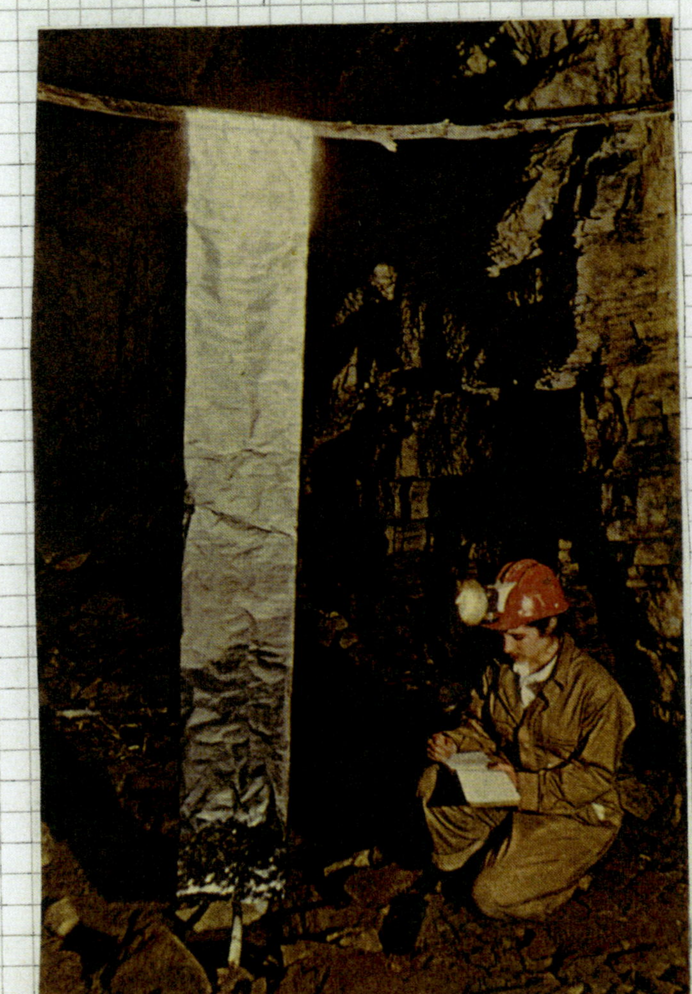

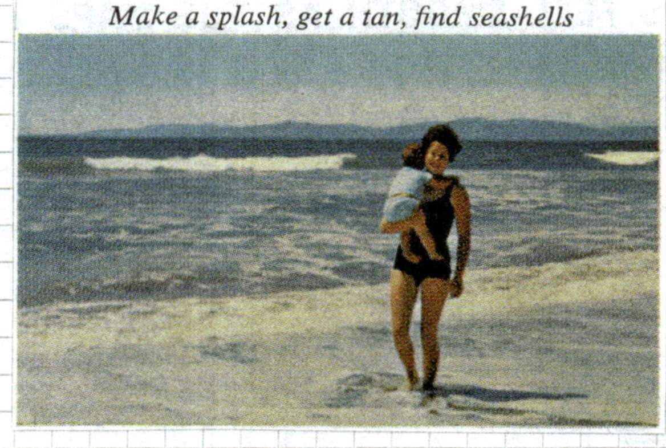

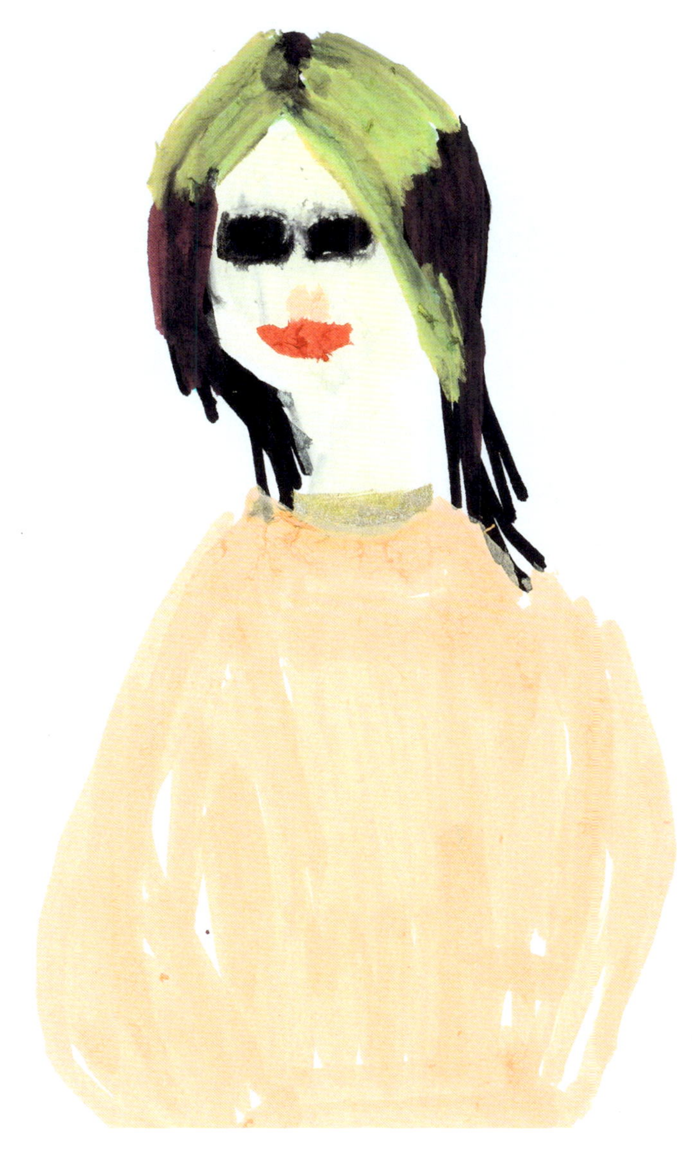

Wie es aussieht, wenn man auf der
Wiese liegt und Enten vorbeifliegen.

(also so ein bisschen an einem Hang)

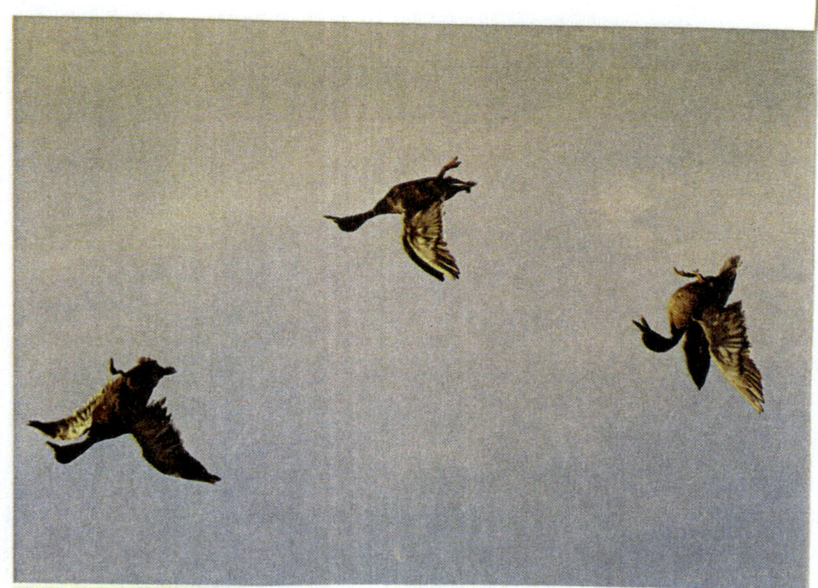

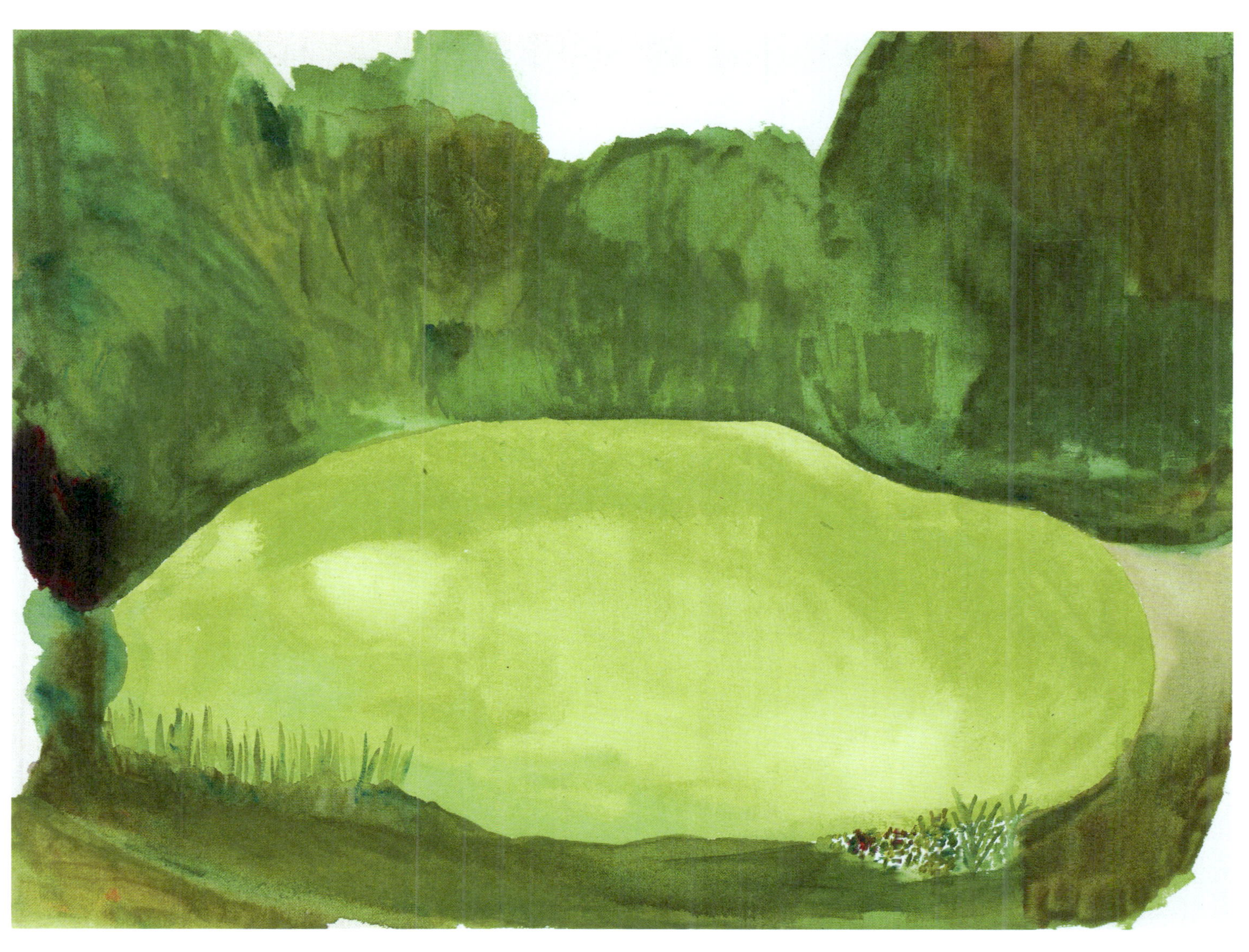

Unerklärliches überall

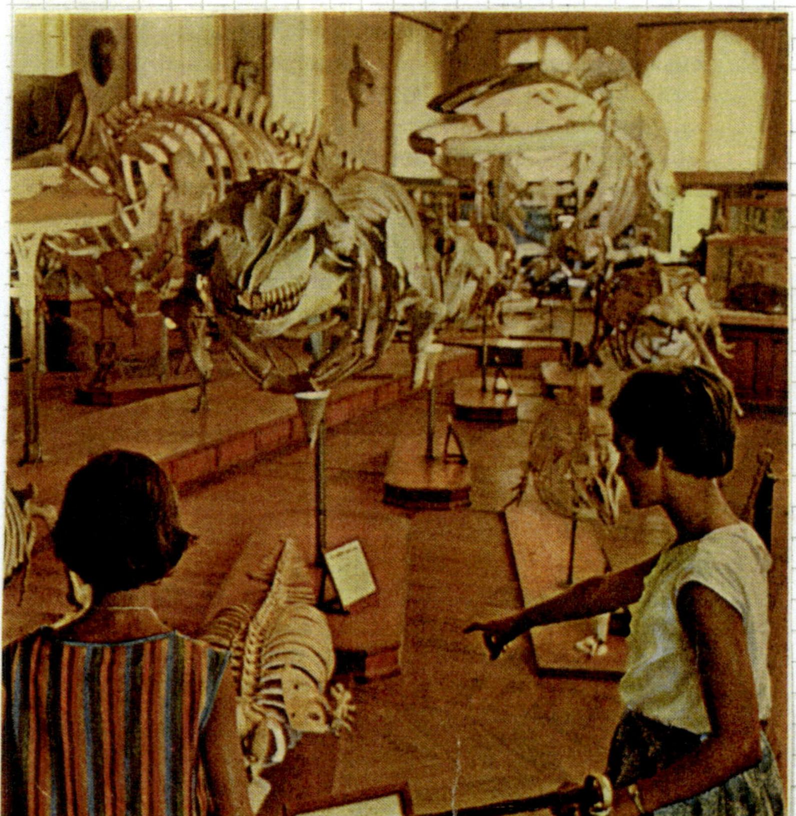

(Auch das können
wir uns nicht
erklären.)

Früher

Früher war alles grösser.

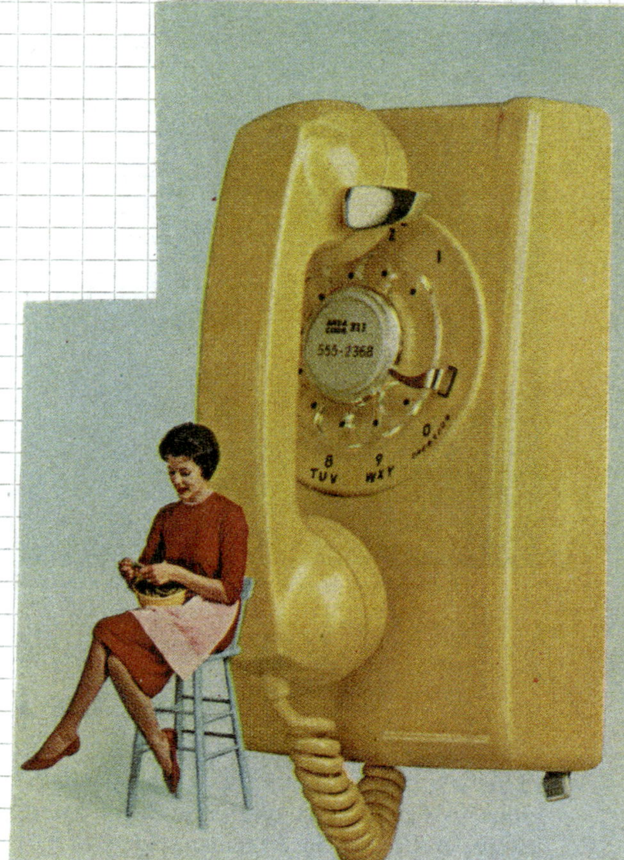

Anzeige

Verschenken Sie Das neue Heft
zu Weihnachten!!! !!

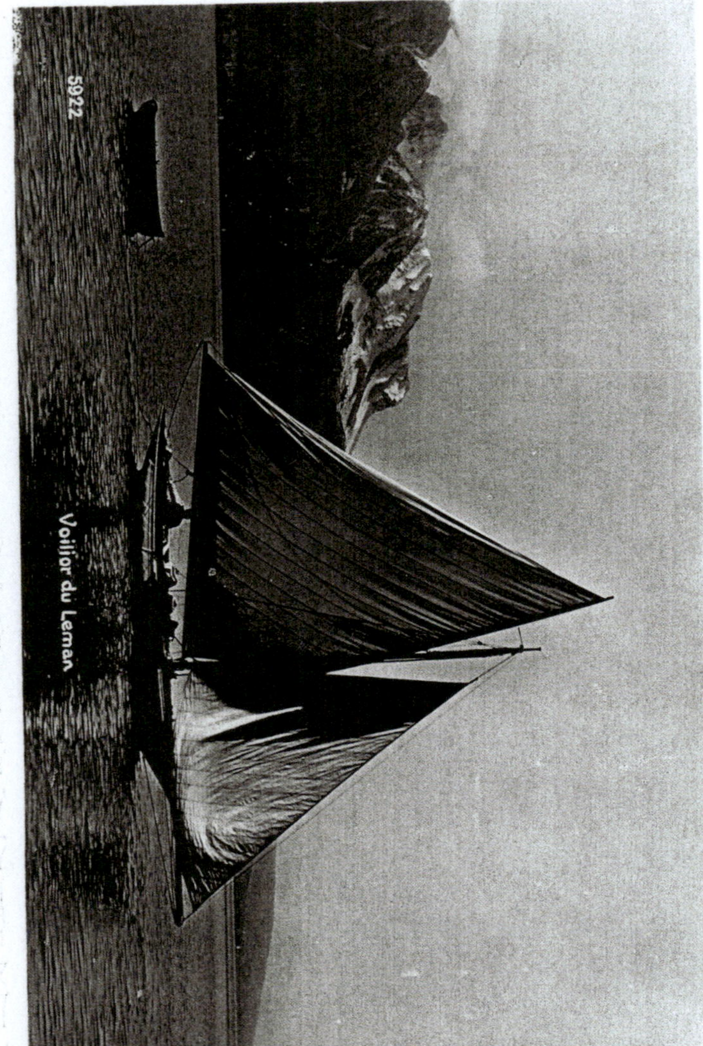

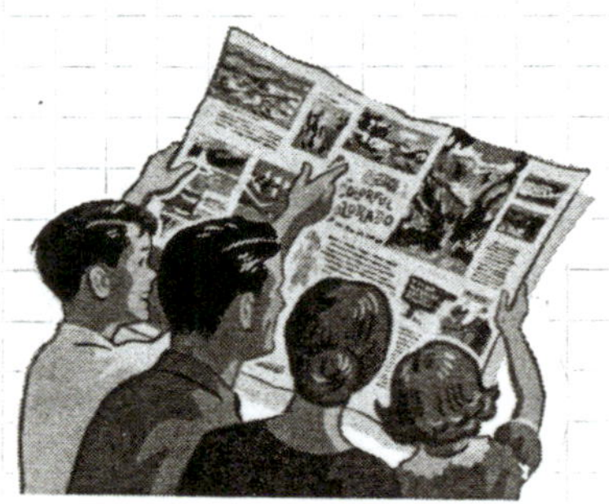

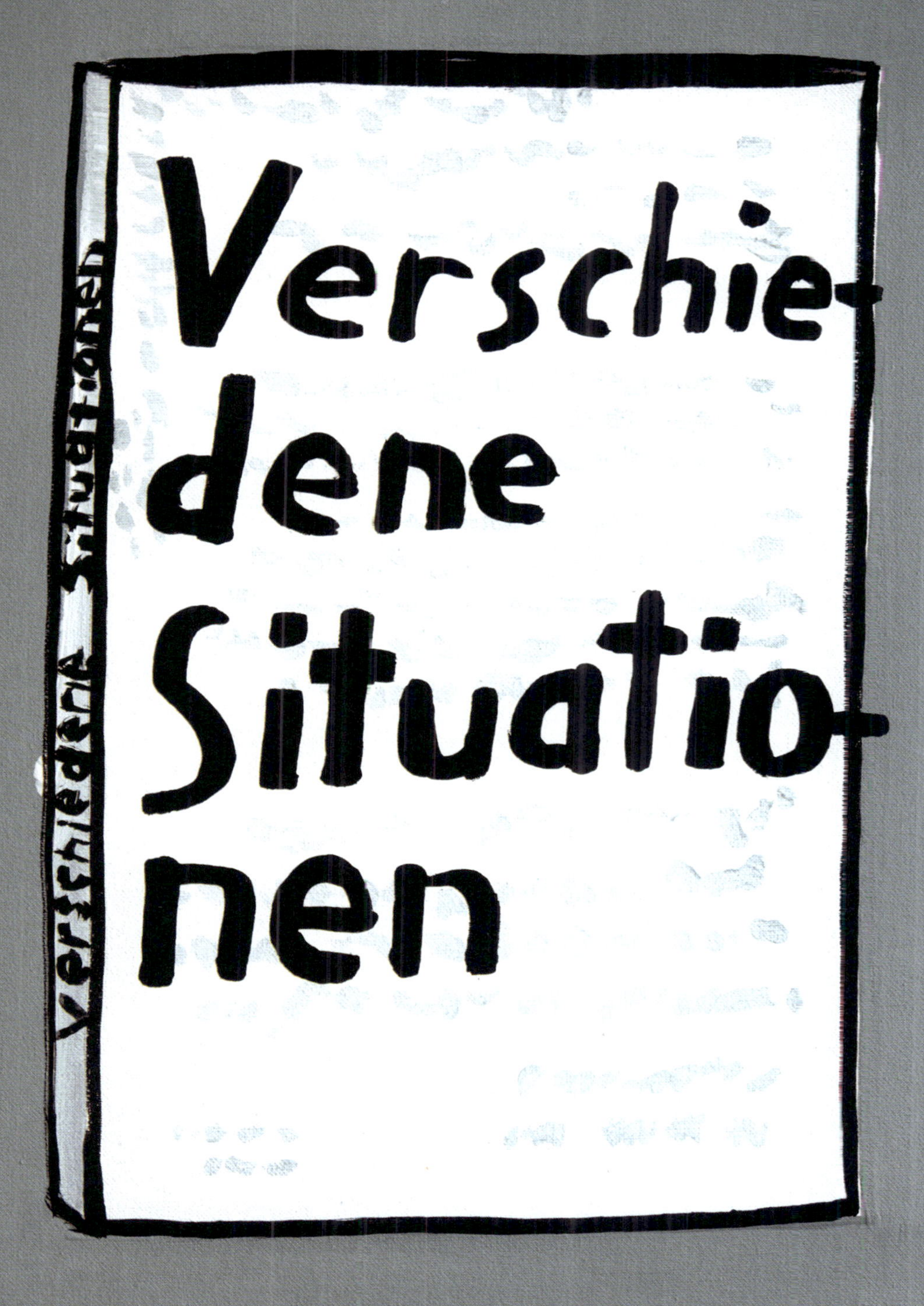

Verschie-
dene
Situatio-
nen
Verschiedene Situationen

Orientierung
in einer immer komplexeren Welt

die Scheibe

1.

2.

3.

129

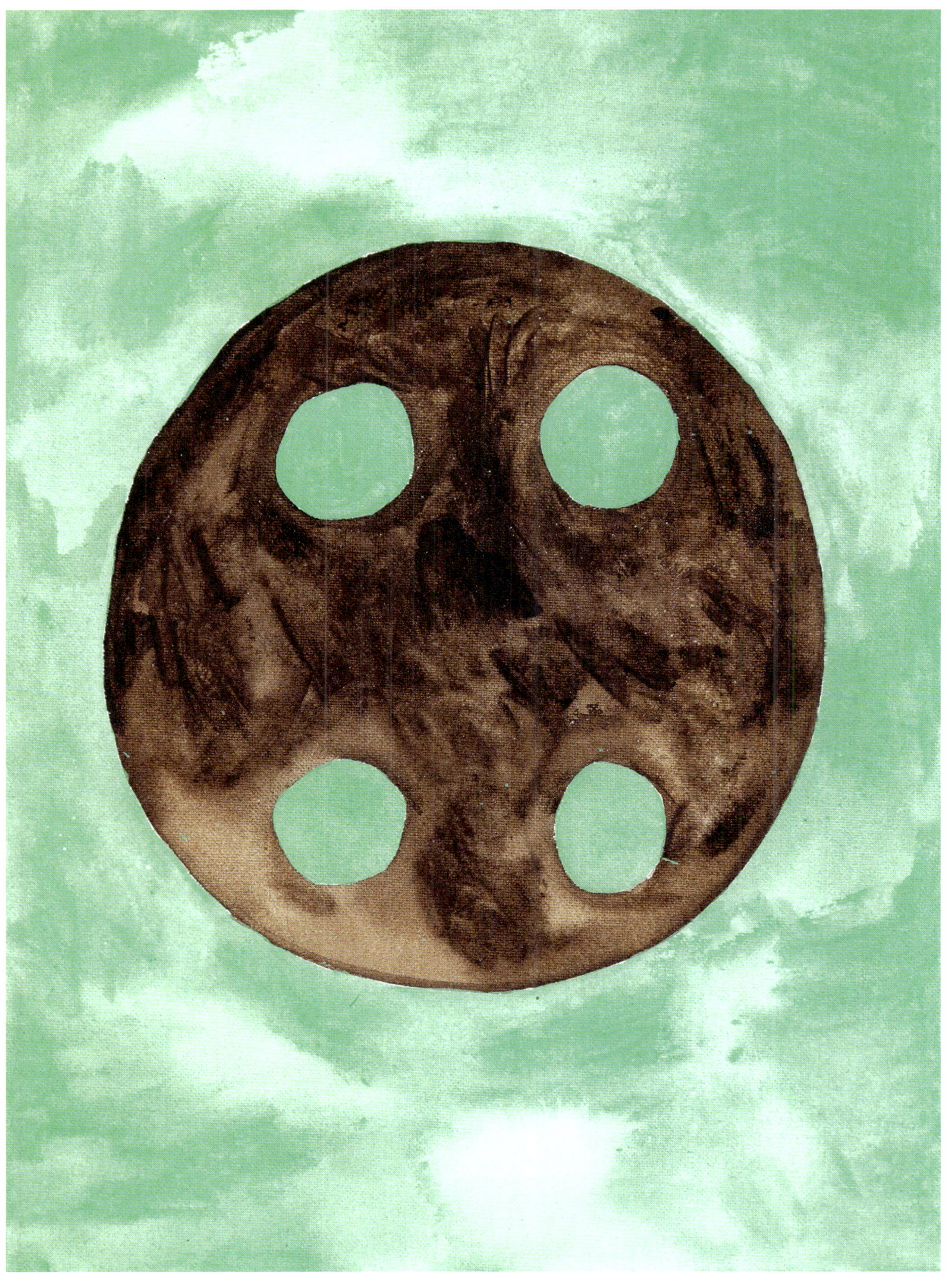

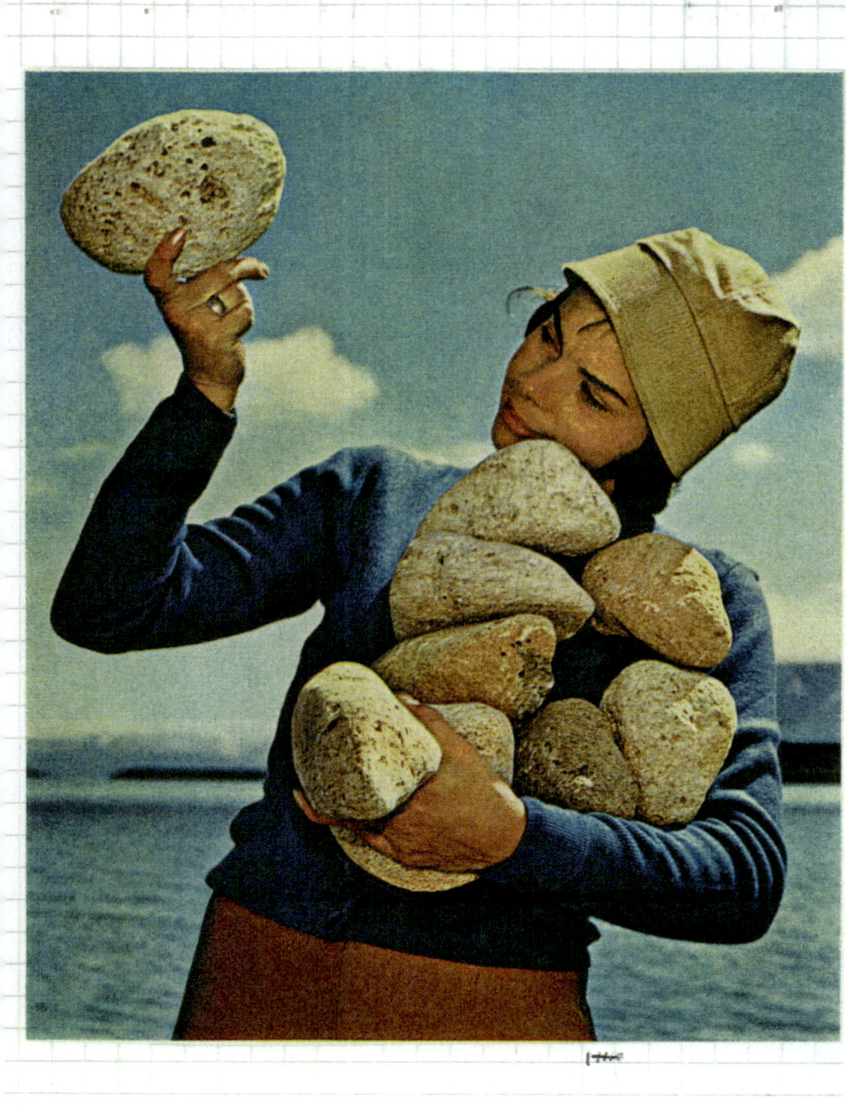

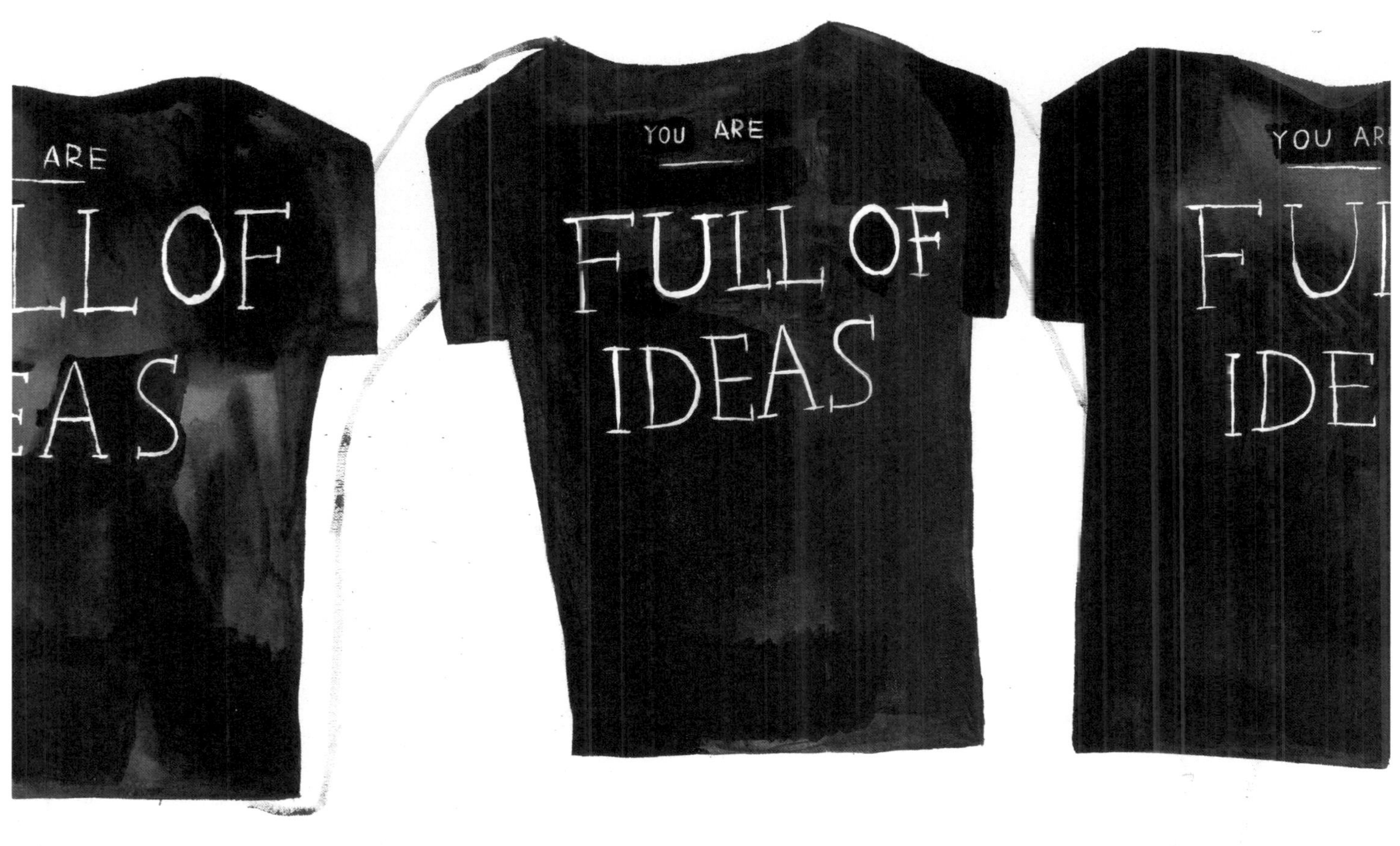

ARE
FULL OF
IDEAS
YOU ARE
FULL OF
IDEAS
YOU ARE
FUL
IDE

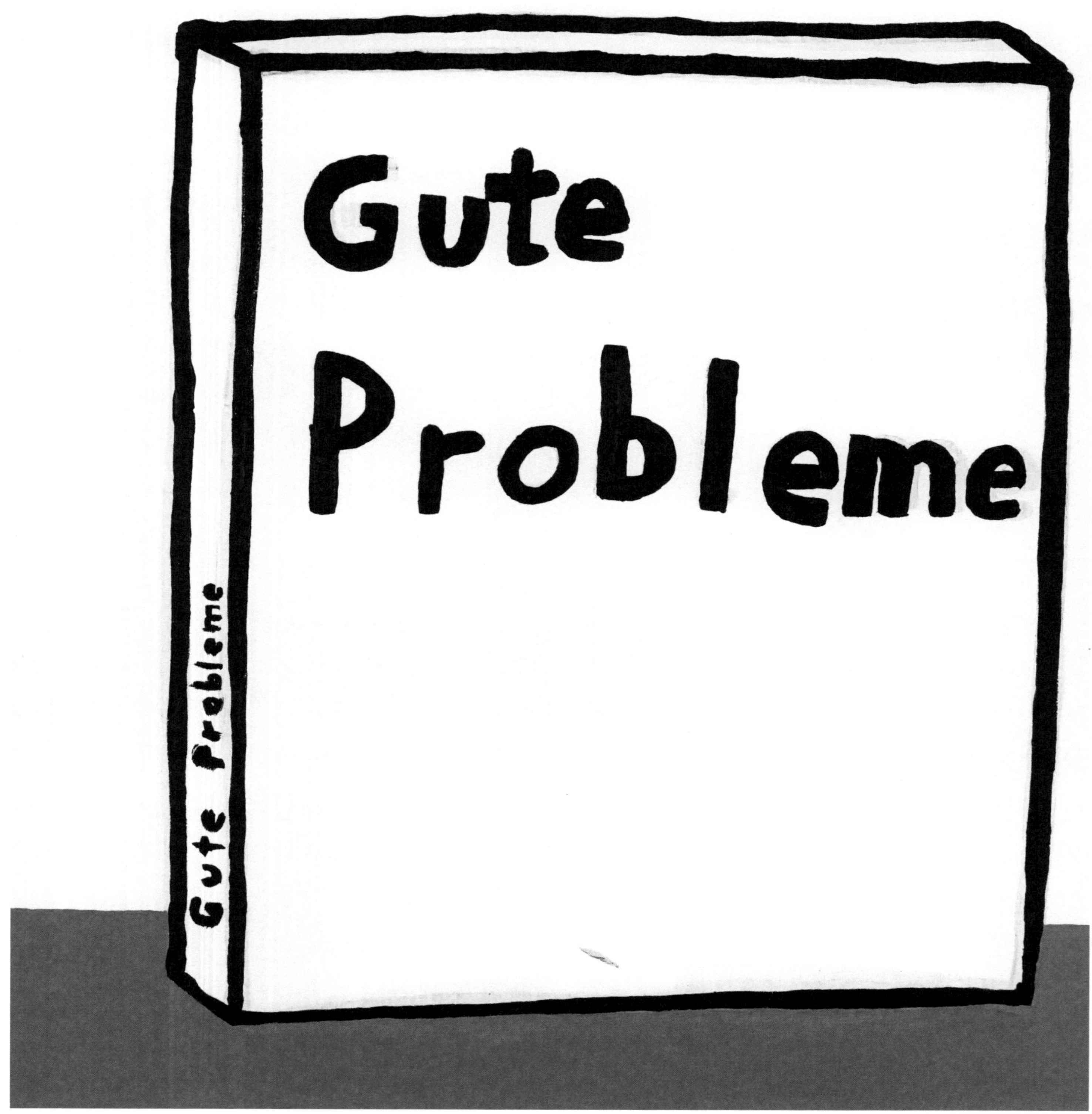

Gute Probleme
Gute Probleme

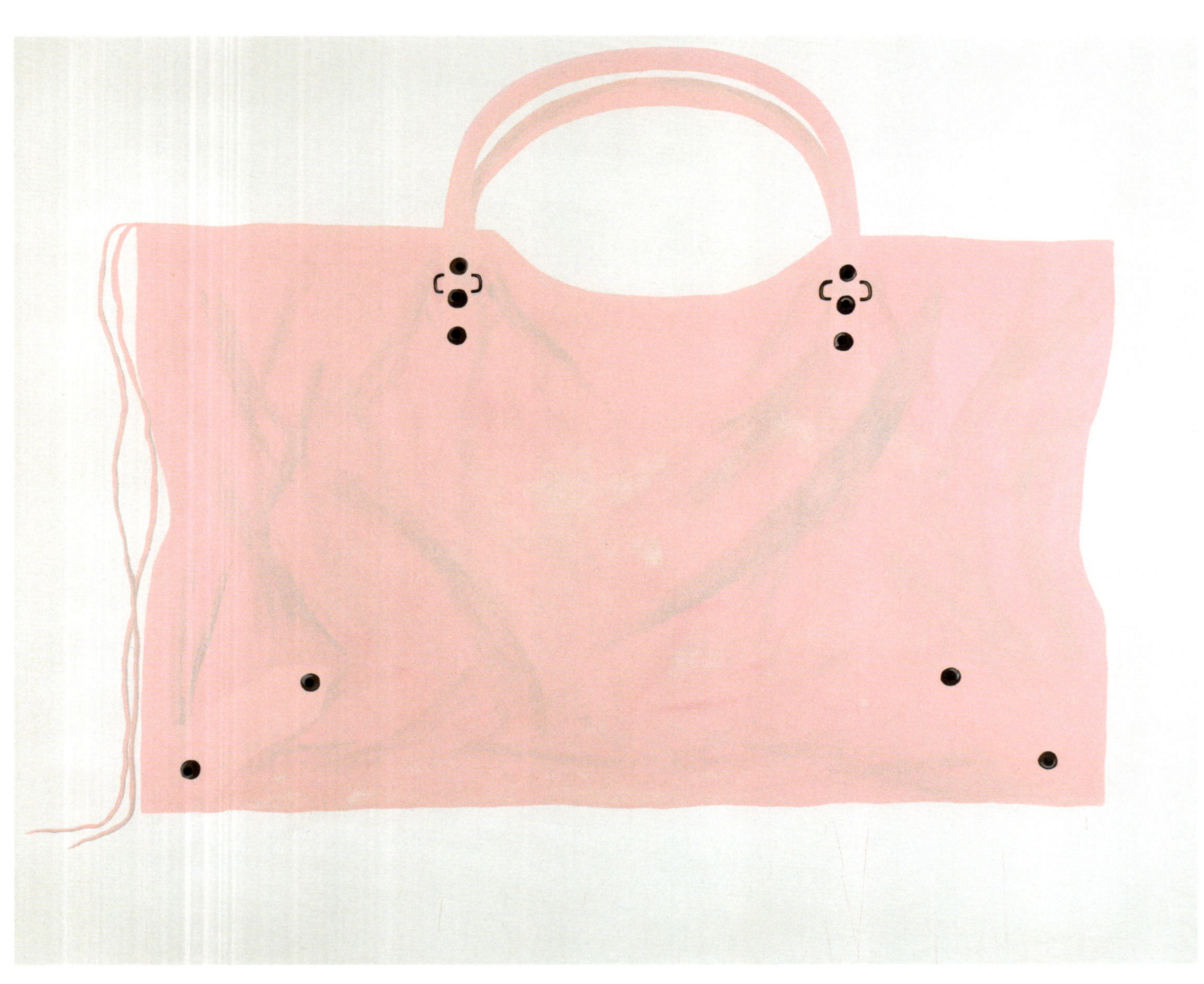

you know
you want it

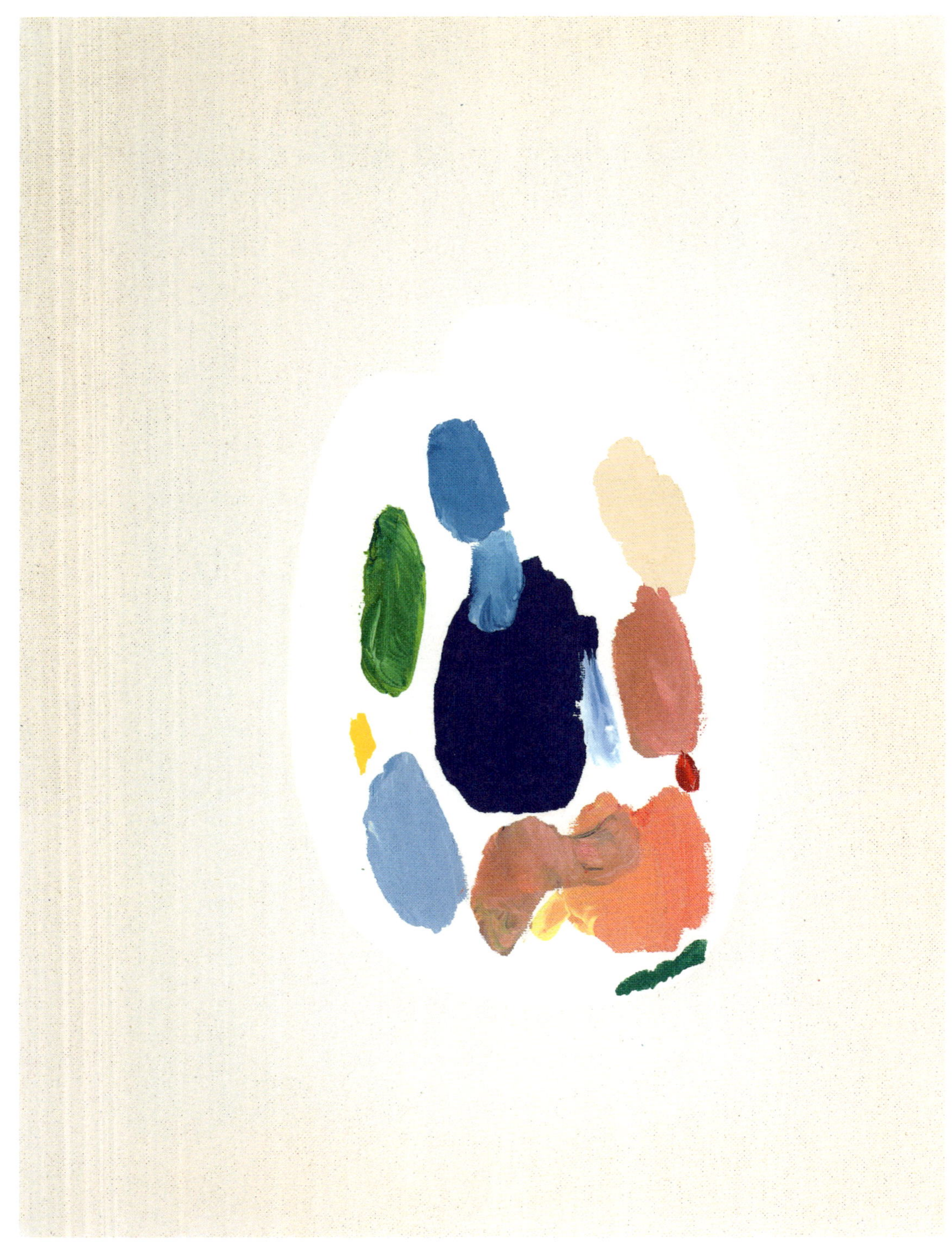

frisch

fix

flexibel

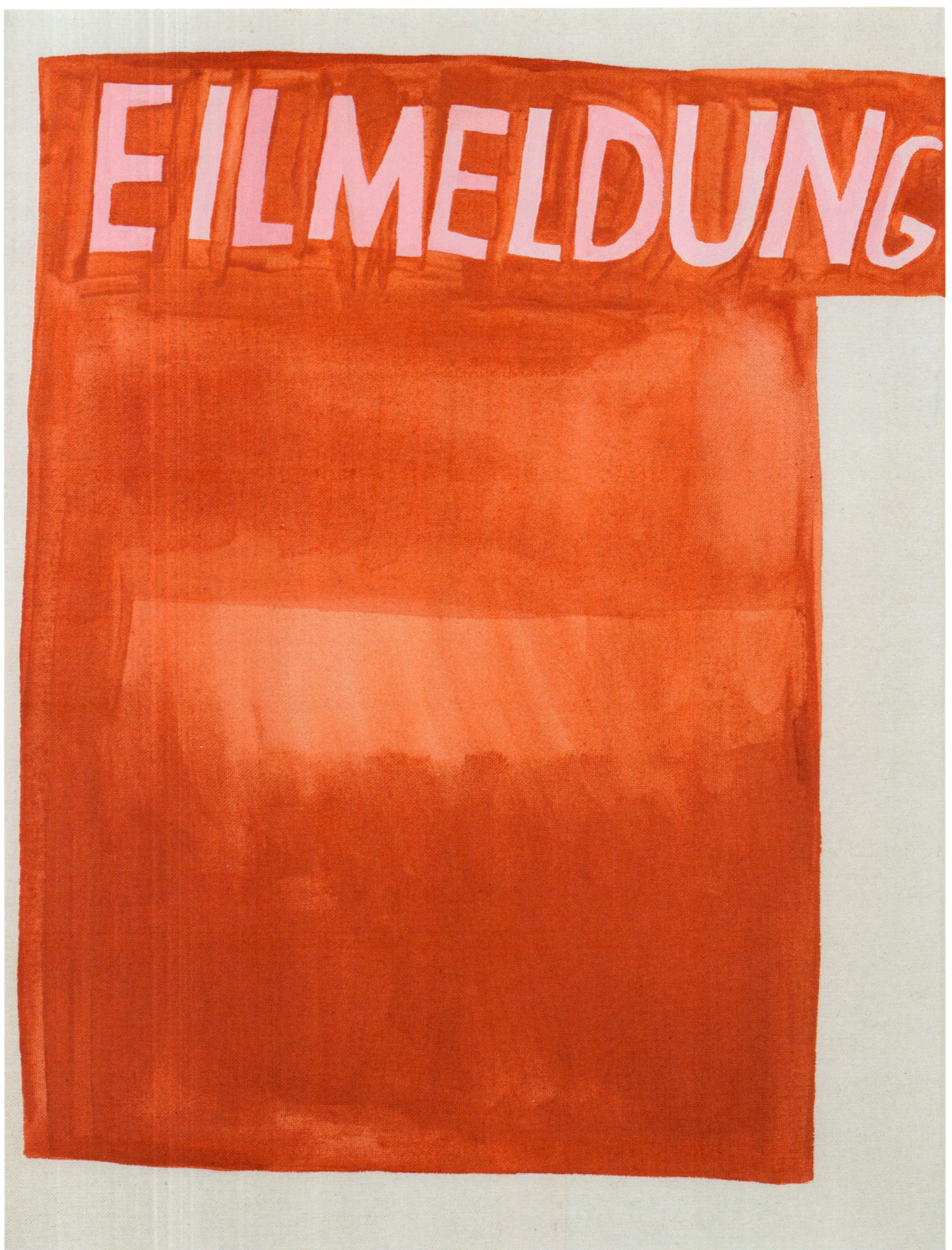

EILMELDUNG

GÖNNEN
SIE SICH
EINEN NEUEN
LOOK

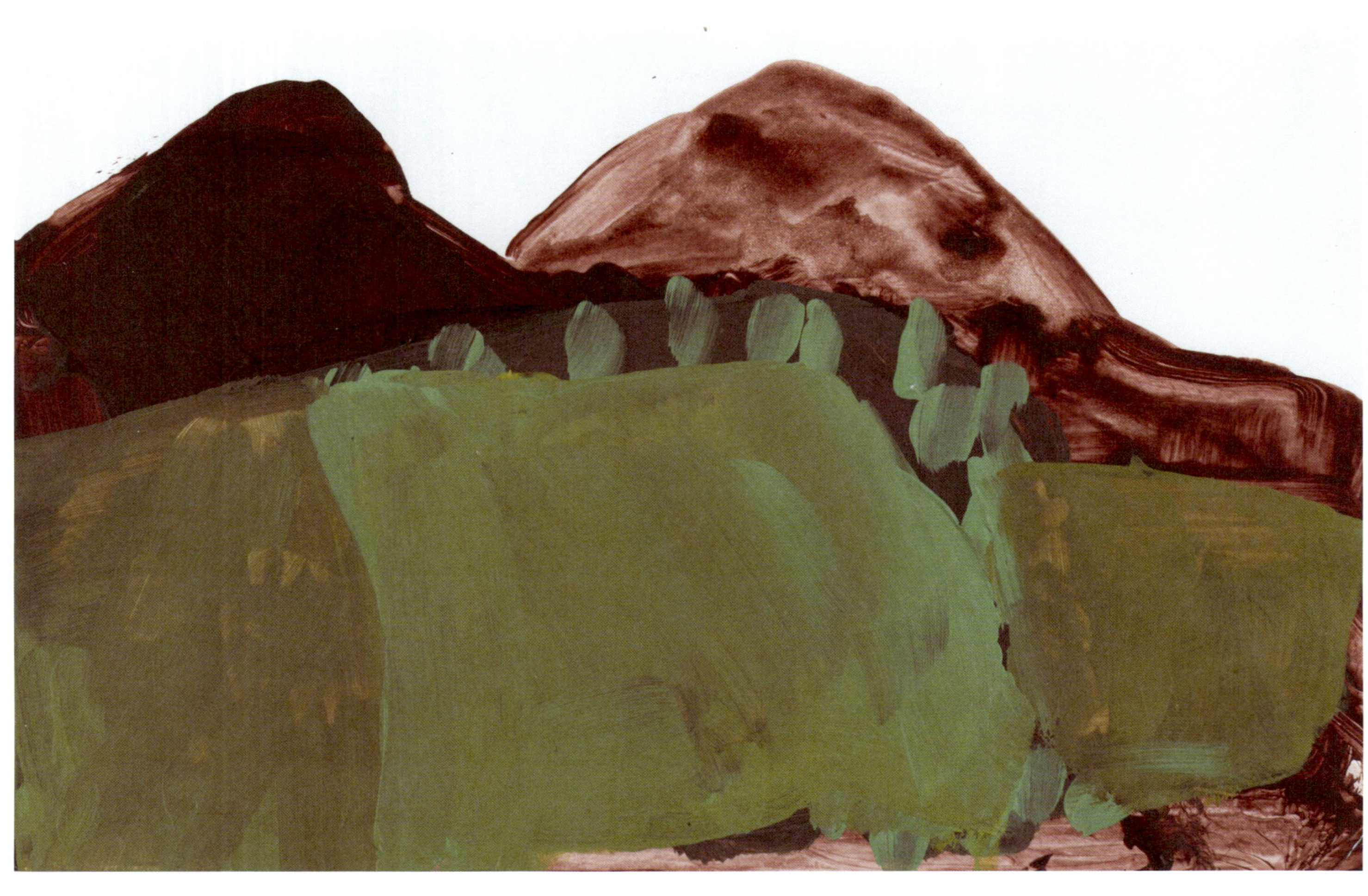

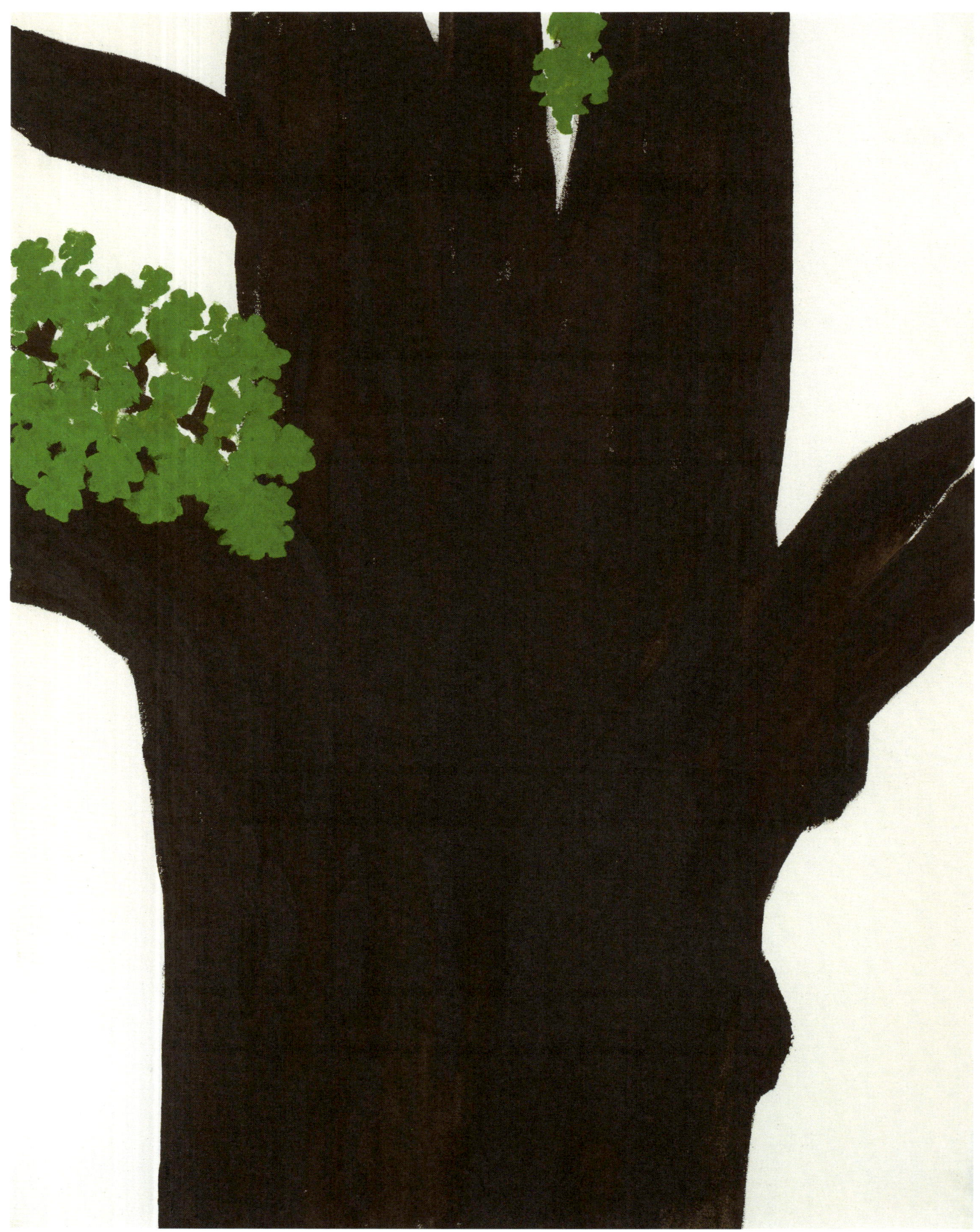

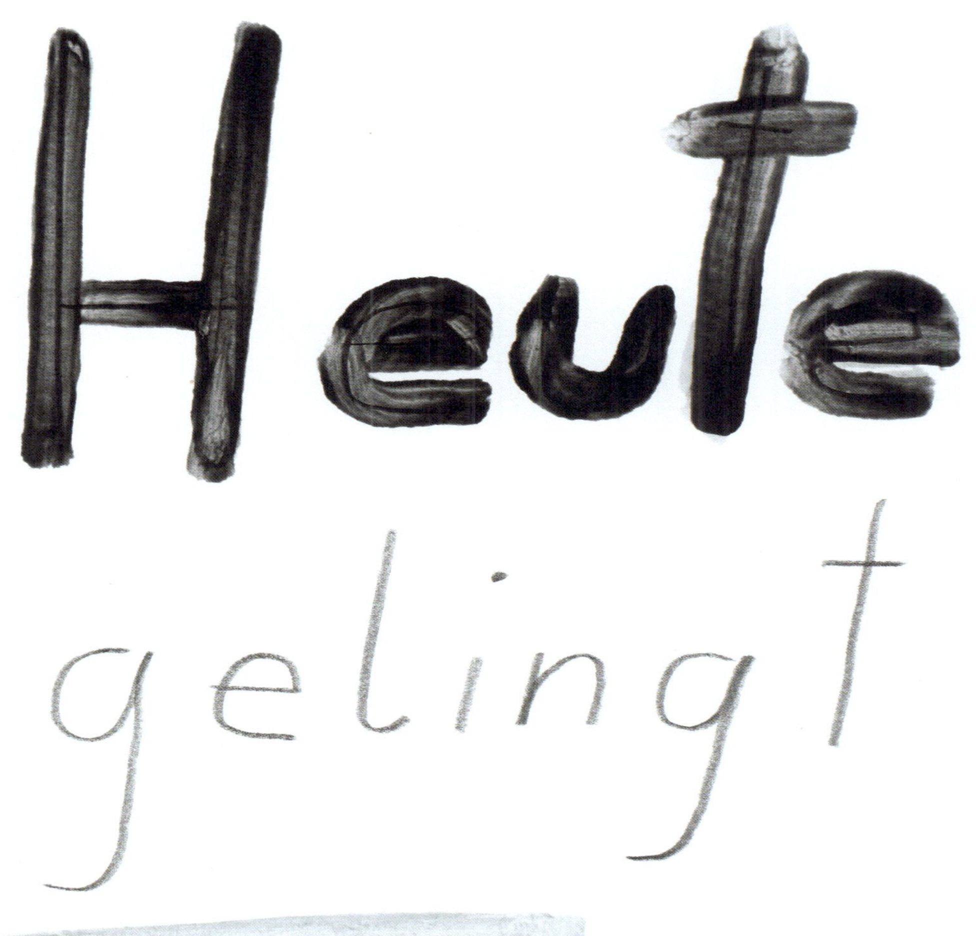

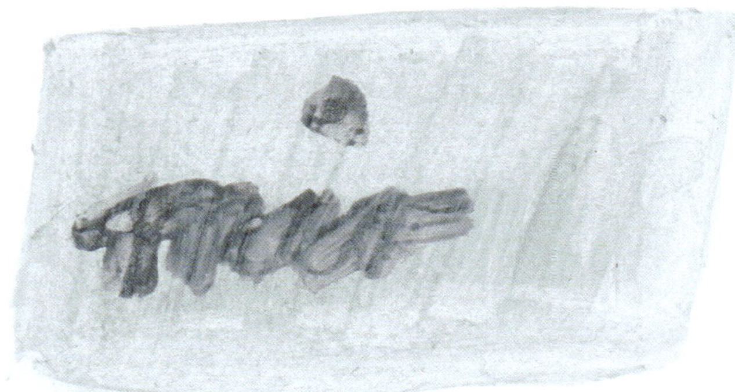

nichts

ISSUE

Heute

Nichts

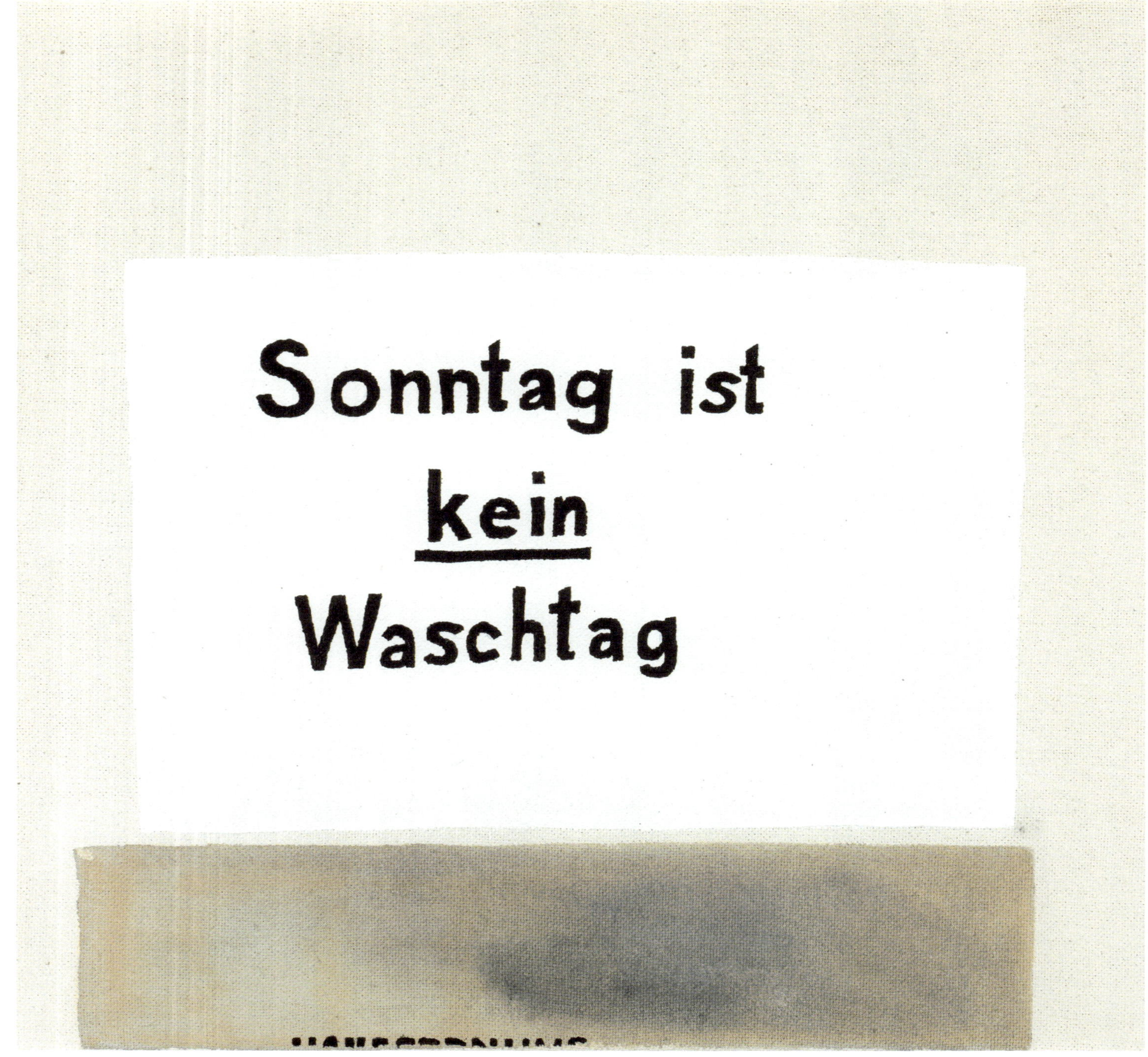

Sonntag ist
kein
Waschtag

Heute

gelingt

mir

nichts

Heute

gelingt

mir

NICHTS

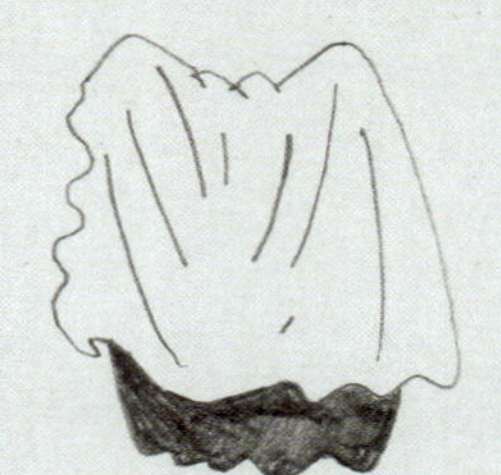

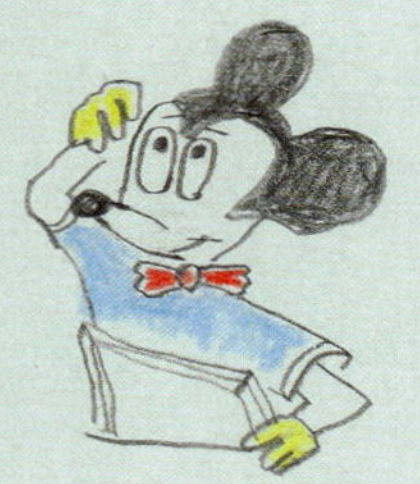

Heute

gelingt

mir

nichts

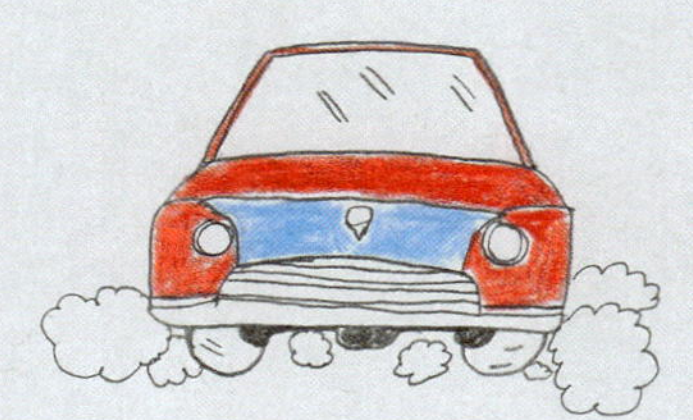
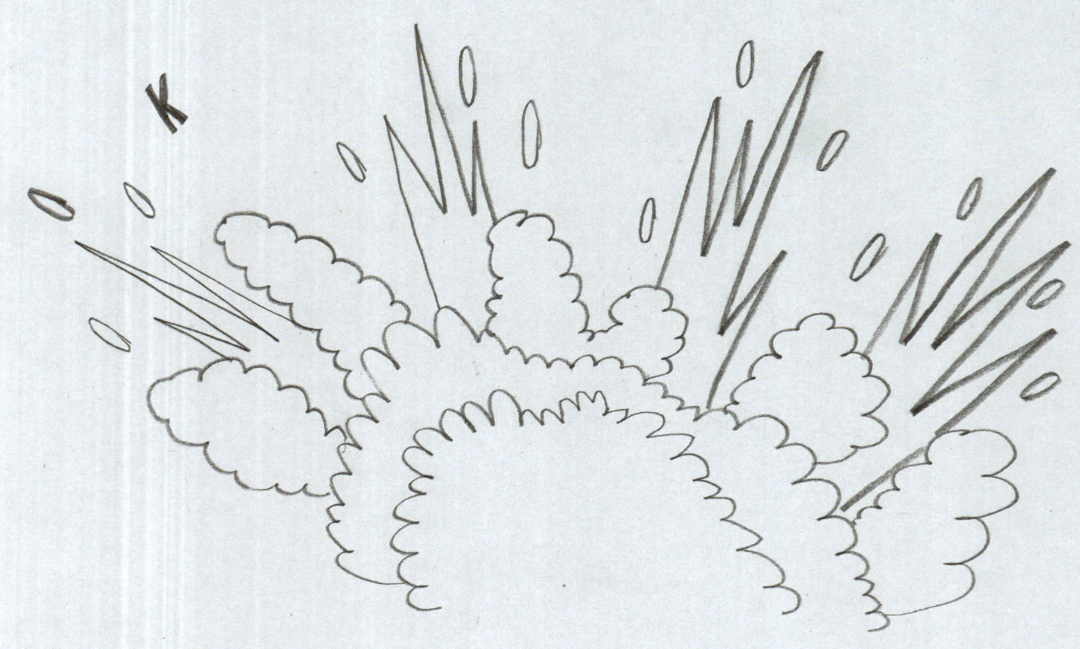
K

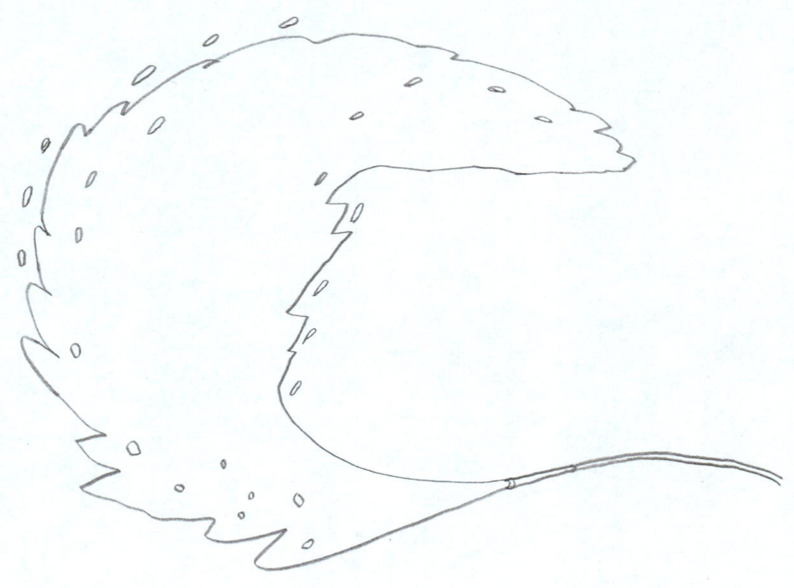

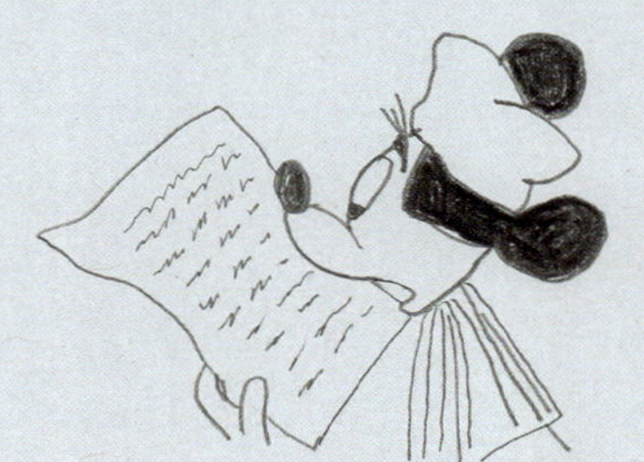

HPS

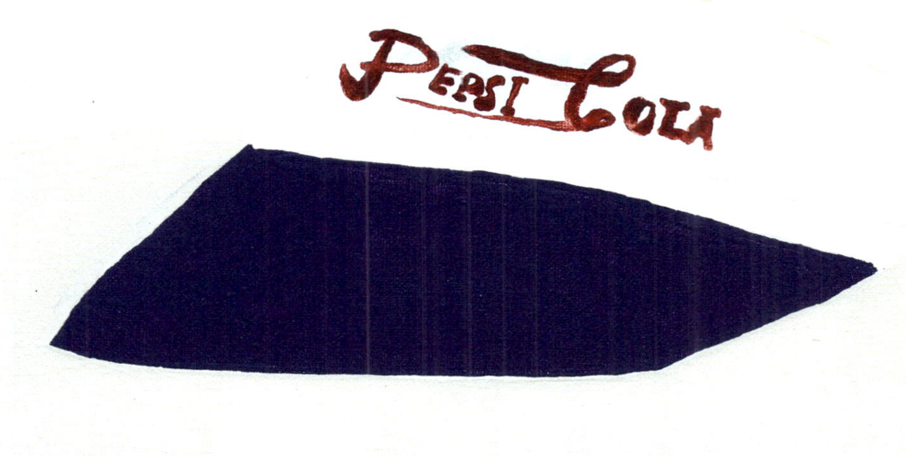

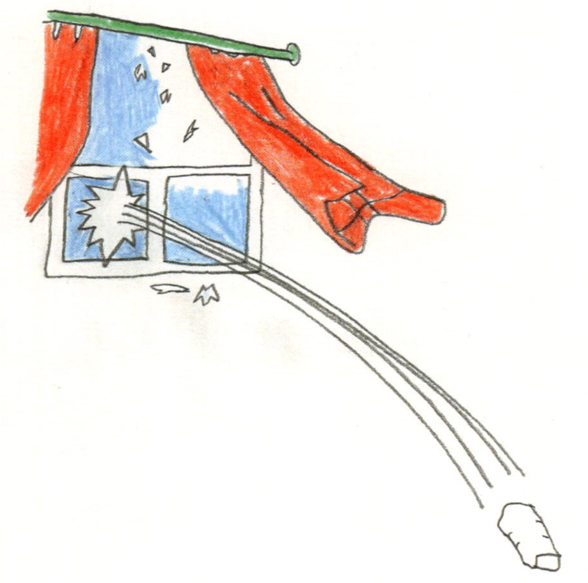

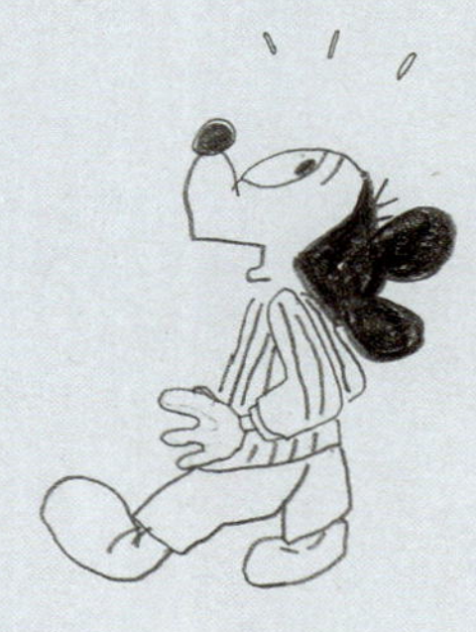

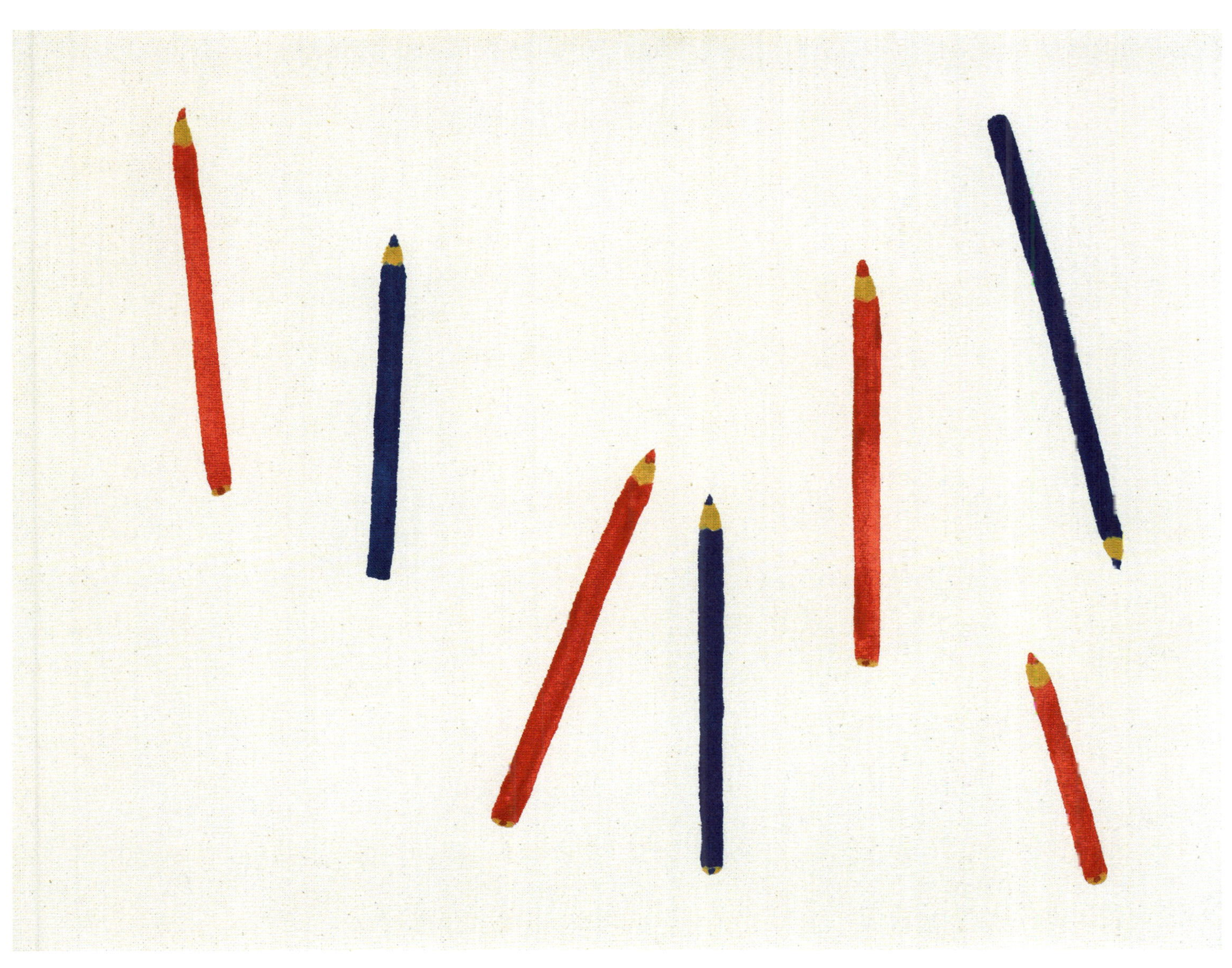

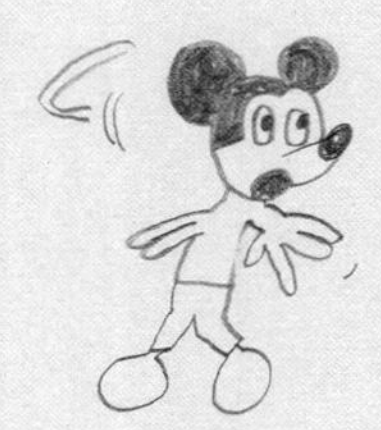

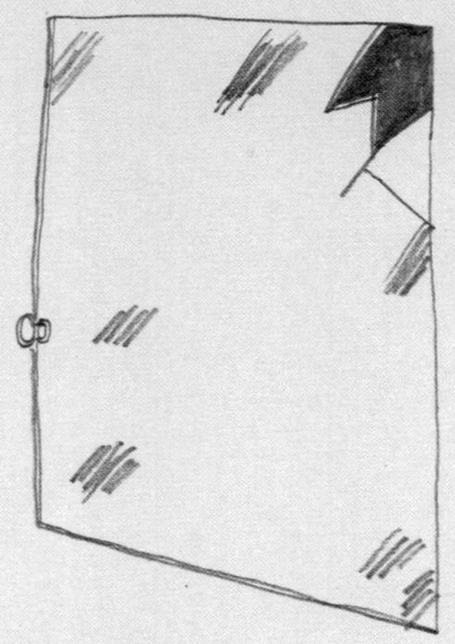

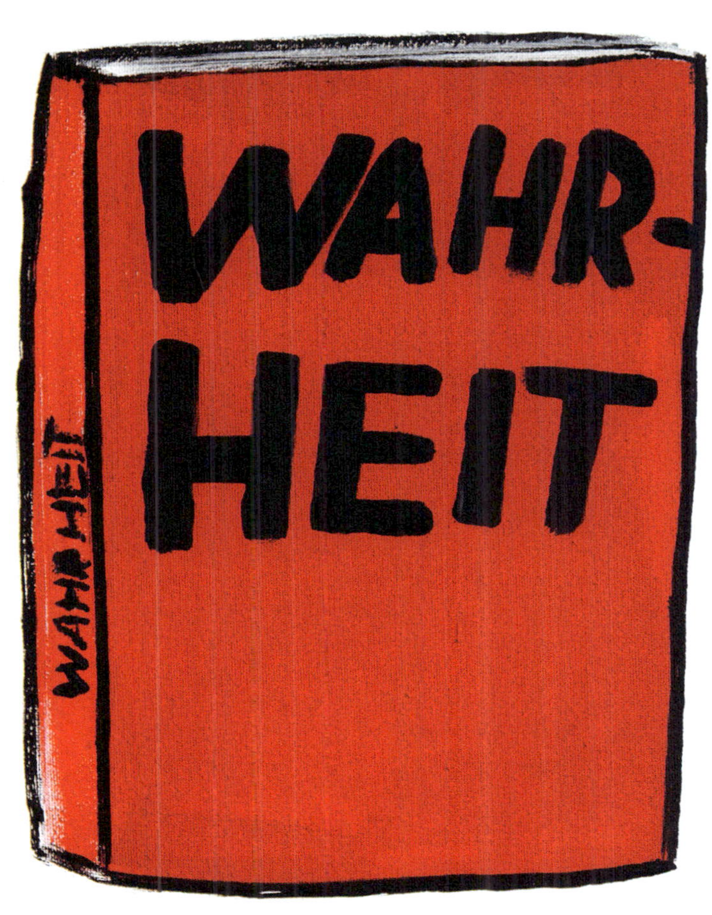
WAHR-
HEIT
WAHRHEIT

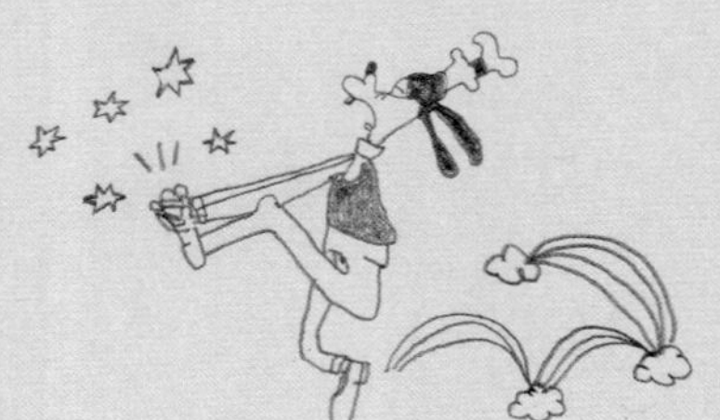

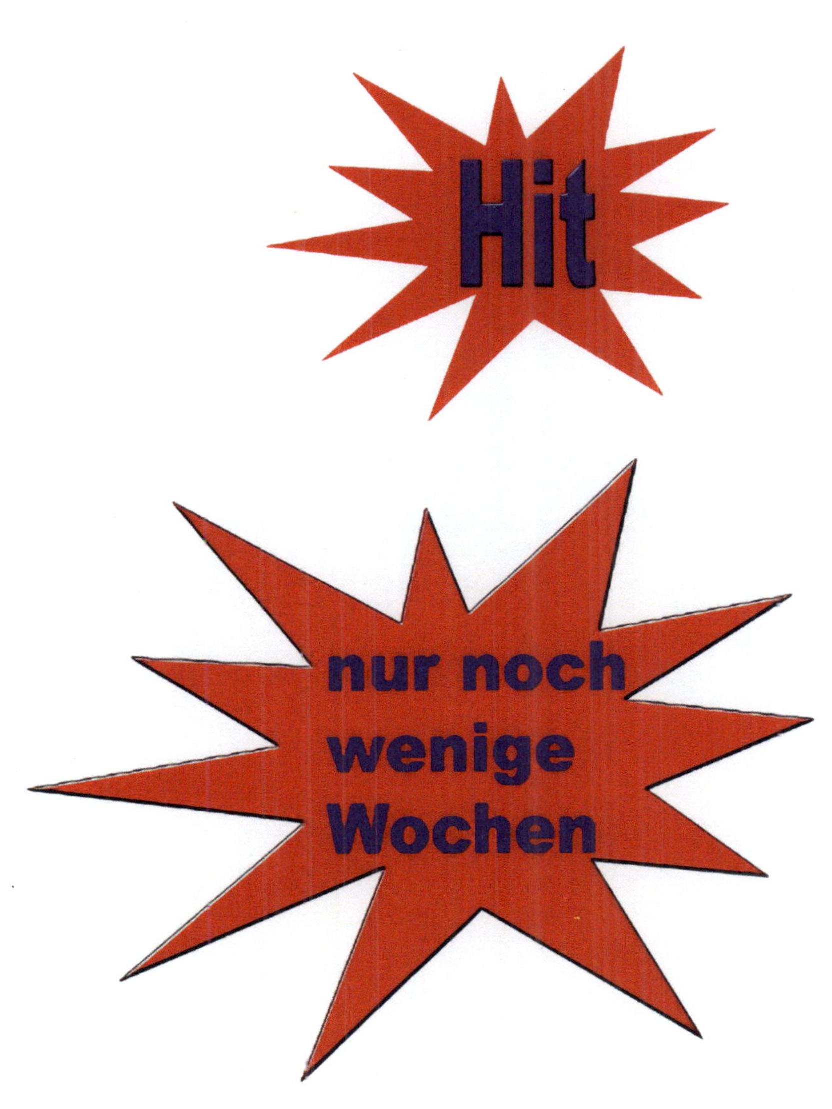

Hit
nur noch
wenige
Wochen

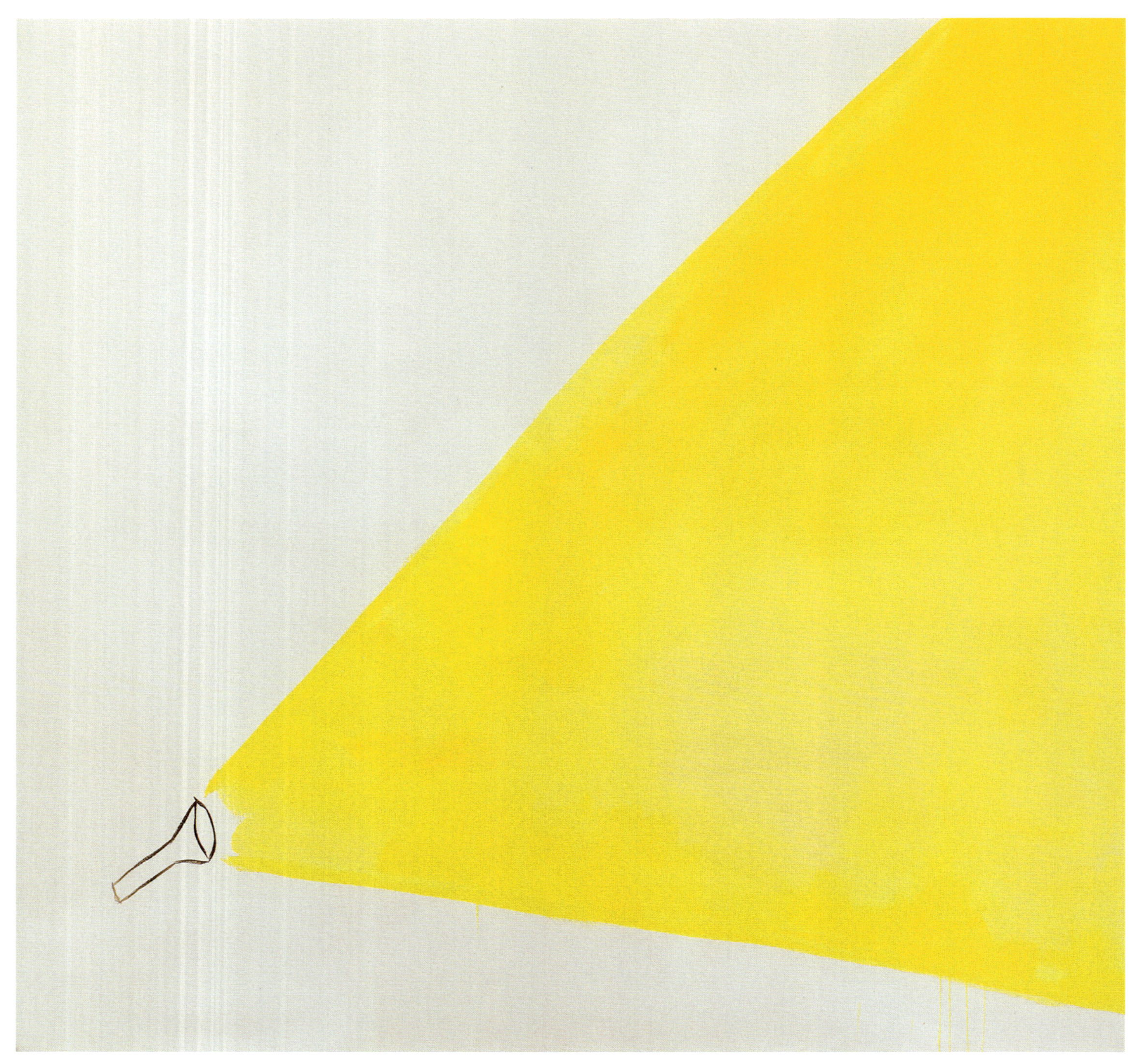

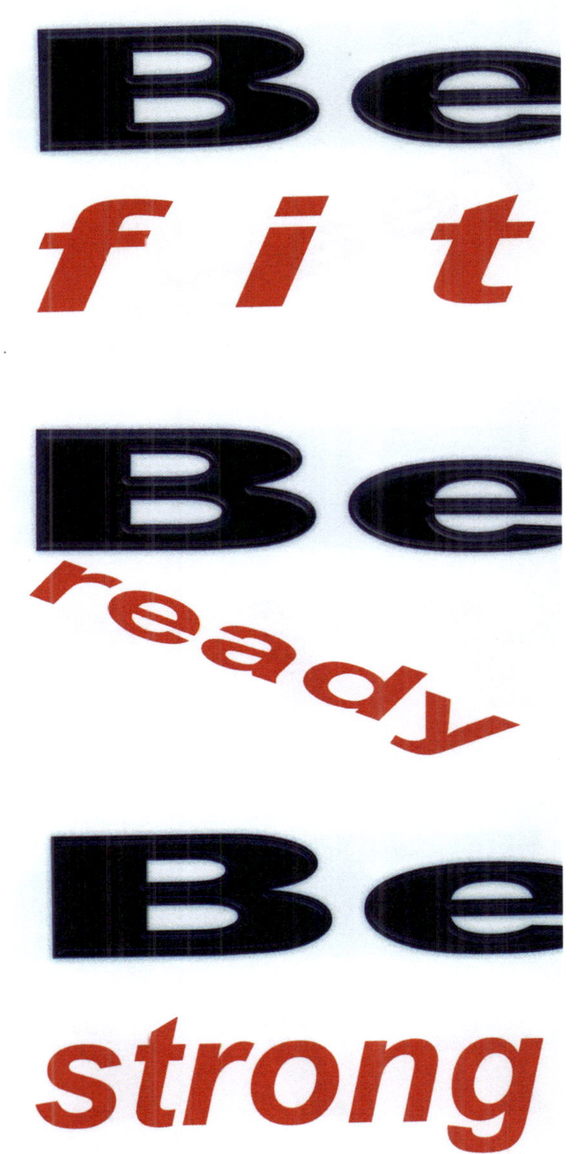
Be
fit
Be
ready
Be
strong

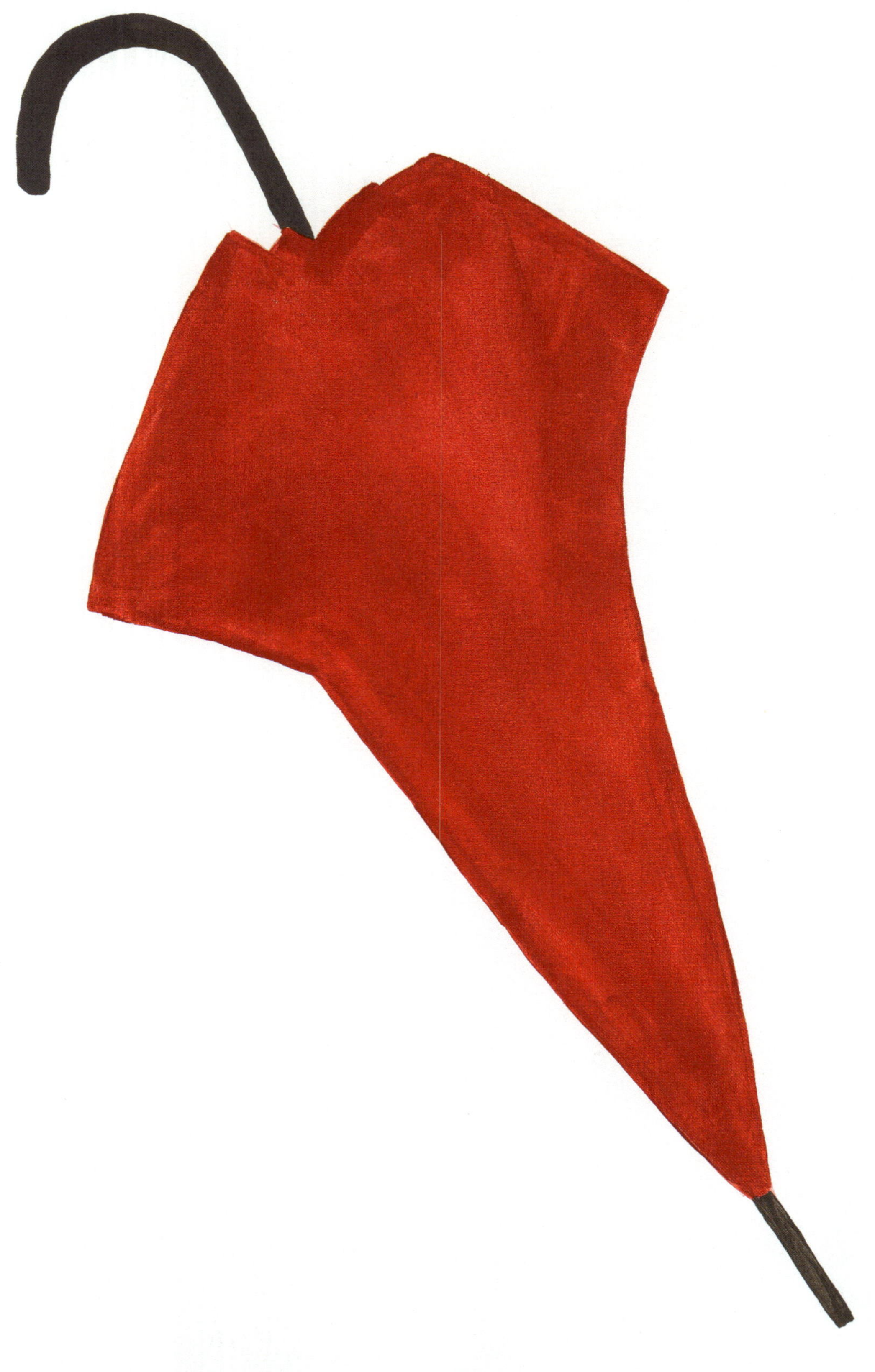

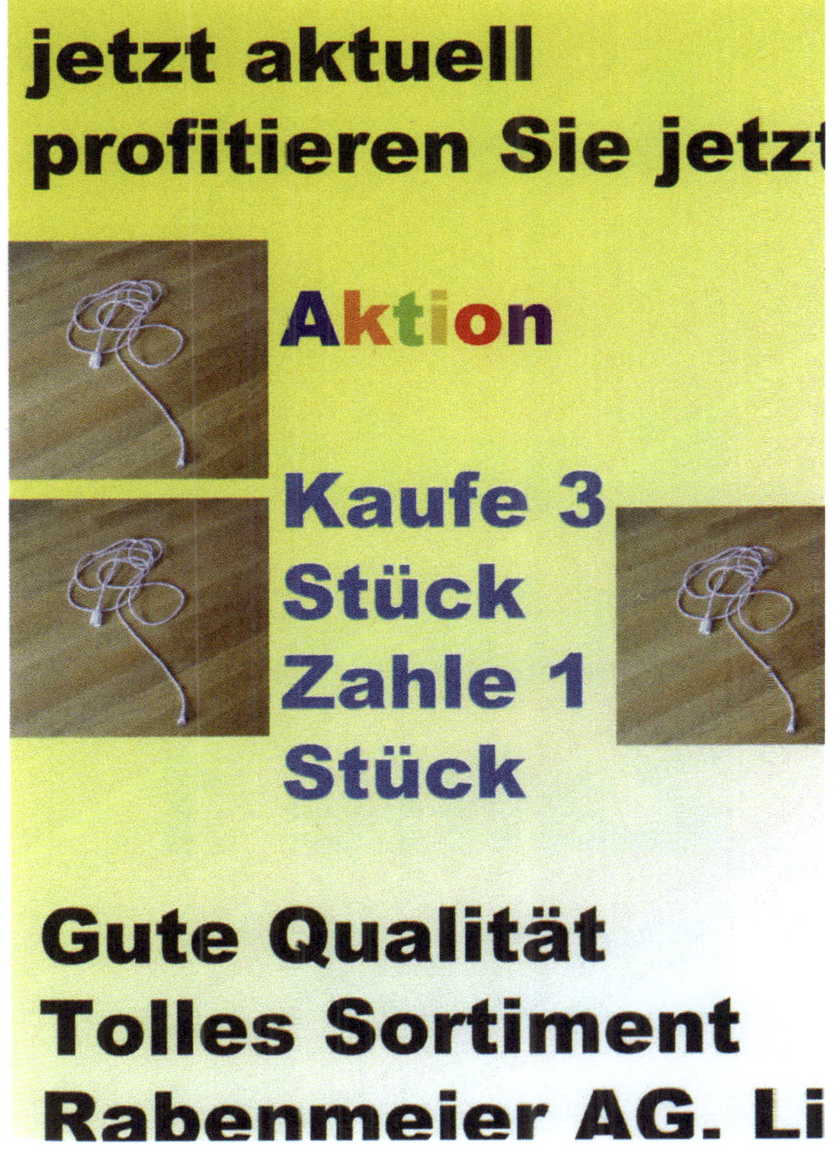

jetzt aktuell
profitieren Sie jetzt
Aktion
Kaufe 3
Stück
Zahle 1
Stück
Gute Qualität
Tolles Sortiment
Rabenmeier AG. Li

Wir sind <u>jederzeit</u> für Sie da.

24/7

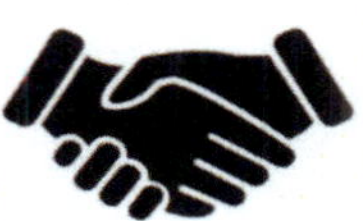

Melden Sie sich gerne

Wenn niemand da,
bitte links

miffy the artist

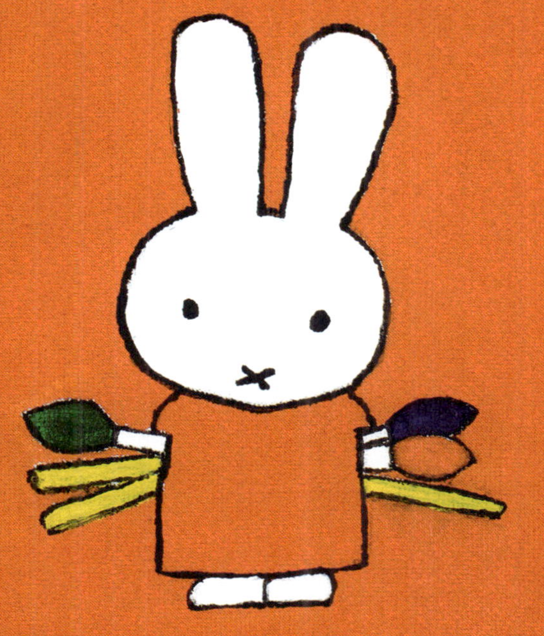

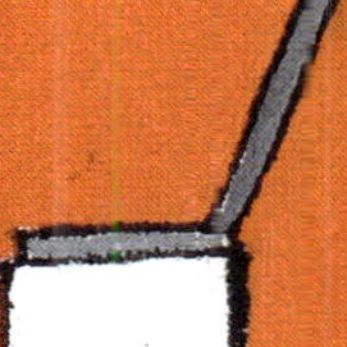

and her side job

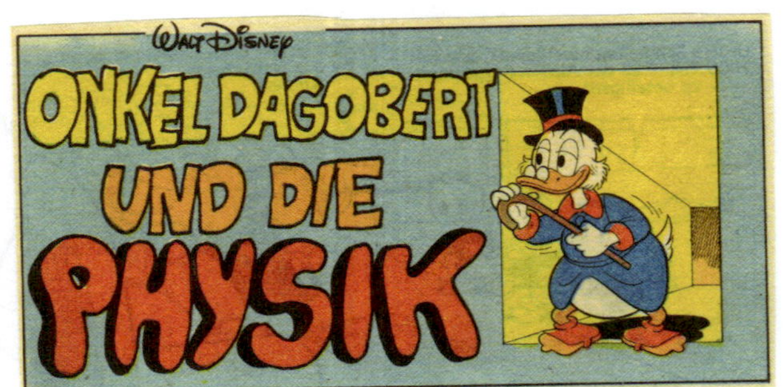

120   2021   MC Nº1

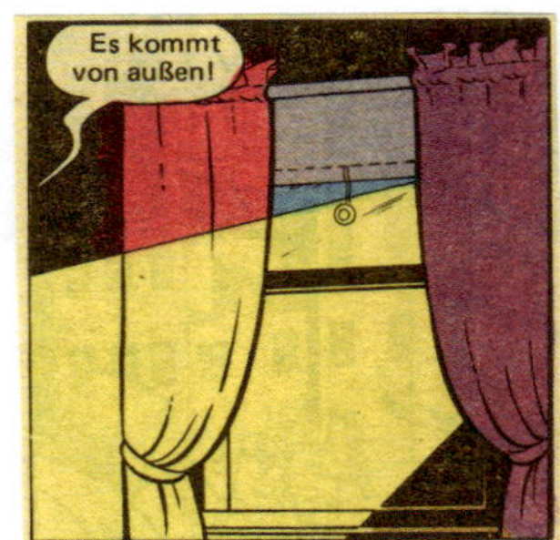

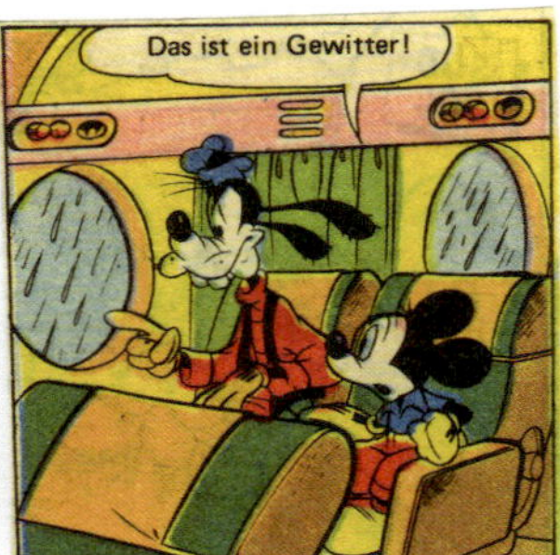

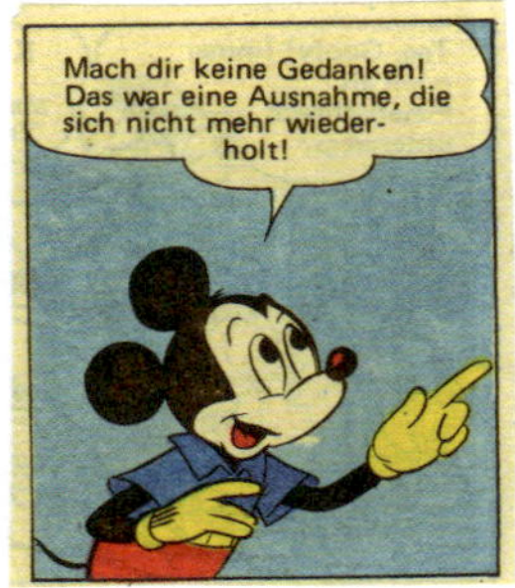

ENDE

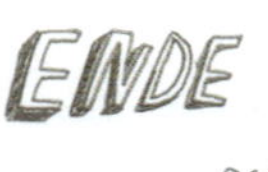

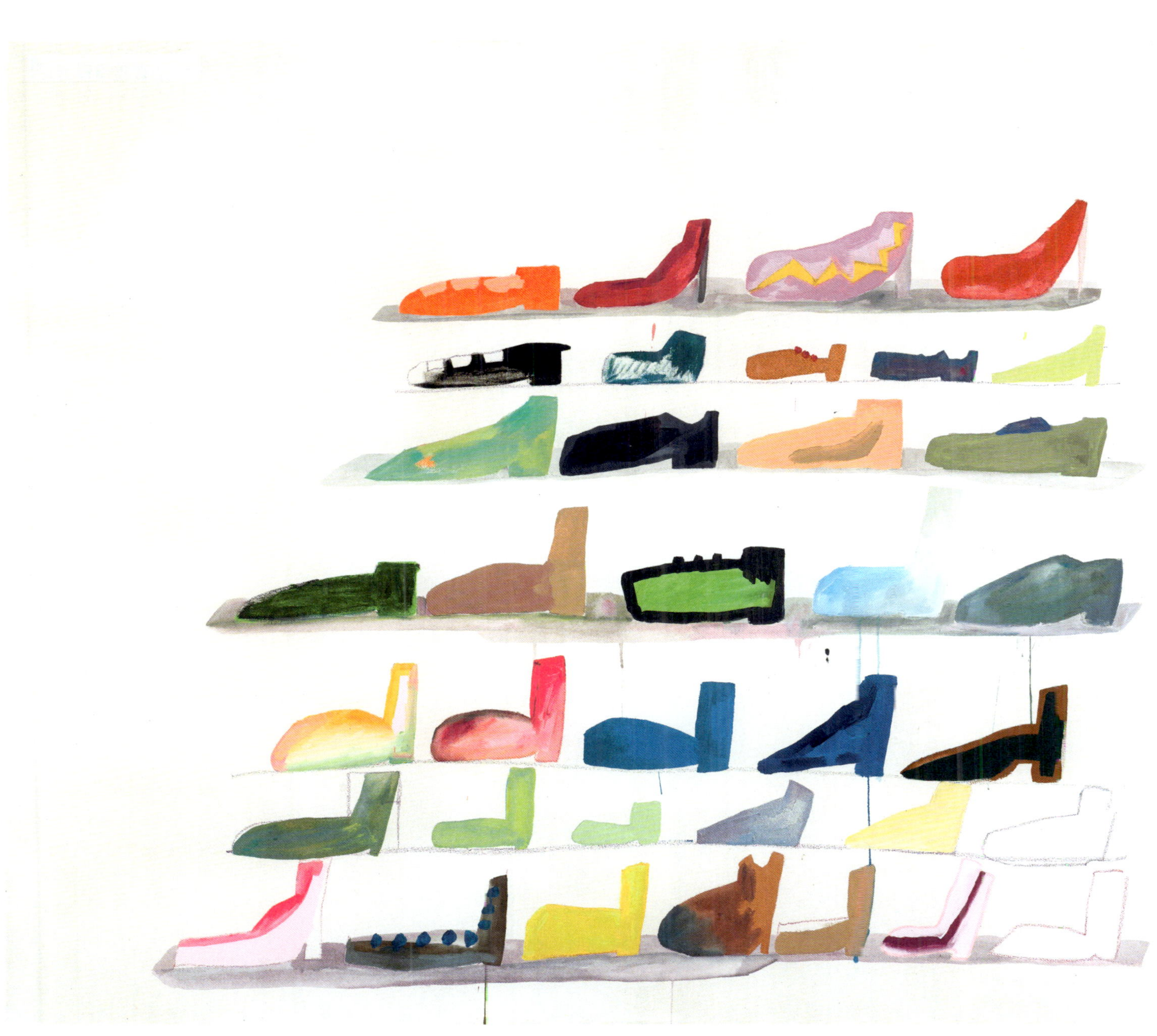

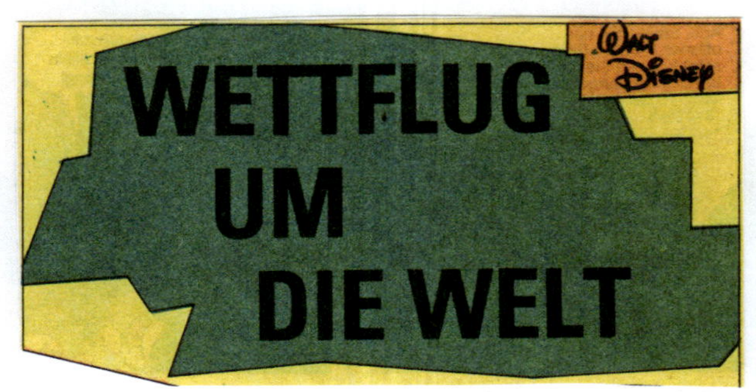

/2d 2d21
MC No. 3

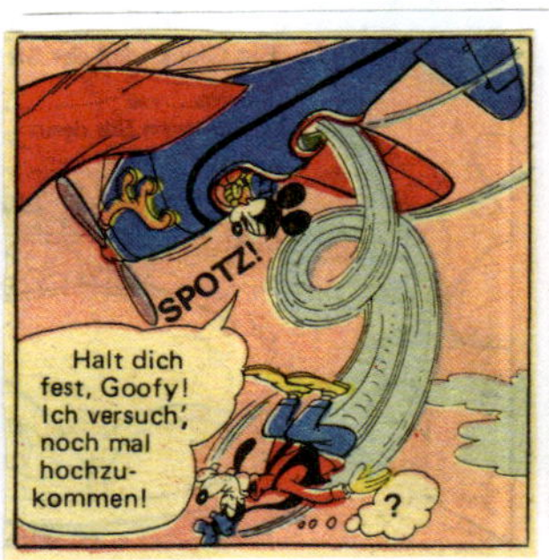

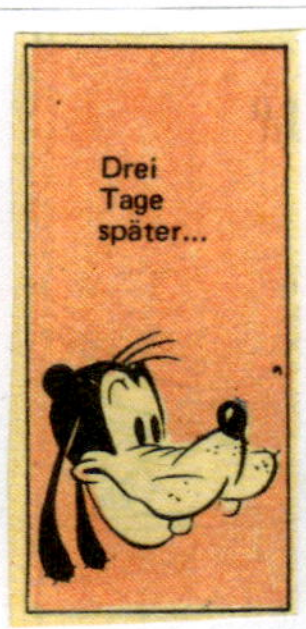

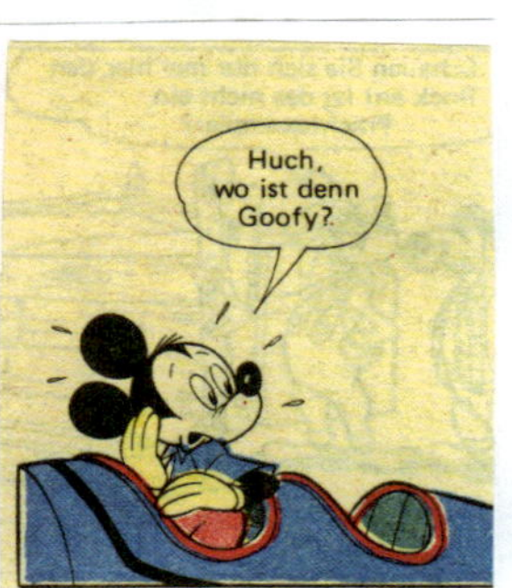

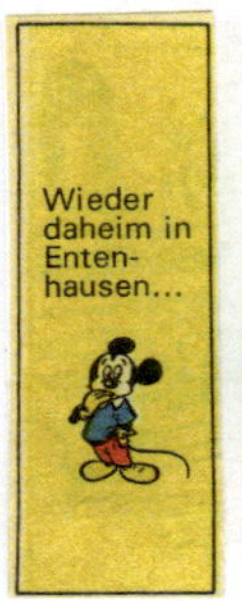

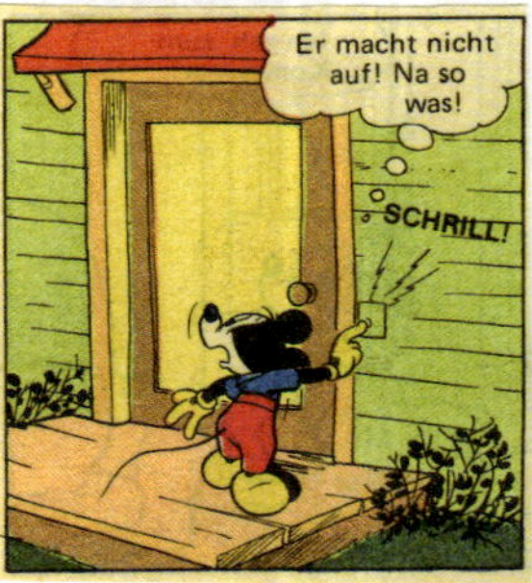

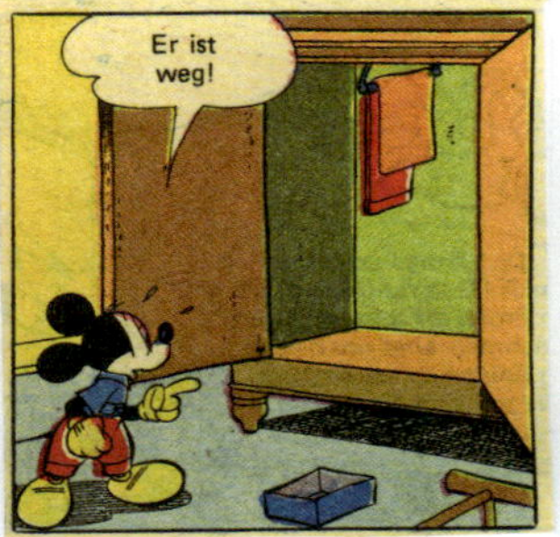
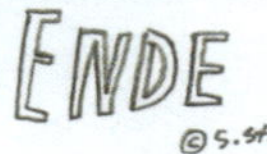

ENDE
© S. St.

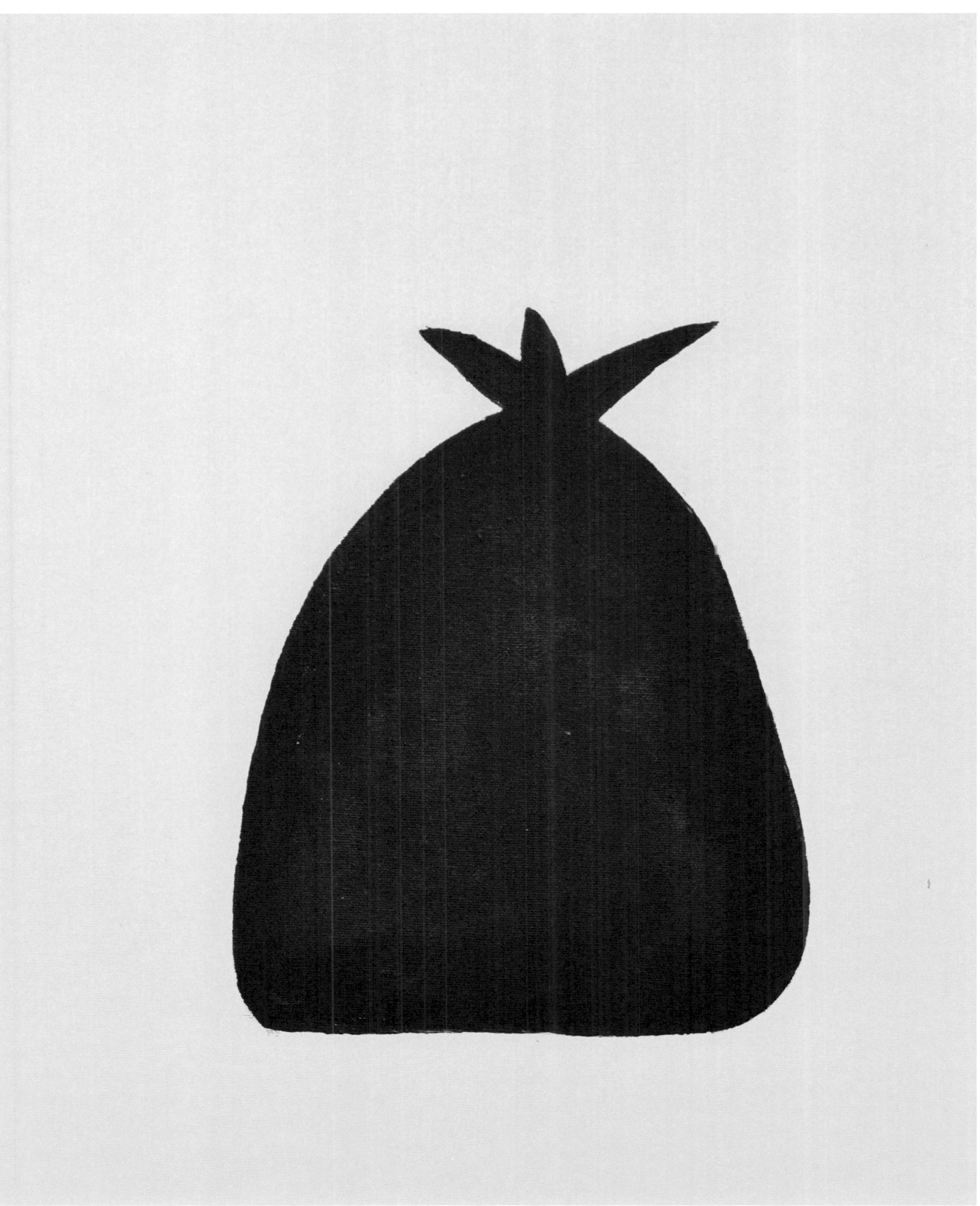

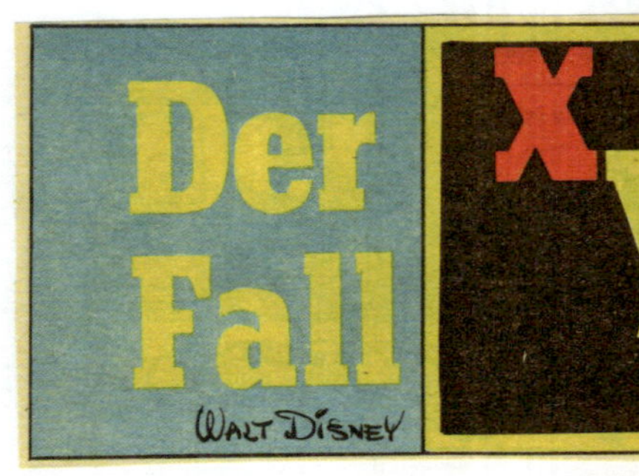
Der Fall
X Y Z
WALT DISNEY
mc Nº2 2021 /20

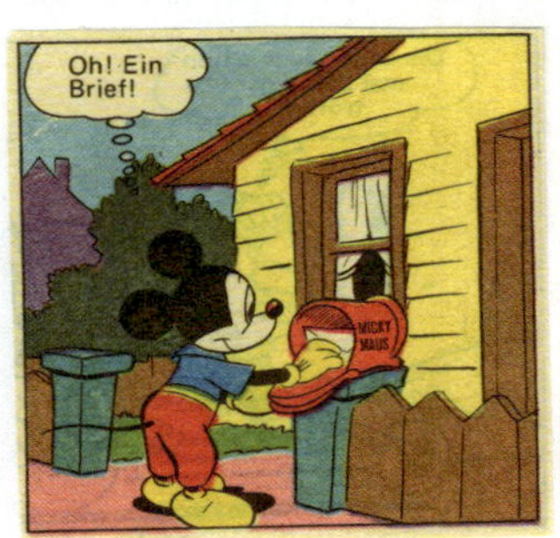
Oh! Ein Brief!

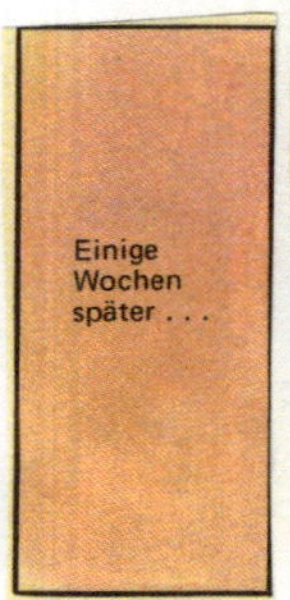
Einige Wochen später . . .

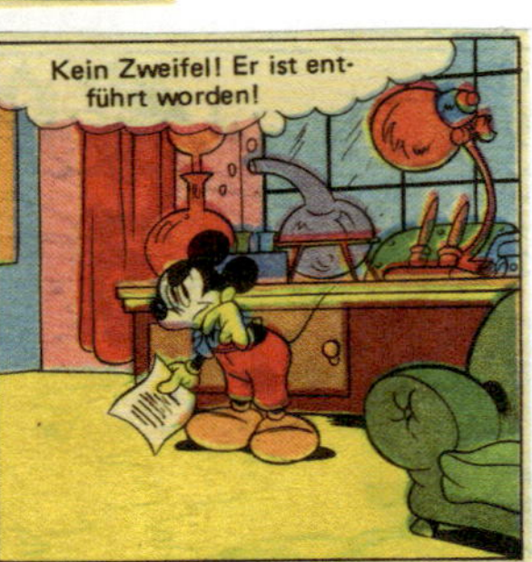
Kein Zweifel! Er ist entführt worden!

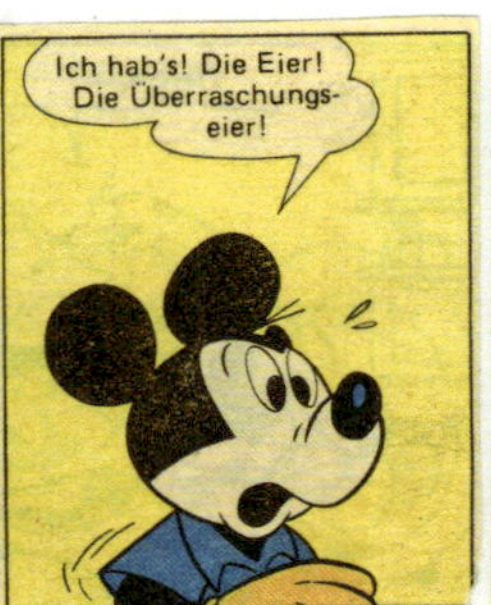
Ich hab's! Die Eier! Die Überraschungseier!

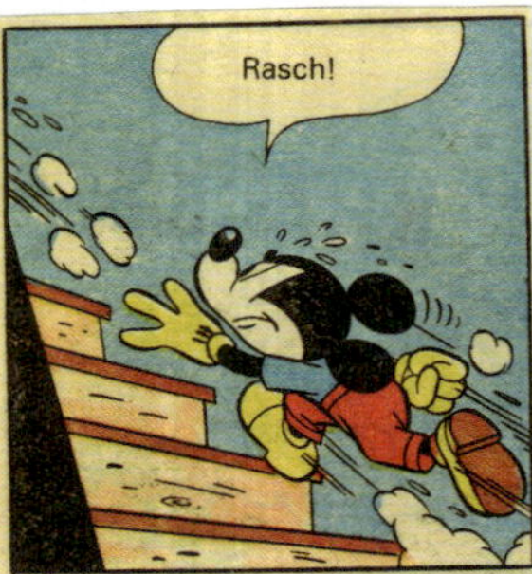
Rasch!

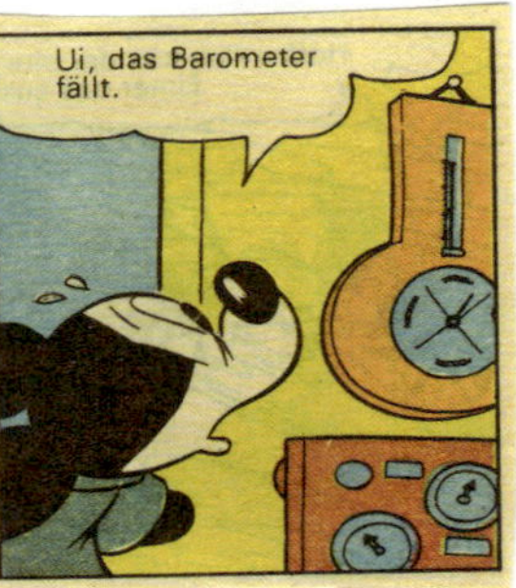
Ui, das Barometer fällt.

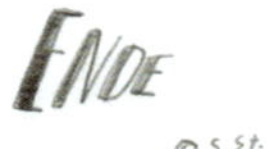
ENDE
© S. St.

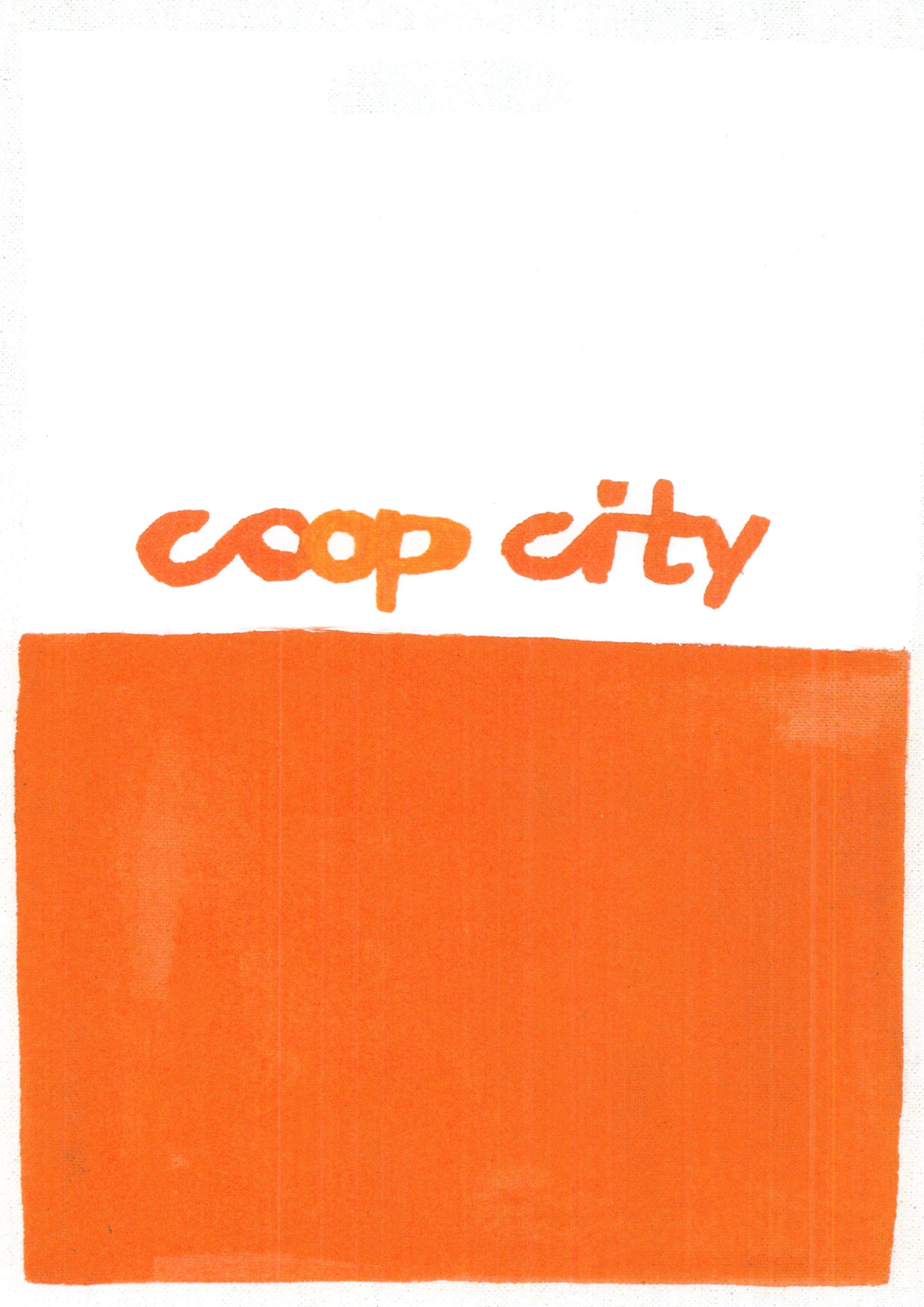

coop city

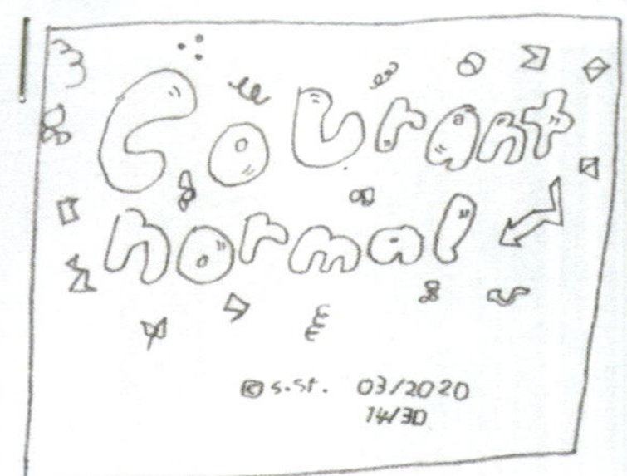

Courant normal
® S.St. 03/2020
14/30

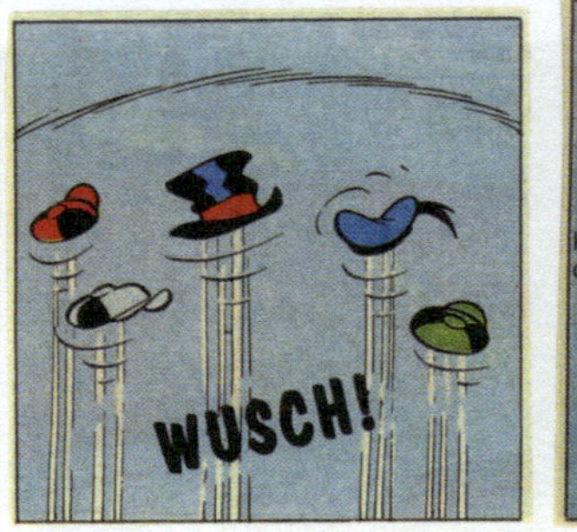

WUSCH!

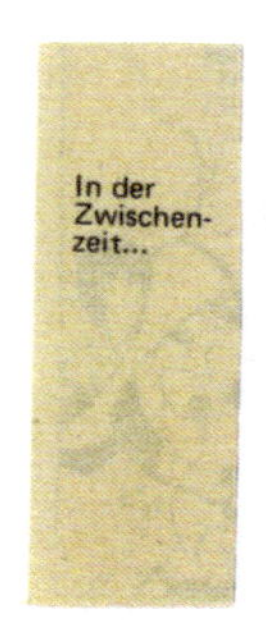

Kurz darauf...

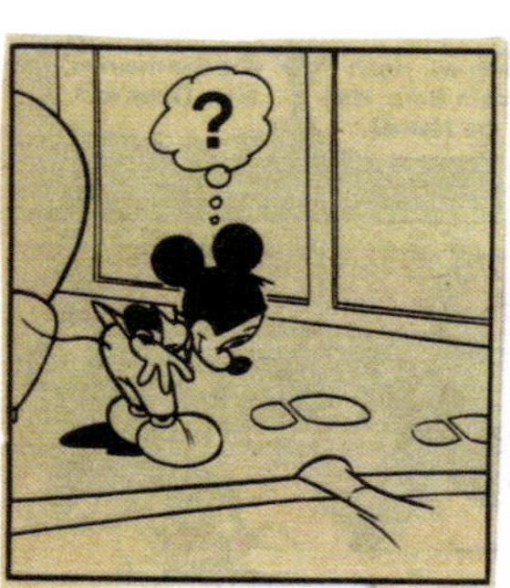

In der Zwischen-zeit...

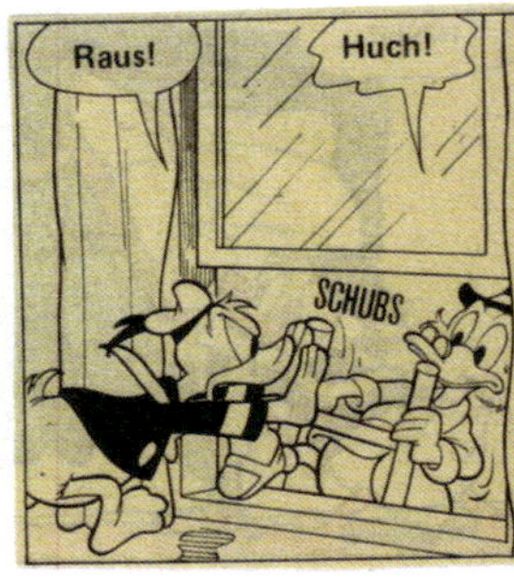

Raus!
Huch!
SCHUBS

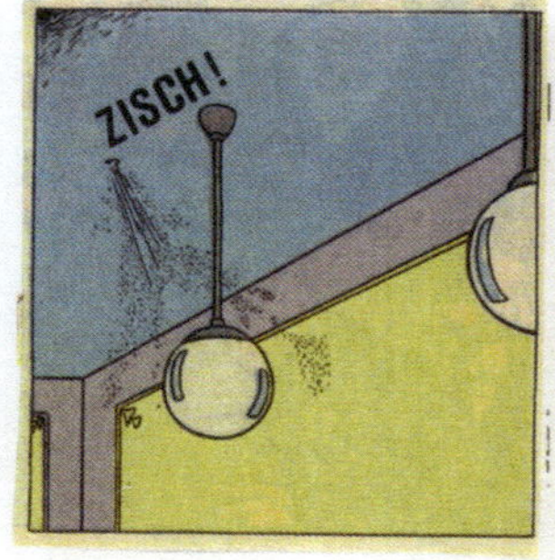

ZISCH!

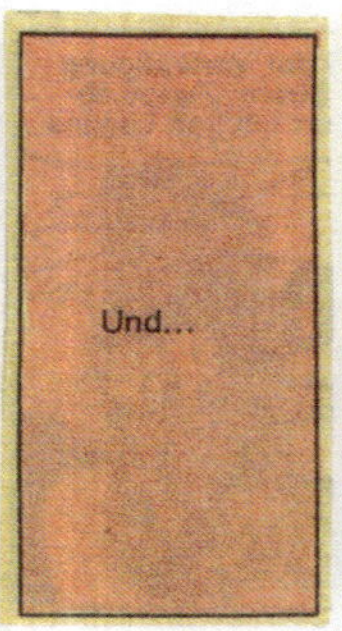

Und...

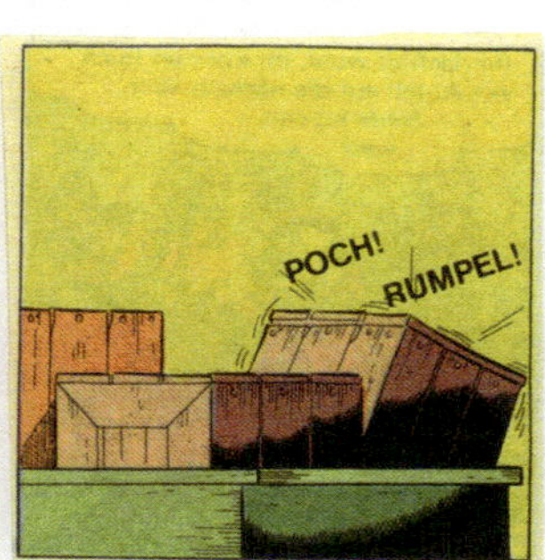

POCH!
RÜMPEL!

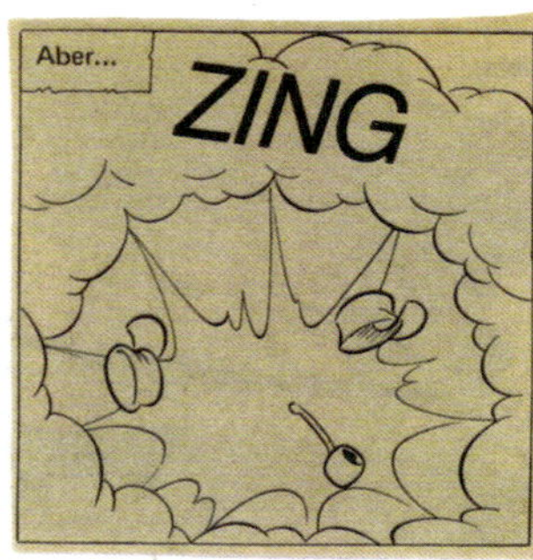

Aber...
ZING

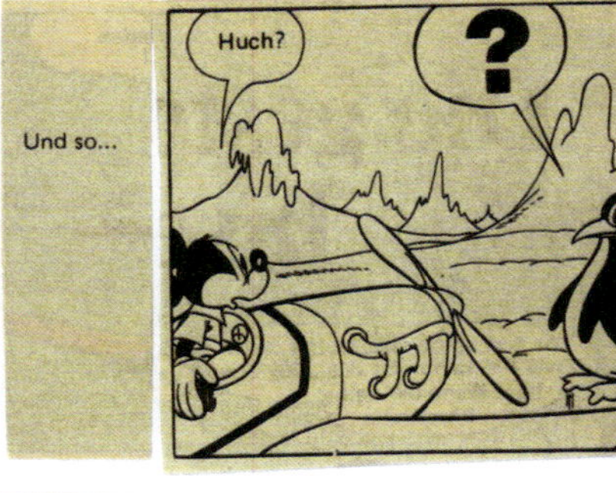

Und so...
Huch?
?

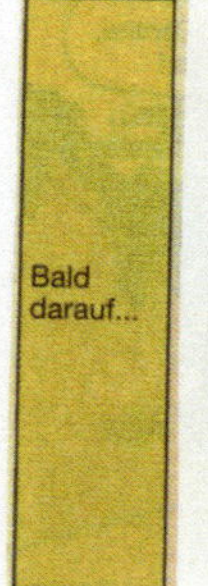

Bald darauf...

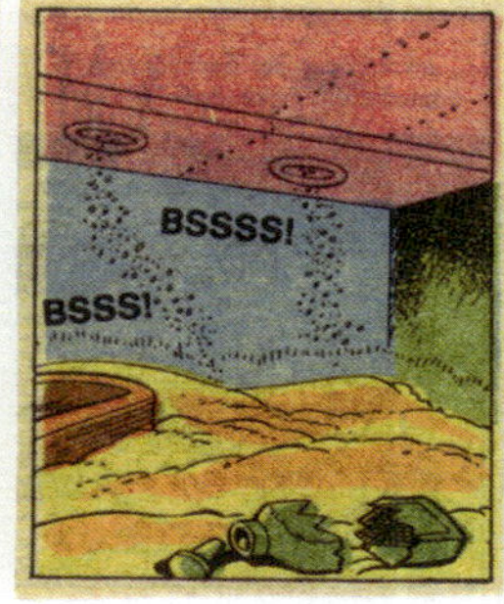

BSSSS!
BSSS!

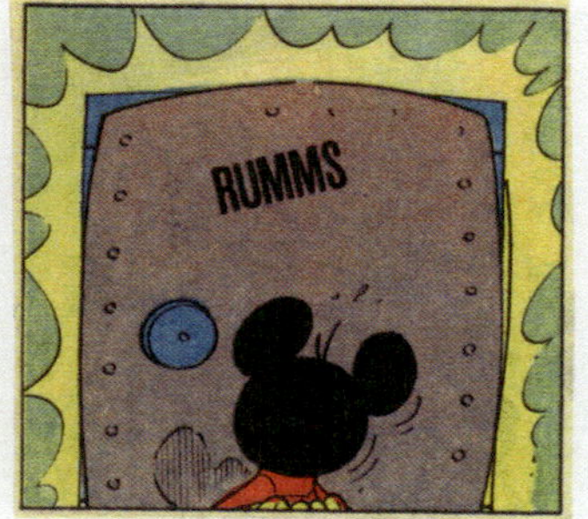

RUMMS

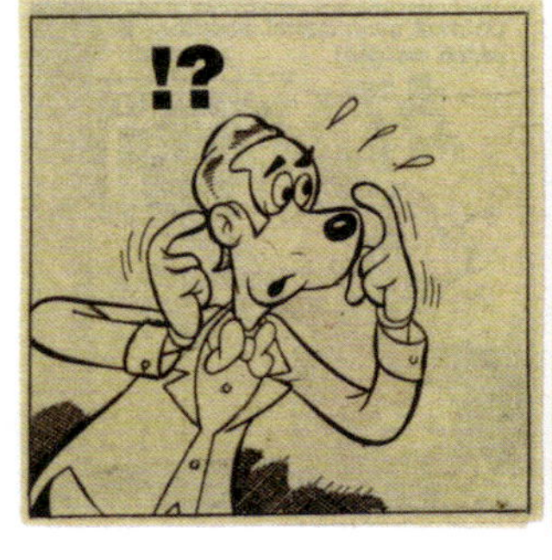

!?

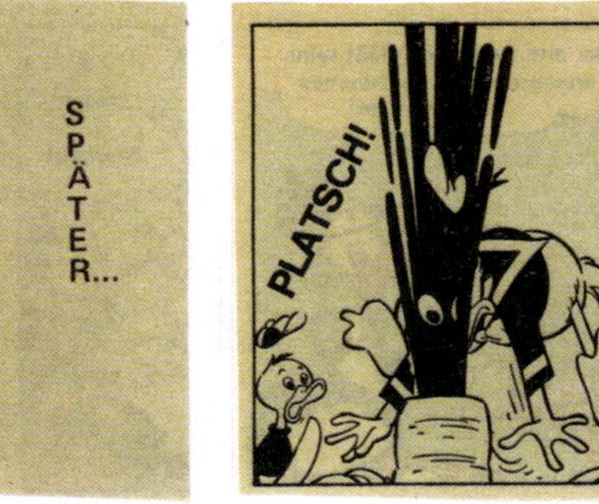

SPÄTER...
PLATSCH!

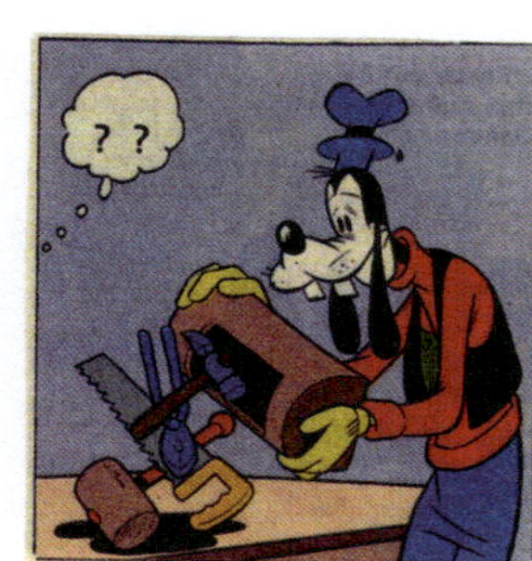

??

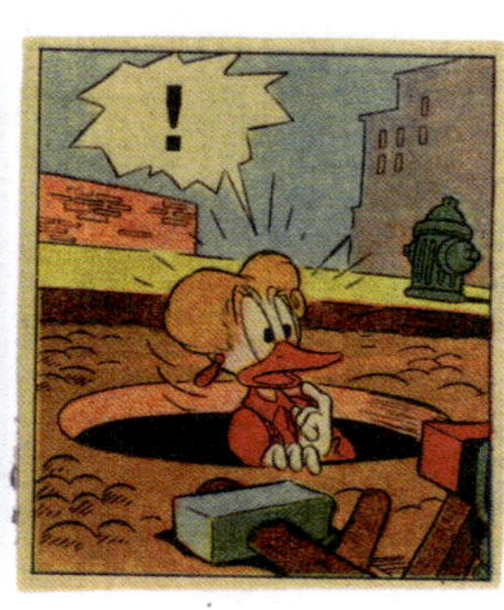

!

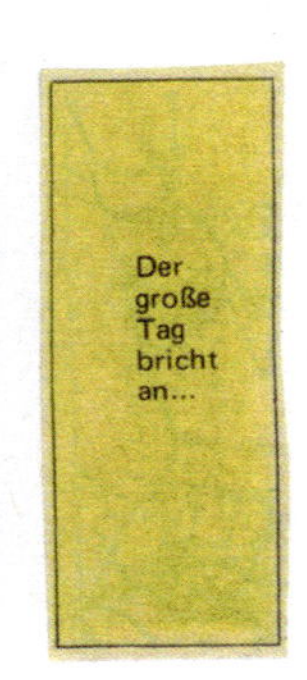

Der große Tag bricht an...

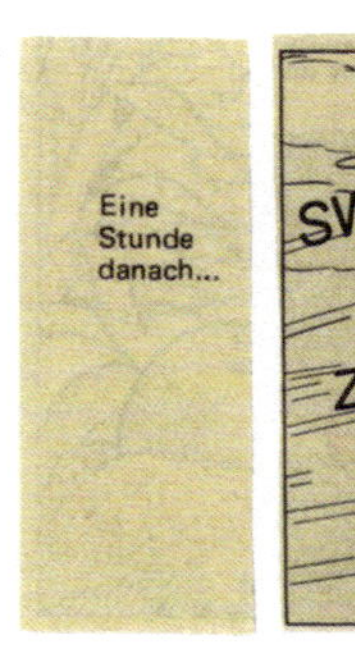

Eine Stunde danach...

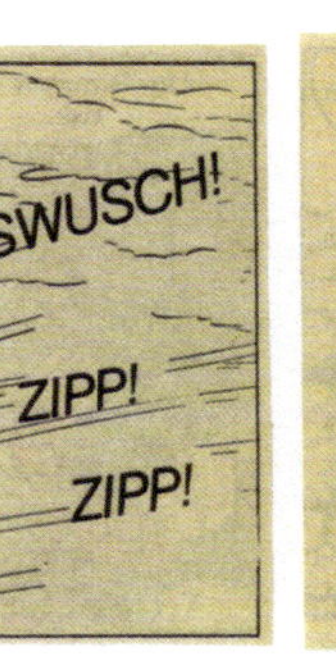

SWUSCH!
ZIPP!
ZIPP!

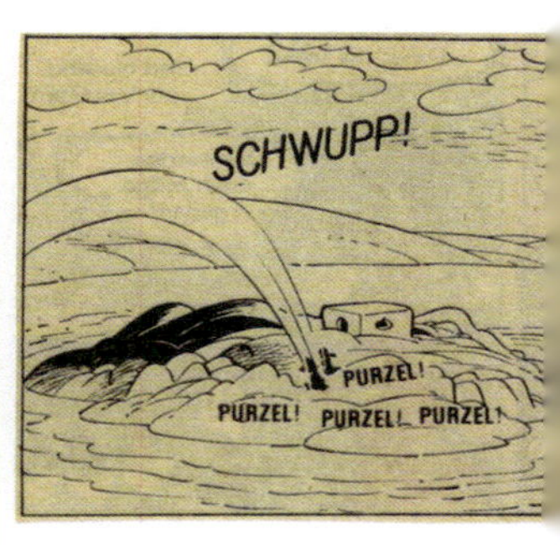

In der Zwischen-zeit...
SCHWUPP!
PURZEL!
PURZEL! PURZEL! PURZEL!

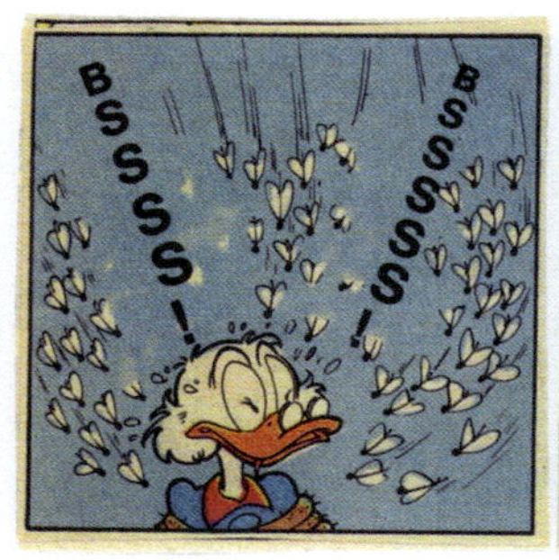

BSSSS!
BSSSS!

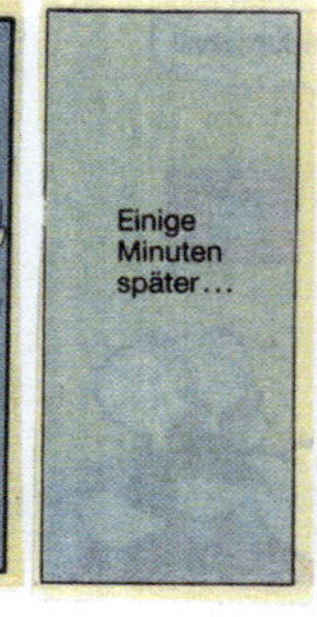

Einige Minuten später...

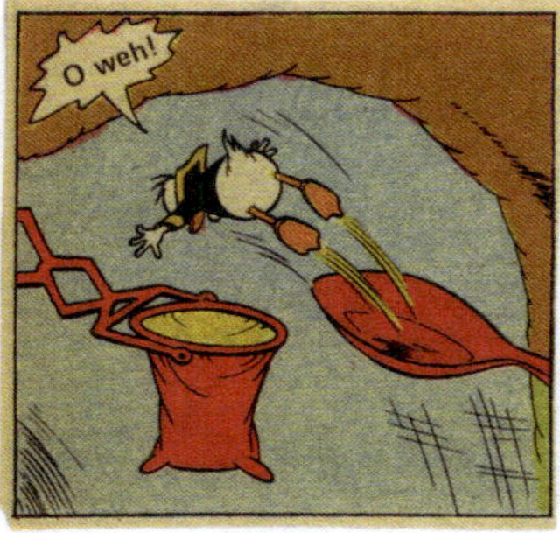

O weh!

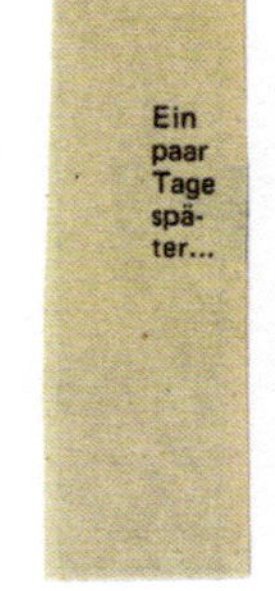

Ein paar Tage spä-ter...

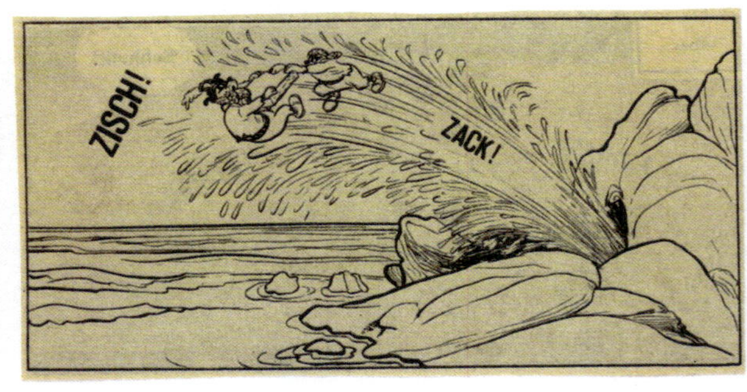

ZISCH!
ZACK!

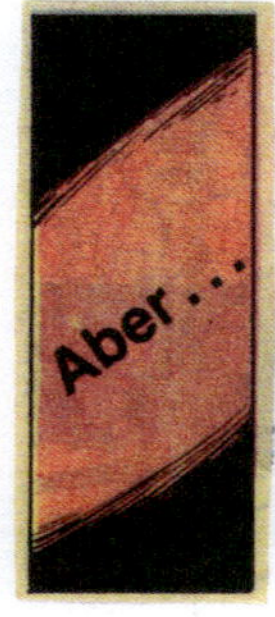

Aber...

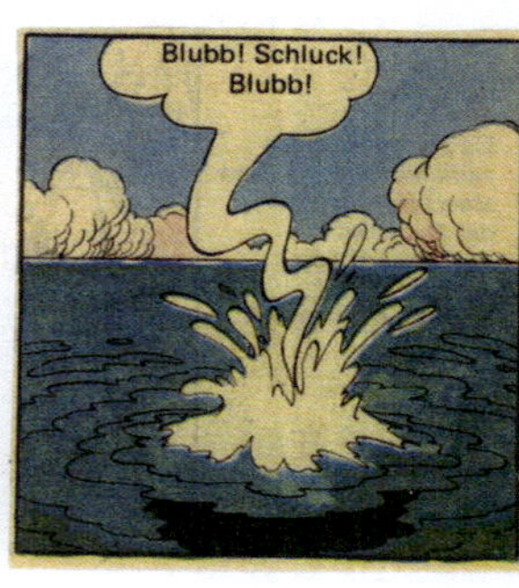

Blubb! Schluck!
Blubb!

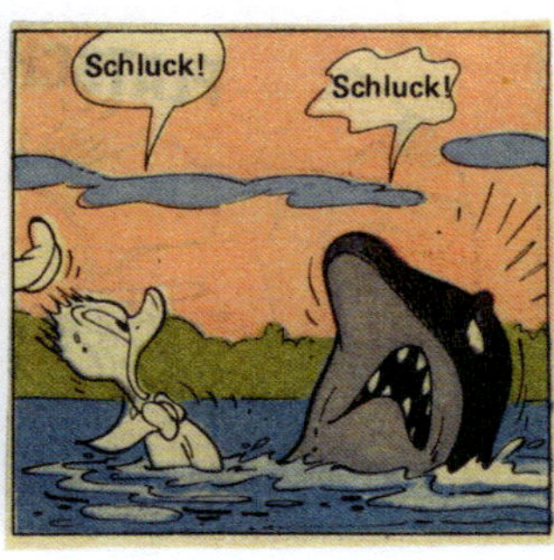

Schluck!
Schluck!

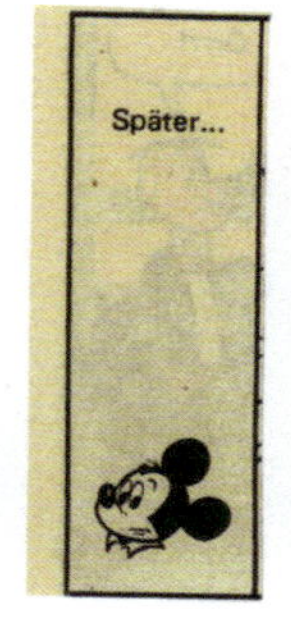

Später...

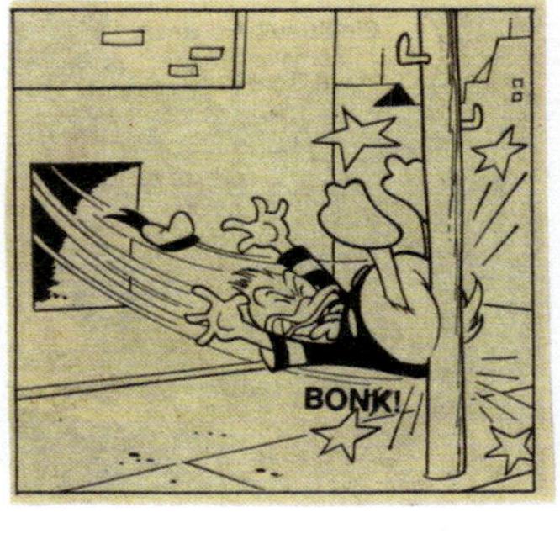

BONK!

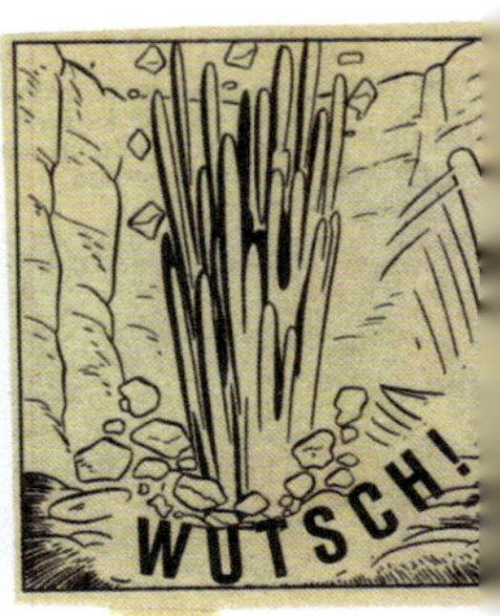

WUTSCH!

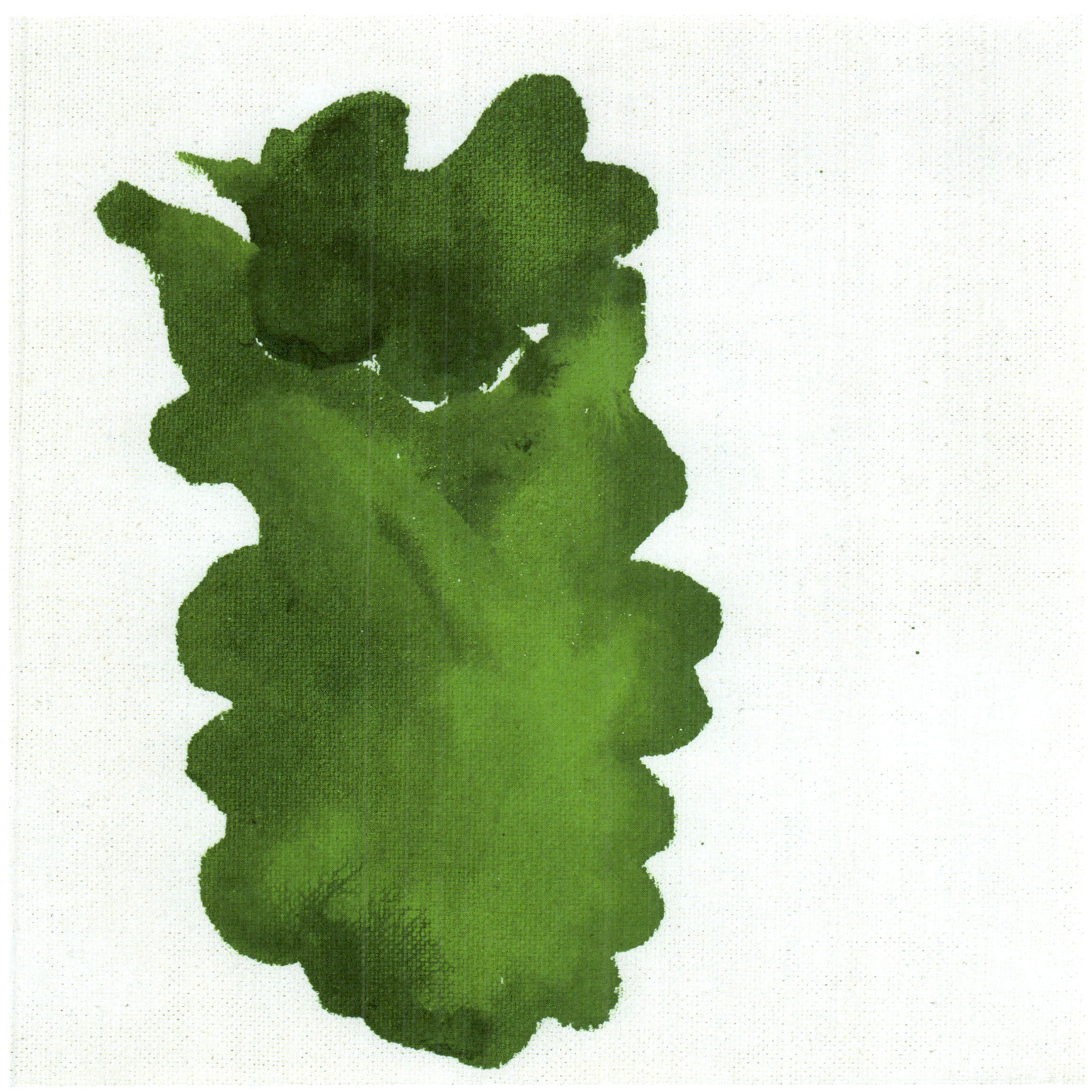

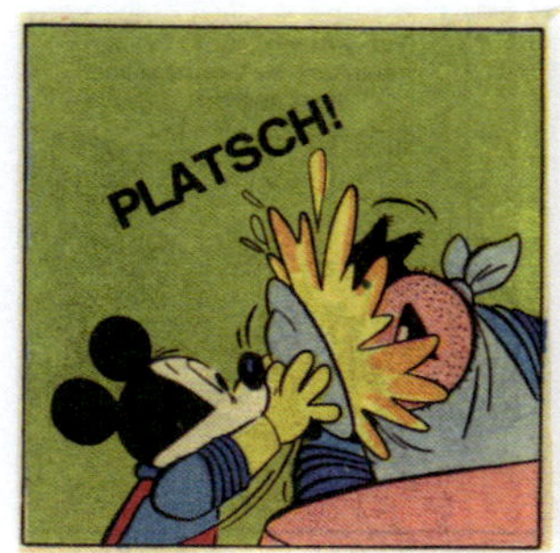

PLATSCH!

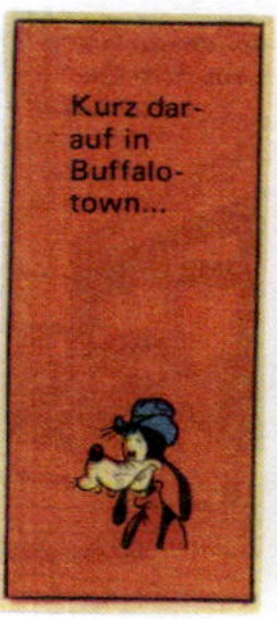

Kurz dar-
auf in
Buffalo-
town...

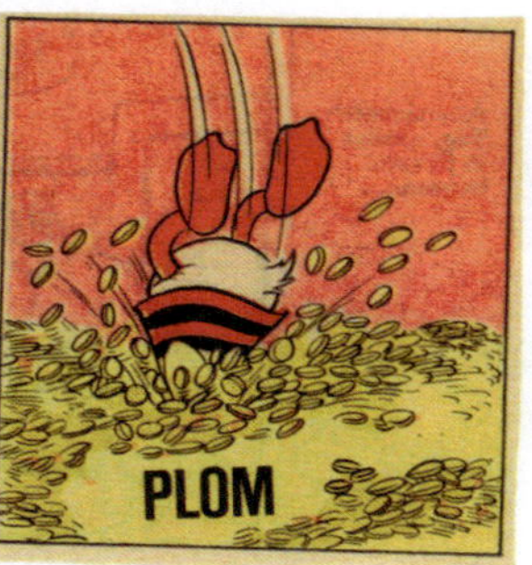

PLOM

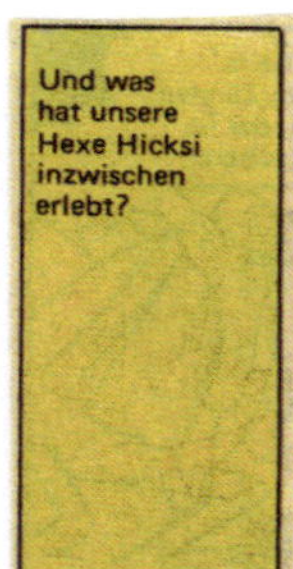

Und was
hat unsere
Hexe Hicksi
inzwischen
erlebt?

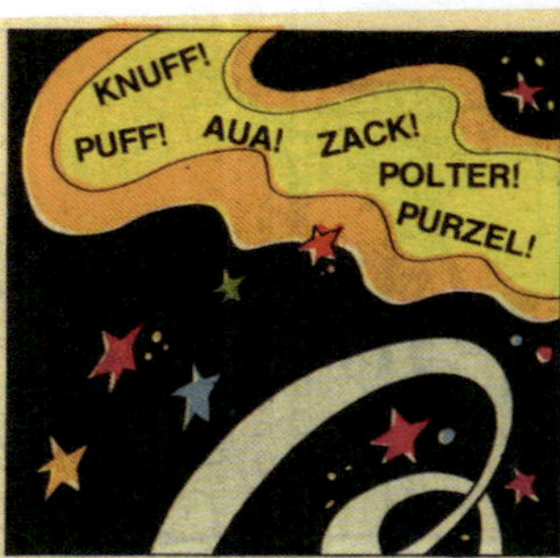

KNUFF!
PUFF! AUA! ZACK!
POLTER!
PURZEL!

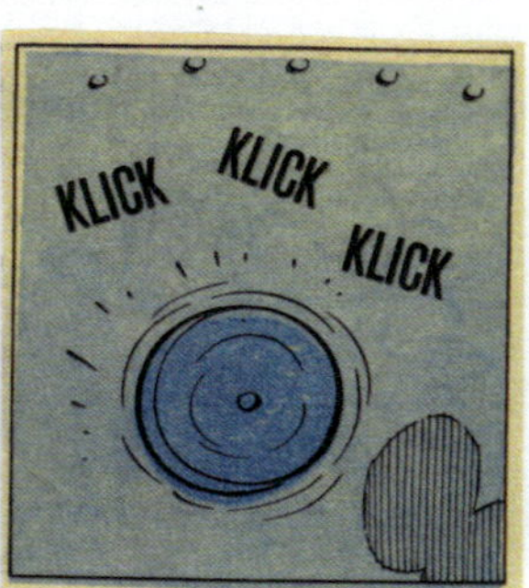

KLICK KLICK
KLICK

Später...

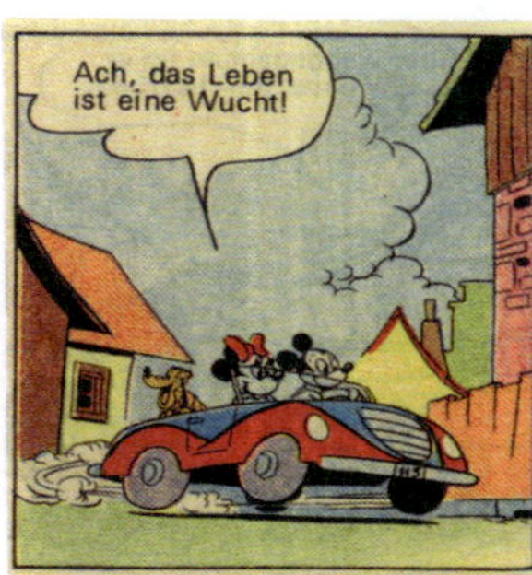

Ach, das Leben
ist eine Wucht!

ENDE

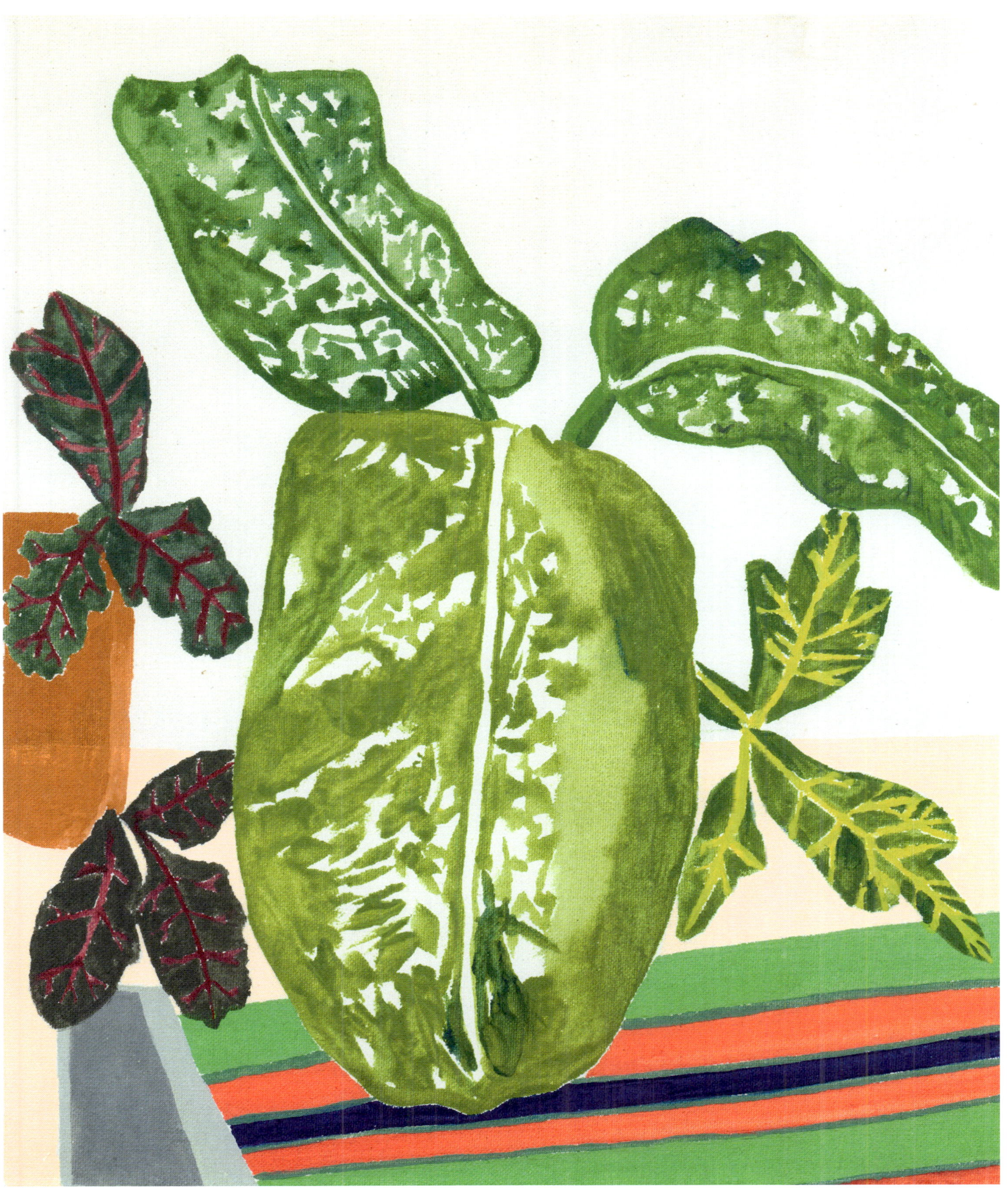

NASS UND UNBEUGSAM

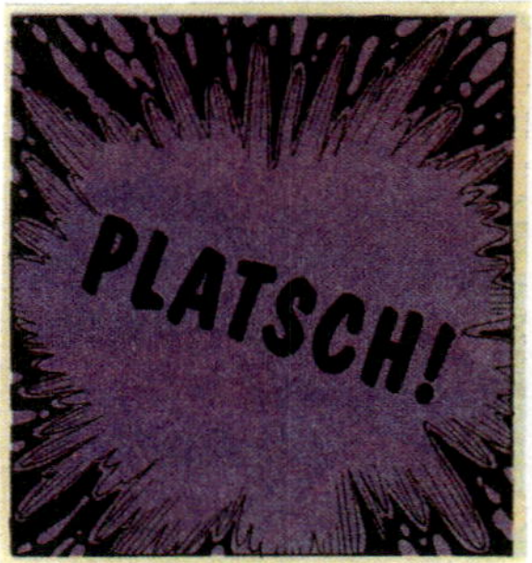

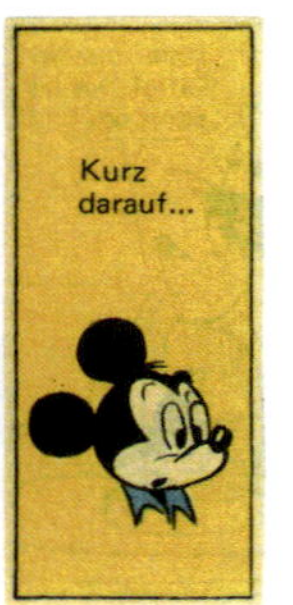

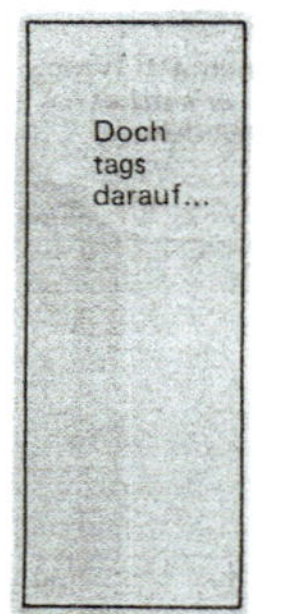

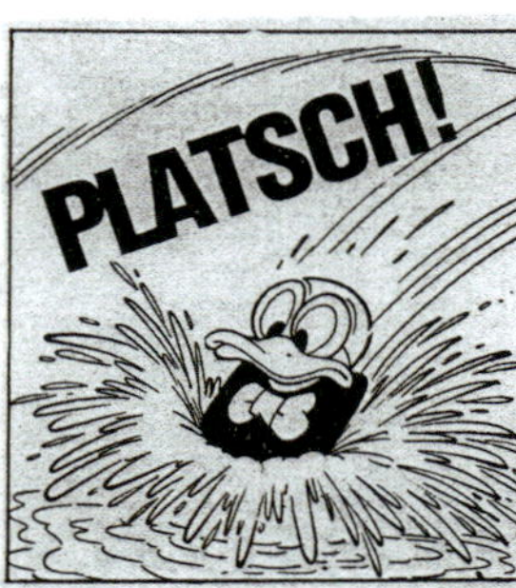

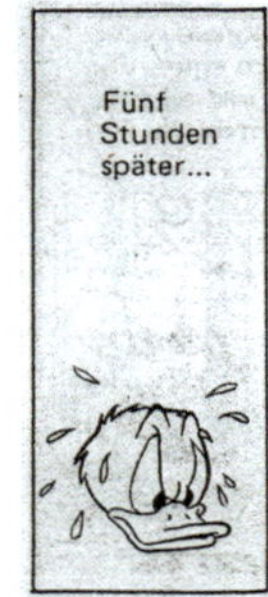

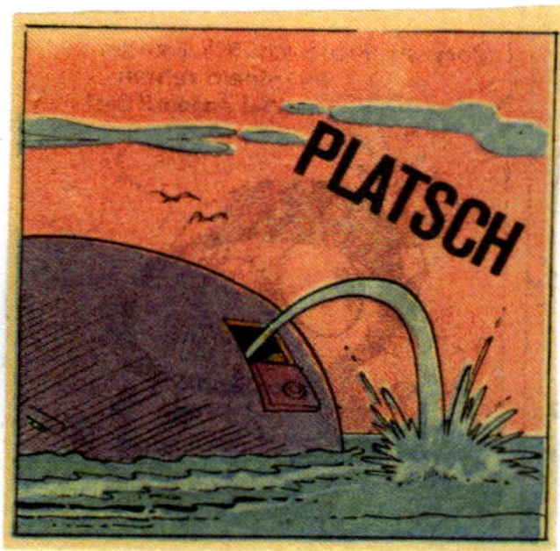

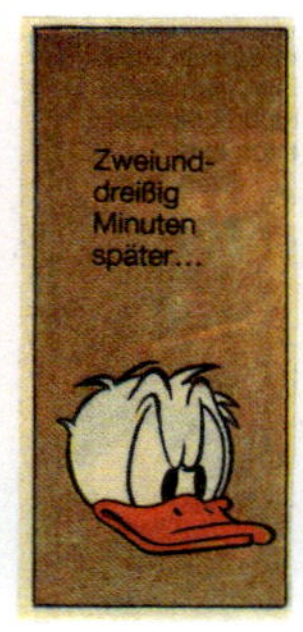

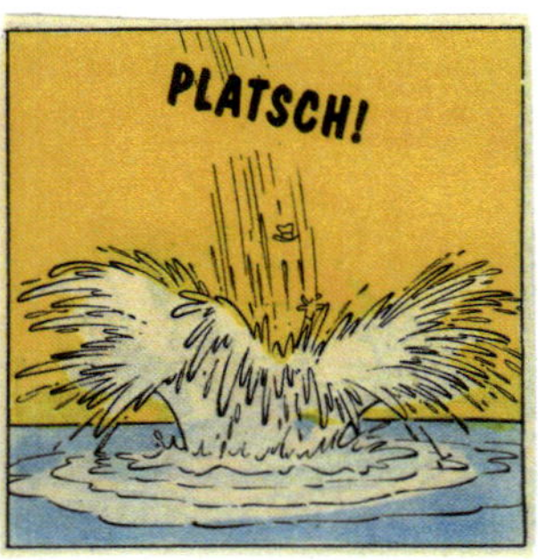

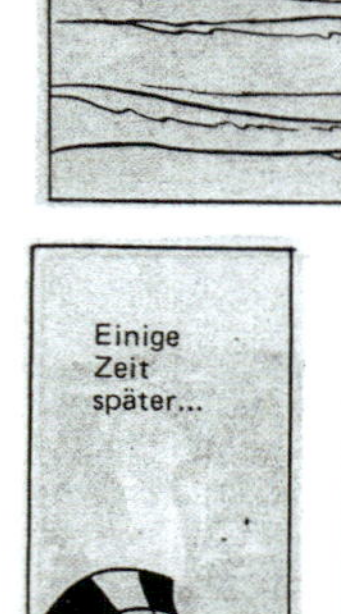

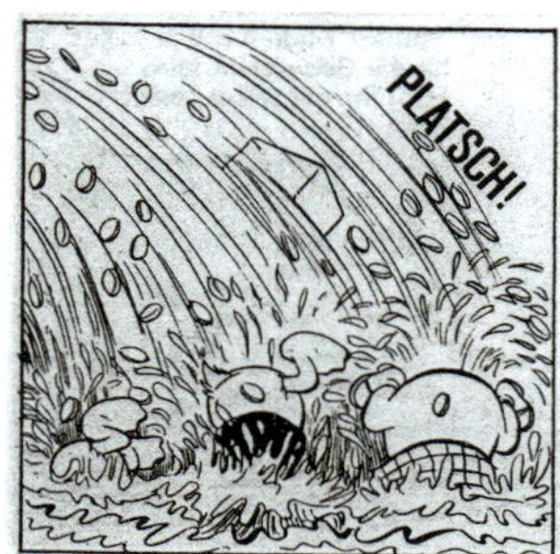

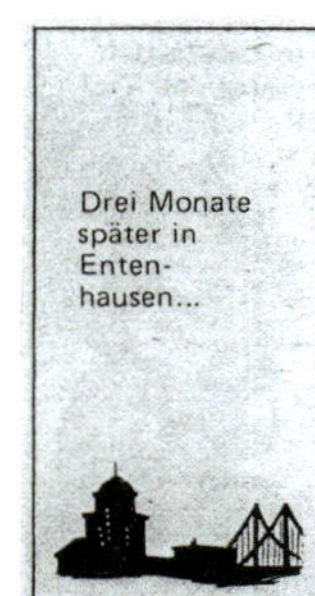

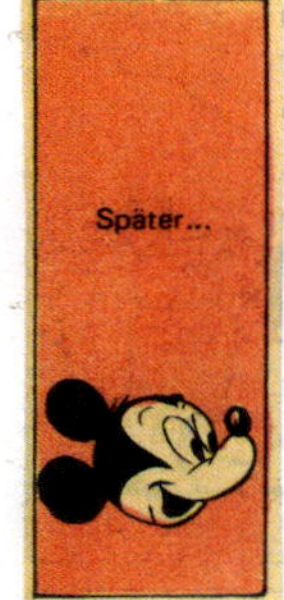

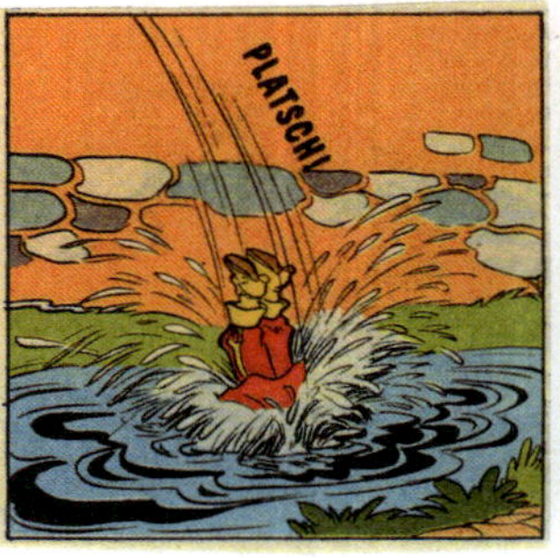

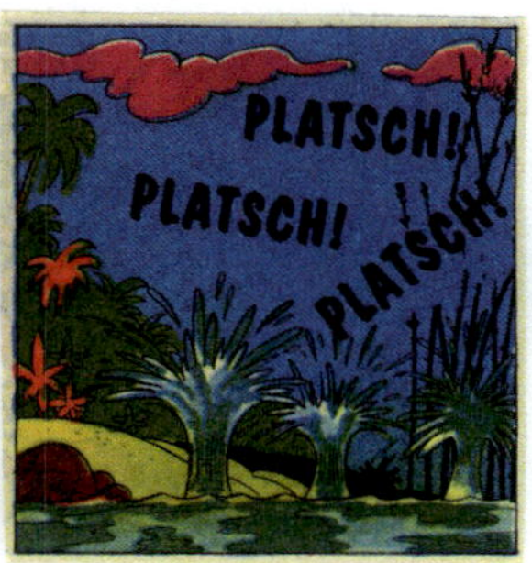

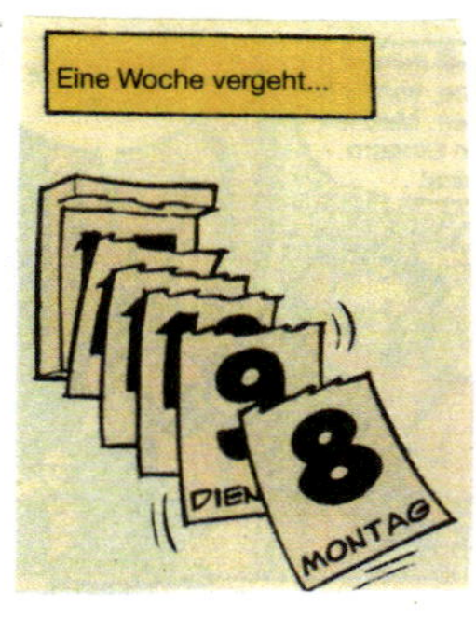

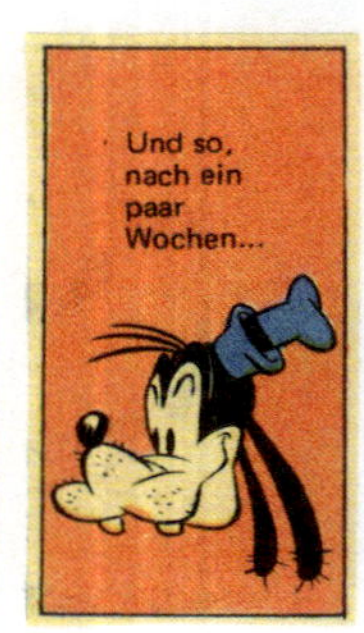

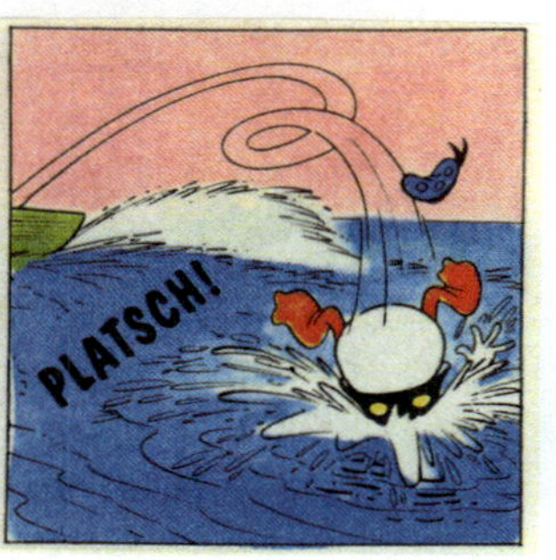

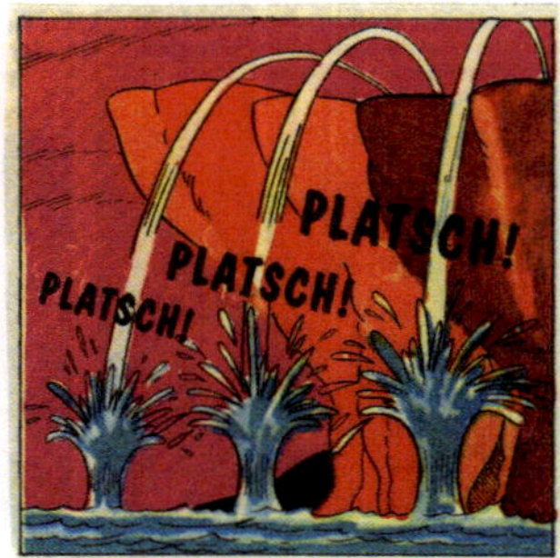

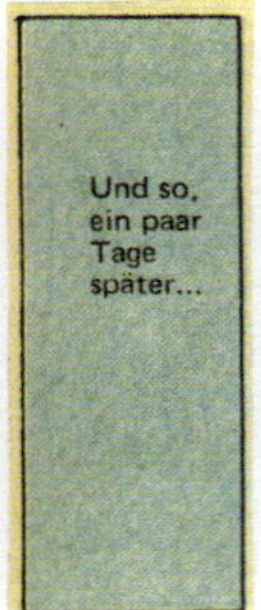

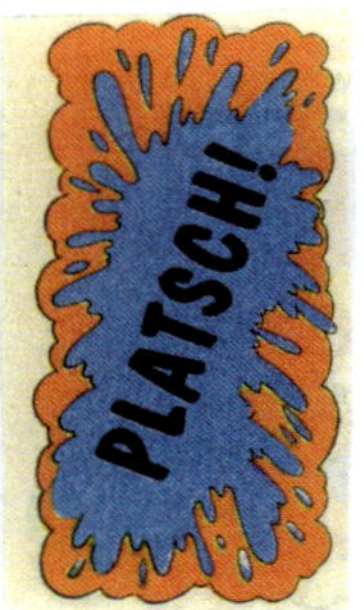

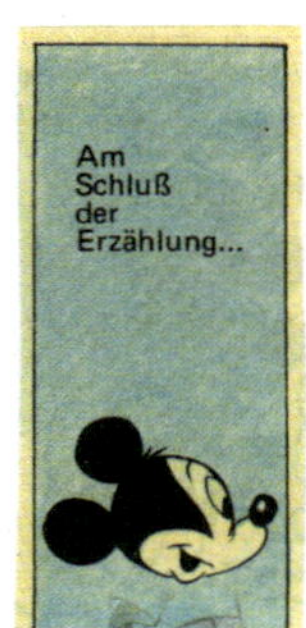

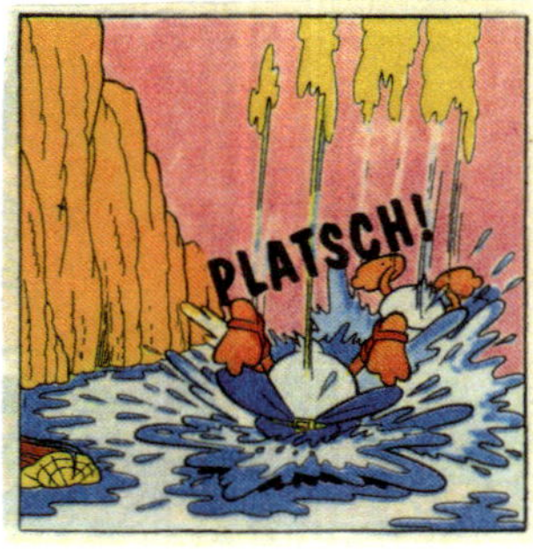

ENDE

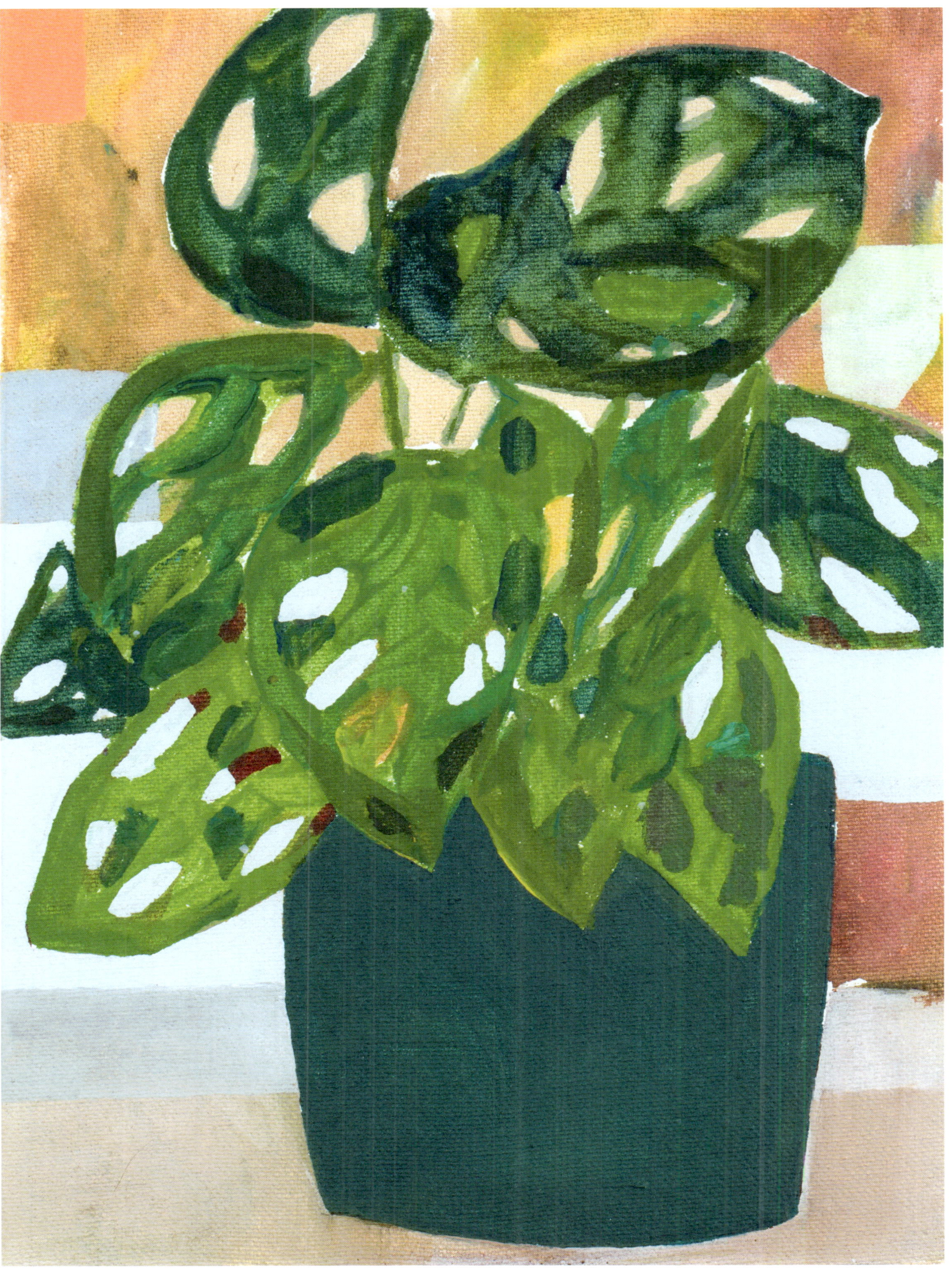

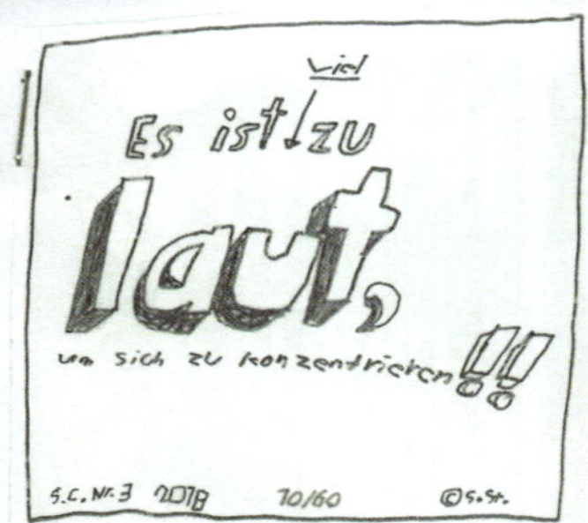

Es ist viel zu laut,
um sich zu konzentrieren!!
S.C. Nr. 3 2018   70/60   © S.S.

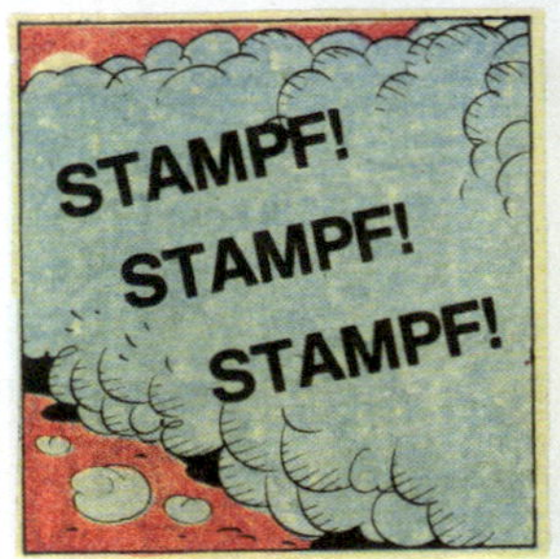

STAMPF!
STAMPF!
STAMPF!

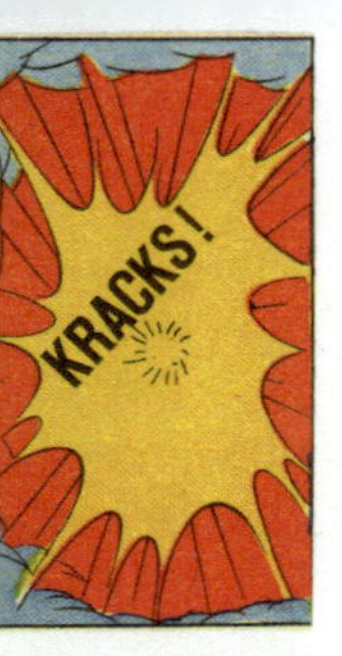

KRACKS!

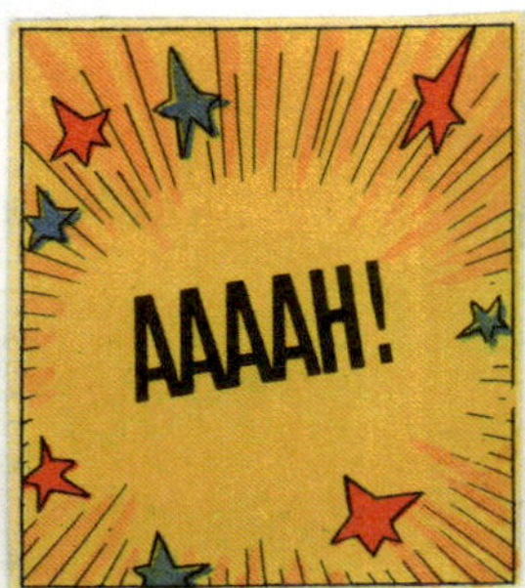

AAAAH!

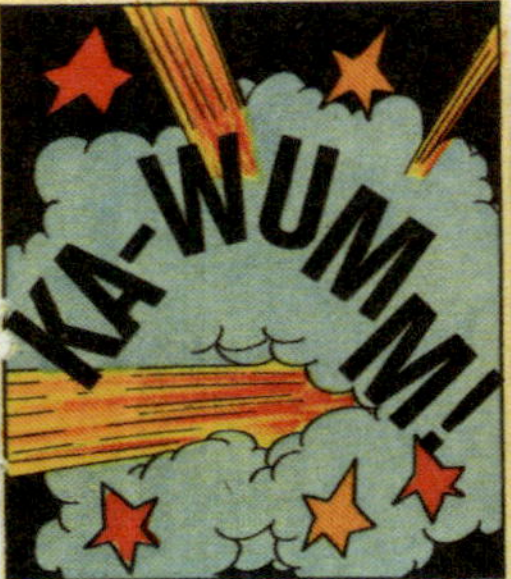

KA-WUMM!

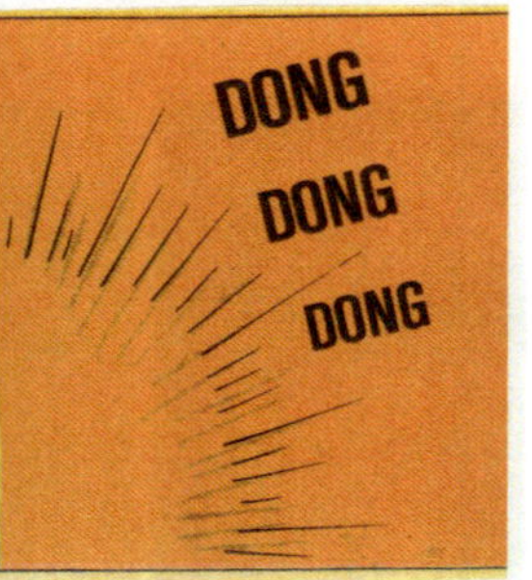

DONG
DONG
DONG

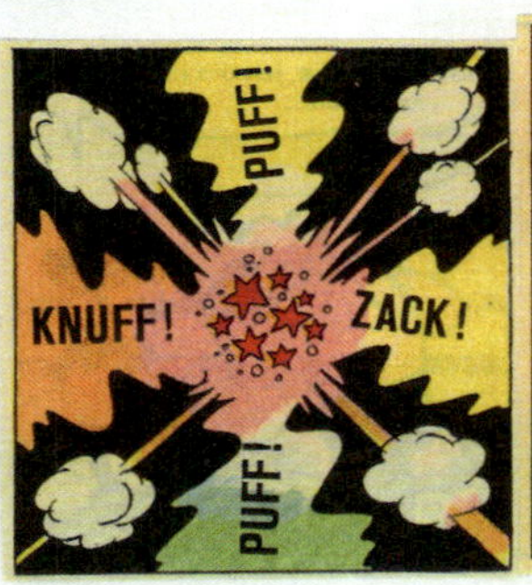

PUFF!
KNUFF!
ZACK!
PUFF!

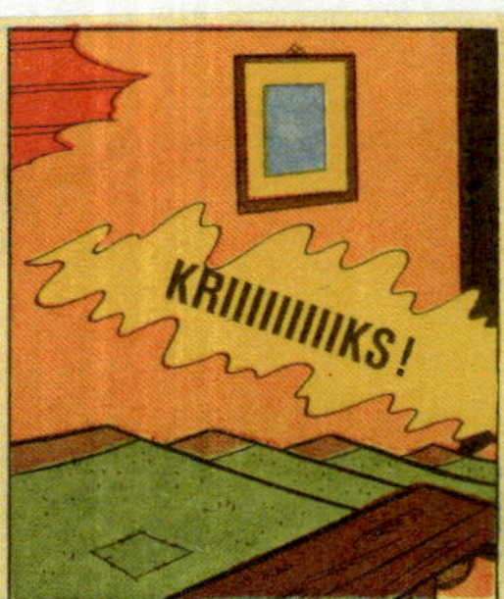

KRIIIIIIIIKS!

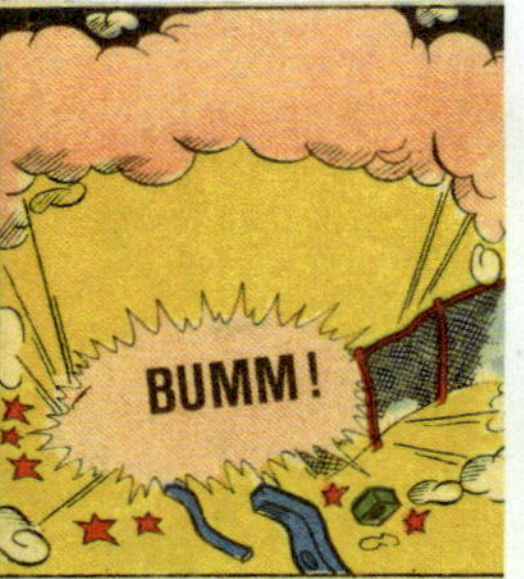

BUMM!

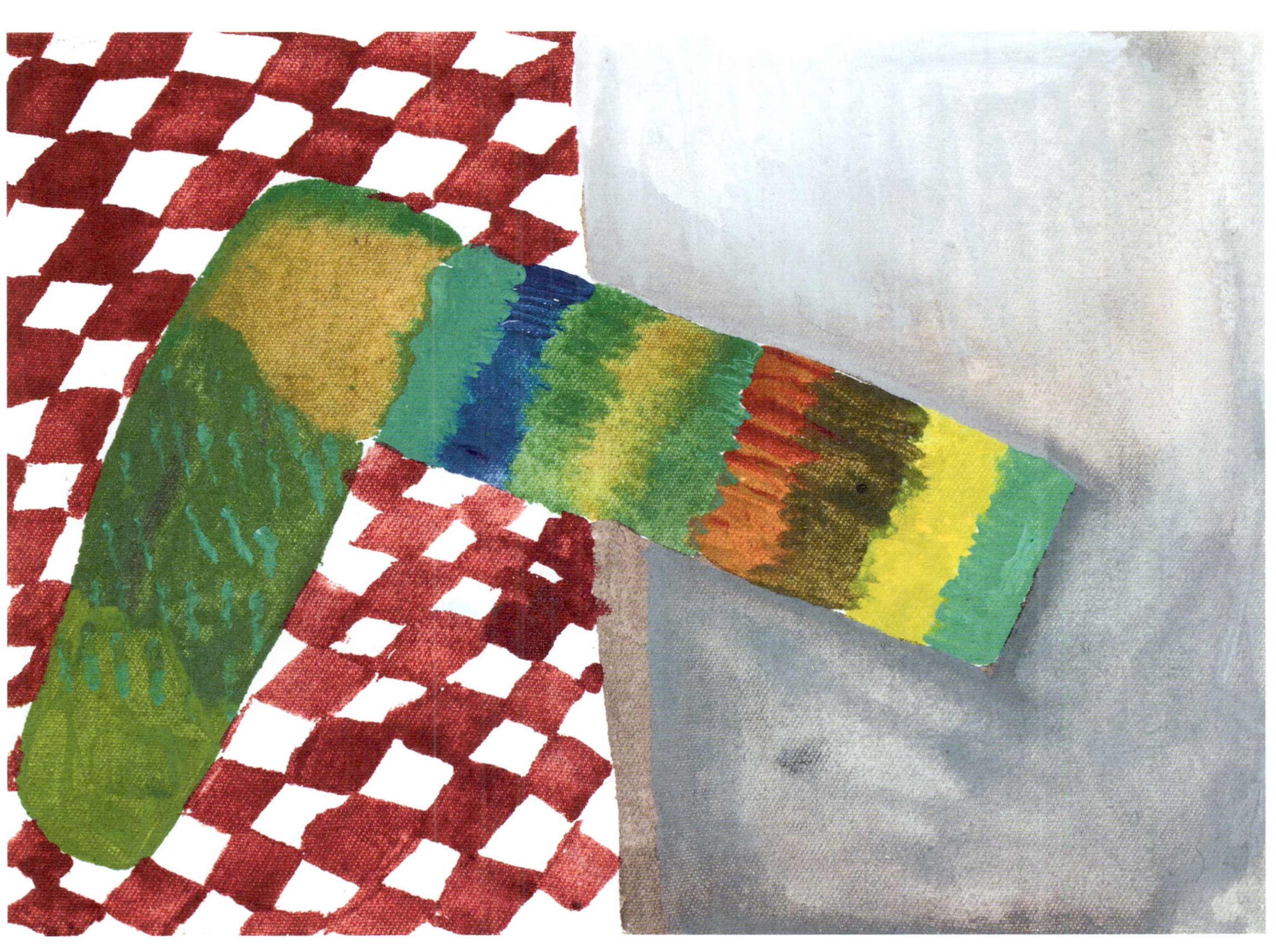

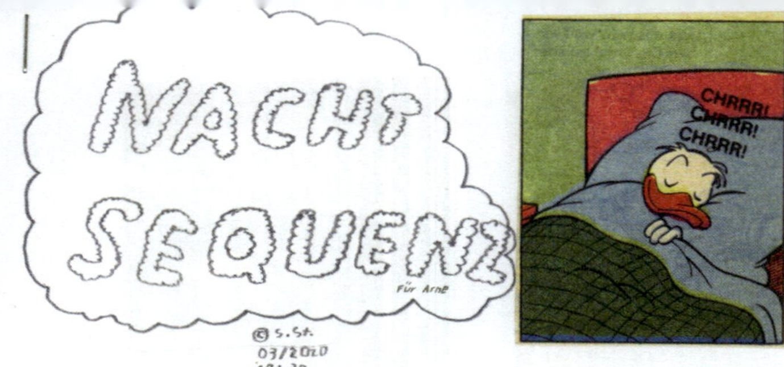

NACHT
SEQUENZ
für Arne
© S.St.
03/2020
CHRRR!
CHRRR!
CHRRR!

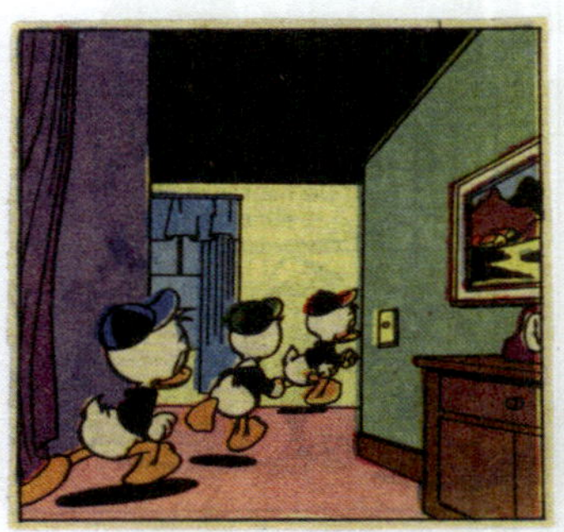

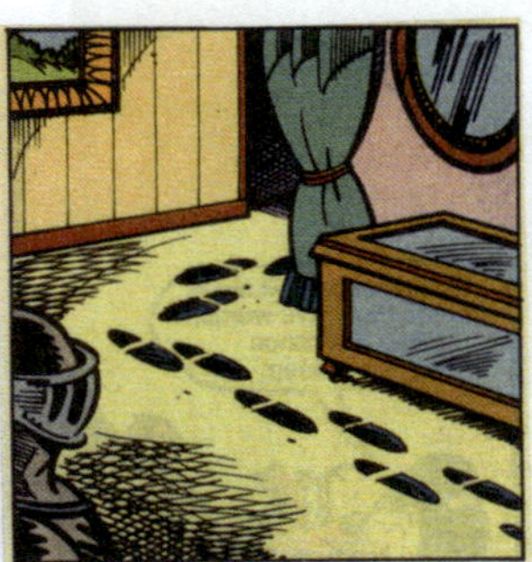

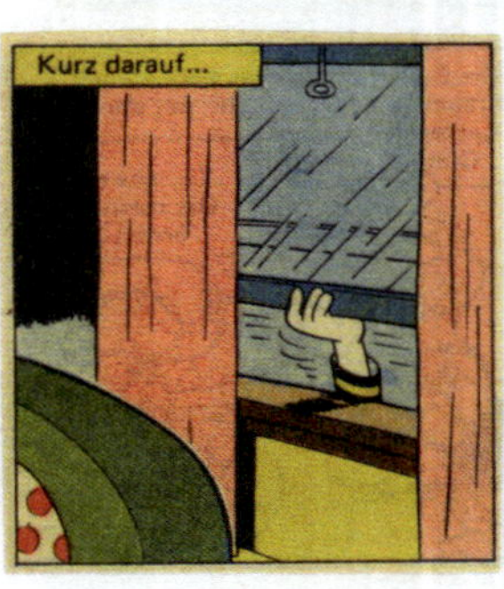

Kurz darauf...

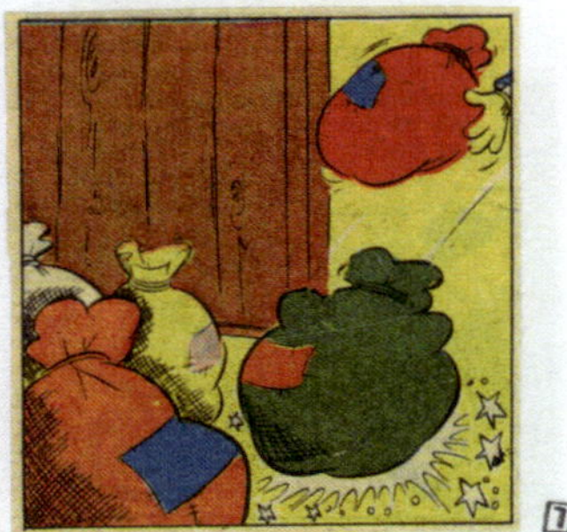

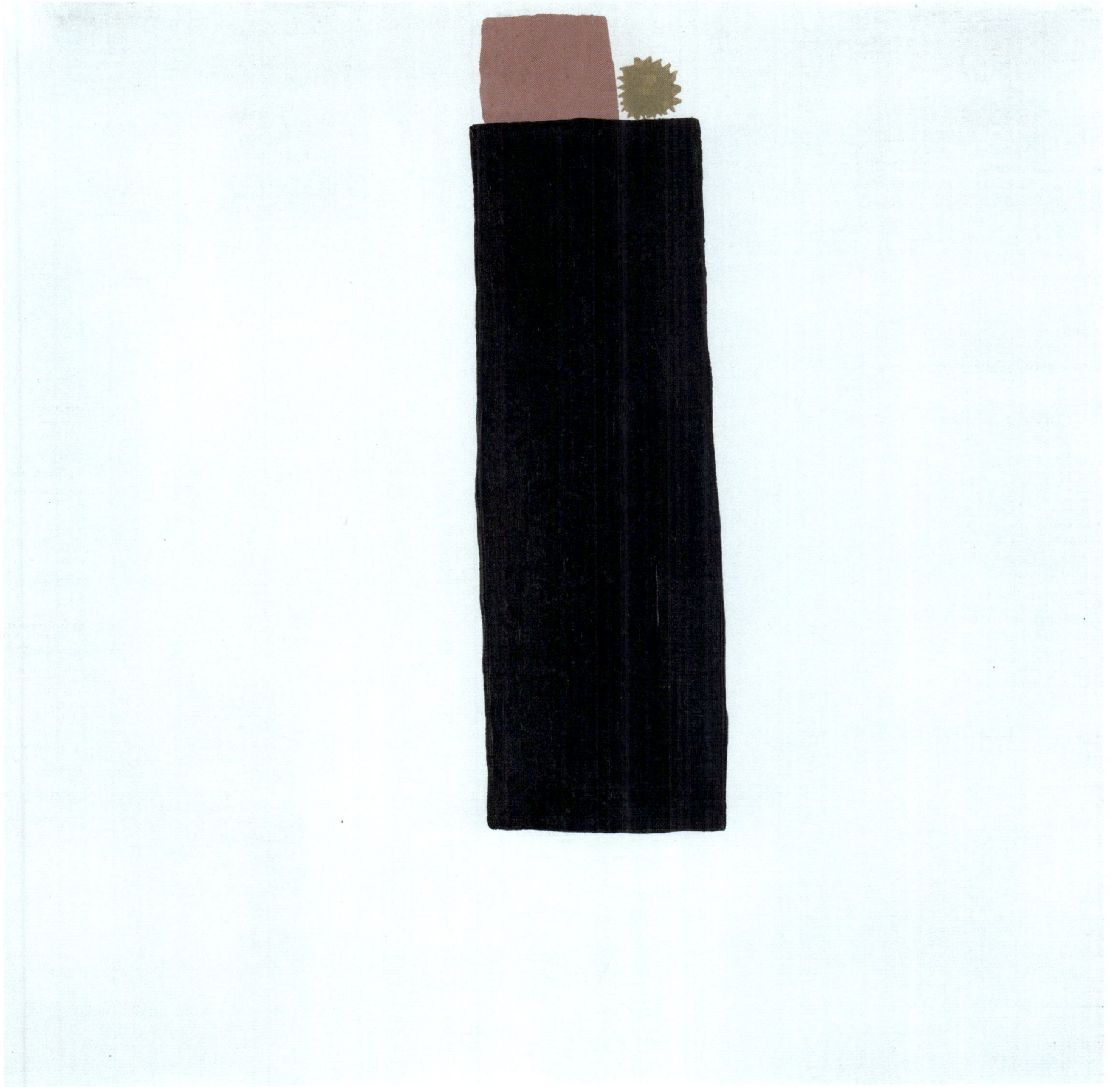

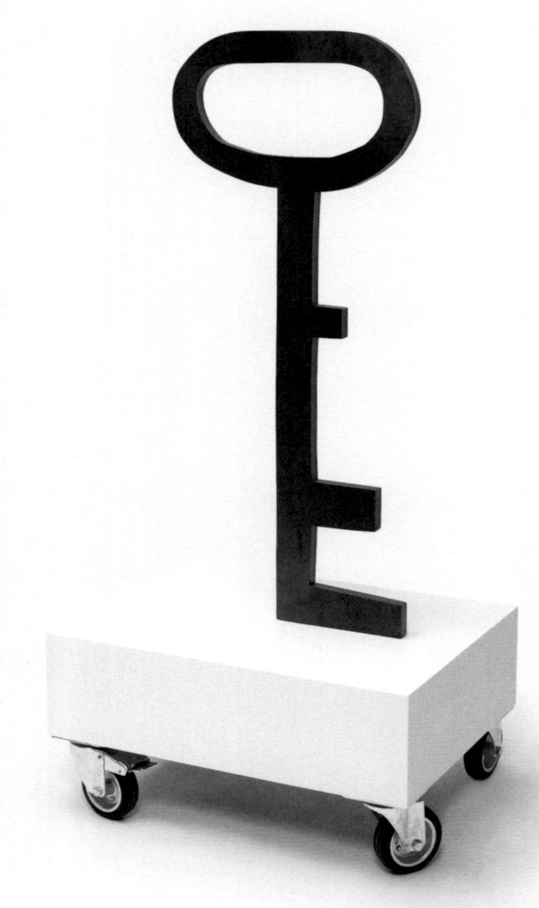

machi   alles.   12:58

bini auf heimweg.   14:43

nun zug. dann einkaufen. dann heim.   14:44

hab kein geld mit.   15:03

komme jetzt heim.   15:04

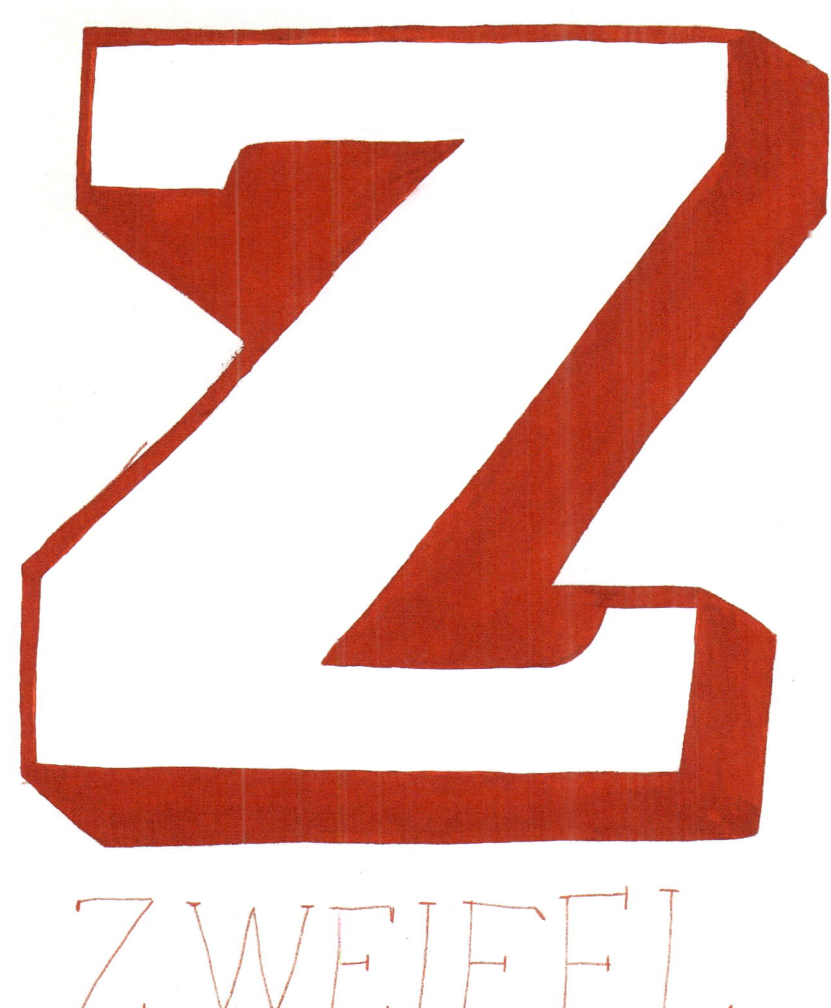

ZWEIFEL

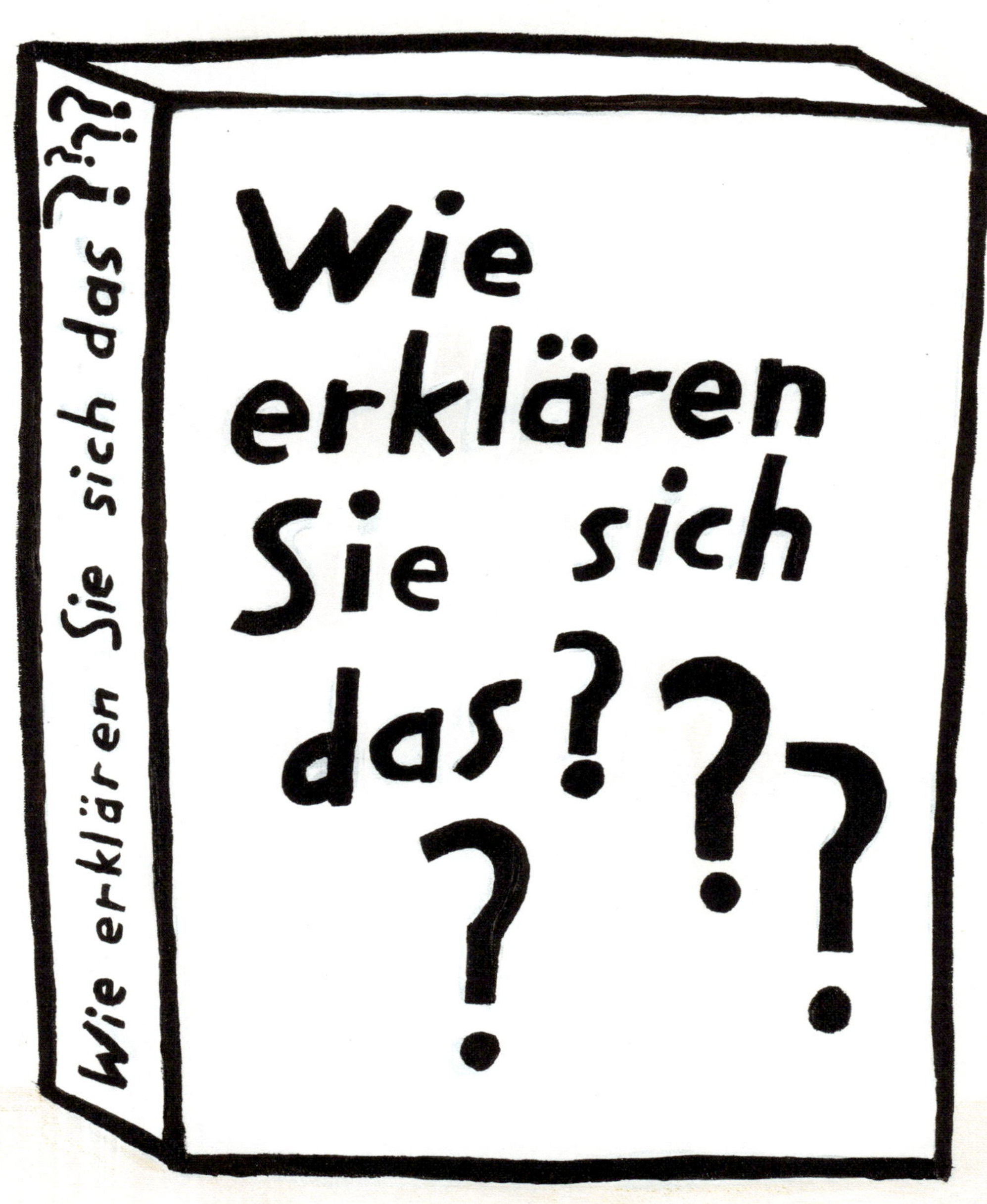

Wie erklären Sie sich das ???
Wie erklären Sie sich das ? ? ? ?

Erbsen, Bücher, Wollsocken und andere
Herzensdinge

Eveline Suter

*Das Ding mit seiner Verlässlichkeit
sorgt dafür, dass der Mensch Fuss
fasst auf der Erde.*[1]

Sereina Steinemann zeigt in ihren Werken
unsere Welt, Dinge im weitesten Sinne,
den Alltag, die Normalität. Das ist an sich
nichts Aussergewöhnliches in der Kunst.
Stillleben sind seit jeher eine Gattung der
Malerei und die Pop-Art hat plakativ die
Objekte des modernen Alltags in den Fokus
genommen.

Ab Mitte der 1950er-Jahre entwickelt
sich die Pop-Art inspiriert von der Werbung, die mit der Ausbildung der Konsum-
gesellschaft immer mehr öffentlichen
Raum einnimmt. Konsumgüter und die Bild-
sprache der Werbung werden zu Themen
von Malerei und Skulptur. Richard Hamiltons
Collage *Just what is it that makes today's
homes so different, so appealing?*[2] gilt
als Ikone der Pop-Art und als ihre Namens-
patin. Für den Katalog der Ausstellung
This is Tomorrow in der Whitechapel Gallery
collagierte der britische Künstler einen
Muskelprotz mit Lollipop-Tennisschläger
in ein Wohnzimmer. Programmatisch sind
dabei nicht nur der Titel, der direkt einen
Werbetext zitiert, und die Beschriftung
«Pop» auf dem Lutscher, sondern auch viele
weitere Gegenstände, die Hamilton mehrheitlich Anzeigen entnommen hat. Hoover-
Staubsauger, Fernseher, Comic-Magazin
oder das Bild der Erde aus dem Welt-
raum stehen für das Lebensgefühl der Zeit,
das von Optimismus und Fortschritts-
glauben geprägt ist. Richard Hamilton
sagte, sein Ziel sei es, «das ganze Leben»
in seinem Werk einzufangen.

Auch Sereina Steinemann fängt unser
Leben ein und arbeitet unter anderem
wie die Künstler*innen der Pop-Art mit bild-
lichen sowie textlichen Werbebotschaf-
ten. So spiegelt ihre Serie *Qualität ist unsere Stärke* (Abb. S. 11–23, 28–34, 67–69,
93–97) den typischen Werbejargon wider.
Die Künstlerin hat die Botschaften allerdings so abstrahiert, dass die Zeichnungen
weniger auf die Produkte verweisen als
auf die impliziten Versprechungen und die
Sehnsüchte, die angesprochen werden.
Richard Hamilton hat 1957 eine Liste mit
den Attributen der Pop-Art erstellt: po-
pulär (für ein Massenpublikum entworfen),
schnelllebig (temporäre Lösung), ent-
behrlich (schnell vergessen), billig, in Massenproduktion hergestellt, jung (an die
Jugend gerichtet), witzig, sexy, effekthascherisch, glamourös, Big Business.[3] Der Ver-
gleich mit dieser Liste zeigt, dass Sereina
Steinemanns Umgang mit dem Alltag und
ihr Blick auf dessen Objekte in vielerlei Hin-
sicht anders ist.

Sereina Steinemanns Werke sind
weder besonders sexy noch glamourös. Im
Zentrum steht vielmehr liebevoll Handge-

machtes, in Bezug auf die Objekte ebenso
wie auf die Darstellungsweise. Durch die
unprätentiöse, bewusst einfache Malweise
erhalten Massenwaren wie eine Coop-
City-Plastiktasche (Abb. S. 133) oder Coca-
Cola-Flasche (Abb. S. 62) einen eigenen,
individuellen Charme und aus dem Saum
der Louis-Vuitton-Hose läuft die Farbe
(Abb. S. 26). Mit dem Zweifel-Chips-Logo
thematisiert die Künstlerin die eigene male-
rische Unsicherheit (Abb. S. 147).

Sereina Steinemanns Werke sind nicht
schnelllebig. Sie erzählen nicht von Flüch-
tigkeit, sondern von Zuwendung, von der
Hinwendung zum Dargestellten, zum Einfachen, zu einer Erbsenschote, einer Tas-
se, einer Socke. Die Art und Weise, wie die
Künstlerin den simplen Dingen Aufmerk-
samkeit und Beachtung schenkt, verleiht
ihnen Bedeutung. Die Konzentration auf
meist nur ein Objekt entschleunigt. «Das
kontemplative Verweilen bei den Dingen,
das absichtslose Sehen» bezeichnet Byung-
Chul Han in seiner kritischen Auseinan-
dersetzung mit der Konsum- und Informa-
tionsgesellschaft als «eine Formel des
Glücks»[4]. Er erläutert, dass die Dinge erst,
wenn sie von ihrer Nützlichkeit und damit
von ihrem Warencharakter befreit sind,
Herzensdinge sein können. Herzensdinge
ermöglichen als Übergangsobjekte einen
Zugang zur Welt, eine Begegnung mit dem
anderen und «sind Ruhepole des Lebens,
die dieses stabilisieren».[5] Eine einzelne ge-
ringelte, vermutlich handgestrickte Woll-
socke (Abb. S. 141) ist ein solches Ding, das
nur noch wenig Nutzen hat, aber sehr
viele Geschichten birgt, sehr viel Leben ent-
hält und erzählt. «Zuwenden» ist ebenso
Fokussierung wie körperliche Bewegung,
verstärkt noch in «zuneigen» und von
da fehlt nicht mehr viel zu «ins Herz schliessen».

Sereina Steinemanns Werke sind
nicht effekthascherisch. Weder die Werke
selbst noch die dargestellten Objekte
sind glatt und makellos. Sie sind weit entfernt von der perfekten Illusion barocker
holländischer Stillleben und die Vögel wür-
den wohl nicht an Sereina Steinemanns
Kirschen picken, wie sie es gemäss der
Legende an Zeuxis' Trauben getan haben.[6]
Gerade die fehlende Virtuosität macht
Sereina Steinemanns Werke treffsicher:
Sie treffen ein Gefühl, sie berühren. Dass
Misslingen produktiv sein und Spass
machen kann, zeigt auch ihre Serie *Heute
gelingt mir nichts* (Abb. S. 101–109) –
charmanter scheitern ist nicht möglich.

Die Pop-Art als Erscheinung der 1950er-
und 1960er-Jahren reflektiert den wirt-
schaftlichen Boom und das Wachstum in
der Nachkriegszeit. Der Konsum und seine
Güter werden meist affirmativ ins Bild ge-
setzt. Der Ausstellungstitel *This is Tomorrow*
ist typisch für den ungebrochenen Fort-
schrittsglauben jener Jahre. Dem heutigen
Lebensgefühl fehlt diese Gewissheit ge-
genüber der Zukunft, Wachstum und Fort-
schritt sind nicht mehr nur positiv konno-
tiert. Vielleicht haftet deshalb Sereina
Steinemanns Werken auf den ersten Blick
eine gewisse Nostalgie an. Für ihre Hefte
(Abb. S. 128–142) – oft Bildkombinationen aus
alten «Lustigen Taschenbüchern» – nutzt
sie den Fotokopierer. Die Socke wirkt,
als hätte sie die Grossmutter gestrickt, die

Schlüssel (Abb. S. 58) wiegen mit ihren
Ringen und Bärten schwer und die ersten
Skulpturen in Sereina Steinemanns Werk
sind von altmodischen, figürlichen Tafeln
inspiriert, vom überdimensionalen Croissant,
das während der Öffnungszeiten vor der
Bäckerei steht, oder vom Riesen-Glacé vor
der Gelateria. So sind auch Sereina Steinemanns Schlüssel (Abb. S. 144) mobil und
stehen nicht immer an derselben Stelle
im Ausstellungsraum. Oder werden sie sogar über Nacht weggeräumt? Dabei sind
Sereina Steinemanns Werke durchaus im
Heute verankert und nicht rückwärts-
gewandt. Es ist die Hinwendung zum Un-
spektakulären, zu einfachen Lösungen und
zum Handgemachten, die nostalgische
Gefühle in uns weckt.

Sereina Steinemanns Werke erzählen
eher von Handwerk und Handarbeit als
von Massenproduktion, auch wenn sie zeit-
genössische Massenprodukte und Werbe-
slogans aufgreifen. Selbst wenn die Künstlerin einen Chat-Dialog vom Mobiltelefon
auf die Leinwand überträgt (Abb. S. 145):
Die Malweise erdet die digitale Kommunika-
tion im Analogen, im Dinglichen von Leinwand und Farbe, in der Handarbeit mit dem
Pinsel. Insofern setzen Sereina Steinemanns Werke einen Kontrapunkt zu Byung-
Chul Hans Zeitanalyse «Undinge verdrän-
gen die Dinge»[7]. Sereina Steinemann macht
in ihrem Werk «Undinge» wieder zu Dingen.
Sie tut dies mit Charme und Zuwendung
und lässt uns darüber schmunzeln. Sereina
Steinemanns Werke sind definitiv humor-
voll.

[1] Byung-Chul Han, *Undinge. Umbrüche
der Lebenswelt*, Ullstein, Berlin 2021,
S. 85.
[2] Richard Hamilton, *Just what is it that
makes today's homes so different,
so appealing?* (Was macht die Wohnun-
gen von heute so anders, so anzie-
hend?), 1956, Collage, 26 × 24.8 cm,
Kunsthalle Tübingen.
[3] Richard Hamilton hat die Liste in einem Brief an die Architekt*innen Alison
und Peter Smithson notiert: «Popular
(designed for a mass audience), Transient (short-term solution), Expendable (easily forgotten), Low cost, Mass
produced, Young (aimed at youth),
Witty, Sexy, Gimmicky, Glamorous,
Big Business.» www.tate.org.uk / visit/
tate-britain/display/modern-and
-contemporary-british-art/richard
-hamilton-sexy-gimmicky-glamorous
-big-business, aufgerufen am
25.02.2025.
[4] Byung-Chul Han, *Undinge. Umbrüche
der Lebenswelt*, Ullstein, Berlin 2021,
S. 16.
[5] Ebd., S. 90.
[6] Zeuxis und Parrhasios liefern sich einen Wettstreit, wer naturgetreuer malt.
An Zeuxis' gemalten Trauben picken
die Vögel, doch Parrhasios gewinnt, da
er sogar Zeuxis mit seiner Malerei
täuschen kann.
[7] Byung-Chul Han stellt fest, dass In-
formationen (Undinge) immer wichtiger
werden, während die Dinge verschwinden Byung-Chul Han, *Undinge. Umbrüche der Lebenswelt*, Ullstein, Berlin
2021, S. 43.

Peas, Books, Woolly Socks and Other
Things Close to the Heart

Eveline Suter

*The thing and its reliability take
care that human beings establish a
firm footing on the earth.*[1]

In her works, Sereina Steinemann shows
our world, things in the broadest sense of
the word, everyday life, normality. In itself, that is not unusual in art. The still life
has long been a genre of painting, and
pop art emphatically made modern everyday life its focus.

Starting from the mid 1950s, pop
art draws its inspiration from advertising,
which takes up more and more public
space as consumer society develops. Consumer goods and the visual language
of advertising become the theme of painting and sculpture. Richard Hamilton's
collage, *Just what is it that makes today's
homes so different, so appealing?,*[2] is
an icon of pop art and may have given
the movement its name. For the catalogue
of the exhibition *This is Tomorrow* at
Whitechapel Gallery, the British artist creates a collage of a muscleman with a
lollipop tennis racquet in a living room. The
title directly quotes an advertising slogan, but this is not the only programmatic
element: the label "pop" can be found
on the lollipop, and there are many more
objects taken by Hamilton from advertisements. The hoover, the TV, the comics
and the image of earth from space all represent the atmosphere of everyday life in
a time shaped by optimism and the belief
in progress. Richard Hamilton said that
his aim was to capture "all of living" in his
work.

Sereina Steinemann also captures our
lives, partly using visual and textual advertising messages, like the creators of pop
art. Thus, her series *Qualität ist unsere
Stärke* (Quality is our Strength, see pp. 11–
23, 28–34, 67–69, 93–97) reflects the language of advertising slogans. However, she
quotes the slogans in such an abstract
way that the drawings do not so much refer
to the products as to the implicit promises
and the longings being addressed. Richard

Hamilton made a list of the attributes of
pop art in 1957: "Popular (designed for a
mass audience), Transient (shortterm solution), Expendable (easily forgotten), Low
cost, Mass produced, Young (aimed at
youth), Witty, Sexy, Gimmicky, Glamorous,
Big Business."[3] Comparing her work with
this list, Sereina Steinemann's response to
everyday life and her perspective on its
objects is clearly different in many ways.

Sereina Steinemann's works are not
particularly sexy or glamorous. Instead, the
focus is on the lovingly handmade, both
in terms of the objects and in terms of the
way they are presented. The unpretentious,
deliberately simple painting style makes
mass-produced objects such as a Coop City
plastic bag (see p. 133) or a Coca Cola
bottle (see p. 62) take on a unique, individual charm, and paint can be found dripping
down from the seam of a pair of Louis
Vuitton trousers (see p. 26). By painting the
logo of the crisp company Zweifel (which
literally means 'doubt'), she addresses her
own artistic uncertainties (see p. 147).

Sereina Steinemann's works are not
transient. They do not tell of impermanence, but of careful attention, of turning
towards the things that are being shown,
towards the simple, a pea pod, a cup, a
sock. By paying attention to simple things,
the artist gives them meaning. She usually
concentrates on just one object at a time,
which means that we slow down. "Lingering on things in contemplation, intentionless
seeing" as Byung-Chul Han writes in his
critical discussion of the consumer and information society, is a "formula for happiness."[4] He explains that objects can only
become "things close to the heart" when
they are freed from their usefulness and
thus from their character as commodities.
Things close to the heart enable us to access the world, as transitional objects;
they enable encounters with the other and
they are "calm centres of life; they stabilize it."[5] A single stripy woollen sock, probably hand-knitted (see p. 141), is one
such thing; it is no longer of much use, but
it contains so many stories and so much
life. Turning our attention to something can
be both a mental act of focusing and a
physical movement, drawing close to it, allowing it to capture our hearts.

Sereina Steinemann's works are not
gimmicky. Neither the works themselves nor
the objects they depict are smooth or flawless. They are far from the perfect illusions
of baroque Dutch still lifes, and the birds
would probably not peck at Sereina Steinemann's cherries as they pecked at Zeuxis'
grapes, as legend has it.[6] It is their lack
of virtuosity that makes her works so unerring: they touch our feelings. Failure can
be productive and even fun, as she shows
in her series *Heute gelingt mir nichts*
(Today I can get nothing right, see pp. 101–
109)—failure has never been more charming.

Pop art as a phenomenon of the 1950s
and 1960s reflects the economic boom
and the growth of the postwar period. Consumerism and its products are generally
presented in a positive light. The exhibition
title *This is Tomorrow* is typical of the undiminished belief in progress during those
years. Today, we lack that certainty about

the future; growth and progress no longer
have entirely positive connotations. That
might be why Sereina Steinemann's works
have a sense of nostalgia about them,
at least at first glance. For her zines (see pp.
128–142)—often combinations of images
from old *Lustige Taschenbücher*, paperback
comic books featuring Disney characters
—she uses a photocopier. The sock looks
as if it was knitted by a grandmother,
the keys (see p. 58) are heavy, with their
old-fashioned shapes, and the first sculptures she has exhibited are inspired by
retro advertising displays, like the oversized
croissant that can be found in front of
a bakery during its opening times, or the
giant ice cream cone in front of the gelateria. Thus, her keys are also mobile (see
p. 144) and are not always found in the
same positions in the exhibition space. Or
are they even cleared away overnight?
Still, Sereina Steinemann's works are very
much anchored in the here and now, and
not backward-looking. It is the way she turns
her attention to the unspectacular, to simple solutions and handmade objects, that
awakens our sense of nostalgia.

Sereina Steinemann's works are more
about craft and working by hand than
about mass production, although they do
respond to contemporary mass production
and advertising slogans. Even when the
artist transfers a chat dialogue from a mobile phone to the canvas (see p. 145), her
painting techniques mean that digital communication is grounded in the analogue,
in the materiality of canvas and paint and
her handiwork with the paintbrush. In
that sense, Sereina Steinemann's works provide a counterpoint to Byung-Chul Han's
analysis of our time, "Non-things supplant
things."[7] In her works, Sereina Steinemann
turns "non-things" into things. She does
so with charm and care, and in a way that
makes us smile. Sereina Steinemann's
works are definitely humorous.

[1] Byung-Chul Han, *Non-things.
Upheaval in the Lifeworld*, Cambridge
2022, p. 70.
[2] Richard Hamilton, *Just what is it that
makes today's homes so different,
so appealing?*, 1956, collage, 26 × 24.8
cm, Kunsthalle Tübingen.
[3] Richard Hamilton included this list in
a letter to the architects Alison and
Peter Smithson: www.tate.org.uk/visit/
tate-britain/display/modern-and
-contemporary-british-art/richard
-hamilton-sexy-gimmicky-glamorous
-big-business, accessed 25.02.2025.
[4] Byung-Chul Han, *Non-things.
Upheaval in the Lifeworld*, Polity, Cambridge 2022, p. 7.
[5] Ibid., p. 74.
[6] Zeuxis and Parrhasius compete
to prove who can paint most naturalistically. The birds peck at Zeuxis'
painted grapes, but Parrhasius wins,
because his painting fools Zeuxis
himself.
[7] Byung-Chul Han argues that information (non-things) is becoming
increasingly important, while things
are disappearing. Byung-Chul Han,
Non-things. Upheaval in the Lifeworld,
Polity, Cambridge 2022, p. 33.

(Das beste Plus für deinen Sommer)
    Sestine

Lucy Duggan

Achtung!!
Das ist eine
Tür, die aufgeht!!
    Schild, Le Crobag, Berlin Spandau

Die Alphabete an der Wand. Das
Fenster daneben: draussen die Graffiti. Der beste
Ort zum Schreiben. Plus:
Nägel, Schrauben, Stifte, Comics. Für
mich ein Raum mit Ausrufezeichen. Deinen
Humor merke ich mir im Notizbuch. Sommer

treibt uns den Hang runter zum Fluss. Sommer
auf den Holzbrettern, eine Frau liest das
Buch: *Besser allein als in schlechter Gesellschaft.* Deinen
nächsten Bildtitel suchst du in Gesprächsfetzen. Die beste
Titelquelle sind aber Flyer: *Wir interessieren uns für
Ihren Wagen. Unbreakable Fun.* Plus:

Elizabeth Murray sagt: «The whole painting was painful.» Plus:
Lily van der Stokker malt: «All day problems. In the evening TV.» Sommer
ist ein langes Gespräch und eine kleine Zeichnung für
eine Freundin. Irgendwann finde ich das
Wort in einer alten E-Mail: Sorgfalt, die beste
Entsprechung für care und carefulness. In deinen

Kartonkisten sind *Stifte, Comics, Leim, Makulatur.* Auf deinen
Bildern sind Zweifel: *Heute gelingt mir nichts. Halt plus
Form. Extra stark.* Stahlblech, die beste
Übersetzung eines Bilds in ein Objekt. Im Sommer
zeigst du drei Schlüssel ohne Tür. Ist das
eine Frage ohne Antwort? Zeichen für

Alphabete ohne Buchstaben. *Mir spruudle vor Idee... Mehr für
dich*: Schlüssel ohne Schloss. In deinen
Bildern spielst du mit Tiefe und Oberfläche: Ist das
Bild eine Tür? *Nägel, Schrauben, Stifte,* plus
Panische Angst, Uhren, Kulturgeschichte. Im Sommer
bist du ins neue Atelier gezogen. Der beste

Ort, um Acrylfarbe in Stahlblech zu übersetzen. Die beste
Parole: *Perfekt aussehen in 1 Minute.* Ein Satz für
Ungeduldige: im Handumdrehen sich verwandeln. Der Sommer
schmilzt den Text, er braucht *Halt + Form.* In deinen
Schlüsseln finde ich Worte aus einer alten E-Mail: seriousness plus
Sorgfalt plus Humor. Kann ich das

alles übersetzen? Da das Fenster, da die Alphabete. Die beste
Antwort. Plus: *Qualität ist unsere Stärke.* Für
meinen Text, kein Schloss. Für deinen Schlüssel, der Sommer.

(The Best Plus for Your Summer)
    Sestine

Lucy Duggan

Caution!!
This is a
door that opens!!
    Sign, Le Crobag, Berlin Spandau

The alphabets on the wall. The
window beside them: outside, the graffiti. The best
place to write. Plus:
nails, screws, pens, comics. For
me, a space with an exclamation mark. Your
humour recorded in my notebook. Summer

carries us down to the river. Summer
on the wooden boards, a woman is reading the
book *Better Alone than in Bad Company.* Your
next title might be gleaned from eavesdropping. But the best
titles come from flyers: *We'll Give You Cash for
Your Car. Unbreakable Fun.* Plus:

Elizabeth Murray says: "The whole painting was painful." Plus:
Lily van der Stokker paints: "All day problems. In the evening TV." Summer
is a long conversation and a small drawing for
a friend. At some point, I find the
word in an old email: Sorgfalt, the best
equivalent for care and carefulness. In your

cardboard boxes are *pens, comics, glue, scrap paper.* In your
paintings, there is doubt: *Today I can get nothing right. Support plus
shape. Extra strong.* Sheet steel, the best
translation of a painting into an object. In summer
you're showing three keys with no door. The
trace of a question without an answer? Signs for

alphabets without letters. *We're bubbling over with ideas… More for
you*: keys without locks. In your
paintings you play with depth and surface: is the
painting a door? *Nails, screws, pens,* plus
fear, clocks, cultural history. In summer
you moved to a new studio. The best

place to translate acrylic paint into sheet steel. The best
slogan: *Look perfect in 1 minute.* A sentence for
the impatient: transformation in a trice. Summer
melts the text, it needs *support + shape.* In your
keys I find words from an old email: seriousness plus
Sorgfalt plus humour. Can I translate the

window, the alphabets? They are the best
answer. Plus: *Quality is our strength.* For
my text, no lock. For your keys, the summer.

154

«Define aura»
  Sereina Steinemanns Stil-Leben

Daniel Morgenthaler

Er *ist* Aura. Walter Benjamin hat immerhin ein Jugendwort geprägt. Als Definition von Aura wird aber heute auf Social Media eher Virgil van Dijk gefeiert. Da steht dann zum Beispiel «Define aura» oder «I think this is called aura» unter einem Foto oder einem Film des niederländischen Nationalspielers und Verteidigers des FC Liverpool. Walter Benjamin hat mit seinem Text *Das Kunstwerk im Zeitalter seiner technischen Reproduzierbarkeit* indirekt Jan van Eyck Aura zugesprochen. «Define aura»: «[…] was im Zeitalter der technischen Reproduzierbarkeit des Kunstwerks verkümmert, das ist seine Aura.»[1] Und im Zeitalter der technischen Produzierbarkeit? Da ist Aura entkümmert. Es ist das Jugendwort des Jahres 2024. Walter Benjamin hat mindestens unendlich Aura-Punkte.

Van Dijk und van Eyck haben beide Aura. Bei van Dijk die öffentliche Person, bei van Eyck die Gemälde. Beide haben Aura wegen ihrer Einzigartigkeit. Weil sie Originale sind. Der eine ist ein Mann, die anderen stammen von einem Mann. Aura zugesprochen hat ihnen ein Mann. Und mehrheitlich männliche fussballinteressierte Jugendliche. Hier zusammengeschrieben hat sie auch ein Mann.

«Walter Benjamins ‹Engel der Geschichte› war kein Autofahrer. Sonst hätte er die Vorzüge eines Rückspiegels zu schätzen gewusst. Anstatt krampfhaft nach hinten zu starren, während er sich doch eigentlich fortbewegt, hätte er mit diesem Hilfsmittel ganz einfach nach vorne schauen können und dabei zugleich das Treiben in seinem Rücken fest im Visier gehabt.»[2] Er war sicher auch noch kein*e Influencer*in, schon klar. Obwohl Influencer*innen in rasender Geschwindigkeit auf sich selbst zurückschauen. Neben der Aura gehört der «Engel der Geschichte» zum Trademark von Walter Benjamin. Und wie der Engel eben noch nicht Auto fahren oder Social Media benutzen konnte, ist auch Aura heute etwas anderes als 1935, als Walter Benjamin mit dem Begriff argumentierte.

Wo stehen Sereina Steinemanns Malereien in dieser Männerwelt, zwischen van Dijk und van Eyck? Drei Arbeiten ziemlich genau in der Mitte: die Malerei einer Louis-Vuitton-Hose (*Hose*, Abb. S. 26), die einer Balenciaga-Tasche (*City Bag*, Abb. S. 92) und die eines Hugo-Boss-Kapuzenpullis (*Boss*). Sie sind ungewöhnlich für Sereina Steinemanns Arbeitsweise, wie ich sie kenne. Sie hat sonst oft etwas komplett Unauratisches wie eine simple Zigarette[3] mithilfe der Technik der Malerei auratisiert. Und zwar wirklich auratisiert, wie ich finde. Nicht fotorealistisch abgebildet – das wäre ja dann eigentlich schon fast wieder die technische Reproduktion der Realität. Sondern ehrlich malerisch. In Sereina Steinemanns Malereien gibt sich die Malerei immer als Malerei zu erkennen. Damit holt sie Aura-Punkte, im Sinne Walter Benjamins.

Und eckt damit auch an. Als ob die Aura einer Malerei vielleicht verkümmern könnte – «Define aura» – wenn sie nur eine Zigi abbildet. Dabei haben auch schon die etwas jüngeren Holländer*innen, ein paar Jahrhunderte nach van Eyck, in ihren Stillleben teils sehr basic Dinge dargestellt. Sogar Verwesendes, um an den Tod zu erinnern. Heute erinnert eine Zigi an den Tod, stimmt doch.

Diese drei Malereien dagegen sind eher Stil-Leben. Mit einer Tasche von Balenciaga. «Das Vulgäre an diesen luxuriösen Handtaschen sind nicht nur die Preise, sondern auch die ominösen Wartelisten, ein Ergebnis der künstlichen Verknappung, der geschäftsantreibenden Noblesse. Bei manchen Häusern herrscht die Anforderung, erst die eigene Kaufkraft und die loyale Verbundenheit mit der Marke durch kontinuierliche Einkäufe unter Beweis zu stellen, um das prominente Teil überhaupt angeboten zu bekommen.»[4] Ein kleiner Selbstversuch: An eine Hermès-Birkin-Tasche, von der hier die Rede ist, komme ich im Internet nicht entfernt ran. Da braucht es den erwähnten Klasse-Trick. Eine Balenciaga-Le-City-Tasche hingegen bringe ich relativ schnell in den digitalen Einkaufskorb. Sie liegt bei 2490 Schweizer Franken.

Also eine vergleichsweise günstige Markentasche. Sie kostet gleich viel wie eine kleinere Malerei von Sereina Steinemann (nicht die vergleichsweise grossformatige des rosa City Bag, die kostet 7000 Franken). Zwischen van Eyck und van Dijk: Die Aura von Mode – im weitesten Sinne die von Virgil van Dijk, den ich mir durchaus in Louis-Vuitton-Hosen in einem Stadionflur voller Leitungsrohre auf Social Media vorstellen kann – hat seit 1935 aufgeholt zur Aura von Jan van Eyck. Jetzt ist auch «Mode … im besten Fall ein Heiligtum».[5] Und ich bezahle nicht die Marke, wie es immer heisst, sondern die Aura der Marke. Sie ist es, die eine in wohl hoher Anzahl hergestellte Tasche (im Falle der Le-City-Tasche made in Italy) mit einem nicht exorbitanten Materialwert gleich teuer macht wie eine one of a kind Originalarbeit mit einem recht niedrigen Materialwert made in Switzerland von Sereina Steinemann.

Sereina Steinemann lässt mit ihrer unverkennbaren Malart (das heisst nicht zwingend, dass sie komplett anders malt als alle anderen Maler*innen, sondern dass sie eben unverkennbar *malt*) die Aura der Marke mit der Aura der Malerei zusammenfallen. Aura hoch zwei. Van Dijk x van Eyck. In der Mitte. Bei der Hose noch mehr als bei der Tasche, da die Hose das Markenemblem von Louis Vuitton einerseits im Rapport vervielfacht. Unten läuft andererseits etwas aus den Hosenbeinen raus. Farbe. Die Farbe lässt sich nicht wegdenken aus Sereina Steinemanns Malereien.

Auch beim Hugo-Boss-Pulli ist sie da und läuft aus dem Ärmel raus – und ein klein wenig ins grosse O von «BOSS» hinein. Die Farbe macht sich sanft bemerkbar. Sogar im Logo, das sich hier seinerseits viel penetranter in den Vordergrund schiebt als noch bei der Vuitton-Hose. Und erst noch etwas heisst. Boss. Chef. Aura? Der Kapuzenpulli ist auch markant günstiger, Sereina Steinemanns Malerei allerdings nicht. Hier driften die Aura von van Dijk, der so einen Pulli ohne hin eher nicht tragen würde, und die von van Eyck wieder auseinander. Richtung Zigi. An die Aura Walter Benjamins erinnert vielleicht noch die Erkenntnis, dass Firmengründer Hugo Boss Nationalsozialist war und im zweiten Weltkrieg Uniformen für die Wehrmacht herstellte.[6]

Walter Benjamins Text zur Reproduzierbarkeit des Kunstwerks ist nämlich 1935 durchsetzt und entsetzt von Vorahnungen des Faschismus. Im Nachwort stehen Sätze wie «…im Gaskrieg hat [die Gesellschaft] ein Mittel gefunden, die Aura auf neue Art abzuschaffen».[7] Das neuerliche Aufkeimen des Faschismus heute könnte im schlimmsten Fall ähnlich enden. Aura ist politisch. Und eine ehrliche Beschäftigung damit wirkt befreiend.

[1] Walter Benjamin, *Das Kunstwerk im Zeitalter seiner technischen Reproduzierbarkeit*, Suhrkamp, Frankfurt 1963, S. 13.
[2] Sven Beckstette über Alex Heim in: *Yesterday Will Be Better*, Aargauer Kunsthaus Aarau, Kerber, Bielefeld 2010, S. 125.
[3] Wobei, die Zigarette hat doch die Aura vieler Menschen lange erheblich gesteigert.
[4] Jovana Reisinger, *Pleasure*, Ullstein, Berlin 2024, S. 77.
[5] Ebd., S. 72.
[6] Vgl.: https://www.deutschlandfunk ku tur.de/historiker-hugo-boss-hat -nachweislich-vom-100.html, Zugriff am 10.2.2025.
[7] Walter Benjamin, *Das Kunstwerk im Zeitalter seiner technischen Reproduzierbarkeit*, Suhrkamp, Frankfurt 1963, S. 44.

"Define Aura"
Sereina Steinemann: Still Life,
Style Life

Daniel Morgenthaler

He *is* aura. Believe it or not, Walter Benjamin coined a "youth word". Though when the definition of aura comes up on social media, it's Virgil van Dijk who tends to be celebrated. Underneath a photo or a video of the Dutch international and Liverpool defender, there will be comments like "Define aura" or "I think this is called aura." In his text "The Work of Art in the Age of Mechanical Reproduction", Walter Benjamin indirectly ascribed aura to Jan van Eyck. "Define aura": "that which withers in the age of mechanical reproduction is the aura of the work of art."[1] And in the age of mechanical production? Aura is thriving. It is the Youth Word of the Year 2024. Benjamin has infinite aura points.

Van Dijk and van Eyck both have aura. With van Dijk, it's his public persona, with van Eyck, it's the paintings. They both have aura because of their uniqueness. Because they are originals. The former is a man, the latter were created by a man. Aura was attributed to them by a man. And by young football fans, most of them male—just like the author of this text.

"Walter Benjamin's 'angel of history' was not a motorist. Otherwise he would have appreciated the advantages of a rearview mirror. Instead of straining to look back, while actually moving on, the angel, with the aid of this device, could have just looked forward and at the same time kept his sights firmly set on the goings-

on behind him."[2] He was certainly not an influencer either, that much is clear. Though influencers look back at themselves while moving at top speed. Along with the idea of aura, the angel of history is a trademark of Walter Benjamin. And just as the angel couldn't yet drive a car or use social media, aura has become something different since 1935, when Walter Benjamin used the term.

In this male world, between van Dijk and van Eyck, where can we find Sereina Steinemann's paintings? Three works are pretty much right in the middle: a painting of a pair of Louis Vuitton trousers (*Hose*, p. 26), one of a Balenciaga bag (*City Bag*, p. 92) and another of a Hugo Boss hoodie (*Boss*). They are unusual for Sereina Steinemann's approach as I know it. Otherwise, her work has often taken something completely lacking in aura, like a simple cigarette,[3] and auratised it using the techniques of painting. And I really mean auratised. Not photorealistically conveyed— in that case we might be talking about the mechanical reproduction of reality. Her approach is painterly and doesn't hide that fact. In Sereina Steinemann's paintings, painting is always recognisable as painting. In this way, she gets aura points, in the spirit of Walter Benjamin.

And sometimes that bothers people. As if perhaps the aura of a painting could wither—"Define aura"—because all it shows is a "Zigi" (Swiss slang for a cigarette). But even in the still life paintings of the slightly more recent Dutch artists, a few centuries after van Eyck, we can already find some very basic objects. Even decaying things, in order to remind people of death. And these days, a cigarette reminds us of death, doesn't it?

But these three paintings tend more towards *style* life than still life. With a bag by Balenciaga. "What's vulgar about these luxury handbags is not just the price but the dubious waiting lists, a result of artificial scarcity and business-driving *noblesse oblige*. In some houses, customers are first required to prove their buying power and brand loyalty through continuous purchases, before they can even be offered the famous item."[4] A little experiment: the bag in question here is the Hermès Birkin, and there's absolutely no way for me to get hold of it on the internet. For that, I'd need the class trick mentioned above. A Le City bag by Balenciaga, on the other hand, can be added to my digital shopping basket pretty quickly. It costs 2490 Swiss Francs.

Which makes it a comparatively low-priced designer bag. It costs the same as a smaller painting by Sereina Steinemann (not the comparatively large one of the pale pink City bag, which costs 7000 Francs). Between van Eyck and van Dijk: since 1935, the aura of fashion—in the broadest sense that of Virgil van Dijk, whom I can certainly imagine wearing Louis Vuitton trousers in a photo on social media that shows him standing in a stadium corridor full of water pipes—has caught up with the aura of Jan van Eyck. These days, fashion, too, is "something sacred, in best case".[5] And I am not paying for the brand, as they always say, but for the aura of the brand. That is what makes a bag

which is probably produced in great numbers (in the case of the Le City bag, made in Italy) with a relatively modest material value just as expensive as a one-of-a-kind original work with quite a low material value, made in Switzerland by Sereina Steinemann.

With her unmistakable method of painting (which doesn't necessarily mean that she paints completely differently from all other painters, but that she does unmistakably *paint*), Sereina Steinemann allows the aura of the brand to coincide with the aura of the painting. Aura squared. Van Dijk x van Eyck. In the middle. With the trousers even more than with the bag, since the trousers—on the one hand— multiply the Louis Vuitton logo in their repeating pattern. On the other hand, something drips down from the bottom of the trouser legs. Paint. In Sereina Steinemann's paintings, paint cannot be ignored.

With the Hugo Boss hoodie, it is there again, dripping out of the sleeve—and a little way into the big O in "BOSS". The paint quietly makes itself known. Even in the logo, which forces its way into the foreground much more insistently here than in the case of the Vuitton trousers. And there is meaning attached to the word. Boss. Aura? The hoodie is also far cheaper, whereas Sereina Steinemann's painting is not. Here, the aura of van Dijk, who would be unlikely to wear a hoodie like this, drifts apart from that of van Eyck. Towards the cigarette. We might still be reminded of the aura of Walter Benjamin by the fact that the company founder Hugo Boss was a National Socialist and made uniforms for the German army in the Second World War.[6]

Because the horrifying prospect of fascism is everywhere in Walter Benjamin's text on the mechanical reproduction of the artwork, which was written in 1935. In the epilogue are sentences like "through gas warfare the aura is abolished in a new way."[7] Today, the recent resurgence of fascism could end in a similar way in the worst case. Aura is political. And an honest engagement with this is liberating.

[1] Walter Benjamin, "The Work of Art in the Age of Mechanical Reproduction", in *Illuminations*, ed. Hannah Arendt, The Bodley Head, London 2015, p. 215.
[2] Sven Beckstette on Alex Heim in: *Yesterday Will Be Better*, ed. Madeleine Schuppli, Aargauer Kunsthaus Aarau, Kerber, Bielefeld 2010, p. 126.
[3] Although for a long time, cigarettes were responsible for increasing many people's auras.
[4] Jovana Reisinger, *Pleasure*, Ullstein, Berlin 2024, p. 77.
[5] Ibid., p. 72.
[6] Cf.: https://www.deutschlandfunk kultur.de/historiker-hugo-boss-hat -nachweislich-vom-100.html, accessed 10.2.2025.
[7] Walter Benjamin, "The Work of Art in the Age of Mechanical Reproduction", in *Illuminations*, ed. Hannah Arendt, The Bodley Head, London, 2015, p. 242.